Empire of Hell

CH00765616

This revisionist history of convict transportation from Britain and Ireland will challenge much that you thought you knew about religion and penal colonies. Based on original archival sources, it examines arguments by elites in favour and against the practice of transportation and considers why they thought it could be reformed, and, later, why it should be abolished. In this, the first religious history of the anti-transportation campaign, Hilary M. Carey addresses all the colonies and denominations engaged in the debate. Without minimizing the individual horror of transportation, she demonstrates the wide variety of reformist experiments conducted in the Australian penal colonies, as well as the hulks, Bermuda and Gibraltar. She showcases the idealists who fought for more humane conditions for prisoners, as well as the 'political parsons', who lobbied to bring transportation to an end. The complex arguments about convict transportation, which were engaged in by bishops, judges, priests, politicians and intellectuals, crossed continents and divided an empire.

HILARY M. CAREY is Professor of Imperial and Religious History at the University of Bristol. She is the author of *God's Empire*, nominated for the Ernest Scott Prize, and co-editor of *Religion and Greater Ireland*. She is Conjoint Professor at the University of Newcastle and Fellow of the Australian Academy of Humanities.

Empire of Hell

Religion and the Campaign to End Convict
Transportation in the British Empire, 1788–1875

Hilary M. Carey

University of Bristol

CAMBRIDGE
UNIVERSITY PRESS

CAMBRIDGE
UNIVERSITY PRESS

University Printing House, Cambridge CB2 8BS, United Kingdom

One Liberty Plaza, 20th Floor, New York, NY 10006, USA

477 Williamstown Road, Port Melbourne, VIC 3207, Australia

314-321, 3rd Floor, Plot 3, Splendor Forum, Jasola District Centre, New Delhi - 110025, India

79 Anson Road, #06-04/06, Singapore 079906

Cambridge University Press is part of the University of Cambridge.

It furthers the University's mission by disseminating knowledge in the pursuit of education, learning and research at the highest international levels of excellence.

www.cambridge.org
Information on this title: www.cambridge.org/9781108716802
DOI: 10.1017/9781107337787

© Hilary M. Carey 2019

This publication is in copyright. Subject to statutory exception and to the provisions of relevant collective licensing agreements, no reproduction of any part may take place without the written permission of Cambridge University Press.

First published 2019
First paperback edition 2021

A catalogue record for this publication is available from the British Library

ISBN 978-1-107-04308-4 Hardback
ISBN 978-1-108-71680-2 Paperback

Cambridge University Press has no responsibility for the persistence or accuracy of URLs for external or third-party internet websites referred to in this publication, and does not guarantee that any content on such websites is, or will remain, accurate or appropriate.

For Bernard
16 December 1946–18 July 2016

Contents

Tables

Acknowledgements

This book concerns religious arguments about convicts which arose in the course of the campaign to end convict transportation from Britain and Ireland to British colonies. As a religious historian, I am in debt to many specialist convict historians who informed me about the complex and interwoven histories of convicts in the British empire. My first thanks are owed to David Roberts of the University of New England in New South Wales who collaborated on the original, AHRC-funded project ('Liberty, Anti-Transportation and the Empire of Morality', 2010–2012 DP 1096538) which led to this book. He kindly read drafts of every chapter and made many valuable contributions throughout. Our preliminary ideas about religious critics of transportation were presented at the workshop organized in September 2010 by Frank Bongiorno at the Menzies Centre for Australian Studies, Kings College London, entitled 'Beyond the Stain: Australian Convict History'. I am grateful to the historians assembled there, including Tim Causer, Ian Duffield, Kirsty Reid, David Roberts and Babette Smith for encouraging me to think a religious history of transportation had value and interest.

In 2014, I moved to the University of Bristol to take up a position as head of the School of Humanities. This had several advantages, including access to British sources, but it did lead to some delay in the completion of this book. On the plus side this meant that I was able to benefit from a number of ongoing convict histories that have usefully informed this study. In 2015, Clare Anderson asked me to provide a keynote lecture for her Carceral Archipelago conference and, as the footnotes reveal, this book owes a debt to the wealth of comparative international studies of convict transportation that she has been uncovering with her team at the University of Leicester. Tim Causer and Chris Holdridge generously shared their PhD theses, on Norfolk Island and the anti-transportation campaign respectively, and I look forward to seeing both in print before too long.

Research papers relevant to this study were presented at meetings of the Ecclesiastical History Society (Exeter and Cambridge), Britain and the World (Austin, Texas), the Australian Historical Association (Launceston, Tasmania), the World History Association (Fremantle, WA) and at research seminars at Macquarie University in New South Wales, the Ourimbah campus of the University of Newcastle in New South Wales, the University of Aberdeen, and the history department at the University of Bristol. Some of the material for Chapter 6 on the horrors of transportation formed part of my inaugural lecture at the University of Bristol in 2015. I am grateful to friends, colleagues and students who provided me with feedback and helped me to hone my arguments and ideas on all these occasions.

I thank my colleagues at the University of Bristol, Helen Fulton and Jessica Moody, for reading and discussing chapters. For encouragement at the right time I thank Josie McLellan. The bulk of the writing for this book was completed while I was on research leave at Clare Hall in Cambridge. In 2013, I benefitted from a visiting fellowship at New College, University of Edinburgh, where I continued research on Alexander Maconochie (Chapter 7). I thank Jay Brown and Brian Stanley who supported my visit. In 2018, a year of research leave from the University of Bristol enabled me to complete the manuscript. For patiently waiting for me to complete the project, and always being supportive and encouraging, I thank Michael Watson at Cambridge University Press.

For hospitality while conducting research at the UK National Archives I am grateful to Patricia and Philip Esler. I thank Rowan and the late Jill Strong for friendship and good company while visiting Fremantle. I am immensely grateful to Rowan for archival notes which are incorporated into Chapter 11. Glenda Strachan and Sid Owen kindly sent me an otherwise unobtainable item from Brisbane which informs Chapter 9. Briony Neilson provided indispensable checking and copy editing.

Finally, I would like to pay tribute to my late husband, Bernard Carey, who died on 18 July 2016 while I was working on this book. Over the course of many years, I visited nearly all the major convict sites that are discussed in the different chapters, sometimes with Bernard and sometimes on my own. But my fascination with the convict past began in 1980 during our honeymoon, spent at my insistence, on Norfolk Island. This book is dedicated to his memory.

Abbreviations

ADB	Australian Dictionary of Biography Online Edition
ANU	Australian National University
BodL	Bodleian Library Oxford
BPP	British Parliamentary Papers
BL	British Library
Col.	Colonel
Col. Sec.	Colonial Secretary
DCB	Dictionary of Canadian Biography
Gov.	Governor
HC	House of Commons
HCJ	House of Commons Journal
HL	House of Lords
HO	Home Office
Lt	Lieutenant
NLI	National Library of Ireland
ODNB	Oxford Dictionary of National Biography
PDS	Prison Discipline Society
RC	Royal Commission
SC	Select Committee
SLNSW	State Library of New South Wales
SPG	Society for the Propagation of the Gospel
SPCK	Society for Promoting Christian Knowledge
SSPCK	Society in Scotland for Propagating Christian Knowledge
SROWA	State Records of Western Australia
TAHO	Tasmanian Archives and Heritage Office
TNA	The National Archives (UK) [formerly Public Record Office]
UOBA	University of Bristol Archives
USPG	United Society for the Propagation of the Gospel
WA	Western Australia

1 Introduction

'Empire of Hell'

You Prisoners of New South Wales,
Who frequent Watch houses and Gaols
A Story To you I will Tell
'Tis of a Convicts Tour to Hell[1] (Francis MacNamara, 1839)

Empire of hell! When will thy cup of abominations be full?[2]

(John Mitchel, 1849)

In 1854, the Young Irelander John Mitchel (1815–1875), published a sensational account of his five years in the world-straddling British penal archipelago.[3] Arrested for publication of seditious material in *The United Irishman*, he was detained at Newgate Prison, tried, found guilty under the Treason Felony Act of 1848, and sentenced to fourteen years transportation.[4] Mitchel was then 'kidnapped', as he put it, and sent to Spike Island in Cork Harbour from whence he travelled by the war steamer *Scourge* to the British convict establishment at Bermuda. After two years, he was transferred again to Cape Colony in southern Africa where the convict transport *Neptune* spent five months at Simon's Bay, south of Cape Town, before it was forced to turn aside by a powerful anti-convict (and anti-Irish) protest and head to Australia instead. As he sailed towards the Cape he listened to the singing of his fellow Irish prisoners and was inspired to excoriate the imperial regime that had sent them into collective exile, 'and then I curse, oh! how fervently, the British empire. Empire of hell! When will thy cup of abominations be full?'[5] Unfortunately for him, Mitchel's trip through hell was not yet over.

---

[1] Francis MacNamara, 'A Convict's Tour to Hell', 23 October 1839, SLNSW C967: 2.
[2] John Mitchel, *Jail Journal, Or Five Years in British Prisons* (New York: The 'Citizen', 1854), p. 187. Entry for 12 September 1849.
[3] Ibid. The *Jail Journal* was serialized from 14 January 1854 to 19 August 1854 in Mitchel's New York journal, *The Citizen*, and subsequently published in book form.
[4] For a transcript of the trial in Dublin under Baron Lefroy, see John George Hodges, *Report of the Trial of John Mitchel for Felony . . . Dublin, May, 1848* (Dublin: Thom, 1848).
[5] Mitchel, *Jail Journal*, p. 187. Entry for 12 September 1849.

1

After eleven months on board the *Neptune*, Mitchel and his fellow transportees reached Van Diemen's Land, the heart of the British penal darkness, on 7 May 1850. Here every prisoner except Mitchel was granted a conditional pardon.[6] While he had some sympathy for his fellow convicts in Bermuda, Mitchel viewed the end products of the British 'reformatory discipline' he encountered in Van Diemen's Land with undisguised horror as 'perfect fiends' who scarcely deserved to live: 'What a blessing to these creatures, and to mankind, both in the northern hemisphere and the southern, if they had been hanged.'[7] Both in the Cape of Good Hope and in Van Diemen's Land he gave enthusiastic support to the anti-transportation movement and the 'efforts of decent colonists to throw off the curse and shame of convictism'.[8] Even before he had made good his escape, Mitchel heard the news that convict transportation to Van Diemen's Land had been abolished. Applauding the plucky colonists who had helped secure this victory, Mitchel made his way to the United States where he renewed his commitment to the armed struggle against British rule in Ireland and the cause of Liberty everywhere – though not for African slaves. Never less than consistent in his opposition to imperial claims to authority, Mitchel would go on to adopt the Confederate cause in the American Civil War and dedicate his supple intelligence to spinning arguments in support of slavery.[9]

An important part of Mitchel's radical opposition to British rule was his refusal to accept that liberal humanitarian projects, such as the abolition of slavery or penal reform, could compensate for the reality of imperial power. While opposition to the imperial project is generally seen to have begun much later, during the Boer War, Mitchel's views anticipate later critics of empire, particularly the Fabians.[10] Mitchel's views were expressed in both the *Jail Journal* and *The Last Conquest of Ireland (Perhaps)* which appeared in 1860. The latter took Mitchel's vendetta against the imperial British to new rhetorical heights, 'The Almighty, indeed, sent the potato blight, but the English created the Famine.'[11]

---

[6] Ibid., 231. Entry for 13 February 1850.   [7] Ibid., 256. Entry for 30 April 1850.

[8] Ibid., 284. Entry for 18 October 1850.

[9] Nini Rodgers, *Ireland, Slavery and Anti-Slavery: 1612–1865* (Houndmills: Palgrave Macmillan, 2007), pp. 293–305.

[10] Gregory Claeys, *Imperial Sceptics: British Critics of Empire 1850–1920* (Cambridge: Cambridge University Press, 2010), p. 151. For the Fenian attack on the liberal empire see also Theodore Koditschek, *Liberalism, Imperialism and the Historical Imagination: Nineteenth-Century Visions of a Greater Britain* (Cambridge: Cambridge University Press), p. 181.

[11] John Mitchel, *The Last Conquest of Ireland (Perhaps)* (Glasgow: Cameron & Ferguson, 1876). For the quotation, see the 'Author's Edition' (Glasgow: Washourne, 1882),

For Mitchel, the countless victims of the famine and the convict fiends of Van Diemen's Land were products of the same demonic power, the British Empire.

Popular opinion has tended to agree with Mitchel that convict transportation was an unmitigated evil, with religious agents complicit in perpetuating its administrative failures and humanitarian abuses. This introductory chapter will address three issues: the role of religion in the penal reform movement that began in the eighteenth century; the history of British and Irish convict transportation in the British empire from 1788; and the tempestuous historiography of British and Irish convict transportation and the anti-transportation movement. It will outline the thesis of this book, which traces the intellectual and religious elements of arguments about convict transportation from John Howard to John West.

Reform and Religion

It is time for a complete rethink of the place of religion in the history of convict transportation. *Empire of Hell* provides this. It poses the radical argument that religious reform was fundamental, not incidental, to convict colonization in the British empire. If this was an 'empire of hell', it was a hell illuminated by Christian reformers from across the denominational and political spectrum. It takes seriously the motivation of those who supported religious reforms to transportation and seeks to understand why they were eclipsed by the end of the transportation era. In the 'age of reform', the reform of criminals was a complex idea with deep religious roots. Parliament debated whether the object of punishment was to be retributive, preventative or reformative and sought to reform the law by making it more consistent, rational and efficient. Religious authorities sustained a much higher, inner and transformative view of reformation than the pragmatic civil authorities, or indeed the convicts themselves. Both the latter understood reformation in terms of passive acceptance of authority under sentence, avoidance of reoffending and integrating successfully in colonial society. Hence the paradox that Evangelical clergy denounced convict morality even while acknowledging the rising wealth and social standing of emancipists and the usefulness of their own convict servants.[12] It was only in response to horror stories from the penal colonies that Christian and secular humanitarians came

---

p. 219. For context see Rodgers, *Ireland, Slavery and Anti-Slavery: 1612–1865*, p. 293 and Christine Kinealy, *A Death-Dealing Famine: The Great Hunger in Ireland* (London: Pluto Press, 1997), p. 29.

[12] See Chapter 2.

together to demand an end to transportation, in part because it was deemed to corrupt rather than reform the criminal.

The idea that criminals could and should be reformed through work and prayer was a key notion for both utilitarian and Christian idealists at the end of the eighteenth century. However, the focus of the reformers was on the prison system and on the individual criminal – not the practice of transportation. John Howard (1726–1790), a lay Dissenter, was the religious face of the movement, and was instrumental in publicizing the deplorable conditions for prisoners throughout Britain and, later, Europe.[13] He produced his own designs for gaols and penitentiaries and stressed that while hygiene and discipline should have paramount importance, there should be separation of different classes of prisoner, and access to religious services and books: 'A CHAPEL is necessary to a Gaol. I have chosen for it [on the accompanying plan] what seems to me a proper situation. It should have a gallery for debtors or women; and the rest may be separated below. Bibles and prayer-books should be chained at convenient distances on each side: those who tear or otherwise damage them should be punished.'[14] Like most utilitarian reformers, Howard believed prisoners should receive their just punishment, but no more than they deserved, and he had no strong objections to transportation.

The secular, utilitarian face of penal reform was supplied by Jeremy Bentham (1748–1832).[15] While Bentham was singularly unsuccessful in securing the reform on which he had set his heart – and a good deal of his own money – namely the construction of the 'Panopticon', his energy, idiosyncratic and striking writing, and persistence, ensured that he had influence well beyond those who directly responded to his ideas.[16] Bentham believed that there was no rational, moral or economic basis for supporting transportation to a distant location where there was no certainty of oversight which could alone ensure consistent punishment for bad behaviour or reward for good. He wrote two pamphlets which set out his position, both expressed in the form of letters to Lord Pelham in 1802. Ten years later he republished them under the title, *Panopticon versus New South Wales*.[17] Bentham summarized the deficiencies of

---

[13] John Howard, *The State of the Prisons in England and Wales, with Preliminary Observations, and an Account of Some Foreign Prisons* (Warrington: William Eyres, 1777); John Howard, *An Account of the Principal Lazarettos in Europe* (Warrington: William Eyres, 1789).

[14] Howard, *State of the Prisons*, p. 48.

[15] John Gascoigne, *The Enlightenment and the Origins of European Australia* (Cambridge: Cambridge University Press, 2002), p. 124.

[16] Ibid., 125.

[17] Jeremy Bentham, *Panopticon versus New South Wales* (London: Robert Baldwin, 1812). For Bentham's unpublished letter on the hulks, see Jeremy Bentham, *Writings on*

transportation when compared with the reformatory in his unmistakable telegraphese: 'Colonizing-transportation-system: characteristic feature of it, radical incapacity of being combined with any efficient system of inspection. Penitentiary system: characteristic feature of it, in its original state, frequent and regular inspection; in its extraordinary and improved state, that principle of management carried to such a degree of perfection as till then had never been reached, even by imagination, much less by practice.'[18] He was particularly cutting in his condemnation of the suggestion that the inclusion of religious training and oversight by convict chaplains could in any way compare with the rigour of architectural oversight. Chaplains, chapels and good books might be provided, but there was a catch: 'Would the books be read? The chapels visited? The chaplains heard?'[19] Bentham was unfortunate in that his conviction that a well-designed penitentiary with effective oversight would inevitably lead to moral reformation was not put to the test in his lifetime. He died frustrated that the penitentiary of his dreams had not been built. Instead, British and Irish convicts were transported and the make-do arrangements and cruelties that plagued the British convict system continued much as before. Change, however, was on the way.

As Howard demonstrated, the rise of the Enlightened prison in the eighteenth century opened the door to more activist, Christian utilitarianism. At home and in the empire, the early nineteenth century saw an explosion in missionary and other religious organizations dedicated to philanthropic, educational and medical causes, catering to all the corporal and spiritual works of mercy, including work with prisoners and religious instruction. The expansion of the settler British empire facilitated Protestant colonial missionary societies, such as the Anglican SPG and SPCK or the Scottish SSPCK which provided religious instruction to colonists, and the expansion of Catholic religious orders who worked mainly with the Irish diaspora.[20] In 1831, the Sisters of Mercy were founded by Catherine McCauley in Dublin to focus entirely on charitable work; they would come to play a particularly important role in the British settler colonies.[21] The first religious women to come to the penal colony of New South Wales were from another charitable order, the

---

Australia V, Third Letter to Lord Pelham, eds. Tim Causer and Philip Schofield (London: The Bentham Project, 2018).

[18] Ibid., 175.   [19] Ibid.

[20] For religious missions to British emigrants and settlers, Joe Hardwick, *An Anglican British World: The Church of England and the Settler Empire, c.1790–1860* (Manchester: Manchester University Press, 2014); Rowan Strong, *Victorian Christianity and Emigrant Voyages to British Colonies c.1840–c.1914* (Oxford: Oxford University Press, 2017); Hilary M. Carey, *God's Empire* (Cambridge: Cambridge University Press, 2011).

[21] Colin Barr and Rose Luminiello, '"The Leader of the Virgin Choirs of Erin": St Brigid's Missionary College, 1883–1914', in Timothy McMahon, Michael Denie and Paul

Sisters of Charity (founded in 1816), four of whom arrived in 1838 at the request of Bishop John Bede Polding (1794–1877) to work with convict women in the Parramatta Female Factory.[22] Collaboration rather than hostility between church and state would be the norm for the emerging philanthropic state of Victorian Britain and its settler empire.

Before this, the Christian monopoly on charitable support for those on the margins of society was challenged by enlightened thinkers who insisted that prisons, hospitals and lunatic asylums should perform a utilitarian function, whether to protect, heal, reform or contain miscreants, and deter crime. For secular utilitarian penal reformers, transportation was regarded as a humane, if often inefficient substitute for execution of criminals. The Italian jurist, Cesare Beccaria (1738–1794), whose most celebrated study, *Dei delitti e delle pene* (Concerning Crimes and Punishments) (1764), was published in English in 1767, presented humanitarian arguments against the 'useless profusion of punishments, which has never made men better', including the death penalty and torture.[23] He denounced the compliant hypocrisy of a church who failed to check unjust authority: 'every noble a tyrant over the people, and the ministers of the gospel of Christ bathing their hands in blood in the name of the God of all mercy'.[24] Yet Beccaria was thoroughly in favour of the practice of transportation as an alternative to execution, which he regarded as a waste of the valuable resource of the prisoner's labour. He noted that thieves were seldom executed in England since transportation to the [American] colonies was substituted for it and this was also the policy in the Russian Empire. Not only was this a thrifty practice, Beccaria argued that it was reformative for convicts sent both to Siberia and the American colonies, noting: 'It has not been discovered that crimes multiply in consequence of this humanity.' In 1837, the Rev. John Dunmore Lang (1799–1978) would cite this passage approvingly when arguing in favour of the continuation of transportation and the creation of new penal colonies against the arguments of Archbishop Richard Whately.[25] On transportation, Howard tended to agree with Beccaria. He does not seem to have felt any particular objection to transportation as a punishment – he

---

Townsend (eds.), *Ireland in an Imperial World* (London: Palgrave Macmillan, 2017), 155–178.

[22] M. Bernadette Shand, '150th Anniversary of the Arrival of the Sisters of Charity in Australia 1838–1988', *Journal of the Royal History Society of Queensland* 13.9 (1989): 331–347.

[23] Cesar Bonesana Beccaria, *An Essay on Crimes and Punishments . . . with a Commentary by Mons. de Voltaire*, trans. Edward D. Ingraham (London: Almon, 1767), p. 102.

[24] Ibid., 20.

[25] John Dunmore Lang, *Transportation and Colonization* (London: Valpy, 1837), p. 41.

had of course seen much worse, both in the lazerettos of Europe and the prisons of Britain. However, he did object to the sentencing of young boys who may not have any chance to return at the end of their sentences:

It is not contrary to justice and humanity to send convicts who are not sentenced for life, to a settlement so remote that there is no probability of their return? And a still greater hardship to those who are sent after they have been four or five years and upwards in confinement, as some were in the last fleet to Botany Bay?[26]

In Enlightened discussions of transportation, both religious and secular penal reformers regarded it as a favour to criminals, an alternative to death and not high on the list of appeals to their humanity.

In their resort to infernal metaphors, modern historians and writers on the prison are reflecting the language used by contemporaries to refer to real sites in the British penal system. In the early nineteenth century, it was common slang to refer to the hulks as the 'floating hell',[27] or sometimes the 'floating academy' or 'Campbell's academy',[28] a wry reference to Duncan Campbell (1726–1803), the wealthy trader with interests in plantations, slaves, convicts and tobacco, who initially had a monopoly on transporting convicts to north America. From 1776 to 1801 Campbell was the overseer of the Thames prison hulks and selected 200 or so convicts for the ill-fated convict colony in East Africa and, with marginally better results, for the first three fleets which sailed for Botany Bay.[29] In popular discourse, convict transports were described as 'hell ships',[30] Norfolk Island as the 'Ocean Hell',[31] prisons and penal stations as 'hell holes'.[32] Fictional narratives were even more likely to depict convict experiences in terms borrowed from the demonic and dystopian otherworld. The attempted escape through the Devil's Blow Hole by Rufus Dawes is one of the most exciting episodes in Marcus Clarke's classic anti-transportation novel highlighting the horrors of the convict

---

[26] Howard, *Lazarettos*, p. 219.

[27] A Member of the Whip Club (ed.), *Lexicon Balatronicum* (London: C. Chappel, 1811), n.p.

[28] Eric Partridge, *A Dictionary of Slang and Unconventional English* 8th edn, edited by Paul Beale (London: Routledge, 1984), p. 408.

[29] Dan Byrnes, '"Emptying the Hulks": Duncan Campbell and the First Three Fleets to Australia', *Push from the Bush*, 24 (1987), 2–23.

[30] Ruán O'Donnell, 'Hellship: Captain Richard Brooks and the Voyage of the Atlas', in Tadhg Foley and Fiona Bateman (eds.), *Irish-Australian Studies* (Sydney: Crossing Press, 2000), 164–174.

[31] J. F. Mortlock, *Experiences of a Convict, Transported for Twenty-One Years*, eds. G. A. Wilkes and A. G. Mitchell (Sydney: Sydney University Press, 1965), p. 67. Alternately, Norfolk Island might be referred to as a 'desecrated Paradise', Ibid., p. 71.

[32] Brian J. Bailey, *Hellholes: An Account of History's Most Notorious Prisons* (London: Orion, 1995).

system in Van Diemen's Land.[33] The gothic allure of Van Diemen's Land ensured good sales for Mitchel's *Jail Journal*, despite the relative comfort in which he served out his truncated sentence of transportation and his total avoidance of the punitive conditions, hard labour and physical punishment meted out to non-political prisoners.[34]

For liberals in the nineteenth century, and for modern citizens of British settler societies, penal landscapes have continued mythic resonance as they represent the past from which contemporaries have escaped to become modern. This is not to deny that transportation could be and often was both terrifying and horrific. All convicts were subject to penal discipline under which the infliction of legally sanctioned violence was an ever-present threat.[35] But the task of untangling myth from reality is complicated by the fact that the horrors of transportation were enhanced, for different reasons, by both advocates and reformers of the system. At the height of the anti-transportation debate, the language of vice, disease and sexual disfunction was used to evoke disgust, galvanize public opinion and change official policies.[36] Historians have been significantly divided on the question of punishment, with older schools of thought more likely to stress the terror and violence of the system designed to constrain the criminal class, while revisionists demur that punishment was constrained and effective, reflecting military rather than demonic norms.[37] More recently, even the sites of secondary punishment in places such as Norfolk Island, Macquarie Harbour, Moreton Bay and Maria Island, intended for the most recalcitrant repeat offenders, have been the subject of re-assessments, rescuing them from injudicious assumptions

---

[33] Marcus Andrew Hislop Clarke, *For the Term of His Natural Life* (London: Richard Bentley and Son, 1874). The novel was published in the *Australian Journal* between 1870 and 1872. Its footnotes included references to scholarly descriptions of the Devil's Blowhole.

[34] Seán McConville, *Irish Political Prisoners, 1848–1922: Theatres of War* (London: Routledge, 2003), pp. 49–52.

[35] D. J. Neal, *The Rule of Law in a Penal Colony: Law and Power in Early New South Wales* (Melbourne: Cambridge University Press, 1991), pp. 49–53.

[36] For images of disease, bestiality and degeneration in the language of the anti-transportation movement as well as paranoia about homosexual vice, see Tim Causer, 'Anti-Transportation, "Unnatural Crime" and the "Horrors" of Norfolk Island', *Journal of Australian Colonial History,* 14 (2012), 230–240; Kirsty Reid, *Gender, Crime and Empire* (Manchester: Manchester University Press, 2007), pp. 211–212; Kirsten McKenzie, *Scandal in the Colonies* (Carlton: Melbourne University Press, 2004), pp. 146–149.

[37] For revisionist views of punishment, see Stephen Nicholas (ed.), *Convict Workers* (Cambridge: Cambridge University Press, 1988). Against the view that convicts were impoverished minor villains, their criminality is stressed by A. G. L. Shaw, *Convicts and the Colonies* (London: Faber, 1966), p. 146.

of exceptional brutality.[38] While the scholarly jury has yet to pass its verdict, the popular imagination continues to be driven by a prurient, and largely ahistorical, fascination with what has been called 'convict Gothic' including the inverted landscape of hell with its sexual deviance, lurid tortures, narrow escapes and salutary lessons.[39]

'Convict Gothic' is hardly new or confined to Australian prisoner narratives; indeed it has a venerable theological and literary genealogy. Precedents include both classical and Christian depictions of journeys to the underworld, Dante's *Inferno* or Milton's depiction of Satan as lord of an 'Infernal Empire' in *Paradise Lost*.[40] That such elevated parallels are not far-fetched is clear from the wickedly satirical evocation of Dante's *Inferno* in 'The Convict's Tour to Hell' by Frank the Poet (Francis MacNamara c.1810–1861).[41] MacNamara's remarkable facility to compose extempore verse was demonstrated at his own trial and, possibly, in a meeting with a young William Bernard Ullathorne (1806–1889), who describes an encounter with a 'poor Irish troubadour', dressed in rags, who 'poured out a stream of hexameter verses' at a meeting in the street.[42] Of all those who have used the metaphor of hell to visualize the convict experience, few have done so with such panache.[43] Following the conventions of a mock-heroic journey to the underworld, Frank the Poet dies and travels across the Styx, where Charon refuses to take any fee before sending him on to Limbo, where Piux VII (r. 1800–1823) rejects him on the ground that Limbo was intended for popes and priests

---

[38] For Moreton Bay: Tamsin O'Connor, 'A Zone of Silence: Queensland's Convicts and the Historiography of Moreton Bay', in Ian Duffield and James Bradley (eds.), *Representing Convicts* (London: Leicester University Press, 1997); Norfolk Island: Margaret Hazzard, *Punishment Short of Death* (Melbourne: Hyland House, 1984); Macquarie Harbour: Hamish Maxwell-Stewart, *Closing Hell's Gates* (Sydney: Allen & Unwin, 2008).

[39] Ken Gelder, 'Australian Gothic', in David Punter (ed.), *A New Companion to the Gothic* (Oxford: Wiley Blackwell, 2012), 379–392.

[40] John Milton, *Paradise Lost*, eds. William Kerrigan, James Rumrich, and Stephen M. Fallon (New York: Random House, 2011), p. 337.

[41] Bob Reece, 'Frank the Poet', in Bob Reece (ed.), *Exiles from Erin: Convict Lives in Ireland and Australia* (Basingstoke: Macmillan, 1991), 151–183. John Meredith and Rex Whalan, *Frank the Poet* (Melbourne: Red Rooster, 1979). For a sceptical re-assessment of the MacNamara legacy, Jeff Brownrigg, 'The Legend of Frank the Poet: Convict Heritage Recovered or Created?', *Journal of Australian Colonial History*, 18 (2016), 1–22. The 'Convict's Tour to Hell' is one of four poems associated with the time MacNamara served with the Australian Agricultural Company.

[42] William Bernard Ullathorne, *From Cabin-Boy to Archbishop* (London: Burns Oates, 1941), p. 65. If MacNamara, this meeting with the unnamed poet cannot have occurred in 1830 as described by Ullathorne, since MacNamara did not arrive in the colony until 1832.

[43] The outstanding recitation by Australian actor, Peter O'Shaughnessy (1923–2013), is available on YouTube www.youtube.com/watch?v=7y_z8vFigG8.

(a place they invented), then Purgatory, then all the way down to Hell where he devises elaborate tortures for all the enemies and authority figures at the penal stations of his acquaintance. As the poem makes clear, MacNamara had an excellent literary and theological education and a clear theodicy in which the poor – and especially poor convict poets – go to heaven and the torturers of the convict system get to burn. Without a glimmer of remorse, he calls down a general anathema on all dukes and mayors, noble judges, traitors, hangmen, gaolers and flagellators, commandants, constables and spies, culminating with Governor Darling. While it is impossible not to enjoy MacNamara's wit (which cost him hundreds of lashes) or Mitchel's venomous pen, it leaves untouched the very hard question of the 'convict voice' and just what the system meant to the vast majority who endured it and who were neither poets nor political hacks.[44] Before returning to the religious critique of the 'empire of hell', it will be useful to briefly sketch the character of the system, its scale and global reach.

British Penal Transportation

Throughout Great Britain and Ireland, prisoners had been exiled as a punishment since the Middle Ages, but it was not until the Transportation Act (1717) that it became a central feature of British law. Working out the numbers of those transported is challenging, one calculation suggests that 204,000 men and 36,000 women left the British Isles as convicts between 1661 and 1870.[45] We know considerably less about the flows of Indian Ocean convicts and transfers between colonies because of limitations in the evidence. In a painstaking piece of historical detective work, Clare Anderson has calculated that 308,000 convicts were transported around the British Empire between 1615 and 1939, including 109,000 (29 per cent) to sites in Asia (see Table 1.1).[46] While Anderson

---

[44] Hamish Maxwell-Stewart, 'The Search for the Convict Voice', *Tasmanian Historical Studies*, 6.1 (2001), 75–89.

[45] Hamish Maxwell-Stewart, 'Convict Transportation from Britain and Ireland 1615–1870', *History Compass*, 8.11 (2010), 1226. For a map of British penal settlements with operational dates, 1815–1945, see Ibid., 1222. His full list of British convict sites includes: 'most American colonies, the Caribbean islands of Barbados, Jamaica, Montserrat, Nevis and St Kitts; the slave factories of Goree and Cape Coast Castle in West Africa; the Australian colonies of New South Wales, Van Diemen's Land and Western Australia; the Indian Ocean Island of Mauritius; Bencoolen, Penang, the Tenasserim Provinces (Burma) and the Strait Settlements (Singapore) in South East Asia as well as Bermuda and Gibraltar'.

[46] Clare Anderson, 'Transnational Histories of Penal Transportation: Punishment, Labour and Governance in the British Imperial World, 1788–1939', *Australian Historical Studies*, 47.3 (2016), 381–397.

Table 1.1 *Convict transportation from Britain and Ireland to penal destinations, 1788–1875*

Origin	Destination	Period	Number
Britain and Ireland	New South Wales	1788–1839	79,278
Britain and Ireland	Van Diemen's Land	1803–1853	68,500
Britain and Ireland	Norfolk Island	1825–1853	6,025
Britain and Ireland	Port Phillip	1844–1849	2,064
Britain and Ireland	Western Australia	1850–1868	9,669
Britain and Ireland	Australian colonies	1807–1868	5,500
Britain and Ireland	Bermuda	1824–1863	9,113
Britain and Ireland	Gibraltar	1842–1875	4,618
Total			184,767

Source: Clare Anderson, 'Transnational Histories of Penal Transportation: Punishment, Labour and Governance in the British Imperial World, 1788–1939', *Australian Historical Studies*, 47 (2016), 382.

is right to note the 'conceptual myopia' that separates studies of the Indian Ocean and Australian penal colonies,[47] the transportation of British prisoners and those sent from other British colonies did form distinct regimes, with relatively little chronological or geographical overlap. This study is only concerned with those convicts, about 185,000 men, women and children, who were transported direct from Britain and Ireland to the Australian penal colonies, Bermuda and Gibraltar, between 1788 and 1875.[48]

As for what drove the system of transportation, empires have a high demand for labour and the resort to convicts as well as other forms of indentured and forced labour for plantations, colonization and military fortifications was part of a global trade in unfree labour.[49] Hamish Maxwell-Stewart refers to convicts, slaves and indentured servants as the 'shock troops of colonialism', who provided a short-lived solution to problems of the supply of labour.[50] In the eighteenth and nineteenth

[47] Ibid., 385.
[48] The most recent survey is Hamish Maxwell-Stewart, 'Transportation from Britain and Ireland, 1615–1875', in Clare Anderson (ed.), *A Global History of Convicts and Penal Colonies* (London: Bloomsbury, 2018), pp. 183–210.
[49] For studies of convict labour in the Roman Empire, medieval and early modern Europe, the Austro-Hungarian, Portuguese and British empires as well as colonial deployment in the British Raj, French Guiana, British colonial Africa, Latin America and the German Third Reich, see Christian Giuseppe de Vito and Alex Lichtenstein (eds.), *Global Convict Labour* (Leiden: Brill, 2015).
[50] Hamish Maxwell-Stewart, 'The Rise and Fall of Penal Transportation', in Paul Knepper and Anja Johansen (eds.), *The Oxford Handbook of the History of Crime and Criminal*

centuries, the Dutch East India Company, French, Portuguese, Russian and Spanish empires also created convict settlements.[51] Apart from the extreme distance from the ports of origin of its convict fleet, it is important to avoid an argument of Australian exceptionalism as a site for British penal colonies. International perspectives on convict transportation have been critical in opening up understandings of convict labour and the extent of its deployment in other spheres of empire.[52] While not insignificant, the scale of the forced labour trade in British convicts does not bear comparison with either the Atlantic or the Indian Ocean trades in both slaves and indentured labour. Britain alone transported more than ten African slaves for every one convict transported across the empire from any port.[53] Even in the Australian colonies, convicts were not the only form of forced labour and, with the end of convict transportation, significant numbers of indentured labourers from China, India, the Pacific, Italy and elsewhere filled the gap in the labour market.[54] Notwithstanding these caveats, transportation was instrumental in the colonization of Australia and important for the construction of naval fortifications in Gibraltar where convicts were transported from 1842 to 1875, and also in Bermuda, where they were sent from 1823 to 1863. While far flung – the British convict system eventually straddled three continents – the most important sites were located in Australia.

Across the British penal archipelago, the flow of convicts continued in fits and starts moderated by a stream of government inquiries, changes in official policy and public opinion. Convicts were transported to New South Wales from 1788 until 1839 when the House of Commons (HC) Select Committee (SC) on Transportation chaired by Sir William Molesworth (1810–1855) recommended an end to transportation.[55]

Justice (Oxford: Oxford University Press, 2016), p. 647. For an estimate that 'transported convicts' made up 7 per cent of the 14.5 million convicts, slaves and indentured servants transported by European empires in modern times, see Ibid., 650.

[51] For a map of these settlements, see Maxwell-Stewart, 'Convict Transportation from Britain and Ireland 1615–1870', 1223.

[52] Christian Guiseppe de Vito and Alex Lichtenstein, 'Writing a Global History of Convict Labour', *International Review of Social History*, 58.2 (2013), 285–325; Clare Anderson (ed.), *A Global History of Convicts and Penal Colonies* (London: Bloomsbury, 2018) provides detailed analysis of eight European convict empires, as well as those in postcolonial Latin America and Japan.

[53] The Trans-Atlantic Slave Trade Database estimates 3,259,441 slaves were transported by Great Britain between 1551 and 1825, www.slavevoyages.org/assessment/estimates (Accessed 12 April 2018). According to the National Archives, 2.6 million Africans were transported to British colonies between 1640 and 1807.

[54] Angela Woollacott, *Settler Society in the Australian Colonies* (Oxford: Oxford University Press, 2015), p. 40.

[55] *Molesworth SC on Transportation* (Report), BPP 1837–1838 (669) XXII.1, p. xli.

The first Australian penal settlements were made in and around Sydney and were extended north to the Coal River (modern Newcastle on the Hunter River) and Port Macquarie and inland to Bathurst and Wellington. Norfolk Island, an uninhabited island halfway between Australia and New Zealand, was one of the earliest settlements established after the arrival of Governor Arthur Philip and the convicts of the First Fleet in 1788. From 1824 to 1852 the island was the site of a much harsher penal settlement for prisoners sentenced to transportation by the courts of Sydney and Hobart. Convicts were also despatched further north to Moreton Bay near modern Brisbane from 1824 to 1850, and south to the Port Phillip District near modern Melbourne from 1803 to 1849. After 1839, transportation was restricted to convicts who had earned their ticket-of-leave whom Earl Grey called 'Exiles'. While convict sites are ubiquitous throughout south-eastern and western Australia, the most important and numerous penal stations were established in Van Diemen's Land, particularly the complex network of probation stations in the natural fortress of the Tasman and Forestier Peninsulas. Smaller, but still significant, convict establishments were maintained at Gibraltar from 1842 to 1875 and Bermuda from 1824 to 1863.[56]

Reformatory penal settlements, like anti-slavery, missions to convert the heathen and humanitarian interventions on behalf of native people formed part of the liberal props that enabled the expansion of the second British Empire.[57] In part, the drive to create a moral empire following the loss of the American colonies was a natural extension of the role of the established church in the imperial British state. Across Christendom, the monastery had been the model for penal discipline in Christian states. While most prisoners were male, prisons for 'fallen' or criminal women were typically directed by women in religious orders, following monastic modes of governance and supported financially by women's work such as washing.[58] In the penal colony of New South Wales, the Irish Sisters of Charity enlisted to regulate the Parramatta Female Factory were following a long tradition of such deployments in the rare context of transported female prisoners. Magdalen asylums were also run by French

[56] For an enumeration of convicts in international convict establishments, with estimates of flows across time, see 'ConvictVoyages', www.convictvoyages.org/statistic (Accessed 7 April 2018), and Anderson, 'Transnational Histories', 381–397.

[57] Andrew Porter, 'Evangelical Visions and Colonial Realities', *The Journal of Imperial and Colonial History*, 38.1 (2010), 145–155; Andrew Porter, 'Trusteeship, Anti-Slavery, and Humanitarianism', *The Oxford History of the British Empire, Vol. III: The Nineteenth Century* (Oxford: Oxford University Press, 1999), 198–221.

[58] De Vito and Lichtenstein (eds.), *Global Convict Labour*, pp. 322–323.

Sisters of Mercy in Lower Canada,[59] where the 1850s saw a steady rise in religious solutions for vulnerable women, juveniles and First Nations prisoners outside the secularized prison complex.[60] Catholic and Protestant missionaries were employed in all the settler colonies to contain, educate and Christianize Indigenous British subjects, sometimes in carceral conditions that resembled those in more overtly secular penal stations. Religious women later conducted missions in northern Australia to Aboriginal lepers housed in lock hospital conditions.[61] However, this takes us away from the particular study of British convict transportation, which was not re-introduced in British North America, with the exception of the political prisoners transported for their role in the rebellions of 1836 and 1837. In all cases, religious provision for prisoners was one aspect of the entanglement of church and the British imperial state, initially Protestant but ameliorated by liberal toleration of other creeds.

A significant feature of British convict transportation was the extent to which it was both tempered and justified by religion. Other European empires also made use of religious personnel and religious ideologies for the management of convict populations, including those sentenced to internal exile or overseas transportation. While all establishments for British and Irish convicts were managed by the state, Protestant societies and Catholic religious orders managed those in other empires, especially for children, women, slaves and ex-slaves, and tribal and indigenous people.[62] These include the Salvation Army in British India and, from 1933, French Guiana, where they supported former prisoners, and schools for convict children in French Guiana and New Caledonia.[63] While not a formal part of the prison system, missions played a significant role in attempts to contain frontier violence, such as those conducted by the London Missionary Society in the warring Kat River Settlement of the Cape Colony.[64] Religious offenders, like political

---

[59] Ted McCoy, *Hard Time: Reforming the Penitentiary in Nineteenth-Century Canada* (Edmonton: Athabasca University Press, 2012), pp. 87–88.

[60] Ibid., 130.

[61] Hilary M. Carey, 'Subordination, Invisibility and Chosen Work: Missionary Nuns and Australian Aborigines, c.1900–1949', *Australian Feminist Studies*, 13.28 (1998), 251–267.

[62] For examples listed, Anderson (ed.), *Global History*, pp. 2–3.

[63] Rachel J. Tolen, 'Colonizing and Transforming the Criminal Tribesman – The Salvation Army in British India', *American Ethnologist*, 18.1 (1991), 106–125; Jean-Lucien Sanchez, 'The Penal Colonization of French Guyana, 1852–1953', ConvictVoyages, www.convictvoyages.org/expert-essays/french-guiana (Accessed 23 August 2018).

[64] Exceptionally, missions also provided training in political theologies of resistance, see Robert Ross, *The Borders of Race in Colonial South Africa* (Cambridge: Cambridge University Press, 2014), pp. 128–129; Elizabeth Elbourne, 'Early Khoisan uses of Mission Christianity', in Henry Bredekamp and Robert Ross (eds.), *Missions and*

prisoners were often seen as more dangerous and requiring particular carceral solutions and isolation. Exile to Siberia was abolished by the Russian Empire in 1900 except for religious and political prisoners.[65] In the nineteenth century, most European nations became committed to enlightened forms of penal discipline in prisons as well as penal colonies and *bagnes* where citizens could be rehabilitated through a combination of work, exile, education and, frequently, religious discipline.[66] In France and Italy, monastic models of confinement were extended to include social criminals, including vagrants, prostitutes, mothers of illegitimate children and boys, such as the celebrated papal reformatory of San Michele in Rome, or the Maison de Force in Ghent.[67] What made the British system different was that, beginning with Colonel Arthur, 'moral machinery' was incorporated into both its home penitentiaries and its distant convict settlements. While subject to continuous criticism, they were recognized as models for convict colonization by other empires, including France and Germany.[68]

Anti-Transportation and Its Historians

Like the flows of convicts, the campaign to end transportation proceeded in fits and starts in reaction to the arrival, or threatened arrival, of convicts in different parts of the empire. As transportation ended in eastern Australia, it began in the west. Convicts were sent to Western Australia from 1849 until 1868. The 1857 Penal Servitude Act nominally abolished transportation as a punishment in the United Kingdom but it continued in various forms beyond this date not only to Western Australia but also to Gibraltar and Bermuda. Colonial opposition ensured that attempts to create additional sites for convicts in tropical northern Australia, southern Africa, New Zealand or the Falkland Islands were ultimately unsuccessful. As with slavery, it required a global

---

Christianity in South African History (Johnannesburg: Witwatersrand University Press, 1993), pp. 65–96.

[65] Sarah Badcock and Judith Pallot, 'Russia and the Soviet Union from the Nineteenth to the Twenty-First Century', in Anderson (ed.), *Global History*, pp. 271–306.

[66] Mary Gibson and Ilaria Poerio, 'Modern Europe, 1750–1950', in Anderson (ed.), *Global History*, p. 337.

[67] See Chapter 6; on San Michele, Mary Gibson, 'Gender and Convict Labour: The Italian Case in Global Context', in De Vito and Lichtenstein (eds.), *Global Convict Labour*, pp. 317–319.

[68] Matthew Fitzpatrick, 'New South Wales in Africa? The Convict Colonialism Debate in Imperial Germany', *Itinerario*, 37.1 (2013), 59–72; Gustave de Beaumont and Alexis de Tocqueville advised against it, but in 1853 Napoleon III ordered transportation, on the British model, to begin to Devil's Island in French Guiana.

campaign which united political and religious forces across the empire to bring about an end to convict transportation from Britain and Ireland.

Convict transportation was not recognized as an absolute moral evil in the eighteenth, or indeed in the first decades of the nineteenth century. However, this position gradually changed, as we will see, in the course of the 1830s and 1840s. In the eyes of liberal historians, the reform of the criminal code and the design of new prisons were among the most distinguished achievements of the age of reform. The herald of the Whig reformist achievement, Thomas Babbington Macaulay (1800–1859), declaiming the violence of a pre-civilized age (that is, before the Whigs came to power), recalled that 'the prisons were hells on earth, seminaries of every crime and every disease'.[69] Liberal governments abolished penal torture, built healthy prisons, attempted to reform transportation and rationalized the law. In this patriotic view, the abolition of convict transportation should be regarded as an accomplishment akin to the abolition of slavery, which merited memorials and self-congratulation in post-colonial states. This was certainly the view of the first historians of the anti-transportation movement such as the Rev. John West (1809–1873). West saw the abolition of convict transportation as one more step in the advance of Christian knowledge and British civilization: 'No believer in the glorious destinies of the Anglo-Saxon race can look upon the events of the last three years without wonder and hope. The American and British empires are seated on all waters; the old and new worlds are filled with the name and fame of England and her children. The lands conquered by Caesar, those discovered by Columbus, and those explored by Cook, are now joined in one destiny.'[70] In these views, West mirrored other Dissenting historians of the empire who saw the expansion of liberal freedoms as the emblematic gift of the British to the world they conquered. The Australian Methodist historian and imperial apologist, W. H. Fitchett (1841–1928), saw the refusal to accept Britain's human detritus as a triumph for the 'common sense and self-respect of the free settlers'.[71] In one of the first attempts to write a national history of Australia, Fitchett depicted convictism as the dismal prelude to the 'golden history' of the new world of the south, secured by the same Providence who guided the steps of British explorers.[72]

[69] Thomas Babington Macaulay, *The History of England from the Accession of James II*, 5 vols. (London: Longman 1849), vol. I, p. 290.

[70] John West, *The History of Tasmania*, 2 vols. (Launceston: Henry Dowling, 1852), vol. I, p. 346.

[71] William Henry Fitchett, *The New World of the South*, 2 vols. (London: Smith, Elder & Co., 1913), vol. II, p. 13.

[72] Ibid., vol. II, p. 355, speaking of Sturt's exploration of the interior.

By the 1970s, revisionist writing by social scientists and historians tore apart liberal assumptions about the progressivism of penal reform. They argued that the creation of the penitentiary was the product of the zeal for social control associated with the rise of industrial society in western Europe and parts of the United States. The classic studies by Michael Ignatieff and Michel Foucault argued that the prison was the material embodiment of the power wielded by ruling elites over the powerless and that breathtaking hypocrisy was the dominant note in religious writing about those convicted and incarcerated.[73] Vic Gatrell's *The Hanging Tree* provided a mercilessly critical survey of the cupidity and heartlessness of gaol chaplains who served to 'comfort' prisoners under sentence of execution,[74] but Foucault got there first. For Foucault, the nineteenth century was a period of retreat from the physical punishment of the body to the disciplining and incarceration of the soul, a process conducted by 'a whole army of technicians who took over from the executioner … warders, doctors, chaplains, psychiatrists, educationalists'.[75] Chaplains were high on Foucault's list of surrogates for the executioner. Clergy had always attended executions and used the gallows in an active way to preach repentance to the crowd assembled for public death.[76] But while there are religious traditions which celebrate the infliction of both pain and incarceration,[77] secular historians tend to regard chaplains as part of the early history of the penitentiary, whose role was rapidly secularized and bureaucratized in the hands of state authorities and subordinated to prison officers, social workers and eventually modern parole and probation officers.[78]

In his bravura epic of the Australian convict world, *The Fatal Shore*, Robert Hughes echoes these views, extending the critique of the prison to convict colonization. He regarded chaplains as an oddity inflicted on a bestial system but who were marginal to its core operations. Referring to the chaplain at Point Puer at Port Arthur, Hughes states that all attempts

---

[73] Michael Ignatieff, *A Just Measure of Pain* (London: Macmillan, 1978); Michel Foucault, *Discipline and Punish*, trans. Alan Sheridan (London: Allen Lane, 1977).

[74] V. A. C. Gatrell, *The Hanging Tree* (Oxford: Oxford University Press, 1996), pp. 371–395.

[75] Foucault, *Discipline and Punish*, p. 1.

[76] For a study of execution sermons in New England which 'warned of the wages of sin, reconciled the convict to both God and the community, and demonstrated the cooperative authority of church and state', see Scott D. Seay, *Hanging between Heaven and Earth* (DeKalb: Northern Illinois University Press, 2009).

[77] Ariel Glucklich, *Sacred Pain* (Oxford: Oxford University Press, 2001), for the origins of pain in the Fall of Adam.

[78] Carolyn Strange, 'The Undercurrents of Penal Culture: Punishment of the Body in Mid-Twentieth Century Canada', *Law and History Review*, 19.2 (2001), 343.

to rejuvenate convict boys by religion were a failure. After five years under his hand: 'a few of the boys could parrot bits of an Anglican catechism, but none could recite the Commandments in correct order or show much grasp of scriptural history'.[79] They could not even sing any hymns. Hughes had a less hostile interpretation of the Rev. Thomas George Rogers (1806–1903), a Protestant religious instructor on Norfolk Island, whom he refers to as a 'dissident friend of the convicts' and 'prototype of the tormented alcoholic chaplain', the Rev. James North, in *His Natural Life*, Marcus Clarke's anti-transportation novel.[80] Clarke provides what have proven to be the two enduring stereotypes of the convict chaplain – either decent but damaged men such as North, who provided some comfort to the anti-hero convict Rufus Dawes, or canting hypocrites such as the Rev. Meekin, 'a Respectable chaplain who is a friend of a Bishop!'. When Meekin tells Dawes to 'read the Bible' and 'humble himself in prayer', Dawes makes the bitter reflection: 'The old, sickening, barren cant of piety was to be recommended, then. He came asking for bread, and they gave him the usual stone.'[81] A recent study of reformist experiments in transportation, including the probation system, continues to focus on the theme of hypocrisy in policy and outcomes.[82]

One of the central assumptions of the 'hell-on-earth' discourse is that penal settlements were devoid of spiritual, moral and intellectual facilities and that convicts lacked an internal, religious life. While convicts in the penal settlements displayed scant interest in institutional religion, Hamish Maxwell-Stewart's work on convict religious tattoos suggests that this was not the whole story.[83] The clergy who ministered to convicts have been lampooned as second-raters without sympathy for their charges or the intellect to reflect on their role in maintaining a corrupt system. In the 1960s, C. M. H. Clark derided the Protestant clergy for serving 'the contemptible, servile, hypocritical function of acting as moral policemen, or sanctimonious spies, for the established moral order'.[84]

---

[79] Robert Hughes, *The Fatal Shore: A History of the Transportation of Convicts to Australia, 1787–1868* (New York: Knopf, 1986), p. 411.

[80] Ibid., 651. Clarke's representation of Rogers (a teetotaller) as the drunken North is misleading on a number of counts, as Hughes realized, Ibid. See also Chapter 8.

[81] Clarke, *For the Term of His Natural Life*, p. 252; the chapter entitled 'The Consolations of Religion'.

[82] Philip Harling, 'The Trouble with Convicts: From Transportation to Penal Servitude, 1840–67', *Journal of British Studies*, 53.1 (2014), 80–110.

[83] Hamish Maxwell-Stewart and Ian Duffield, 'Skin Deep Devotion: Religious Tattoos and Convict Transportation to Australia', in Jane Caplan (ed.), *Written on the Body: The Tattoo in European and American History* (London: Reaktion, 2000), p. 282.

[84] C. M. H. Clark, *A History of Australia II: New South Wales and Van Diemen's Land, 1822–1838* (Melbourne: Melbourne University Press, 1968), p. 108.

Alan Grocott, the only historian to have written a book-length study of convict clergy, represented them as essentially part of the punishment regime which prisoners had to endure.[85] His main thesis, relentlessly pursued, was that in New South Wales convicts were either hostile or indifferent to all forms of religion, something which supported the views of Grocott's doctoral supervisor, Russel Ward, and his argument about the role of the 'nomad tribe' of anti-clerical rural workers as foundational to the Australian national identity.[86] The harshest criticism of all has been reserved for figures such as the second colonial chaplain of New South Wales, the Rev. Samuel Marsden (1764–1838), denounced chiefly on the basis of his duties as a magistrate and his undeniably harsh record for flogging convicts.[87] If not actually sadistic, clergy have also been accused of providing the rhetorical and moral justification for the much harsher punishment regimes which replaced the supposed free and easy days of assignment. Even the role of clergy in the anti-transportation campaign has come under attack.[88] The historian Babette Smith has extended the finger of accusation at both the Catholic Vicar General, William Bernard Ullathorne (1806–1889) and the Rev. John West (1809–1873), the Congregationalist minister chiefly responsible for launching the Australasian Anti-Transportation League which was instrumental in unifying colonial forces in Australia and New Zealand in opposition to continued transportation. Smith's central thesis is that, in cahoots with Molesworth, Ullathorne, West and their clerical comrades were guilty of orchestrating a homophobic panic which was as self-interested as it was destructive for the convicts who deserve to be remembered dispassionately as the real founders of Australia.[89]

Empire of Hell challenges the historical stereotypes which equate religious intervention with malevolent social control. It takes a lead from the

---

[85] Allan M. Grocott, *Convicts, Clergymen and Churches* (Sydney: Sydney University Press, 1980).

[86] Ward's preface declares his satisfaction that Grocott's findings were 'not basically different from what I had stated them to be', Ibid., p. ix.

[87] Matthew Allen, 'The Myth of the Flogging Parson: Samuel Marsden and Severity of Punishment in the Age of Reform', *Australian Historical Studies*, 48.4 (2017), 486–501. See also Michael Gladwin, 'Flogging Parsons? Australian Anglican Clergymen, the Magistracy, and Convicts, 1788–1850', *Journal of Religious History*, 36.3 (2012), 386–403.

[88] For the reception of the anti-transportation debate, see David A. Roberts, 'Beyond the Stain: Rethinking the Nature and Impact of the Anti-Transportation Movement', *Journal of Australian Colonial History*, 14 (2012), 205–279.

[89] Babette Smith, *Australia's Birthstain: The Startling Legacy of the Convict Era* (Sydney: Allen & Unwin, 2008), p. 10 et passim. For critique of Smith, see Hilary M. Carey, 'Clerics and the Beginning of the Anti-Transportation Debate', *Journal of Australian Colonial History*, 14 (2012), 241–249.

'religious turn' in historical writing about the penitentiary, including the rediscovery of the religious foundations of early prison reform. The object is not to elevate and celebrate these religious threads – simply to make them visible and integral to the historical tapestry of the convict system. Simon Devereaux, for example, in an article which examines the background to the English Penitentiary Act of 1779, suggests that too much emphasis has been placed on the modernizing, secular and Enlightenment roots of prison reform to the neglect of its weighty, religious elements.[90] Penal reform was dominated by Evangelical religion as much as utilitarian sciences, according to Richard Follett.[91] When Sir William Blackstone (1723–1780) and William Eden set out to reform the penal code, they proposed the creation of a model penitentiary which would replace the poorly regulated and disease-ridden holding pens that had been condemned by the reforming John Howard with moral reformatories which were designed to bring the prisoner back to a know-ledge of their correct place in society. It is the next stage of the reform process which has been neglected by researchers; for ongoing religious reform we need to turn our attention south. As discussed in Chapter 2, although John Howard's model penitentiary with the chapel at its heart was never built (and neither was Jeremy Bentham's Panopticon), Evan-gelical reformist aspirations were invested in the decision to establish a penal colony in New South Wales. It was not until 1816 that the first model penitentiary at Millbank was opened, to almost universal condem-nation. In the 1830s, as Follett has suggested, Evangelicals hoped that their 'new models of prison discipline' would lead offenders back to an ordered life which was bounded by lawful and moral citizenry.[92] *Pace* Hughes, the era of convict transportation to Australia belongs to the most optimistic phase of the prison reform movement which continued until the 1850s, during which the British imperial state committed itself to an explicitly reformist project in which religion played a key role. It was not until the end of the transportation era that there was a move away from moral reformism back to old-fashioned deterrence and severity.

John Mitchel had a privileged vantage point from which to view the British convict empire, and reveals much about the nature and extent of religious interventions in the later stages of the British convict system. Despite his commitment to the violent overthrow of the British

---

[90] Simon Devereaux, 'The Making of the Penitentiary Act, 1775–1779', *The Historical Journal*, 42.2 (1999), 404–433.

[91] Richard R. Follett, *Evangelicalism, Penal Theory, and the Politics of Criminal Law Reform in England, 1808–30* (New York: St. Martin's Press, 2000), p. 9.

[92] Ibid.

government in Ireland, Mitchel was not without religious sensibilities, as might be expected of a son of the Manse: his father was a Presbyterian minister before making a late conversion to Unitarianism. Mitchel's journal makes it clear that clergy, religious instructors and schoolmasters were available everywhere on his convict travels and appear to have done the best job they could on limited resources. On his first Sunday in Bermuda, he attended service on deck with the prisoners. Afterwards the chaplain, a Scot, visited him and offered to lend him books: 'I rather like the man: he did not cant, as so many of those persons.'[93] There were religious instructors for the men and school masters for the boys, and while Mitchel felt no wish to be one of the convicts, he appreciated the visits by educated clergy who gave him news and let him feel a gentleman despite his situation. At the Cape, while the *Neptune* was delayed by the anti-convict protest, the Anglican bishop of Cape Town, Dr Robert Gray (1809–1872), came on board, preached to the convicts and afterwards came to see him. Mitchel noted that Gray 'called the poor convicts, "My dearly beloved brethren"', whereas the religious instructor, called them 'my men'. Gray made a good impression on Mitchel in both his appearance and his views on transportation: 'He is a young man for a bishop, but wears a highly orthodox shovel-hat, and a most peremptory silk apron girt round his loins. I found him a very agreeable person: he heartily approves of the anti-convict movement.'[94] He also found Van Diemen's Land fully fortified by established and Dissenting clergy. While Mitchel is scarcely an impartial observer, such observations confirm that by the 1850s clergy were well integrated into the convict system and were by no means passive agents of an imperial power. At the very least, Mitchel demonstrates the need for a reassessment of religion in both the working of the convict system and in the anti-transportation campaign he witnessed in Bermuda, the Cape Colony and Van Diemen's Land.

Empire of Hell traces the religious arguments about convict transportation from its origin in 1788 until its end in Gibraltar in 1875. The chapters which follow mostly flow chronologically and geographically and they cover every colony which received convicts direct from the United Kingdom and Ireland from 1788 to 1875. Five chapters are focused on four different religious traditions that contributed to the debates about transportation. Chapter 2 considers the rise of Evangelical Anglicans to positions of influence which allowed them to press for reformation as a fundamental object of prison discipline. While

---

[93] Mitchel, *Jail Journal*, p. 64.   [94] Ibid., 204.

Evangelicals generally opposed transportation and supported moves for home-based penitentiaries, Chapter 3 examines the work of Sir George Arthur who sought to create a reformist penal colony on Evangelical principles in Van Diemen's Land from 1824 to 1836. Beginning with Arthur but reflecting changes to the management of the prison system in Great Britain and Ireland, clergy began to have an increasing role within the convict system, whether as chaplains, magistrates, religious instructors or schoolteachers. Enshrined in legislation that put them at the heart of the reformative prison movement, their role became more significant after the Bigge Reports (1822–1823) recommended the enhancement of private assignment and harshening the regime of punishment in the colonies. Chapter 4 examines the special role played by the Quakers, Rational Dissenters who initiated the penal reform movement in the United States, which was duly brought to Australia by Quakers travelling 'under concern', notably James Backhouse and George Washington Walker in the 1830s. Backhouse and Walker recommended that reformation and training was implemented for both convicts and Australian Aborigines but continued to support transportation in the form created by Colonel Arthur.

Just as religious ideas were essential to the design and reform of penal systems, so they were in the overthrow of convict transportation. Chapter 5 focuses on the Liberal Anglicanism of Richard Whately (1787–1863), archbishop of Dublin, who first articulated a Christian utilitarianism hostile to the continued maintenance of the flow of convicts and supportive of systematic colonization using free labour. Whately's arguments were incorporated into the findings of the Molesworth SC on Transportation (1838), which demonized convicts and their settler masters. Chapter 6 examines the campaign to denounce the 'horrors of transportation' and its sectarian strands, represented by the trade in insults between the judge, Sir William Westbrooke Burton (1794–1888), and Ullathorne in New South Wales. Both Catholics and Protestants had reasons to condemn the moral failings of the convicts and free the colony from private assignment, which was regularly, if erroneously, equated with slavery. While Molesworth was sure that his Report had dealt a death blow to transportation, in fact it continued with renewed vigour, buoyed by religious models of reformative transportation promoted by senior members of both Whig and Tory administrations. Chapters 7 and 8 examine a number of penal reformatory experiments, of which Captain Maconochie's term in the 'Ocean Hell' of Norfolk Island was the most controversial. The high watermark for religiously based transportation was reached by the probation system, considered in Chapter 9, which attempted to implement the Evangelical straightjacket of Pentonville with a mobile army of religious instructors in the probation stations of Van Diemen's Land. By the 1840s, no corner of the British penal empire was entirely free of religious and reforming influences, though the attempt to reform the hulks, Bermuda and Gibraltar, considered in Chapter 10, defeated the best efforts of Governor Sir Charles Elliot (1801–1875) and other administrators.

While Archbishop Whately initiated a Christian debate about the utility and morality of transportation, it was not until attempts were made to resume transportation to eastern Australia that the anti-transportation campaign began in earnest, considered in Chapter 9. The spiritual leader of the movement was the Congregationalist minister and journalist, the Rev. John West, whose Dissenting liberalism helped create a loyal, non-sectarian alliance opposed to transportation on moral grounds. As with the institution of slavery, convictism did not end when the transports ceased to arrive in eastern Australia. It continued in the 'floating hells' of the hulks, Bermuda and Gibraltar. The final days of the hulks were hastened by the timely intervention of a clerical whistle-blower, the Rev. John Guilding, featured in Chapter 10. Chapter 11 looks at the last gasp of transportation, which included the development of Pentonville across the sea in Western Australia where Bishop Mathew Hale (1811–1895) advocated reformative rather than punitive colonization. A concluding chapter assesses the legacy of transportation and its challenging religious history.

It is necessary to demarcate the limits of this study. Except by way of illustration, it is not about convict religion, the relationship between convicts and their pastors or religious elements of convict discipline, though these are important subjects which deserve attention. Rather, it concerns religious arguments made by elites about convict transportation, initially to support its reformative possibilities against the rival claims of the penitentiary (Chapters 2, 3, 4 and 8) and later to demand its abolition (Chapters 5, 6 and 9). While individuals often held strong opinions about transportation, the debate between ecclesiastical and government authorities was at its most active in the 1830s, 1840s and 1850s when the liberal empire provided a vast arena for reformative experiments in penal discipline. This period forms the main focus of study though it includes analysis of every major penal establishment to where British and Irish convicts were transported as well as considering the views of every major Christian denomination that participated in the anti-transportation debate.

Conclusion

This introductory chapter has argued that the British convict transportation system has been dominated by representations which stress the horror, cruelty, vice and irrationality of the system. In the pithy words of John Mitchel, it was an 'empire of hell'. Such a designation has traditionally served to demonize the convict system. In the nineteenth century, it was the convicts who were regarded as morally repugnant. In the course of revisionist historiography of the convict system and in celebratory popular history, the demonic agents have changed their identities. Historians have rediscovered the agency and integrity of convict men and women and recognized their contribution to the founding of Australian society. Now it is the figures of authority, the British politicians and bureaucrats, the local governors, convict administrators and clergy who are more likely to be derided, along with the braying colonists with their bourgeois pretensions and foibles, including far too much interest in convict sex. This narrative of origins marginalizes much that was important to the transportation debate and tells us more about contemporary identity politics than the convicts and their legacy.

This book argues that religion played a central role in shaping the ideology and discipline of the convict system as it evolved over the course of more than eighty years. Reformist regimes, heavily influenced by religious ideals, were just as important to the convict colonies as they were to home-based British penitentiaries and reformatories. Enlightened penal reform was the product of a partnership between religious and secular reformers, including John Howard and other rational Evangelicals and Dissenters, Samuel Romilly and even the anti-clerical Jeremy Bentham. When Bentham debated whether his Panopticon or transportation to New South Wales was the best solution for crime in Britain, he was recommending prison reforms which had already been trialled in the United States along lines supported by the Religious Society of Friends. In the nineteenth-century campaign to end convict transportation, Anglican Evangelicals, Liberal Anglicans, Quakers and other advocates of Rational Dissent, as well as Catholics, would play different roles in reforming and then campaigning for an end to convict transportation. The next five chapters will consider how these different religious traditions of penal reform evolved and why it proved so challenging for their combined forces to bring down the 'empire of hell'.

Religion is the most powerful engine that can be applied to the human mind; and surely if there be any spot upon this earth, in which more than in any other it may expect attention, that spot is within the walls of a prison.[1]

(George Holford, 1821)

[T]here are but few, even among the most guilty, who may not, by proper discipline and treatment, be subdued and reclaimed.[2]

(William Wilberforce, 1822)

Following the abolition of the Atlantic slave trade in 1807, a reforming wave swept through the British Empire. While Mitchel bemoaned the extension of the empire of hell, reformers proposed the establishment of a moral empire which might compensate for the loss of the thirteen American colonies. Although the moral empire was not exclusively or even a majority achievement of clerical or specially religiously committed reformers, it was affected by three related religious movements: Rational Dissent, which included enlightened advocates for penal reform inspired by John Howard; the evangelical revival, especially the serious Anglican interpretation of the movement spearheaded politically by William Wilberforce (1759–1833); and the Methodists with their heightened awareness of the social dimension of Christianity sparked, in some cases, by the expectation of an imminent Second Coming. This chapter will consider the way in which one of those strands, Anglican Evangelicalism, or the 'low church' party of the United Church of England and Ireland,[3]

---

[1] George Holford, *Thoughts on the Criminal Prisons of This Country* (London: Rivington, 1821), pp. 69–70.

[2] Prison Discipline Society, *Fourth Report of the Committee of the Society for the Improvement of Prison Discipline* (London: Bensley, 1822), pp. 10–11.

[3] From this point, Evangelicalism is capitalized to refer to the Anglican Evangelical tradition and put in lowercase when referring to evangelicalism as a wider movement that included most Dissenters (i.e., Baptists, Quakers, Congregationalists and Methodists) as well as some Anglicans. For analysis, see Gareth Atkins, 'Anglican Evangelicalism', in Jeremy Gregory (ed.), *The Oxford History of Anglicanism, Volume II: Establishment and Empire, 1662–1829* (Oxford: Oxford University Press, 2017), 452–473; David W. Bebbington, *Evangelicalism in Modern Britain: A History from the 1730s to the*

came to influence ideologies of penal discipline at home and how this impacted the penal colonies of New South Wales, including Norfolk Island and Van Diemen's Land (which became a separate colony in 1825).

Evangelicals were open to plans for reform though they were initially hostile to convict transportation, which they saw as a less moral solution than the construction of well-designed penitentiaries at home. They hoped that the reformatory regime which underpinned the Gaol Chaplains Act (1773), which required the appointment of chaplains in every prison, and the Penitentiary Act of 1779, might be extended to the colonies.[4] In effect, reformers opted for the creation in Botany Bay of what Mayhew would later call a 'penal purgatory'.[5] While Anglicans did not believe in purgatory, they were open to plans to create an earthy equivalent in the penal colonies.[6] Not all colonial officers shared this Evangelical ambition, indeed most governors were pragmatic naval or military men focused on keeping order and doing their duty, not religion. However, it was promoted by a number of the more articulate and influential governors as well as most of the colonial chaplains, and their views were endorsed by the Colonial Office and figures of influence in Parliament. To understand how this happened, we need to know more about the 'age of atonement', a period dominated by the Tories in government and the established church in religion, who ruled together from the arrival of the First Fleet in New South Wales in 1788 until 1830.

Age of Atonement

So great was the gloom which descended following the French Revolution that Boyd Hilton has termed the period from 1795 to 1865 an 'age of

1980s (London: Unwin Hyman, 1989), pp. 3–17; Timothy Larsen, 'Defining and Locating Evangelicalism', in Timothy Larsen and Daniel Treier (eds.), *The Cambridge Companion to Evangelical Theology* (Cambridge: Cambridge University Press, 2007), 1–14; John Wolffe, *The Expansion of Evangelicalism: The Age of Wilberforce, More, Chalmers and Finney* (Downers Grove, IL: InterVarsity Press, 2007).

4 For the ideology of the 1779 Penitentiary Act, see Laurie Throness, *A Protestant Purgatory: Theological Origins of the Penitentiary Act, 1779* (Aldershot: Ashgate, 2008); The Gaols Act (1823) mandated regular visits to prisoners by chaplains.

5 Henry Mayhew and John Binny, *The Criminal Prisons of London and Scenes of Prison Life* (New York: Kelley, 1862), p. 147, referring to Pentonville.

6 Anglican belief in Purgatory was countermanded by Article 22 of the Thirty-Nine Articles (1571), where it is defined as 'a fond thing, vainly invented'. In Catholic theology, Purgatory was a place of suffering where the souls of the departed, who had not expiated their sins in this life, await final judgment; Andrew Skotnicki, 'God's Prisoners: Penal Confinement and the Creation of Purgatory', *Modern Theology*, 22 (2006), 85–110.

atonement' in contrast to the 'age of enlightenment' which preceded it.[7] The Evangelical Party in the Church of England rose up partly to challenge the popular religious revival sparked by the emergence of the Methodists, whose spiritual optimism and enthusiasm were roundly criticized in the years following the death of John Wesley in 1791.[8] 'Atonement' lies at the core of Christian doctrine. In the New Testament St Paul teaches: 'we were reconciled to God through the death of his Son' (Romans 5:10), and 'Christ died for our sins' (1 Corinthians 15:3). In a range of metaphors employed by early Christian thinkers adopted from the Old Testament, Christ was the Paschal or Passover lamb sacrificed to God by the Israelites on the night before the Exodus which allowed the angel of death to pass over their households (Exodus 12).[9] Hence, Christ's death was the ransom paid to release the Israelites from Egyptian bondage; His blood was poured out as a sacrifice for all, the single perfect offering (Hebrews 10:12); once slaves to sin, Christ's death has made us free (Romans 6:20). In the eighteenth century the interpretation of the atonement underwent a significant shift, away from the 'coldness' of Protestant orthodoxy, to a warmer, more subjective experience expressed in pietism on the continent and Methodism in Britain.[10] Evangelicals preached a return to the orthodox Calvinist models of the relationship of God and humanity, where the world was regarded as a place of atonement and suffering, a spiritual penal colony like the material colonies being created in the southern world where convicts were exiled to atone for their sins.

The interpretative shift in understandings of atonement is evident in the Arminian hymns of Charles Wesley (1707–1788), which are particularly rich in representations of the atonement and its symbols of lambs, blood, sacrifice, prayer, death and hoped for – but never guaranteed – pleas for pardon and release from bondage (to sin).[11] In *Hymns and*

---

[7] Boyd Hilton, *The Age of Atonement* (Oxford: Clarendon, 1988).

[8] For a study that stresses the fluid political alliances which subverted partisan Anglican boundaries and linked Anglicans with like-minded Dissenters, such as the Quakers and former Quakers who were prominent in prison reform see J. C. D. Clark, 'Church, Parties and Politics', in Jeremy Gregory (ed.), *The Oxford History of Anglicanism, Volume II: Establishment and Empire, 1662–1829* (Oxford: Oxford University Press, 2017), pp. 289–313.

[9] For the significance of the Book of Exodus for Protestant anti-slavery, see John Coffey, *Exodus and Liberation: Deliverance Politics from John Calvin to Martin Luther King Jr* (Oxford: Oxford University Press, 2013), pp. 79–106.

[10] Simeon Zahl, Atonement in Nicholas Adams, George Pattison and Graham Ward (eds.), *The Oxford Handbook of Theology and Modern European Thought* (Oxford: Oxford University Press, 2013), p. 635.

[11] Joanna Cruickshank, '"Appear as Crucified for Me": Sight, Suffering, and Spiritual Transformation in the Hymns of Charles Wesley', *Journal of Religious History*, 30.3 (2006), 311–330.

Sacred Poems, published in 1743 and intended to support Anglican services, the lamb appears dozens of times in hymns that are generally uplifting and confident of salvation: 'Pardon and Peace in Him I find/ But not for me alone/ The Lamb was slain; for all Mankind/ His Blood did once atone'.[12] Christ is the one who liberates slaves who are captives to sin, just as he led souls from captivity in the harrowing of hell:[13] 'Christ; who now gone up on high/[14] Captive leads Captivity'.[15] Over a century later, a shift in mood is evident in the work of Charles Simeon (1759–1836), the leading Anglican Evangelical clergyman, whose sermons and hymn collection reflect the strains and anxieties of the age. In his expository preaching Simeon focused on the lamb who atoned for the sins of the world, but whose mercy is not certain: 'Sinners, behold the bleeding LAMB!/ To him lift up your longing eyes,/ And hope for mercy in his name'.[16] Simeon objected to the wild notions of the Methodists, some of whom believed in the doctrine of sinless perfection which caused them to 'wink hard at their own imperfections'.[17] No such winking was permitted in the Calvinist tradition preached by Simeon, which instead stressed the extreme depravity of human nature.[18]

Although the Evangelical temper was consciously antagonistic to utilitarian humanism and Methodist optimism, the three movements had certain things in common and came to similar conclusions about what ought to be done in relation to crime and punishment. In the first place, none of the movements were liberal or democratic in their sympathies. Prisoners, slaves and the heathen were souls to be saved, who owed a debt to society, not citizens or potential citizens whose woes should be ameliorated by economic or social reform. Punishment, pain and suffering were conditions to be relished if they achieved a moral purpose and it was assumed that whether prisoners were to be reformed or deterred from sinning again, pain was necessary to affect the hardened

---

[12] John Wesley and Charles Wesley, *Hymns and Sacred Poems* 4th edn (Bristol: Farley, 1743), p. 259.

[13] The allusion here is to the tradition that Christ visited Hell immediately after the crucifixion, bringing out a number of select souls, before proceeding to his Resurrection, a belief defined for Anglicans as Article 4 of the Thirty-Nine Articles, *The Book of Common Prayer* (Cambridge: John Baskerville, 1760).

[14] Ibid., p. 148.

[15] John Wesley and Charles Wesley, *Hymns and Sacred Poems* 4th edn (Bristol: Farley, 1743), p. 148.

[16] *A Collection of Psalms and Hymns*, compiled by C. Simeon, 17th edn (Cambridge: Page, 1835), p. 76.

[17] Charles Simeon, *Memoirs of the Life of the Rev. Charles Simeon*, edited by William Carus (London: Hatchard & Son, 1847), p. 161.

[18] For Simeon's conversation with Wesley on the differences between Arminian and Calvinist views of human nature, see Ibid., 182.

heart.[19] Besides a general indifference to the particular modes by which a prisoner might be punished, the first part of the nineteenth century would be dominated by theologies which stressed humanity's sinful nature, gloried in the suffering of Christ on the cross, and looked forward with anxious dread to a future life which, in all probability, would be filled with an eternity of suffering and torment. In some ways, this sounded like the fate of the prisoners transported to remote penal colonies in Australia. Punishment, pain and judgement were not, in this view, the particular burden of prisoners but the common expectation of all sinful humanity.

Evangelical theology was generally nationalistic and outward looking, rejecting the personal, privatized piety of European pietism and older Dissent and seeking to create a 'national morality', uniform and rigorous across social and geographical boundaries.[20] Its importance stemmed from the way it was embraced as the core value system by middle-class professionals and intellectuals who made up the ruling class of the British Empire, common to the established Church of England and Ireland and also to the Church of Scotland. William Wilberforce was its parliamentary leader, but the Evangelical movement extended much more widely than the 'Saints' associated with Wilberforce in Parliament and the 'Clapham Sect'.[21] Today, Wilberforce and the Evangelical circle of influencers are often seen as conservatives (Tories). However, this is misleading: Claphamites were just as likely to regard themselves as Whigs, because this was the party, as James Stephen explained, of 'Peace, Reform, Economy and Toleration',[22] In their Claphamite garb, early Evangelicals were socially conservative, reflected in their establishment of organizations such as the Sunday School movement (c.1780), the Bettering Society (1797) and the Bible Society (1804). But in other ways they were progressive and outward looking, as evidenced in their work for the colony of Sierra Leone, the Church Missionary Society and the penal colony of New South Wales. It is therefore anachronistic to draw a linear progression between contemporary conservative and liberal political

---

[19] Martin J. Wiener, *Reconstructing the Criminal* (Cambridge: Cambridge University Press, 1990), pp. 111–113.

[20] For national morality which concerned law, governance, war and worship, see F. D. Maurice, *Social Morality* 2nd edn (London: Macmillan and Co., 1872).

[21] The perceived influence of the Clapham Sect owes much to the hagiographical reminiscences of Sir James Stephen, 'The Clapham Sect', *Edinburgh Review*, 80.161 (1844): 204–307. Sir James Stephen (1789–1859) was Under Secretary of State for the Colonies from 1836 to 1847. His father, the politician James Stephen (1758–1832), was a member of the group; Ian Bradley, *The Call to Seriousness* (London: Jonathan Cape, 1976); Ernest Marshall Howse, *Saints in Politics* (London: Allen and Unwin, 1971).

[22] Stephen, 'The Clapham Sect', 255.

movements and the Whigs and Tories of the eighteenth century or to pigeonhole the Evangelicals into one or another category. The main distinguishing feature of the Claphamites, besides their activism in relation to the slave trade, was their commitment to practical Christianity, as championed by Wilberforce.[23] The heyday of the group was quite short, from 1797 to 1808 after which the major figures moved away from Clapham while retaining their religious, intellectual and political activism and family connections with the original circle. Despite the group's short life, Wilberforce had ample time to entrench his views on the proper management of penal colonies, support for penitentiaries and opposition to transportation.

Evangelicals and Penal Colonies

In relation to penal reform, the major activists were not figures regarded as central to the Clapham Sect but rather Quaker evangelicals (or 'ex Quakers'), such as Thomas Fowell Buxton (1786–1845), Samuel Hoare (1751–1825), Elizabeth Fry (1780–1845) and William Tallach (1831–1908).[24] They allied with Tory defenders of the exclusive rights of the established church, who would later mobilize to defend the reformist experiment of the Millbank Penitentiary, such as the politician George Peter Holford (1767–1839),[25] Governor of Millbank Penitentiary and the Rev. Daniel Nihil, both of whom advocated reformist prison discipline and opposed transportation.[26] Buxton, though 'heartily attached' to the Whig Party, declared that he was 'not a Whig', but 'one of those amphibious nondescripts called Neutrals'.[27] Such equivocation was a useful stance for a moral crusader. Wilberforce and his friends lent their support to penal reform at home, but it was not mentioned as a cause by James Stephen in his account of the group.[28] Even when abolition had cleared the way for other Evangelical projects to progress, it was never high on their extraordinary list of Christian

---

[23] John Wolffe, 'Clapham Sect (act. 1792–1815)', *ODNB*.

[24] For church parties referred to, see Ford K. Brown, *Fathers of the Victorians* (Cambridge: Cambridge University Press, 1961), pp. 349, 51; W. J. Conybeare, 'Church Parties, ed. Arthur Burns', in Stephen Taylor (ed.), *From Cranmer to Davidson* (Woodbridge: Boydell, 1999), pp. 213–386. Tallach was the first secretary of the Howard League for Prison Reform (1866). For Quakers and penal reform, see Chapter 4.

[25] Holford, *Thoughts on the Criminal Prisons*.

[26] Daniel Nihill, *Prison Discipline in Its Relation to Society and Individuals* (London: Hatchard, 1839), p. 36.

[27] Buxton to John Henry North, 19 April 1819, Charles Buxton (ed.), *Memoirs of Sir Thomas Fowell Buxton* (London: John Murray, 1848), pp. 91, 294.

[28] Stephen, 'The Clapham Sect', 204–307.

objectives. The Rev. William John Conybeare (1815–1857), in a celebrated essay on Anglican 'church parties' in 1855, presented the Evangelical Party in the Church of England as the agents responsible for 'those acts of national morality, which will give an abiding glory to the present century'.[29] Conybeare credited Wilberforce, Macaulay, Stephen, Thornton, Buxton and other 'Evangelical champions' with almost all the social reforms of the Victorian era, from the suppression of the slave trade to penal reform, the abolition of suttee and the protection of miners and factory workers.[30] This representation was far from just to the broad alliance of reformers, from across the denominational and political spectrum, who worked towards the same social goals. Nevertheless, Evangelicals were opinion leaders on questions of national morality, and this mattered in debates about penal reform and penal colonies.

In the late eighteenth century concerns about public morality had given rise to numerous voluntary associations within the Church of England which had the general purpose of the 'reform of manners', among them the Society to Effect the Enforcement of his Majesty's Proclamation Against Vice and Immorality (better known as the Vice Society) which was formed in 1788, the same year as the First Fleet arrived in Botany Bay.[31] Anglican Evangelicals were concerned at the potential threat to public order posed by religious enthusiasm outside the established church, including among the new Methodists, who caused constant irritation through their habits of itinerancy and direct spiritual appeal to people outside the parish system, and the older Dissenters with their traditions of radical objections to state power. At home they sought to emulate the Dissenters' committed missionary dedication to the uplift of the poor, recognizing that some of John Wesley's most dramatic and effective preaching was conducted in prisons and to prisoners.[32] Anglican Evangelicals were also concerned that religious work in the empire was being left in the hands of societies outside the Church, such as the Baptist Missionary Society (1792) and the London Missionary Society (1795), while the older established societies, such as the Society for the Propagation of the Gospel and the Society for Promoting Christian Knowledge (SPCK), were unwelcoming to Evangelical candidates.

It was within this context that the Eclectic Society first met in 1783, made up of Anglican Evangelical and Dissenting clergy and laity, many

---

[29] Conybeare, 'Church Parties', p. 263.   [30] Ibid.

[31] Joanna Innes, 'Politics and Morals: The Reformation of Manners Movement in Later Eighteenth-Century England', in Eckhart Hellmuth (ed.), *The Transformation of Political Culture* (Oxford: Oxford University Press, 1990), pp. 57–118.

[32] P. J. Collingwood, 'Prison Visitation in the Methodist Revival', *London Quarterly & Holborn Review*, 180 (1955), 285–292.

of whom had an interest in overseas missions.[33] The Eclectic Society's most significant achievement was the formation of the Church Missionary Society in 1799.[34] However, the group's earliest meetings were concerned more generally with the best means for propagating the gospel in British colonies. Although the records for these meetings have not survived, some sense of the topics discussed can be gleaned from the memoir of Josiah Pratt (1768–1844), the long-time secretary of the Church Missionary Society. For instance, Pratt notes that the question appointed for discussion on 30 October 1786 was: 'What is the best method for planting and propagating the Gospel in Botany Bay?' It was intended that this meeting would include the Rev. Richard Johnson (1756–1827), who had been appointed chaplain to the penal colony of New South Wales. Johnson, a Methodist at a time when the followers had not yet decisively split from the Church of England, was not present on 13 November when the Society discussed the new penal colony.[35] A letter written by Henry Venn (1725–1797) on 28 October 1786 indicates that Johnson's appointment as chaplain to Botany Bay had been thanks to the intervention of William Wilberforce with Prime Minister William Pitt the Younger. Venn considers this an opening for the gospel in a new world. The fact that this was to be a convict colony, however, seems to have rather escaped his mind:

With what pleasure may we consider this plan of peopling that far–distant region, and other openings connected with the heathen, as a foundation for the Gospel of our God and Saviour to be preached unto them – when a vast multitude, whom no man can number, shall call upon His name – when the wilderness shall become a fruitful field, and all the savageness of the heathen shall be put off, and all the graces of the Spirit shall be put on … To be the means of sending the Gospel to the other side of the globe – what a favour![36]

Venn further adds that Johnson had the approval of both the archbishop of Canterbury and Sir Charles Middleton (1726–1813) – the naval officer and, from 1784, a Tory Member of Parliament, who was a devout Evangelical and one of the earliest opponents of the slave trade.

---

[33] Josiah Pratt and John Henry Pratt, *Memoir of the Rev. Josiah Pratt* (London: Seeleys, 1849), p. 10.

[34] Elizabeth Elbourne, 'The Foundation of the Church Missionary Society: The Anglican Missionary Impulse', in John Walsh, Colin Haydon and Stephen Taylor (eds.), *The Church of England c.1689–c.1833* (Cambridge: Cambridge University Press, 1993), pp. 247–264.

[35] Johnson's humane sympathy for the convict is evident from his letters and preaching such as his sermon to all the colonists, free and unfree. Richard Johnson, *An Address to the Inhabitants of the Colonies Established in New South Wales and Norfolk Island* (London: The Author, 1792). He also served as a magistrate.

[36] Pratt and Pratt, *Memoir of the Rev. Josiah Pratt*, p. 464; Venn's *Life and Letters*, p. 416.

Subsequent meetings of the Eclectics considered the best method of propagating the gospel in the East Indies (1789) and, in the presence of the Rev. Melville Horne, Chaplain of Sierra Leone, the best method for Africa (1791).[37] Significantly, it appears to anticipate that the chief purpose of Botany Bay would be as an 'opening to the heathen' rather than as a site for the conversion of the convict colonists; they were a necessary means for the sending of the gospel rather than its object.

Success for all these imperial Evangelical ventures was, however, far from assured. The turning point in ambitions for a much wider role for Christianity in effecting change in the empire came with the end of the Napoleonic wars. Until this point all activity in overseas territories was subordinated to ensuring the security of the state. Yet even before the final defeat of Napoleon and his exile to Saint Helena, British Evangelicals proclaimed a special duty laid on Britain to spread the gospel not just in Europe but also to the world. In this way, Botany Bay could be regarded as a colony in the empire of mercy, a place of regeneration of Britain's spiritual credentials. Such an imperial view of the penal colonies is reflected in the *Christian Observer*, the journal founded as a vehicle for the Clapham Sect. Published from 1802 until 1874, its editors included leading Evangelical laymen, initially Josiah Pratt and then Zachary Macaulay, from 1802 to 1816. Among other imperial activities, the *Christian Observer* provided coverage of events in the penal colonies and the South Seas. There were reports on the zealous activity of the New South Wales Bible Society, reports from the South Sea Islands, where the Gospel of St Luke had been translated into the Tahitian language, and the Rev. Samuel Marsden wrote of the excellent progress of the young New Zealanders under his care in Parramatta, where he had taken them to admire his orchard and vineyards: 'When I tell them that there is but one God, they advance many arguments to prove my assertion incredible.'[38] Apart from Marsden, news of the penal colonies among Evangelical readers came from reports of the various societies, such as the British and Foreign Bible Society (founded 1804), which had sent out almost nine hundred copies of Bibles and Testaments for the 'inhabitants of the villages, and the prisoners on board the convict ships'.[39] By the 1820s, New South Wales auxiliaries of the major Evangelical societies, including the British and Foreign Bible Society, Religious Tract and Book Society and Church Missionary Society, had been set up on the instigation of

---

[37] Ibid.   [38] *Christian Observer*, vol. 19 (1820), p. 774
[39] *Christian Observer*, vol. 19 (1822), p. 834. A New South Wales Auxiliary of the British and Foreign Bible Society was formed in 1817 with Governor Macquarie as its patron.

either the Rev. Samuel Marsden or the Rev William Cowper (1778–1858).[40]

The *Christian Observer* also reviewed books, magazines and sermons. In 1820, it assessed a collection of sermons by Thomas Chalmers (1780–1847). Evangelicals stressed that the world was a fallen place, that convicts were no more fallen relative to the perfection of God than prisoners were from human society:

We want to urge upon you this lesson of Scripture, that this world differs from a prison house, only in its being a more spacious receptacle of sinners, and that there is not a wider distance, between a society of convicts, and the general community of mankind, than there is between the whole community of our species, and the society of that paradise, from which, under the apostasy of our fallen nature, we have been doomed to live in dreary alienation.[41]

For Evangelicals, the whole world was open for reform and structural change: 'Now is the time for reviewing our commercial system; for reforming our poor laws, that fruitful source of some of the most baneful evils which afflict society; for extending and perfecting plans of education; for affording additional facilities of public religious instruction; for improving our code of criminal laws and our system of prison discipline.'[42] These were not separate objectives and campaigns but part of a united assault on the root and branch of evil in society both at home and abroad.

Meanwhile, in the newly created penal colonies, the Evangelical stamp of church establishment had been assured through the character and personality of the first chaplains appointed to New South Wales, including Johnson, Marsden and the Rev. William Cowper (1778–1858). Interestingly, Cowper's eldest son would go on to become one of the leaders of the anti-transportation movement in New South Wales.[43] All three early chaplains had obtained their theological training through the Elland Society which provided funds for Evangelicals to attend Oxford and Cambridge and secured their colonial appointments through the patronage of the Clapham Sect. *The Eclectic Review* heaped their efforts with praise, declaring Marsden, 'a character that seems expressly formed by Providence to produce an entire and most beneficial change throughout not only the limited tract of New South Wales, but the vast extent of Australasia; to christianize and civilize the barbarians that constitute its original inhabitants, and to re-christianize and re-civilize the horde of

[40] *Sydney Morning Herald*, 10 July 1858, p. 5. Cowper also served as diocesan secretary of the SPG and SPCK.
[41] *Christian Observer*, vol. 18 (1820), p. 398.   [42] Ibid. (1819), p. 823.
[43] See Chapter 9.

wretched culprits that are vomited by our prison-ships upon its shores.'[44]
All rewarded their patrons by remaining staunchly attached to their
Evangelical principles, despite the unpopularity of their views with the
more easy-going of the early governors and their civil and military officers. Unwavering in their view of the moral failings of the large body of
settlers, both free and unfree, their dismal outlook has not endeared them
to contemporary historians.[45]

The appointment of Anglican clergy as magistrates in New South
Wales and Van Diemen's Land has further contributed to historians'
hostility concerning the role played by established clergy in the penal
regime. In her colonial portrait of the Rocks in Sydney, for instance,
Grace Karskens argues that the settlement should be seen as an early
modern or 'pre industrial' community.[46] By this she means that patterns
of work, family, village and societal norms were not those of modern
industrialized people, but were much more like those described in Peter
Lazlett's 1965 classic, *The World We Have Lost*.[47] Although a useful
insight, it is only true to a certain extent. The peculiar circumstances of
Sydney's foundation as a penal colony ensured that there were many
important differences in the administration and social profile of New
South Wales and comparable port communities in the United Kingdom
or colonial America.

One of these differences was in the condition of the established church,
which was not quite as it was at home. In England, the integral relationship between church and state was reflected in the substantial legal role
played by the church courts. These courts gradually lost their powers to
enforce their jurisdiction during the late eighteenth century.[48] One
reason for this was the rise of the Justice of the Peace or magistrate who
filled the void which had formerly been taken by the church courts in
resolving local conflict and socially disruptive behaviour such as drunkenness, vagrancy and promiscuity. Since magistrates were unpaid, the
role was often discharged by leaders of the local gentry and clergy. By
1831, more than one in five English magistrates were clergy and this may

[44] 'Voyage to Australasia', *Eclectic Review* 5.2 (1809), p. 988.
[45] John Hirst, 'The Australian Experience: The Convict Colony', in Norval Morris and
David J. Rothman (eds.), *The Oxford History of the Prison* (Oxford: Oxford University
Press, 1995), pp. 235–265.
[46] Though noting challenges of nomenclature raised by E. P. Thompson, Grace Karskens,
The Rocks (Carlton: Melbourne University Press, 1997), p. 12.
[47] Peter Laslett, *The World We Have Lost* (London: Methuen, 1965).
[48] R. B. Outhwaite, *The Rise and Fall of the English Ecclesiastical Courts, 1500–1860*
(Cambridge: Cambridge University Press, 2006), pp. 100–101.

have been a factor in anti-clericalism in some rural areas.[49] The rising status, education and respect for the rural clergy led to increasing reliance on the established clergy to agree to act as magistrates (which attracted no salary). This comfortable arrangement was challenged by reaction to the Peterloo Massacre of 1819, when up to eighteen people were killed following a peaceful demonstration calling for parliamentary reform. Two clerical Justices of the Peace on the magistrates' committee, the Revs. W. R. Hay and Charles Ethelstone, were pilloried by the Radical press for their ineffectual involvement, with Hay accused of being drunk and incompetent and Ethelstone, aged eighty-eight, characterized as decrepit and hypocritical. This event did much to lessen respect for clerical magistrates and associate them with a harsh administration of the law which punished the poor and favoured the 'old corruption'.[50] Influential Evangelicals such as Charles Simeon disapproved of clerical magistrates and insisted clergy be trained for their own, religious profession, not as servants of the state.[51] However, clergy remained important until Parliament moved to provide funding which would make possible the rise of an independent secular magistracy in rural areas.[52] Importantly, the second generation of Evangelicals, scarred both by political controversy and rising tensions between high and low church parties, tended to withdraw from public office. In line with Simeon's recommendation, the Rev. William Cowper was adamant in refusing Governor Macquarie's requests that he serve as a magistrate.[53]

In the penal colonies, which lacked both a gentry class and a clerical hierarchy ruled by a bishop, there were no church courts and greater and lesser offences were perforce dealt with by settler magistrates many of whom had little experience or social standing to equip them for the task. The governors responded by putting pressure on colonial chaplains to take on the role, as was common in England and Ireland. Michael Gladwin notes there were half a dozen clergy magistrates in colonial New South Wales, Norfolk Island and Van Diemen's Land, including a number of vigilant critics of convictism, such as Thomas Rogers,

---

[49] E. J. Evans, 'Some Reasons for the Growth of English Rural Anti-Clericalism c.1750–c.1830', *Past & Present*, 66.101 (1975), 101.

[50] Eugenio F. Biagini, Liberty, *Retrenchment and Reform* (Cambridge: Cambridge University Press, 1992), p. 232.

[51] Nigel Yates, 'Internal Church Reform, 1780–1850: Establishment under Fire', in *The Churches*, edited by Joris van Eijnatten, Paula Yates (Leiden: Leuven University Press, 2010), p. 45.

[52] Peter Virgin, *The Church in an Age of Negligence* (Cambridge: James Clarke, 1989), p. 125.

[53] N. S. Pollard, 'Cowper, William (1778–1858)', *ADB*.

Thomas Naylor and John Ison.[54] Their number also included one former convict, the Rev. Henry Fulton (1761–1840), a minister of the Protestant Church of Ireland transported for his role in the rebellion of the United Irishmen in 1798, who received a full pardon in 1805.[55] In Van Diemen's Land, Colonel Arthur put a stop to the appointment of clergy to the magistracy when he replaced all the settler magistrates with stipendiary 'police magistrates', who presided over police courts and did his bidding.[56] In New South Wales, stipendiary magistrates were first created in 1825, but this was not enough to prevent honorary magistrates using the bench as a vehicle to circumvent the governor, as occurred in 1834 when Tory magistrates clashed with the liberal reforms of Governor Bourke.[57] Clerics were gradually eliminated as magistrates in all colonies, including Western Australia, by 1850.[58]

Other than their service as magistrates, the activities of the colonial chaplains sent to the penal colonies focused on liturgical duties of divine service, baptisms, weddings and burial services, including attendance at executions. The chief limitation on the effectiveness of the chaplains who were in the colony was simply lack of personnel. When interviewed before the 1812 SC on Transportation, the Rev. Richard Johnson (1756–1827) frankly admitted that to make a difference they would have to pay more than the ten shillings per day or £182 per year that he was receiving.[59] During Johnston's time, the supply of Anglican clergy consisted of himself, Fulton on the Hawkesbury River and the Rev. Samuel Marsden for everyone else, with his own church supported by a convict clerk. The former New South Wales governor, Vice Admiral John Hunter (1737–1821), testified that although convicts attended divine service 'very properly and attentively', no more than five or six people were listening to Johnston's sermons.[60] He tried to set an example by attending himself. He also sent around constables with instructions to jail anyone found drunk on Sunday. Of the convicts who testified, most confirmed that they hardly ever saw a clergyman and the captains were not reading prayers on convict voyages. On the other hand, considerable

---

[54] Michael Gladwin, *Anglican Clergy in Australia, 1788–1850* (Woodbridge: Boydell and Brewer, 2015), pp. 125–128.
[55] Fulton was emancipated and allowed to practice his ministry, first in the Hawkesbury and then on Norfolk Island, effectively replacing the Rev. Richard Johnson on his departure.
[56] W. D. Forsyth, *Governor Arthur's Convict System* (Sydney: Sydney University Press, 1935), pp. 56–58.
[57] Neal, *Rule of Law*, p. 124.   [58] Gladwin, *Anglican Clergy*, p. 114.
[59] 'Testimony of the Rev. Mr Johnston', 25 March 1812, *SC on Transportation*, BPP 1812 (341) II.573, p. 67.
[60] 'Testimony of Admiral Hunter', 19 February 1812, Ibid., p. 23.

practical reformation was happening as convicts obtained their freedom and did well if they could avoid alcohol. When asked if he thought the punishment at Botany Bay was 'calculated to produce any reformation in the moral and conduct' of those sent there, Thomas Robson, a former convict who had been a clerk in the Navy Office, replied that he did not think them reformed, but that they were 'in general treated better than they deserved'.[61] A more optimistic account was given by William Richardson, who had been Johnson's schoolmaster and clerk. According to Richardson, the convicts were treated with respect and 'a great reformation took place among them; those [who] were the most notorious villains in this country became in that country very good members of society'.[62] The Commissary John Palmer also agreed that many of the people sent to the colony were reformed there and this included women who had married and started families.[63] Perhaps what was most telling was Hunter's comment that most convicts chose to stay in the colony on the completion of their sentences and, among those who did return, he received many applications for permission to go back, 'for they find they could live there, but they could not live here'.[64]

Gaol Chaplains

The passing of the Penitentiary Act in 1779 led to a firm redirection of official thinking towards reformatory and away from punitive modes of prison discipline. Although the actual process of reform, and the funding needed to build prisons which could bring these Christian visions of the penitentiary to life, took some time to arrive, the change is reflected in a wealth of new writing on the prison. Gaol chaplains led the way here and, prior to the repeal of the Test Acts in 1828, they were all drawn from the established church and many were Evangelicals. A good example of the implementation of Anglican teaching to the prisoner, influenced by Methodist trends, is reflected in the 'Select Manual of Devout Exercises' written by Rev. W. C., chaplain of the New Bailey Prison, Manchester.[65] Although the initials appear incorrect, 'W. C.' may be the Rev. Nicholas Mosley Cheek (1745–1805), founder of St Stephen's Church and

[61] 'Testimony of Thomas Robson', 2 March 1812, Ibid., p. 52.
[62] 'Testimony of William Richardson', 20 March 1812, Ibid., p. 57.
[63] 'Testimony of Mr J. Palmer', 20 March 1812, Ibid., p. 60.
[64] 'Testimony of Admiral Hunter', 19 February 1812, Ibid., p. 23.
[65] Rev. W. C., Chaplain of the New Bayley Prison Manchester, *The Prisoner's Select Manual of Devout Exercises: Including Forms of Visitation and Select Psalms* (Manchester: Swindells, 1791).

chaplain of the New Bailey.[66] Dedicated to the prisoners, the contents include prayers with texts from scripture which were intended to both comfort and reprove. These include, 'On coming into solitary confinement', 'For a Prisoner under great Trouble of Mind', 'For a young Prisoner who is destitute of Parents and Friends', or 'At the time of execution': 'O HOLY JESUS, Who of Thine infinite Goodness didst accept the conversion of a Sinner on the cross, open Thine eye of Mercy upon this Thy servant.'[67] Notes indicate that W. C. conducted a Sunday School and his words were directed at younger inmates for whom, traditionally, there was greater hope of rejuvenation. Writing a generation after W. C., the Rev. John Clay's collection of sermons for prisoners is more assertively Evangelical in tone.[68] Clay was one of the new class of official gaol chaplains given increasing responsibilities to report and implement the prison policies of the day. Although published in 1827, it is unclear whether the sermons were delivered in that form to prisoners, though the subtitle (in a great degree adapted to a country congregation) suggests that some modifications had been made. Clay's execution sermon was characteristically lengthy on the justice of the law and light on its mercy. In it, he urges the men to think on the fate of the man just executed and ask if they had been guilty of sins that would take them to the gibbet. The specific sins he mentions as most likely to lead in this direction were drunkenness, Sabbath-breaking and poaching, demanding: 'Do not imagine within yourselves that there is yet time to reform – what time have you?'[69]

In the penal colonies, chaplains working with prisoners made use of a range of similar prayer books, such as the *Manual of Instruction and Devotion*, published by the SPCK in 1827.[70] One copy, now in the Ferguson Collection in the Australian National Library, has the inscription: 'This Book was given by the Society for Promoting Christian Knowledge – to the Parochial Lending Library at Port Macquarie in the Colony of New South Wales, in the Diocese of Australia, 1836,'

---

[66] William E. A. Axon, *Annals of Manchester* (Heywood, Manchester, 1886), p. 133. Cheek was a Methodist travelling preacher from 1765 to 1768 and published psalms and hymns for the use of St Stephen's, Salford. See Henry D. Rack, 'The Providential Moment: Church Building, Methodism, and Evangelical Entryism in Manchester, 1788–1825', *Transactions of the Historic Society of Lancashire and Cheshire* 141 (1991), 247.

[67] Rev. W. C., *Prisoner's Select Manual*, p. 57.

[68] See the memoir of his father, written by Walter Lowe Clay, *The Prison Chaplain: A Memoir of the Rev. John Clay* (Cambridge: Macmillan, 1861).

[69] John Clay, *Twenty-Five Sermons Preached to the Inmates of a Gaol* (London: Rivington, 1827), pp. 330–331.

[70] Duke Yonge, *A Manual of Instruction and Devotion, for the Use of Prisoners* 4th edn (London: Society for Promoting Christian Knowledge, 1827).

which thereby associates it with the philanthropic work of Sir William Edward Parry (1790–1855), commissioner of the Australian Agricultural Company from 1829 to 1834, or possibly his successor, Colonel Henry Dumaresq (1792–1838), both of whom showed benevolent interest in the convict servants of the Company. From the Commissioner's house at Carrington, Port Stephens, Parry led a ministry which included regular Sunday services, distributing 100 Bibles to convicts which he acquired from the Naval and Military Bible Society, as well as SPCK prayer books, while Lady Parry opened a school and set up a lending library. He created a cricket club, made Saturday a holiday and played a game every Saturday afternoon while acting as parson in residence, which he described in a letter to Sir John Stanley (later his son-in-law) as 'somewhat arduous'. Besides writing a sermon every week and preaching two each Sunday, Parry christened children, churched women, visited the sick and buried the dead: 'In all these things,' he wrote to his mother, 'we trust that a new tone, and a beneficial one, has been given'.[71] Parry's lay ministry was not unique; with so few clergy in the penal colonies, governors also made use of visiting missionaries to itinerate and preach to convicts.

At about the same time as Parry was preaching and playing cricket with convicts in Port Stephens, the Rev. Wilton Pleydell (1795–1859) published *Twelve Plain Discourses Addressed to the Prisoners of the Crown*, dedicated to Archdeacon Broughton.[72] A well-educated clerical landowner and employer of convicts, Pleydell was appointed chaplain to the convicts and incumbent of Christ Church, Newcastle, New South Wales, in 1831.[73] He was particularly expressive about the sin of flouting authority: 'Have you submitted yourselves to all your governors, teachers, spiritual pastors and masters?'[74] Having presumably caused his listeners to squirm with guilt, he then turned to accusation: 'The crime for which you were sent out to this colony, was an offence against one or other of the ten commandments, and against how many of the others, unknown to your fellow creatures, or undiscovered, or not exactly punishable by the laws of man have you not offended?'[75] Another set of prayers written for the use of prisoners and chaplains was compiled in Van Diemen's Land by the Rev. W. H. Browne (1800–1877), also

[71] Sir Edward Parry to Mrs Parry, 7 July 1830; to W. H. Hooper, 13 May 1830; to Sir John Stanley, n. d. 1830. Edward Parry, *Memoirs of Rear-Admiral Sir W. Edward Parry, Kt* 3rd edn (London: Longman, 1857), pp. 222–230.

[72] C. Pleydell N. Wilton, *Twelve Plain Discourses Addressed to the Prisoners of the Crown, in the Colony of New South Wales* (Sydney: Stephens and Stokes, 1834).

[73] Herbert Marshall, 'Wilton, Charles Pleydell (1795–1859)', *ADB*.

[74] Wilton, *Twelve Plain Discourses*, p. 21.   [75] Ibid.

printed with Broughton's sanction.[76] A presentation copy, now in the Ferguson Collection of the National Library of Australia, bears an inscription on the front cover to Lt Governor Arthur, 'with Rev. Dr Browne's respectful compliments'.[77] In his introduction, Browne explained that it was intended as an aid for prisoners without instructors, as well as 'Lecturers of Road Parties in the Interior'. Browne's selection is not so fiery as Pleydell's, and the 'Prayers for Persons Under Sentence', were thoughtfully chosen to emphasize the atoning power of a merciful Saviour, 'we humbly commend the soul of this thy servant into thy hands, . . . wash it, we pray thee, in the blood of that immaculate lamb that was slain to take away the sins of the world'.[78] After the execution took place, he prayed that those 'who survive in this and other daily spectacles of mortality', take warning and amend their lives.

Other colonial chaplains also wrote sermons and prayers to be delivered at the time of the execution of prisoners. The Rev. Robert Knopwood (1763–1838), not generally considered the most benign or active of chaplains, nevertheless wrote orthodox prayers on behalf of the souls of condemned prisoners which acknowledged their sin: '[T]hey are accounted as one of those that go down to the pit', but pleaded for mercy: 'O Lord convince them, that their sins are not greater than thy mercy can permit'.[79] His harsh and uncompromising sermon on the occasion of an execution is addressed to the condemned man, 'it hath pleased Almighty God in his justice, to bring you under the sentence and condemnation of the Law. You are to suffer death in such a manner, that others, warned by your example, may be the more afraid to offend'.[80] The sermon was possibly preached by Knopwood to two boys, Thomas Smith, aged sixteen, and George Kirby, aged seventeen, condemned for their role in a murderous attack by bushrangers at New Norfolk in Van Diemen's Land. On 24 May 1815, the day before their scheduled execution, he prayed with the prisoners all day, then 'preached a condemned sermon to them' attended by 'a great many of the inhabitants'.[81] The next day, after a melancholy and sleepless night, Knopwood went again to pray with the prisoners after which he visited Lt Governor Thomas Davey (1758–1823) with a petition from the officers and inhabitants asking him to spare the lives of the two young men. In a dramatic denouement,

[76] Rev. W. H. Browne, *Jail Manual* (Launceston: H. Dowling, 1834).   [77] Ibid.
[78] Ibid., 13–14.
[79] Robert Knopwood, 'Prayers for Convicts Condemned to Death', SLNSW DLMS: 51, 13–14, 19.
[80] Ibid., 16–18.
[81] Robert Knopwood, *The Diary of the Reverend Robert Knopwood, 1803–1838*, ed. Mary Nicholls (Hobart: Tasmanian Historical Research Association, 1977), p. 205.

acted out at the foot of the scaffold, Smith and Kirby were reprieved, but their accomplices were hanged. Knopwood, delighted, records that he 'had them all in the room and had them return thanks to Almighty God for his goodness in sparing their lives, and likewise all the people prayed'.[82]

Scenes of this type formed a standard part of sensationalist trials and executions and were a target for penal reformers such as Samuel Romilly who condemned the 'uncertain administration of justice' which, for the same offence, sent one man to the gallows or to Botany Bay and another to a few months imprisonment.[83] Clergy who attended death scenes supplied graphic descriptions of executions and final confessions, which sold readily to the popular market.[84] Nevertheless, such public displays of justice and religious intercession were becoming uncommon. Knopwood's intervention was only possible because Lt Governor Davey had condemned the men following an illegal declaration of martial law.[85] Such arbitrary acts of retribution and mercy were not the norm in the penal colony. These colonial prayers and sermons provide an insight into the kind of religious instruction provided to prisoners of the Crown. Allan Grocott has argued that convicts were 'irreligious, profane and anti-clerical', that positive responses to religion were the acts of 'unctuous hypocrites' and that harshly judgemental teaching was responsible for convict contempt of Protestant parsons.[86] This is to misunderstand the theological function of penal religious instruction which mined conventional themes of guilt, penitence, forgiveness and spiritual rejuvenation. It also underestimates the religious commitment of convicts and clergy, including many devout and conscientious pastors who diligently promoted the moral teachings of the day with the means at their disposal.[87]

The Penitentiary Movement

While attempts were made to patch up the deficiencies of the ramshackle penal system using traditional religious tools, the most significant experiment which aimed to reform as well as punish prisoners and provide an

---

[82] Ibid.
[83] Samuel Romilly, *Observations on the Criminal Law of England as It Relates to Capital Punishments* (London: Cadell & Davies, 1810), p. 19.
[84] Andrea McKenzie, 'From True Confessions to True Reporting? The Decline and Fall of the Ordinary's Account', *The London Journal*, 30.1 (2005), 55–70.
[85] James Boyce, *Van Diemen's Land* (Melbourne: Black Inc, 2008), p. 75.
[86] Grocott, *Convicts*, pp. 200, 24.
[87] For a defence of convict clergy, see Gladwin, 'Flogging Parsons?', 397.

alternative to transportation was Millbank Penitentiary. This came with the staunch support of the established church which had more or less exclusive access to prisoners detained there in lieu of being transported. After exhaustive discussion of rival models for a national prison, the 'General Penitentiary at Millbank' was constructed from 1816 to 1821 at the then staggering cost of half a million pounds.[88] The first governor was the politician and penal reformer George Peter Holford (1767–1839), who had led the House of Commons Committee set up in 1810 to reconsider the question of national penitentiaries and ending the practice of transportation. Like enlightened reformers such as Bentham, Cesare Beccaria and Samuel Romilly, Holford was a principled opponent of convict transportation. He supported home-based reformative institutions in which the governor, the chaplain and the surgeon had much enhanced powers of regulation over prisoners.[89]

Despite mounting evidence of the system's ineffectiveness and serious deficiencies in almost all aspects of its operation, Holford was a fervent believer in its efficacy. According to the account of Major Arthur Griffiths (1838–1908), which was admittedly rather jaundiced, the low point in the management of Millbank was reached between 1837 and 1844 when the roles of governor and chaplain were combined under the Rev. Daniel Nihil.[90] The regime at Millbank was minutely interrogated by the 1831 SC on Secondary Punishments in the course of which the chaplain, William Whitworth Russell (1795–1847) defended the reformist policies, including its revolutionary avoidance of corporal punishment, education programme and advocacy of shorter sentences.[91] Although writing with humour and insight about crime and punishment,[92] Griffiths clearly had an axe to grind in denouncing the attempt at religious governance in place of the more professional, secular regime he himself represented. Under

---

[88] Seán McConville, *A History of English Prison Administration, Vol. I 1750–1877* (London: Routledge & Kegan Paul, 1981), p. 111.

[89] Ibid., 129–30.

[90] Arthur Griffiths, *Memorials of Millbank and Chapters in Prison History* (London: Chapman and Hall, 1884), p. 155. For the collapse of Millbank as a penitentiary, see M. Heather Tomlinson, 'Penal Servitude 1846–1865: A System in Evolution', in Victor Bailey (ed.), *Policing and Punishment in Nineteenth-Century Britain* (London: Croom Helm, 1981), 126–149. For Nihil's views, see Nihill, *Prison Discipline*, pp. 36–37.

[91] 'Testimony of Rev. Whitworth Russell', 29 March 1831, *Select Committee on Secondary Punishments*, BPP 1831 (276) VII.519, pp. 26–27.

[92] For this view of Griffiths, a prolific writer who presented the foibles of past criminal practice as the foil for the rational practice of the present British prison system, see Christine Marlin, 'A Prison Officer and a Gentleman: The Prison Inspector as Imperialist Hero in the Writings of Major Arthur Griffiths (1838–1908)', in Jason W. Haslam and Julia M. Wright (eds.), *Captivating Subjects* (Toronto: University of Toronto Press, 2005), p. 229.

Nihil, 'The Chaplain's Reign', as Griffiths described it, led to a collision of ideology since, in his view, it was impossible to reform criminals by religious means, and the attempt to do so was not only futile but led to unrest among the prisoners and hypocrisy among the warders.[93]

In defence of Millbank, Holford published a series of tracts promoting the use of separation and categorization in prison, and asserting the importance of the prison chaplain and the essential role played by religion, which he called: 'the most powerful engine that can be applied to the human mind'.[94] Advocating religiously based prison reform, Holford called for more funding for religious provision to existing prisons. He served on a series of prison reform committees, consistently championing the use of Anglican chaplains alone in prisons. In speech after speech in the House of Commons, and inquiry after inquiry, Evangelical reformers such as Holford convinced themselves that if only prisoners could make good use of their time in confinement it would be possible to make them better men and women. Holford's poems collected in *The Convict's Complaint in 1815, and the Thanks of the Convict in 1825*, that is before and after Milbank, present this view in mawkish rhyme:

> Thanks be to those who plann'd these silent cells,
> Where Sorrow's true-born child, Repentance, dwells;
> Where Justice, sway'd by Mercy, doth employ
> Her iron rod to chasten, not destroy.[95]

Initially, prisoners themselves and their families agreed with Holford; petitions to the Home Office carry pleas for prisoners to be selected for the penitentiary instead of transportation. Robert and Sarah Bennett, for example, begged that their son, John Bennett, convicted of petty theft in the City of Bath, not be transported to New South Wales: 'The Boy only 15 years of age is truly penitent and may be reclaimed.'[96] Ministers of religion supported criminal petitions on behalf of convicts seeking reform (and a shorter sentence) in the penitentiary, such as the Bristol horse thief, James Shepherd convicted in 1821 and sentenced to death commuted to seven years transportation.[97] As reports of the conditions in Millbank emerged, however, the petitions died away.

---

[93] Griffiths, *Millbank*, p. 162.   [94] Holford, *Thoughts on the Criminal Prisons*, pp. 69–70.
[95] George Holford, *The Convict's Complaint in 1815, and the Thanks of the Convict in 1825* (London: Rivingtons, 1825), p. 21.
[96] Robert and Sarah Bennett to Lord Sidmouth, 25 June 1819, in TNA PC 1/67.
[97] Petition for James Shepherd, 1821, TNA HO 17/39/31. For other criminal petitions signed by ministers of religion relating to the penitentiary, see TNA HO 17/9/10 (1823); HO 17/34/72 (1824); HO 17/7/17 (1824); HO 17/34/72 (1824); HO 17/8/18 (1825); HO 17/11/41 (1827); HO 17/98/11 (1827); HO 17/12/20 (1828); HO 17/12/33 (1828); HO 17/26/12 (1828); HO 17/103/101 (1830); HO 17/73/35 (1830).

Apart from Milbank, the most important breakthrough for organized prison reform arose when Evangelicals in Parliament came together with reformers among the Whigs and Liberals. This same alignment was responsible for the effective transformation of British anti-slavery from a local, pietistic concern among the Methodists and Quakers, into a national movement.[98] The major vehicle for the alliance of 'Saints' (Claphamite Evangelicals) and Whigs was the Society for the Improvement of Prison Discipline and the Reformation of Juvenile Offenders, better known as the Prison Discipline Society (PDS), which secured support from all parties to this common cause.

Prison Discipline Society

Formed in 1816 at the initiative of the Quaker philanthropists, Thomas Fowell Buxton (1786–1845) and Samuel Hoare II (1751–1825),[99] the PDS was originally intended to provide support for the work of their sister-in-law, Elizabeth Fry, in Newgate and to improve, if possible, conditions for prisoners in English gaols.[100] The PDS was for the issue of penal reform what the Society for the Abolition of the Slave Trade (1787) and the Anti-Slavery Society (1823) were for the anti-slavery movement, and what the Aborigines' Protection Society (1837) was for Indigenous people in British colonies, that is a society created by secular and religious activists, including politicians, clergy and business people, to lobby for changes to the law relating to a particular cause, creating a network of local societies to coordinate the work and build a financial and social base.

With the formation of the PDS, Whigs and Saints secured an organization to promote Christian principles of penal reform on a broader canvas and with legislative bite. The Society was also a conduit to knowledge about penal reform elsewhere in both Europe and America. Like many of the early reformers, Thomas Buxton was particularly interested in the gaols of Antwerp and Ghent.[101] At the Maison de Force at Ghent, the

[98] A. D. Kriegel, 'A Convergence of Ethics: Saints and Whigs in British Antislavery', *Journal of British Studies*, 26.4 (1987), 435–450.

[99] Samuel Hoare was a wealthy Quaker whose philanthropic work included prison reform, anti-slavery and the establishment of Sunday Schools. In 1797, he was one of twelve founding members of the Society for the Abolition of the Slave Trade. According to the *Memoirs of Samuel Hoare by His Daughter Sarah and His Widow Hannah*, edited by F. R. Pryor (London: Headley, 1811), Hoare opposed capital punishment, but was not 'a projector of the improvement of prison discipline' (p. 39).

[100] Buxton (ed.), *Memoirs of Sir Thomas Fowell Buxton*, p. 64: 'The exertions of Mrs Fry and her associates had prepared the way, public attention had been drawn to the subject; and in 1816 the Society for the Reformation of Prison Discipline was formed.'

[101] Ibid., 68–72.

women were held in separate cells, there was industry which supported the prisoners and there were neither fetters nor soldiers other than guards at the gates.[102] The first efforts of the Society were personal and infused with charitable sympathy for the poor. Buxton led his own investigation of the trail of misery left by inadequate and punitive prisons upon the distressed poor.[103] Another early and important report was initiated by Elizabeth Fry and her brother, Joseph John Gurney, which followed literally in the footsteps of John Howard by visiting and reporting on conditions in prisons.[104] Fry went on to report on female prisoners in 1827.[105] As interest in penal reform evolved, separate campaigns and separate societies developed, focussing around particular issues, including capital punishment, juveniles, women and conditions on convict transports, with individuals contributing to penal causes personal to them.[106] In general, the PDS opposed transportation and supported penitentiaries in place of the prisons denounced by Howard and a legion of inspectors who followed in his footsteps.

As the Society developed, it shifted its membership up the social scale to include more Anglican Evangelicals and fewer Dissenters. PDS meetings were regularly reported in the *Religious Intelligencer* or the *Christian Observer*, which thus provide insight into Claphamite views on penal reform. In 1819, the PDS approved resolutions moved by Wilberforce and others in support of proper classification of prisoners; the separation of men, women and juveniles; and the regime of 'humane treatment, constant inspection, moral and religious instruction, judicious classification, and well regular labour', which were said to 'seldom fail, under the Divine blessing, to reclaim the most guilty'.[107] The same message was repeated on every possible occasion: 'Without reformation, the object of prison discipline cannot be attained: without religious impressions,

---

[102] Society for Diffusing Information on the Subject of Capital Punishment and Prison Discipline, *An Account of the Maison de Force at Ghent from the Philanthropist, May 1817* (London: Taylor, 1817), p. 7.

[103] Thomas Fowell Buxton, *An Inquiry, Whether Crime and Misery Are Produced or Prevented, by Our Present System of Prison Discipline* 5th edn (Edinburgh: Constable, 1818).

[104] Joseph John Gurney, *Notes on a Visit Made to Some of the Prisons in Scotland and the North of England in Company with Elizabeth Fry* (London: n.p., 1819).

[105] Elizabeth Gurney Fry, *Observations on the Visiting, Superintendence and Government of Female Prisoners* (London: John and Arthur Arch, 1827). See also Chapter 4.

[106] The Society for the Diffusion of Knowledge upon the Punishment of Death and the Improvement of Convict Discipline began in 1812 but was taken over by the Juvenile Delinquency Committee. The original Society was relaunched in 1828. For the origin of the PDS, see Buxton's *Memoirs*, p. 33; *The Origin and Object of the Society for the Diffusion of Knowledge upon the Punishment of Death* (London: McCreery, 1812), pp. 7, 12.

[107] 'Prison Discipline Society Report', *Christian Observer*, vol. 19 (1820), p. 424.

reformation is utterly hopeless.'[108] With the revision of its membership away from the Quaker elite and towards the Evangelical middle class, the religious and emotional sympathies of the Society were impregnated with a more belligerent and quasi-official tone. Besides the dominance of politicians, the Society began corresponding and investigating the status of county gaols in England and compiling data for the House of Commons SC on Gaols (1818, 1819), the first of many committees it effectively directed. The committee itself was chaired by the banker Samuel Hoare III (1783–1847), who had broken with his father's Quakerism and become an Anglican, and included six politicians – all of them Whigs and Radicals, including the Hon. Henry Grey Bennet (1777–1836) and Stephen Lushington (1782–1873).

The PDS consistently opposed transportation, basing their view on information received from the Rev. Samuel Marsden in New South Wales, as well as the testimony of clergy, officers and convicts and former convicts to a series of parliamentary select committees. Throughout the 1810s, as the merits of the penitentiary were debated in Parliament, Bennet, Wilberforce, Romilly and other penal reformers continued to make objections to transportation and promote the virtues of properly conducted prisons and penitentiaries in Britain and Ireland and oppose transportation. In 1812 Romilly objected that transportation had been in place in New South Wales for twenty-five years without any proof of the benefit of the system.[109] By 1819, when the government was awaiting the outcome of the SC on Gaols, the leading penal reformers of the day including Bennet, Wilberforce and Sir James Mackintosh, were again actively lobbying for drastic changes to the system, making use of Marsden's correspondence for conditions in the colony.[110] In a very long speech, Bennet made a detailed condemnation of the system in New South Wales which was corrupting to women and children and made little if any provision for the religious instruction of Catholics.[111] At the same time, the number of convictions for serious crimes was so high that it was clear that all hope that transportation had been reformative were seriously mistaken.[112] In its eighth report for 1819, the PDS noted the 'prevalent feeling among offenders in [this] country that transportation is but a separation from connexions, and affords a prospect of successful

---

[108] *Christian Observer*, vol. 22 (1822), p. 821.
[109] Hansard, HC Deb, vol. 21, col. 6044, February 1812.
[110] Samuel Marsden, *The Letters and Journals of Samuel Marsden, 1765–1838*, ed. J. R. Elder (Dunedin: Otago University Council, 1932), p. 31. Marsden's letters were originally sent to friends in the Elland Society.
[111] Hansard, HC Deb, vol. 39, col. 464–509, 18 February 1819.
[112] Hansard, HC Deb, vol. 39 col. 472, 18 February 1819.

enterprise and advantageous settlement'.[113] Both transportation and imprisonment on the hulks were seen as 'inefficient' and unlikely to lead to the primary, elusive goal of reforming the guilty, which only scientific and moral penal systems could provide.[114] It would be decades before the PDS secured the changes it felt were necessary, including the construction of penitentiaries and the abolition of transportation and the hulks. A more immediate achievement was the dispatch of Commissioner John Thomas Bigge (1780–1843).

Bigge Reports

Bigge received his commission to inquire into the colony of New South Wales on 5 January 1819 at a time when there was a rising tide of concern that transportation was not tough enough, that corruption and maladministration were responsible for the rising crime rate and that Governor Macquarie's regime was overly generous to serving prisoners and emancipists. The three volumes of the Bigge Reports represent the most comprehensive analysis of a penal colony ever attempted in the colonial era as well as a watershed for the history of convict transportation.[115] Bigge was appointed by Henry Bathurst (1762–1834), Secretary of State for War and the Colonies from 1812 to 1827 in the Tory ministry of Lord Liverpool, to undertake a review of the colonial administration of New South Wales, including its 'Laws, Regulations and Usages, Civil Military and Ecclesiastical'.[116] A moderate Tory who sympathized with William Wilberforce, Bathurst favoured the amelioration rather than the abolition of slavery.[117] His instructions to Bigge were to change the direction of the colony from one intended to support its economic growth for the benefit of the settlers and former convicts to one of punishment: 'Transportation to New South Wales is intended as a severe Punishment applied to

---

[113] *Eighth Report of the Committee of the Society for the Improvement of Prison Discipline* (London: Bensley, 1832), p. 5.

[114] Ibid., 6.

[115] There were three volumes presented to Parliament and subsequently printed: *The State of the Colony of New South Wales*, 19 June 1822, BPP 1822 (448) XX.539; *The Judicial Establishments of New South Wales and of Van Diemen's Land*, 21 February 1823, BPP 1823 (330) X.515; and *The State of Agriculture and Trade in the Colony of New South Wales*, 13 March 1823, BPP 1823 (136) X.607. The large appendix, including transcripts of interviews with witnesses, TNA CO 201/127, was not printed but extensive extracts were included in John Ritchie and John Thomas Bigge, *The Evidence to the Bigge Reports: New South Wales under Governor Macquarie*, 2 vols. (Melbourne: Heinemann, 1971).

[116] Earl Bathurst to John Thomas Bigge, 6 January 1819, *Instructions to Bigge*, BPP 1823 (532) XIV.633, p. 4.

[117] 'Bathurst, Henry (1762–1834)', *ADB*.

various Crimes, and as such must be rendered an Object of real Terror to all Classes of the Community'.[118] He was also to consider how best to encourage education and religious instruction in the colony. Bathurst urged that the purpose of punishment was the prevention of crime, not the improvement of the prisoner. In curiously poetic language he confirmed that transportation should be dreaded: 'It is their sad Estrangement from the sweets and comforts of a Life, which their Guilt has forfeited, and the Mercy of His Majesty has spared', not merely endured.[119]

Opposition to transportation came from a number of sources, including the radical Whigs and conservative Evangelicals who for different reasons believed it was not severe enough to deter crime. A month after Bigge received his commission, Wilberforce rose in the House of Commons to address a motion concerning transportation to New South Wales.[120] Wilberforce's speech was delivered with his characteristic moral force, and he used his platform to denounce conditions on the hulks, the moral character of the penal colony of New South Wales and the regime of Governor Macquarie. He objected first to the conditions under which prisoners were transported basically as caged animals: 'Was it not a fact, that the whole voyage was passed in gambling, in singing indecent songs, in every species of vice?'[121] Wilberforce then stated with approval his knowledge of 'a person' (Commissioner Bigge) who had set out to enquire into the state of the prison system but that Parliament still had a role. He objected, in sequence, to the cost of the colony, news that Governor Macquarie had appointed former convicts as magistrates, and that prisoners had been neither terrified by their experience of transportation nor reformed. For Wilberforce, the correct procedure was to turn the gaols into 'schools for reformation' instead of depravity.[122] In response to these slurs, Lord Castlereagh suggested that Wilberforce had put too much confidence in his sources in the colony (i.e., Samuel Marsden), and that he should not expect the same standards in Botany Bay as he would in Warwickshire, the one a den of crime and the other 'one of the counties of this civilized, and he hoped he might call it moral country'.[123] The point was that Wilberforce did demand this, as did other Evangelicals and lobbyists for the PDS. Across the empire, they argued, there should be one, consistent moral regime and they were hopeful that Commissioner Bigge would help them achieve it.

---

[118] Bathurst to Bigge, 6 January 1819, *Instructions to Bigge*, p. 4.   [119] Ibid., p. 5.
[120] Hansard, HC Deb, vol. 39, col. 464–509, 18 February 1819.
[121] Hansard, HC Deb, vol. 39, col. 467, 18 February 1819.
[122] Hansard, HC Deb, vol. 39, col. 486, 18 February 1819.
[123] Hansard, HC Deb, vol. 39, col. 487, 18 February 1819.

Bigge's report on the state of ecclesiastical establishments in New South Wales and Van Diemen's Land was included in the third of his reports on New South Wales.[124] It enumerated the religious and charitable institutions of the colony, including clergy, chaplains and schools, and was focussed substantially on the established church. Reporting on the Bible Society, Bigge concluded: 'there has existed no want of zeal in the local authorities of New South Wales and Van Diemen's Land, in the clergy of the established church, or in those who are not members of it, to promote the interests of religion and morals amongst the lower classes of the inhabitants'.[125] Detailed recommendations beyond this dry assessment, which said next to nothing about religious services for convicts, owed much to Thomas Hobbes Scott (1783–1860), who was later appointed archdeacon of New South Wales with a mandate to implement a plan for the establishment of the Church of England in the colony. Much more information about religion in the colony was gathered as evidence about ecclesiastical establishments, schools and charitable societies, forming part of the vast unpublished appendix of 600 folios to the report.[126] In presenting a picture of the religious condition of the colony, Bigge recorded hundreds of letters, notes of interview and brochures of the colony's many religious and philanthropic societies. Charities favoured by the 'exclusivist' (anti-emancipist) faction showed their aversion to the children of the colony rising above themselves. For instance, *The Rules and Regulations of the Female Orphan Institutions* (1818) directed: 'The Children of this Institution are to be educated only in View to their present Condition in Life, and future Destination; namely, as the Wives or Servants of common Settlers, Mechanics and labouring People.'[127]

Bigge was more than happy to listen to adverse gossip about all in authority from Governor Macquarie to the Colonial Chaplain, Samuel Marsden, and included this frequently ill-considered and hostile range of material in the appendix. Bigge interviewed seven clergy resident in New South Wales: Rev. R. Cartwright, Rev. J. Cross, Mr Bowden, Rev. Mr Cooper, Rev. S. Marsden and the Rev. Mr Hill, along with the two colonial chaplains in Van Diemen's Land, the Revs. Robert Knopwood (1763–1838) and John Youl (1773–1827). He paid attention to the emancipist lawyer, Edward Eager (1787–1866), the leading Methodist

[124] 'State of the Ecclesiastical Establishments in New South Wales and Van Diemen's Land', *Commissioner Bigge on Agriculture and Trade*, BPP 1823 (136) X.607, pp. 68–77.
[125] Ibid., p. 78
[126] 'Appendix to Commissioner Bigge's Report', 1822: Ecclesiastical Establishments, Schools & Charitable Societies', TNA CO 201/127.
[127] *Rules & Regulations Established for the Future Management and Improvement of the Female Orphan Institution* (Sydney: Howe, 1818), pp. 8–9, 'Appendix to Commissioner Bigge's Report 1822', TNA CO 201/127: 151–151v.

layman in the colony, though only in respect of Eager's critique of the failings of Judge Barron Field (1786–1846).[128] Bigge seems to have ignored the lively Catholic, Presbyterian and smaller Dissenting ministries who, though few in number, might have challenged his final recommendations. Settlers, officers and clergy were asked whether they saw any evidence of reformation by convicts and former convicts, a key claim of Macquarie. To a man, they said not. Major George Druitt (1775?–1842), an Irish-born former soldier and Chief Engineer of the Colonial Establishment, thought 'more complete separation' might be useful for the convicts, especially the boys: 'as their reform in the present State appears to be hopeless'.[129] When asked about a chapel for the convict barracks in Sydney's Hyde Park, he stated that there was no chapel, 'but the Clergyman reads prayers & gives a lecture every Wednesday Evening to such as chose to attend; & on Sundays Divine Service is performed by him when all are obliged to attend'. Druitt was also asked whether a chapel and school should be built in the barracks. He approved the construction of a chapel in the school, largely because this would prevent escapes which occurred when prisoners were marched to church in town.[130]

In relation to religion and education, Bigge was provided with evidence from the Rev. William Cowper (1778–1858), the Anglican Evangelical minister of St Philip's, Sydney, who had fallen out with Macquarie. Unlike Marsden, Cowper steadfastly refused to act as a magistrate in Macquarie's regime, reflecting a strict view of the need to separate church and state characteristic of the second generation of Evangelicals. Cowper was quizzed as to whether applications for marriage were only sent to him 'with a view merely to the Improvement of their condition as Prisoners'. Cowper thought this likely. He recognized a 'great Deal of concubinage in Sydney', but he baptized the illegitimate children regardless and registered the children with the names of the parents.[131] Like other Evangelicals, Cowper held a low view of convict morality and capacity for Christian conversion. When asked if there were any instances of 'reformed Lives & habits' among the convicts, he denied it, stating: 'There are several Instances of Temporary Reform, but I think few in whom I cd. say there was a radical change in their Principles.'[132] In the Hawkesbury, Bigge heard much the same from the Rev. Robert Cartwright (1771–1856), who shared Cowper's sentiment as to the religious feeling of the people. Cartwright stated that he thought the order for compulsory religious attendance was useful – and the only way he

---

[128] Lauren A. Benton and Lisa Ford, *Rage for Order: The British Empire and the Origins of International Law, 1800–1850* (Cambridge: Harvard University Press, 2016), p. 5.
[129] Ritchie and Bigge, *Evidence*, p. 114.   [130] Ibid., I.15.   [131] Ibid., I.150.
[132] Ibid., I.151.

would get a congregation.[133] Cartwright put his greatest hope in the coming generation, reflected in his energetic work in establishing schools in the colony.[134] He agreed that the offspring of the convicts afforded the best prospects, adding, 'I should have quitted the Colony long ago, but for this circumstance.' He also noted that the convicts were interested in advancing the education of their children.[135]

The impact of the Bigge Report on Transportation was augmented by changes to prison management in England. These ensured that for the next twenty years, there would be a strong Evangelical strand dominating most theories and practices of penal reform. The Bigge Report opened up new sites for penal transportation across the settler colonies, including Macquarie Harbour in Van Diemen's Land, which operated from 1822 to 1833, Norfolk Island which reopened in 1824 and Moreton Bay which operated from 1824 to 1839. The main purpose of these additional penal settlements was to harshen the experience of transportation and make it more of a deterrent to crime at home, in line with Bathurst's instructions to Bigge. The Gaol Act of 1823 precipitated further change, imposing the requirement of reporting centrally to Parliament and more rigorous standards for prison officers, especially the chaplain. The chaplain was slowly transformed from a religious counsellor to the most senior reporting official, other than the governor, in every prison, penal station and penitentiary. In this way, Evangelical religion, supported by the Tories in government, became associated with some of the most infamous and repressive institutions in the British Empire. This was not the intention of Evangelicals engaged in penal reform, who consistently advocated for the humane reform of prisoners in place of the punitive and bloody code of an earlier era. However, it was the effect of the action of the PDS and the creation of the Milbank penitentiary and the new sites of ultra-penal isolation and punishment.

Conclusion

This chapter has examined the Evangelical contribution to the penal reform of the empire, a project which was embraced by a small number of Claphamites, including William Wilberforce, as part of the grand plan to improve the empire. The age of atonement, reflected in the theology and politics of post-Revolutionary Britain, saw the coming together of a

---

[133] Ibid., I.153.
[134] William Macquarie Cowper, *The Autobiography and Reminiscences of William Macquarie Cowper, Dean of Sydney* (Sydney: Angus & Robertson, 1902).
[135] Ritchie and Bigge, *Evidence*, p. I.157.

coalition of Tory, Whig and what Buxton called 'neutral' forces to renew the criminal code and reform penal discipline. The main vehicle for this was the Penal Discipline Society, which consistently opposed transportation and promoted the penitentiary as a better alternative. Where Bentham had presented secular arguments in favour of the Panopticon and against New South Wales, the PDS was not so convinced that there would be a single, best solution to the problem of how to reform rather than simply punish criminals. The experiment of Millbank, greeted as the fulfilment of the ideals of John Howard, was captured by its Evangelical advocates, such as George Holford. The failure of the first penitentiary to meet the unreasonable expectations placed on it for reform by religion and work alone meant that transportation would continue for the foreseeable future. While a wide range of voices were involved in the cause of penal reform, with Anglican Evangelicals only one part of a hearty chorus, they represented those who were most committed to penal reform as an aspect of the unified church state and the realization of the moral empire. The real strength of the Prison Discipline Society was the alliance that it forged between Anglican Evangelicals, leading Quaker advocates of penal reform and Whigs and Radicals who supported penal reform in parliament. As the expertise of the Society developed, it became an effective advocate in favour of penitentiaries and reformist solutions at home rather than transportation abroad, with the testimony of Samuel Marsden, Elizabeth Fry and sympathetic convict surgeons about the vulnerability of convict women critical to the campaign.

But transportation had plenty of time still to run. So long as there was one established church in England and Ireland and one in Scotland, imperial institutions would reflect the hierarchy and values of the church establishment overseas as well. With the bringing down of the Bigge Reports, the task which now confronted all Anglican penal reformers was how to reform the hulks and penal colonies springing up in Australia in the direction of greater uniformity and harsher punishment so that it would be truly a 'terror to evil doers'. Bigge encouraged the creation of colonial church establishments in both New South Wales and Van Diemen's Land, which were intended to provide 'national' (that is, Anglican) personnel and institutions, including churches, schools and prisons, to uphold the existing social order. Taken together, these reforms were intended to reform and moralize the penal colonies until the happy day when adequate penitentiaries, constructed for this purpose in the home country, might do away with the necessity for transportation altogether. One governor, Sir George Arthur, believed that it was possible to build an Evangelical system of penal reform in the penal colonies. His attempt to make this happen in Van Diemen's Land is the subject of the next chapter.

'Hell upon Earth': Sir George Arthur in Van
Diemen's Land, 1823–1837

This Colony must be considered in the light of an extensive Gaol to the
Empire, the punishment of criminals and reformation of criminals, the
grand objects, in its penal character, to be obtained to, and these, under
Providence, can alone be affected by the presence of a respectable Military
Force; -by the erection of proper places for confinement:- by an active
judicial establishment;- by a more general diffusion of knowledge, and by
the powerful operation of Religion.[1]   (George Arthur, 1826)

[D]uring the last twelve years Colonel Arthur had possessed despotic
powers for the sole purpose of framing a system of atrocious and
unheard-of cruelty, such as stood unparalleled in the annals of
nations; his sole object was to inflict pain—intense pain—to render
the condition of the convict most wretched and degraded—to make
Van Diemen's Land what it now is, a hell upon earth—a fitting abode
for the criminals, whom he by his tortures had converted into still
worser fiends.[2]   (William Molesworth, 1837)

The moral and penal landscape of Van Diemen's Land was largely
created under the regime of a deeply religious, authoritarian former
soldier, Col. George Arthur (1784–1854), who was Lt Governor succes-
sively of British Honduras (1814–1822), Van Diemen's Land
(1823–1837) and Upper Canada (1838–1841) before ending his colonial
career as Governor of Bombay (1842–1846).[3] Arriving in Van Diemen's
Land after the handing down of the three volumes of the Bigge Reports in
1822 and 1823, Arthur fully embraced his instructions to make the penal
colony, as Bigge was charged to ensure, a 'fit receptacle for convicts' with
conditions of 'salutary terror' to deter criminals from committing crimes.
The Bigge Reports were a turning point in the transportation system,

---

[1] Arthur to Bathurst, 27 April 1826, TNA CO 325/28.
[2] Sir William Molesworth, 'Affairs of Canada', Hansard, HC Deb, vol. 39, col. 1462–1463,
22 December 1837.
[3] For studies of Arthur, see Michael C. Ivan Levy, *Governor George Arthur* (Melbourne:
Georgian House, 1953); A. G. L. Shaw, *Sir George Arthur, 1784–1854* (Melbourne:
Melbourne University Press, 1980); A. G. L. Shaw, 'Arthur, Sir George
(1784–1854)', ADB.

marking a decisive move towards increased severity, greater institutional oversight and fewer opportunities for convicts to benefit materially from their sentences.[4] His twelve years in Van Diemen's Land made Arthur the longest-serving administrator of any penal colony in the empire, and his views and methods weighed heavily with both Tory and Whig administrations. When convicts, critics and reformers referred to Van Diemen's Land as 'hell upon earth', they were largely referring to the penal system Arthur called 'Gaol to the Empire'.[5] The gaol was capacious: about 75,000 convicts were transported to Van Diemen's Land between 1803 and 1853, a bit less than half of all convicts sent to Australian penal colonies.[6]

What has not been sufficiently taken into consideration in assessing Arthur's regime was his committed Anglican Evangelicalism which impacted on all aspects of his personal and public life. In the 1830s, he was the chief defender of convict transportation against its critics. It was Arthur who believed – and acted – on the assumption that transportation was a key element of a coherent programme of penal discipline, and that it was both morally and administratively sound. It was Arthur, in collaboration with Archdeacon Broughton, who published a rebuttal of Archbishop's Whately's arguments against the reformative claims of transportation. Against the scandalous allegations of the Molesworth SC on Transportation, before which he appeared as a witness, Arthur defended his system with considerable authority. He saw off Maconochie's accusation that it lacked science, humanity, justice and reason,[7] and Molesworth's denunciation that transportation was 'inefficient, cruel and demoralizing'.[8] When Arthur was appointed Governor to Upper Canada, Molesworth could hardly contain his rage before the House of

---

[4] R. Evans, '"Creating an Object of Real Terror": The Tabling of the First Bigge Report', in Martin Crotty and David A. Roberts (eds.), *Turning Points in Australian History* (Sydney: University of New South Wales Press, 2009), pp. 48–61.

[5] Arthur to Bathurst, 27 April 1826, TNA CO 325/28: 13v–14v.

[6] For statistics, Hamish Maxwell-Stewart, 'Convicts', *The Companion to Tasmanian History* (Hobart: Centre for Tasmanian Studies, 2006), n.p. The history of the convict system in Van Diemen's Land is extensive, beginning with John West, who saw the ending of transportation as essential to the birth of the Australasian nation. West, *History of Tasmania*; Alison Alexander, *Tasmania's Convicts* (Sydney: Allen & Unwin, 2010); Boyce, *Van Diemen's Land*. For Aborigines: Lyndall Ryan, *Tasmanian Aborigines* (Sydney: Allen & Unwin, 2012); Henry Reynolds, *Fate of a Free People* (Ringwood: Penguin, 1995).

[7] Alexander Maconochie, 'Report on the State of Prison Discipline in Van Diemen's Land', BPP 1837–1838 (121) XL.237, p. 8.

[8] William Molesworth, *Report from the Select Committee of the House of Commons on Transportation* (London: Henry Hooper, 1838), p. 1v. The phrase does not appear in the BPP.

Commons, referring to Arthur as a despot and torturer whose chief object was the infliction of pain.[9]

Modern historical assessments of Arthur's system have been divided, possibly because the concept of a 'good' administrator of a penal colony is as challenging to modern sensibilities as claims for a 'good' manager of a slave colony (and at different times Arthur governed both convicts and slaves).[10] Without attempting to reconcile these opposing views, this chapter will assess the religious elements of Arthur's penal system and consider the extent to which he was able to implement a moral vision for the empire's leading penal colony. It includes a detailed analysis of his plans for reformatory religious and penal establishments in Van Diemen's Land and his pamphlets on transportation, written in response to Archbishop Whately. Arthur's religious and penal reforms were critical to the changing view of transportation by governing elites. Condemned as 'hell on earth', it was nevertheless the penal system most congruent with the Evangelical values of sin, crime, penitence and punishment examined in the previous chapter.

Arthur the Evangelical

Sustained by well-placed Evangelical friends, Arthur's regime in Van Diemen's Land had something of the character of Zachary Macaulay's in Sierra Leone, the colony of former and freed slaves founded by Evangelicals to spearhead the conversion of Africa a generation earlier. Catherine Hall has called Macaulay's governorship of Sierra Leone 'a new imperial experiment, a laboratory for the benevolent empire of God', values Arthur shared for Van Diemen's Land.[11] Macaulay served as governor from 1794 to 1799 before returning to England and devoting himself to the anti-slavery cause, as well as to numerous other charitable and religious societies.[12] Before, during and after his appointment to Van Diemen's Land, Arthur corresponded with leading Evangelicals, including William Wilberforce, James Stephen, Thomas Fowell Buxton and Zachary Macaulay, who encouraged his work of humane and Christian

---

[9] Sir William Molesworth, 'Affairs of Canada', Hansard, HC Deb, vol. 39, col. 1462–1463, 22 December 1837.

[10] For a range of views of Arthur, see Clark, *A History of Australia, Volume II*, p. 141; Shaw, *Sir George Arthur, 1784–1854*, p. 285; W. D. Forsyth, *Governor Arthur's Convict System* (Sydney: Sydney University Press, 1970), p. 8.

[11] Catherine Hall, *Macaulay and Son: Architects of Imperial Britain* (Yale: Yale University Press, 2012), p. 22.

[12] Penelope Carson, 'Macaulay, Zachary', in Donald M. Lewis (ed.), *The Blackwell Dictionary of Evangelical Biography, 1730–1860*, 2 vols. (Oxford: Blackwell, 1995), vol. II, p. 707.

governance.[13] Following the death of Arthur's eldest son, James Stephen devoted a Sunday afternoon to writing him a lengthy letter of condolence and encouragement. He comforted Arthur by stressing the significance of his work in laying the foundations for a powerful future state which might be a force for good or evil: 'Of what incalculable importance will not the establishment of a christian nation & enlightened state be in the centre of the eastern hemisphere & within reach of the Chinese Hindoo & Mahommedan nations which surround you.'[14] Stephen's advice was to use practical means for this object: 'Schools, missionaries, Bibles, prayer books are the things you want & the weapons you must use.'[15] Reports of Arthur's support for Evangelical projects, including the New Zealand missions of the Church Missionary Society were duly reported in the *Christian Observer*,[16] as was his earlier intervention on behalf of female slaves.[17] Arthur was instrumental in facilitating the attempt by George Augustus Robinson (1791–1866) to 'save the remnant' of the Tasmanian Aborigines in the wake of the failed military exercise aimed at their removal as a threat to colonists.

As a penal administrator, Arthur was scrupulous and fair-minded. His efforts were highly regarded by the Colonial Office and on his retirement, he was loaded with honours, including, in 1848, an honorary degree of Doctor of Civil Law from the University of Oxford. Arthur's activism divided his contemporaries. In 1832, the *Launceston Advertiser* referred to his penal reforms with approval as 'a complete and wholesome system of discipline of prisoners'.[18] At the same time he was vilified by critics, such as the journalist Henry Saxelby Melville (who was imprisoned by Arthur's Supreme Court), as Lt Governor of Hell.[19] His penal system was admired by the Quakers James Backhouse and George Washington Walker during their six-year visitation of the Australian colonies.[20] Arthur facilitated their tour of Van Diemen's Land, allowing them to visit and report on every penal station on the island as well as

[13] Alan Lester and Fae Dussart, 'The Genesis of Humanitarian Governance: George Arthur and the Transition from Amelioration to Protection', in Alan Lester and Fae Dussart (eds.), *Colonization and the Origins of Humanitarian Governance* (Cambridge: Cambridge University Press, 2014), pp. 37–76.

[14] J. Stephen to Arthur, 4 January 1824, Arthur Papers, vol. 4, SLNSW, MS A2164: 481.

[15] Ibid.   [16] *Christian Observer* 25 (April 1825), p. 839.

[17] *Christian Observer* 25 (April 1825), p. 176.

[18] *Launceston Advertiser*, 28 March 1832.

[19] Henry Saxelby Melville, *The History of the Island of Van Diemen's Land, 1824–1835* (London: Smith & Elder, 1835), p. 241.

[20] James Backhouse, *A Narrative of a Visit to the Australian Colonies* (London: Hamilton, 1843), p. 15.

interviewing convicts on road gangs.[21] Arthur enjoyed the full support of the colonial chaplains, whom he respected and whose Evangelical churchmanship he generally shared. He accepted the advice of Samuel Marsden, corresponding with him on agricultural matters and exchanging views on the religious prospects of the colony.[22] In 1824, Marsden was delighted that Arthur had begun to secure clerical reinforcements for the penal colony, considering it: 'one of the greatest Blessings that divine Providence could have bestowed upon your Land'.[23] Arthur was on good terms with the higher clergy including Archdeacon Scott and Archdeacon, later Bishop William Grant Broughton (1788–1853), who visited Van Diemen's Land several times in the course of his long episcopate. Broughton would later support Arthur when he defended the moral qualities of the convict transportation system. Other clerical critics were less impressed. The Presbyterian journalist and lay preacher, Frederick Maitland Innes (1816–1882), who personally toured many of Van Diemen's Land penal establishments in the late 1830s, condemned the 'cruelty and moral wickedness' of private assignment, asserting that it was impossible for a well-disposed master to have effective religious oversight of his convict servants, declaring, 'every interest is now outraged by the penal arrangement in force in this country'.[24]

Evangelical religion was mixed up in all of Arthur's schemes for Van Diemen's Land, something which appalled Melville: 'It may be as well to remark that this Government is generally termed a religious administration . . . but whilst this outward show – this over righteousness is so conspicuous – this place wherein the strayed sheep are penned, is considered by them a worldly hell.'[25] William Forsyth acknowledged that he underplayed the role of religion in Arthur's penal system as only having 'some value' as an agent of reformation of convicts.[26] Later historians rightly challenged this assessment.[27] Arthur's plans for a 'natural penitentiary' in Van Diemen's Land followed the same principles as the artificial penitentiaries favoured by Evangelicals in the Prison

---

[21] See Chapter 5.

[22] There are eight letters from Marsden to Arthur written between 18 December 1824 and 8 June 1836, and just one from Arthur to Marsden, on 20 May 1836. See Oxford, Bodleian Library, United Society for the Propagation of the Gospel USPG C/AUS/TAS 4 [Hereafter BodL USPG].

[23] Marsden to Arthur, 30 April 1825, BodL USPG C/AUS/TAS 4.

[24] Frederick Maitland Innes, *Secondary Punishments* (London: John Ollivier, 1841), p. 54.

[25] Melville, *History of Van Diemen's Land*, p. 258. For press attacks on Arthur, see Forsyth, *Governor Arthur's Convict System*, pp. 169–203.

[26] Forsyth, *Governor Arthur's Convict System*, p. vii.

[27] Ibid., v–vi, referring to Levy, *Governor George Arthur* and Clark, *A History of Australia*, vol. II.

Discipline Society.[28] He implemented fundamental changes to the penal system in Van Diemen's Land towards the reformatory model, creating an effective bureaucracy and building on the self-interest of setters and convicts.[29] His radical solution to the convict threat was to confine dangerous prisoners in the impregnable peninsular fortress of Port Arthur, complemented by a rigorous system of private assignment. According to Richard Ely, Arthur's objective was to ensure punishment was effective, by which he meant that no misdeed would go unpunished. The object of chaplains was to generate a sense of 'mind': 'Thus "minded" shamed as well as hurt by punishment, the convict would be led, step by step, to develop the "inward regulator", which conforms conduct of the laws of God and man.'[30] Arthur's system was designed to pay for itself by giving masters an investment in the effective management and reform of their convict servants.

Beyond the penal establishment, Arthur wanted a complete religious system to serve both civil and convict society. He acted on Earl Bathurst's mandate to Thomas Hobbes Scott (1783–1860), the first archdeacon of New South Wales (and Bigge's secretary), who in 1824 tasked Scott with devising an Anglican ecclesiastical establishment for New South Wales, including clergy, churches and schools. Accompanying Commissioner Bigge to Australia, Scott's knowledge of the colony was unrivalled, however he was officious and unpopular with his own clergy and showed little sympathy for the needs of the convicts. Bigge reported that colonial efforts to promote religion were not wanting but that the dispersed nature of the settlements and the 'depraved habits of the people' were impediments to religion and education.[31] While there was evident need for churches and schools, Scott's assumption of the ascendancy of the Church of England antagonized Methodist, Presbyterian, Congregationalist and Catholic colonists who were essential to their successful operation.

Arthur shared their doubts about the extent to which Archdeacon's Scott's plan was suitable for Van Diemen's Land, especially for the convicts who constituted about half the population. Nevertheless, he threw himself into the project with his customary thoroughness and eye for detail and system, preparing memoranda to accompany Scott's

---

[28] Ibid.   [29] Shaw, *Convicts and the Colonies*, pp. 226–228.
[30] Richard Ely, 'Arthur, Sir George', in *Blackwell Dictionary of Evangelical Biography*, vol. I, p. 30.
[31] For New South Wales, see Ritchie and Bigge, *Evidence*; For Van Diemen's Land, the testimony of witnesses appears in the unpublished appendix.

Reports of 21 April 1826, 14 April 1828 and 19 August 1830.[32] In the first memorandum, Arthur aimed to create an Anglican establishment for the colony of Van Diemen's Land like those already in place in Nova Scotia (1787), Quebec (1793), Calcutta (1814), Jamaica (1824) and Barbados (1824).[33] However, the legislative standing of the established church had been undercut by the repeal of the Test Acts (1828) and the Roman Catholic Relief Act (1829), securing new rights for dissenting Protestants and Catholics. While Arthur made an open avowal of his support for the Church of England: 'I have at heart the extension of the Church to which my family and myself are so warmly attached', he was not rigidly sectarian. He opposed the excessive claims for the established church advanced by Scott and Broughton.[34] He wrote to James Stephen that, having discovered Broughton was a high churchman 'strongly exclusive & strictly opposed to the Evangelical clergy', he hoped he would have no power to appoint ministers for the colony.[35] For pragmatic reasons, he supported the Wesleyans, whom he thought best suited to the convicts, as well as Evangelicals for everyone else. If a full church establishment was to be erected, it must also be generously subsidized by the home government.

To the disappointment of both Scott and Arthur, Bathurst regarded Scott's initial proposal as far too expensive, thus requiring Arthur to make energetic efforts to secure its survival. Scott's second visit elicited another lengthy memorandum from Arthur, dated 14 April 1828. The third memo, dated 19 August 1830, was in response to the visit by William Grant Broughton, who had succeeded Scott as archdeacon and would go on to become the first (and only) bishop of Australia. Broughton used this occasion to deliver a charge to the Van Diemen's Land clergy, which reveals his views of the moral condition of the colony. Broughton was more optimistic than Scott about the prospects of Van Diemen's Land and its progress under Arthur's administration, though there was no cause for complacency: 'The religion which we teach is the religion of Jesus Christ; and the appointed work of our ministry is to set him forth as the great agent in recovering the world from the dominion of sin.'[36] He urged his

---

[32] Arthur, 'Memoranda on New South Wales and Tasmania Clergy', 1826–30, TNA CO 325/28.

[33] H. W. Tucker, *The Spiritual Expansion of the Empire* 4th edn (London: SPG, 1900), p. 124; Rowan Strong, *Anglicanism and the British Empire, c.1700–1850* (Oxford: Oxford University Press, 2007).

[34] Shaw, *Sir George Arthur*, p. 145.

[35] Arthur to James Stephen, 23 April 1835, Arthur papers, vol. 4, SLNSW A2164 [CY Reel, p. 675].

[36] W. G. Broughton, *A Charge Delivered to the Clergy of Van Diemen's Land* (Hobart: James Ross, 1830), p. 10.

clergy to attack this problem with the tools of their Protestant faith, the Bible, the Book of Common Prayer and 'some one or more comprehensive Manuals of the Doctrines and Duties of the Christian Religion'. He recommended that they support the Society for the Propagation of the Gospel (failing to mention the Church Missionary Society, its Evangelical rival, which was patronized by Colonel Arthur), and establish parochial schools. Parents, 'who were themselves vicious', were to be prevailed upon to send their children to school, where their sense of sin might be appropriately moderated. Apart from this gentle hint, there is no reference to the penal population of Hobart; rather this was a pastoral message from a high church bishop with a sense of his duty to lead, comfort and unite his clergy.

Ministering to Convicts

One of Arthur's most original reforms was to secure Dissenters rather than Anglicans as salaried catechists to penal stations. For his scheme of establishment, Scott had requested ten additional clergy, including one for each of the penal stations of Macquarie Harbour and Maria Island, as well as a rural dean to cover for him during his absences.[37] While Scott assumed that all these appointments would come from the established church, Arthur demurred. In 1825, he wrote to James Stephen requesting 'reinforcement of the Church and School Establishment – especially of Ministers suited to this Colony', by which he meant those sympathetic to his own low churchmanship.[38] A year later he suggested that convict chaplains might as well be Methodists: 'Their Services may no doubt be obtained at a very moderate charge, and I should conceive they would be better qualified for the Office than any Gentlemen who have received a Liberal University Education.'[39] Ever diligent, Arthur had already contacted the resident Wesleyan missionary in Hobart, Benjamin Carvosso (1789–1834), and discussed with him the appointment of two convict chaplains which he was willing to support so long as the government contributed to their salaries. Arthur's request was put to the Wesleyan Methodist Conference, who approved the appointment of the first missionaries in 1826, one for Macquarie Harbour and another for Maria Island. In 1827 William Schofield (1790–1878) arrived in Hobart Town from where he was appointed, with initial reluctance on his part, as

---

[37] Arthur to Bathurst, 27 April 1826, TNA CO 325/28.
[38] Arthur to Stephen, 23 April 1835, Arthur Papers, vol. 4, SLNSW A2164 [CY Reel, 675].
[39] Arthur to Bathurst, 27 April 1826, TNA CO 325/28: 9.

Wesleyan catechist to the remote penal station at Macquarie Harbour.[40] Macquarie Harbour has a reputation that is possibly the most terrible of all the penal stations in Australia.[41] This reputation was deliberately heightened by government authorities in order to increase its deterrent effect, but the evidence shows that this was a particularly hostile environment for prisoners and officers both. Its most celebrated horror, highlighted by the Molesworth SC on Transportation,[42] was the cannibalism of a party of prisoners who absconded on 20 September 1822, of whom only one survived, Alexander Pearce. In one narrative said to be based on his interrogation by the Rev. Robert Knopwood in 1824, Pearce admitted that he had survived by devouring his colleagues; the first to die was allowed to say his prayers.[43] He was not believed and Pearce was returned to Macquarie Harbour. When he escaped again, this time with a single companion, human remains (or remains assumed to be human) were found in his pocket when he gave himself up.[44] Executed on 19 July 1824, Pearce was attended by Father Philip Connolly (1786–1839), the Catholic chaplain of Van Diemen's Land. At Pearce's request, 'in order to humble himself, as much as possible in the sight of God and Man', Connolly provided a detailed account of Pearce's confession to the crowd assembled around the scaffold minutes before the execution. This stressed that the condemned man was 'more willing to live than to die', approved the Providential justice to which he was subject and called on all present to 'offer up their prayers, and beg of the Almighty to have mercy upon him'.[45]

Despite these horrors – and others associated with the hard labour and punishment regime in Macquarie Harbour – the Wesleyans made progress in their mission.[46] For readers of the *Wesleyan Methodist Magazine*, Carvosso provided an account of the mission to Macquarie Harbour exulting that: 'men had returned from that place of sin and sorrow, walking in uprightness of life, and with their mouths filled with praises to the great Ruler of events; who, in his beneficent and inscrutable providence, had made banishment to Macquarie Harbour subservient

[40] G. L. Lockley, 'Schofield, William (1793–1878)', ADB.
[41] Maxwell-Stewart, *Closing Hell's Gates*, p. 1: 'Pluto's Land', 'The Rubbish Pit of the British Empire'.
[42] *Molesworth SC on Transportation*, BPP 1837–38 (669) XXII.1, p. xvii.
[43] Alexander Pearce, 'Narrative of the Escape of Eight Convicts from Macquarie Harbour in September 1822', 1824, SLNSW DLMS 3: 14.
[44] Ian Brand, *Macquarie Harbour Penal Settlements* (West Moonah: Jason, 1984), pp. 56–57.
[45] *Hobart Town Gazette*, 6 February 1824, p. 3
[46] Brand, *Macquarie Harbour*, pp. 45–46.

to their conversion to God'.[47] On 31 October 1828, Schofield began a class meeting with seventeen prisoners who 'feared the wrath to come' and eventually recommended that they be released on ticket-of-leave. Arthur was not convinced of the conversion of Schofield's men, though he did provide employment for two of them as gardeners at Government House. There was also a school for fifty-eight prisoners taught by six convict schoolmasters; none received payment other than the commendation of the chaplain and a reprieve from more arduous penal labour. Independent confirmation of the effectiveness of the religious instruction – albeit to a small number – is provided by the evidence from the visit to Macquarie Harbour in June 1832 by James Backhouse and George Washington Walker.[48] In their report, they noted that the duties of the missionaries included separate services for convicts and for officers and soldiers on Sunday, with an additional, voluntary service for prisoners on Sunday evening. There was evening school for prisoners three times a week and an adult school on Thursday. Friday was reserved for the Class Meeting and on Saturday there was choir practice. There was no provision for Catholic prisoners who were nominally the responsibility of Father Connolly, the Catholic chaplain in distant Hobart.

Schofield remained at the challenging post of Macquarie Harbour for four years until he was replaced by John Allen Manton (1807–1864) in 1832. On Macquarie Harbour's closure shortly afterwards, and the prisoners' transfer to Port Arthur, Manton went with them to become Port Arthur's first resident religious officer. There he officiated at its elegant church, overseeing the school as well as cooperating with religious instructors in probation stations to general satisfaction. Following the disruptive intervention of Bishop Francis Nixon, the fourteen-year experiment with Methodist ministry to the convicts came to an end. At Port Arthur, the replacement of Manton with a prickly Anglican chaplain led to a major battle (considered in Chapter 8).[49] In a despatch issued in 1834, Eardley Wilmot reported to the colonial secretary, Lord Stanley (1799–1869) on the impact of Durham's arrival, noting that the news of Manton's replacement by Durham had 'created a sensation', with significant consequences. Whereas before Christians of all denominations, including Presbyterians, Wesleyans, Independents and Roman

---

[47] Benjamin Carvosso, 'Methodism in Van Diemen's Land', *Wesleyan Methodist Magazine*, 49 (1831), 250–51.

[48] Backhouse, *Visit to the Australian Colonies*, pp. 44–59.

[49] For the convict protest about Durham's replacement of Manton, see Ian Brand, *Port Arthur 1830–1877* (Launceston: Regal, 1996), pp. 39–40. For Manton, who arrived in Sydney in 1831, see James Colwell, *The Illustrated History of Methodism* (Sydney: W. Brooks, 1904), p. 163.

Catholics, had been happy to attend the one place of worship at Port Arthur, the arrival of a Church of England clergyman with claims of precedence and plans to consecrate the church for the use of the established church had led to a general strike: 'all of these different creeds inform us that they cannot conscientiously attend the Church of England Service'.[50] Durham was to find equal difficulty in trying to wrest control of the school from the independent schoolmaster.

At the same time as Scott and Broughton were hoping to entrench Anglican establishment, including exclusive support for Church of England schools, there was a change of government and with it a change in policy from quasi-establishment, which favoured the Church of England, to liberal support for major Christian denominations on the basis of their colonial population.[51] Colonial church establishments were dismantled, including the expensive apparatus of clergy reserves in Upper Canada, New South Wales and Van Diemen's Land, and in their place multi-denominational arrangements were installed, pioneered in New South Wales by the liberal governor, General Sir Richard Bourke (1777–1855), and implemented through the Church Acts for New South Wales (1836) and Van Diemen's Land (1837).[52] This involved dissolving the arrangements created to support the Clergy and School Lands Corporation, despatched by Earl Bathurst in 1825 to Governor Sir Thomas Brisbane.[53] The Church of England lost both its entitlement to one-seventh of all lands in New South Wales and its right to support an exclusively Anglican or 'national' education system. On the other hand, Governor Bourke's Church Act of 1836, which required communities to contribute to the funding of churches and schools, led to an immediate and gratifying improvement in the staffing and construction of churches and schools.[54] Suddenly there was an opportunity for most parts of the Colony of New South Wales (and later other colonies as well) to meet community demand for religion and education.

With great satisfaction, Bourke wrote to Lord Glenelg (Secretary of State for the Colonies in the Whig administration of Viscount Melbourne), enclosing a letter received from Broughton with a list of places

---

[50] Eardley Wilmot to Lord Stanley, 1843; Brand, *Port Arthur 1830–1877*, p. 39.
[51] Peter Burroughs, 'Lord Howick and Colonial Church Establishment', *Journal of Ecclesiastical History*, 25.4 (1974), 381–405.
[52] David Stoneman, 'Richard Bourke: For the Honour of God and the Good of Man', *Journal of Religious History*, 38.3 (2013), 341–355.
[53] For despatches relevant to these changes between Governor Richard Bourke and Glenelg, see BPP 1837 (112) XLIII.21.
[54] See John Barrett, *That Better Country* (Melbourne: Melbourne University Press, 1966), pp. 16, 17, 79 and 81, for maps showing churches and stationing of clergymen in New South Wales and Van Diemen's Land before and after the Church Acts.

which had all subscribed more than £300 and were therefore, under the terms of the Church Act, entitled to a clergyman. Bourke suggested that the men selected for these appointments might be offered passage in a convict ship: 'I am persuaded that great benefit would accrue to the convicts from the opportunity which would thus be afforded of imparting religious instruction during the Voyage.'[55] Over the next few years, the Society for the Propagation of the Gospel (SPG), in coordination with the Colonial Office, approved the appointment and passages – on either convict or emigrant ships – of a stream of clergy, including a small number intended to provide religious instruction on convict hulks and transports and convict establishments. Catholic clergy also served as religious instructors on ships leaving Ireland, though this created other difficulties.[56] Finally, the governor of New South Wales, Sir George Gipps (1791–1847), wrote to the home secretary, Constantine Phipps, the Marquis of Normanby, asking him to stop approving any additional appointments because of the dramatic impact it was having on colonial finances which had risen almost three-fold, from an estimated £13,242 in 1834 to £34,066 in 1840.[57] The end of convict transportation to New South Wales in 1840 put a further brake on government support. On 8 August 1840, Lord John Russell wrote to the archbishop of Canterbury rejecting his request for additional religious instruction for the convicts in New South Wales.[58] Thanks to Bourke, Arthur and their successors, in a little over ten years, religious provision for free and convict people of the penal colonies had been put in place. From very different political perspectives, Arthur and Bourke both believed that religious training would allow for the reformation of the criminal from within, creating that moral realm which was the proper objective of all Christian rulers.

'Gaol to the Empire'

Apart from the two pamphlets on transportation (1833, 1835), which will be reviewed shortly, Arthur wrote no general account of his theories of penal discipline. This needs to be inferred from his testimony to government inquiries, such as the Molesworth Committee, before which he testified in June 1837, or his despatches to the Colonial Office. The drive

---

[55] Bourke to Glenelg, Sydney 29 November 1836, BodL USPG C/AUS/GEN 1.
[56] See Chapter 8.
[57] George Gibbs to Marquis of Normanby, 3 December 1839, BodL USPG C/AUS/ GEN 1.
[58] Russell to Archbishop of Canterbury, 8 August 1840, BodL USPG C/AUS/GEN 1.

to justify the expense of establishment, supplemented by the Methodist ministry, inspired Arthur to articulate a considered philosophy for the penal colony, one which was simultaneously nationalistic and moral, as well as worth the expense. In 1826 Arthur wrote grandly to Lord Bathurst (1762–1834):

This Colony must be considered in the light of an extensive Gaol to the Empire, the punishment of criminals and reformation of criminals, the grand objects, in its penal character, to be obtained to, and these, under Providence, can alone be affected by the presence of a respectable Military Force; – by the erection of proper places for confinement:– by an active judicial establishment;- by a more general diffusion of knowledge, and by the powerful operation of Religion.[59]

All this could be accomplished with the outlay of a few thousand pounds, which would be money well spent and a saving to the empire. Laying on the flattery, Arthur had the vision to see the convict establishment as setting the foundation for a future, free colony: 'when transportation shall cease, and all its Chains and Trammels disappear, a flourishing country will be at once exhibited, one of the finest monuments of Your Lordship's long Administration'.[60]

Alas, it was all too late, for in the never-ending whirl of cabinet officers, Bathurst had already been replaced by Viscount Goderich, and it would be William Huskisson (1770–1830), who took over as Secretary of State for War and the Colonies in 1827 and had to deal with Arthur's plans. Arthur doggedly argued for more chaplains and suggested that if Parliament made the funds available then the benefit would be repaid in the decrease in crime.[61] True to his Evangelical principles, Arthur was pleading not just for more clergy, but for a system of punishment which would offer prisoners something other than pain:

Convicts may be worked in Chains, lashed to the Tread mill, locked within the Walls of a solitary Cell, and their Bodies reduced by scanty fare but their Minds remaining unchanged, the dread of punishment always sinks under the power of temptation, – and they are no sooner liberated from the Trammels of confinement than they enter with renewed zest, upon scenes of Villainy, daring an ignominious death or, Macquarie Harbour, which they say is worse than death.[62]

Arthur urged the need for better religious provision: for the convicts, for the free settlers and for the rising generation. Scott had asked for a rural dean to officiate for him in his absence, but Arthur asked instead for an

---

[59] Arthur to Bathurst, 27 April 1836, 'Memoranda on New South Wales and Tasmania Clergy', TNA CO 325/28: 13–14.
[60] Ibid.   [61] Arthur to Huskisson, 14 April 1828, TNA CO 325/28: 13–14.   [62] Ibid.

archdeacon for Van Diemen's Land. In due course Van Diemen's Land would receive its own bishop, Francis Russell Nixon (1803–1879), who was consecrated bishop of Tasmania in Westminster Cathedral in January 1843. Instead of an Anglican establishment, Van Diemen's Land would be governed by the Church Acts of 1836 (New South Wales) and Van Diemen's Land (1837), which, as Frederick Innes pointed out with accurate disdain, provided no specific allocation for convicts, while doing away with the exclusive rights of the Church of England: 'Here we have religion ministered to those who can receive it with pomp or external decency; here it is virtually denied to the poor, the naked, the blind, and the miserable.'[63]

To Arthur's further plea for chaplains to reform the colony in the records of the Colonial Office, there is a pencilled comment – presumably from Huskisson – which queried what effect they would have if settlers and their convict servants 'cannot be induced to attend to their religious duties and receive Moral Instruction'.[64] Even more damning were the calculations of the full cost of creating a church establishment which was no less than £11,200. The pencil furiously objected to the high salaries, higher than in New South Wales, and noted the claims made by Governor Darling that the people of New South Wales were also anxiously waiting for additional churchmen. A briefing note prepared in 1829 for yet another incoming colonial secretary, Sir George Murray, on the measures proposed by Archdeacon Scott, with Arthur's approval, three years earlier reflect the cooling of enthusiasm in the Colonial Office for providing financial support for religion in Van Diemen's Land.[65]

In New South Wales, even Sir Ralph Darling, a religiously committed Tory high churchman, was reluctant to see the establishment of a cumbersome Church and School Corporation with endowed lands which, if unsuccessful, would leave a heavy capital burden on the colonial government. In Van Diemen's Land, Arthur suggested that there should be a separate fund administered by the Lt Governor and a committee of public officers: 'By this arrangement the fund would still be saved from the interference of any future Legislative Assembly.'[66] This last comment suggests another factor driving the evident anxiety of both Scott and Arthur for a solution. They were both aware that the religious character of the colonies was not exclusively Anglican and that once a more democratic mode of government was established it was unlikely that a

---

[63] Frederick Maitland Innes, 'The Convict System of Van Diemen's Land', *Monthly Chronicle*, 5.27 (1840), 437.
[64] Pencilled note, Arthur to Huskisson, 14 April 1828, TNA CO 325/28: 13–14.
[65] 'Briefing note for Sir George Murray', c.16 February 1829, Ibid.   [66] Ibid.

fund intended for the benefit of the church established in England (but not in the Australian colonies) would survive. But Arthur was nothing if not pragmatic and he adjusted well to the opportunities provided by the Church Act. By January 1836, he could provide an intimately detailed account of the expenditure on places of worship for all the major denominations, including Wesleyans, Independents, Roman Catholics as well as members of the established church (Anglicans); he was less sure about the Presbyterians and Quakers.[67] He continued to regard provision for the poor and prisoners as a mission best suited to the Wesleyans: 'Their system of instruction appears to be admirably adapted to attract the lower classes, and to win them especially from low, degrading vices.'[68] By the end of his administration he had increased the number of government schools from two to twenty-nine, including one for the boys of Point Puer at Port Arthur, and the number of churches from four to eighteen, with grants for Catholic, Presbyterian, Baptist and Independent (i.e., Congregational) chapels, as well as Anglican churches at Richmond and New Town. It was a respectable and relatively even-handed provision.[69]

As much as the churches and schools he built, the lengthy proposal and discussion about church establishment for Van Diemen's Land, including provision for convicts, provides strong evidence for Arthur's religious vision for the penal colony. Even though stillborn, it demonstrates the compatibility of his evangelical outlook with his strict plan for regularity and efficiency in penal discipline. It was also compatible with the programme of increasing surveillance, pain and 'terror to evil doers' that was now entrenched as government policy. Throughout his administration, Arthur had to constantly battle to convince the Home Office that his regime for convicts was sufficiently punitive. Far from overstepping the bounds of humanitarian decency, Arthur was effective in mitigating the most draconian impulses of a series of distant and politically insecure governments. In August 1833, Stanley wrote to Arthur instructing him to send 'criminals of the most hardened character' direct to Norfolk Island or Macquarie Harbour with a view to overcome the view that transportation was 'rather a boon and a benefit, than a state of suffering and punishment'.[70] Forsyth notes that Arthur did not actually fulfil this instruction, regarding it as inconsistent with his own plan to concentrate

---

[67] Arthur to Glenelg, 26 January 1836, *Religious Instruction*, Australia, BPP 1837 (112) XLIII.21, pp. 68–72.
[68] Ibid., p. 70.   [69] Forsyth, *Governor Arthur's Convict System*, pp. 38–39.
[70] Stanley to Arthur, 26 August 1833, *Molesworth SC on Transportation*, appendix, No. 1 'Correspondence Respecting Secondary Punishment', p. 12, BPP 1837 (518) XIX.1.

prisoners on the Tasman Peninsula.[71] As he explained to James Stephen, Arthur believed private assignment, including immediate and consistent punishment of breaches of prison discipline backed by an effective police force, was the most effective path to good order and reformation.[72]

Arthur was well aware that the problem was not so much that he had not done all in his power to make transportation properly severe, or 'as severe a punishment as any human being ought to be subjected to', but that this message was not understood at home.[73] In response to the objections to transportation when opposed to the construction of penitentiaries either at home or in the colony, Arthur put forward a considered plan to abandon the separate penal stations at Maria Island and Macquarie Harbour and concentrate prisoners on the Tasman's Peninsula.[74] By this stage Port Arthur had already been in operation for three years and Arthur knew there would be little choice but to accept this as a fait accompli. This was his 'natural penitentiary', which was free from the kinds of objections that the SC on Secondary Punishments had raised 'against hulks, gaols and penitentiaries, and every other pace of imprisonment and confinement in England'.[75] In every way, including morally and religiously, Arthur thought this was preferable to penitentiaries at home – a belief he maintained throughout his life.

Arthur v Whately

Arthur's main opportunity to defend his vision arose in response to yet another government inquiry, the long-running SC on Secondary Punishments (1831–1832), closely monitored by the PDS.[76] The debate between Whately and Arthur, supported by Broughton, needs to be seen in the light of its deliberations. Prior to the Molesworth SC, this was the most important parliamentary committee to inquire into the prison and transportation system. The PDS continued to argue that both transportation and imprisonment on the hulks were seen as 'inefficient' and unlikely to lead to the primary, elusive goal of the reformation of the

[71] Forsyth, *Governor Arthur's Convict System*, p. 135.
[72] Arthur to James Stephen, 23 April 1835, Arthur Papers, vol. 4, SLNSW A2164 [CY Reel 186, p. 675]: '[I]n the Assignment Service ... the beauty of the system exists, so far as the reformation of the Prisoners be an object to be gained.'
[73] 'Testimony of Colonel G. Arthur', 27 June 1837, *Molesworth SC on Transportation*, BPP 1837 (518) XIX.1, p. 292.
[74] Arthur to Viscount Goderich, 15 February 1833, appendix, No. 1 'Correspondence respecting Secondary Punishment', Ibid., p. 46.
[75] Ibid.
[76] *Select Committee on Secondary Punishments*, BPP 1831 (276) VII.519; BPP 1831–1832 (547) VII.559.

guilty which only scientific and moral penal systems could provide.[77] The committee attracted considerable attention with important contributions made not just by those who testified to the SC but also by those across the political and religious spectrum who were engaged by the issues it raised: what was the most effective punishment for those who committed crimes for which the erosion of the 'bloody code' meant that execution was no longer a final solution?[78]

The transportation debate was also influenced by Edward Gibbon Wakefield (1796–1862), whose accounts of his prison experiences, begun while he was still under sentence in Newgate, asserted that transportation was an unmitigated boon for criminals and advocated 'systematic' colonization by free rather than convict settlers.[79] Wakefield's views were promoted through the influential quarterlies which shaped public opinion: he was favourably reviewed by Charles Dodd in the *Quarterly Review*,[80] and, together with the SC *Report on Secondary Punishments*, in the *Law Magazine*.[81] The *Law Magazine* affirmed the common view, heavily endorsed by Wakefield, that transportation was not a punishment, and that private assignment of convicts in penal colonies was nothing other than 'domestic slavery'.[82] The appearance of Wakefield's books was a significant moment in the moral debate around transportation. It represented an early salvo in the campaigns of the Colonial Reform Society, soon to play a prominent role in advocating colonial self-government, free emigration and an end to convict labour.[83]

Observations on Secondary Punishments (1833)

As the leading advocate of transportation to the colonies, Arthur wasted no time in responding to Whately with his own *Observations upon*

---

[77] Prison Discipline Society, *Eighth Report*.

[78] For the impact of the debate on penal settlements, see Lisa Ford and David A. Roberts, 'New South Wales Penal Settlements and the Transformation of Secondary Punishment in the Nineteenth-Century British Empire', *Journal of Colonialism and Colonial History*, 15.3 (2014): n.p.

[79] Robert Gouger (ed.), *A Letter from Sydney, the Principal Town of Australasia* [by Edward Gibbon Wakefield] (London: Joseph Cross, 1829); Edward Gibbon Wakefield, *Facts Relating to the Punishment of Death in the Metropolis* (London: James Ridgway, 1831).

[80] [Charles Edward Dodd], 'Punishment of Death – Wakefield on Newgate', *The Quarterly Review*, 47 (March 1832), 170–216.

[81] Anonymous, 'Secondary Punishments', *Law Magazine* 7 (1832), 1–43.   [82] Ibid., 9.

[83] Philip Temple, *A Sort of Conscience: The Wakefields* (Auckland: Auckland University Press, 2002), p. 431. Wakefield formed the Society for the Reform of Colonial Government with Charles Adderley and John Robert Godley in 1849.

Secondary Punishments.[84] Initially printed in Hobart by James Ross in 1833, a copy of Arthur's riposte found its way to Whately. Never one to resist controversy, Whately responded with his 1834 *Remarks on Transportation*, including a specific response to the arguments raised by Bishop Broughton.[85] By this stage Arthur was entering the final hour of his negotiations about church establishment in Van Diemen's Land with the Colonial Office, making good use of the controversy with Archbishop Whately to strengthen his position. In a dispatch to Stanley, Arthur alluded to Whately's argument about the 'contaminating effects' of convicts on the community, noting that while 'no doubt overstrained', it demonstrated the need, indeed the 'moral necessity' to provide, 'by extraordinary means, upon an extensive scale', for religious and moral instruction, especially schools for the education of the children of the colony.[86] In 1835, Arthur responded again with his *Defence of Transportation*, which, reflecting the widening circle of those interested in the debate, was published in London.[87] The entire exchange, initiated by Whately and countermanded by Arthur, was the intellectual high point in the religious debate about the validity of transportation as both an effective deterrent to crime and an opportunity for the reform of the criminal.

In his lengthy, eighty-one-page letter to Archbishop Whately, penned in Hobart in May 1833, Arthur observed that he had initially been gratified rather than annoyed that so eminent an authority as the archbishop of Dublin had taken an interest in colonial affairs.[88] Despite its tone of scrupulous politeness, Arthur was deeply unimpressed by what he regarded as Whately's ill-informed attack on transportation. Far from failing by comparison with the American penitentiaries, Arthur countered that many Americans had told him they regretted the lack of penal colonies to which they might exile their 'wicked fellow countrymen'.[89] In relation to the deterrent effect on crime, Arthur insisted that it was just as important to expatriate the criminal, something which could not be achieved by penitentiary and prison discipline alone, no matter how effective and beneficial the work performed by religious instructors. He

---

[84] George Arthur, *Observations upon Secondary Punishments ... to Which Is Added a Letter upon the Same Subject by the Archdeacon of New South Wales* (Hobart: James Ross, 1833).
[85] Richard Whately, *Remarks on Transportation, and on a Recent Defence of the System; in a Second Letter to Earl Grey* (London: Fellowes, 1834).
[86] Arthur to Stanley, 15 October 1834, *Religious Instruction, Australia*, p. 64, BPP 1837 (112) XLIII.21.
[87] George Arthur, *Defence of Transportation, in Reply to the Remarks of the Archbishop of Dublin in His Second Letter to Earl Grey* (London: George Cowie, 1835).
[88] Ibid.   [89] Arthur, *Observations upon Secondary Punishments*, p. 9.

made this point with one of his more long-winded and belaboured metaphors: 'While I would support and encourage in their holy offices the ministers of religion, while I would promote the spread of religious information, while I would depend upon the labours of zealous and pious men as among the most desirable agents of crime prevention; I would expel those ... who choke the good seed sown by them.'[90] Arthur also made the valid point that penitentiary convicts in England and America were just as much slaves, with no property in their own labour, whereas in Van Diemen's Land, effectively classified, subject to the oversight of stipendiary police, private assignment provided them with some hope. 'The spirit of the convict', Arthur claimed, 'is not subdued by unmingled severity' but, with good behaviour, led to a ticket-of-leave and a gateway to free society.[91] At the same time, the 'worst men' were isolated in penal settlements. The system worked because the private master had a direct interest in the reform of prisoners, on whom he depended to secure the success of his farm.[92] As for the claim that the colony was a 'community of felons', the reality was that property was as safe as it was in England: 'The most respectable families, even in the interior are free from annoyance and live in comfort.'[93] What is more, they were generous in their support of religious, charitable and educational causes, which Arthur saw as a matter of imperial pride and evidence that 'the best feelings of the British character retain their original lustre even in this penal colony'.[94] If the colony was to prosper, moreover, it needed labour, which Arthur considered to be more important than ensuring the free character of all who settled there. In another back-handed dig at Whately, he compared his own system of punishments and rewards, with its prospect of joining an increasingly prosperous colony, to Whately's alternative proposal of forced labour on the Irish bogs. Finally, Arthur concluded, transportation really did lead to reform; it prevented crime and contributed to the rise of the colonies.[95] If only the system had worked as well as Arthur claimed, the transportation of convicts might have continued for decades.

Included with Arthur's *Observations* was a letter from Archdeacon Broughton, printed in Hobart on 22 June 1833.[96] Although expressed in deprecating courtesies to his clerical superior, Broughton took considerable trouble to respond fully to Whately's arguments against

---

[90] Ibid., 17.
[91] Ibid., 26–27. On the other hand, Arthur had no compunction in calling convicts the equal of slaves, as noted in the *Molesworth SC on Transportation*, BPP 1837–1838 (669) XXII.1, p. vii.
[92] Ibid., 30.   [93] Ibid., 35.   [94] Ibid., 36.   [95] Ibid., 80.   [96] Ibid.

transportation, giving as his opinion that the chief cause of the rapid increase in crime was a 'decay of faith in the truths of religion'.[97] Reflecting on his experience in English parishes, Broughton claimed that the problem of rising crime was not related to any change in the efficacy or mode of punishment, but from a 'diminished prevalence of the fear of God'. Broughton denigrated the archbishop of Dublin's discussion of crime, noting that he made no reference to morality. Such a defect, he noted, was unexpected in a bishop and theologian, but left him instead 'among the ranks of a jurist and a politician'.[98] Whately, the only liberal Anglican appointed to the House of Lords, would soon reply in kind to this slur on his moral credentials (see Chapter 5). As the collective voice of church and state for the penal colony, Broughton and Arthur were doubly authoritative, which is no doubt why Arthur invited Broughton to join him in replying to Whately. Broughton drew attention to the alliance in his letter, recalling their visit to a convict road party where Broughton performed divine service: 'you will testify I think that there could not possibly be a congregation displaying more fixed attention than these men, who continued standing during the prayers and sermon'.[99] Broughton then returned to his main assertion, namely that transportation had been condemned too quickly, that it was as effective a means of reformation as other forms of secondary punishment and, even if not 'improved in morals', by their removal to the penal colony convicts were less of a danger to society than if they remained at home.[100]

This was a full and well-reasoned response, showing humanity to the convicts, respect for their capacity to reform (even while recognizing this as rare) and arguing that transportation was better than the alternatives. It accorded with the view of convicts which Broughton developed in his recommendation to Arthur about the structure of a proposed church to serve the Hobart penitentiary, which he thought should incorporate space for free and unfree members of the congregation to worship together. Broughton's arguments about transportation were also based on his extensive colonial experience and his diligent travels around both New South Wales and Van Diemen's Land. His interventions were sincere and well-argued and emphatically rejected the view that abolishing transportation would have any impact on crime at home whereas it may, in Broughton's view, provide better outcomes for colony and convict in the empire. Broughton decried the 'fashionable feeling' of wanting a church 'pure from the contamination of a convict congregation'.[101] Since outwardly convicts continued to be members of the

[97] Ibid., 85.   [98] Ibid., 87.   [99] Ibid., 109.   [100] Ibid., 110–111.
[101] Broughton to Sir George Arthur, 6 August 1830, USPG C/AUS/TAS 4.

church, they therefore had every right to participate in its services: 'we have no right to banish them from the general assembly of the congregation'.[102] Broughton saw participation in communal religious service as a key part of the reformative training.[103] While an admiral theory, the penal associations and awkward arrangements in the Penitentiary Chapel designed by colonial architect John Lee Archer (1791–1852) in 1829 (which included thirty-six cells for solitary confinement beneath the Chapel floor) ensured it was not a success with Hobart's free churchgoers.

Defence of Transportation (1835)

In his first pamphlet, Arthur had invited Whately to change his mind. Unsurprisingly, Whately made no concessions at all to the case raised by either Arthur or Broughton.[104] In his *Defence of Transportation*, Arthur was determined to overthrow Whately's case that transportation to the colonies was ineffective as a counter-inducement to crime or that it damaged the colony economically.[105] Arthur began by questioning many of Whately's assumptions, including that convict labour, like slave labour, was invariably less efficient than the labour of free men, or that settlers acted in relation to their convict assigned servants as if they were slaves, treating them with similar disregard and severity.[106] As far as the condition of emancipists and ticket-of-leave men were concerned, Arthur argued that whereas in former times their conditions were, at one time, very favourable, this was no longer the case: 'unless he be a steady, hard working man, he can obtain little more than a bare subsistence'.[107] Arthur also took issue with the assumption that the interests of England and her convict colonies were at variance. In fact, he maintained, they were all part of the one empire. Beyond the strict economic benefit of convict labour, there was the question of the reform of the prisoners. If nothing more than the aversion of crime was hoped for, then why not simply revert to the 'filthy and noisome dungeons of former times?' Because public perceptions carried with them national expectations: 'And let it never be forgotten, that it is the true interest of England, that transportation should reform, as well as afflict the offender.'[108] Arthur here clearly placed himself on the side of the PDS, who believed that reform was the principal objective of penal systems. He also saw

---

[102] Ibid.   [103] Ibid.
[104] Whately, *Remarks on Transportation*. For discussion, see Chapter 5.
[105] Arthur, *Defence of Transportation*.   [106] Ibid., 16–17.   [107] Ibid., 40.
[108] Ibid., 48.

transportation as a way to reduce the overall load of criminality in the empire, by removing criminals from the 'excitement' of their original circumstances and the conditions of want characteristic of large cities.[109] With Archdeacon Broughton (and against Archbishop Whately), Arthur therefore renewed the call for additional religious and clerical services as a way to reduce crime. In an extraordinary phrase, he refers to ministers of religion as 'parts of a moral mechanism' which might be engaged to stop crime 'at its fountain head', that is in the hearts of criminals.[110] As we have seen, Arthur was trying to persuade the Colonial Office to strengthen the 'moral mechanism' of Van Diemen's Land with an adequate ecclesiastical establishment. The public pamphleteering should be seen as part of his frustration at the slow progress of his private lobbying with government.

In contrast to this positive message about convict redemption, Arthur condemned Whately's utilitarian pessimism. For Arthur, the prospect of reform was integral to the Protestant mode of governance:

The religion of the Protestant Church is not a system either of empty form or of mere doctrinal declamation. It is emphatically a religion of motives. It alone is calculated to establish within every breast an armoury, by weapons drawn from which each dishonest solicitation may be opposed in its beginnings.[111]

As a means to reinforce the 'moral restraint', which was the surest guard against criminality, Arthur concluded that transportation was a better option than any other. By recommending the abolition of private assignment, Molesworth would place an intolerable burden on the small cadre of religious instructors and clergy charged with achieving the same kind of reformative effect, with none of the financial inducements supplied by Arthur's highly regulated system.

Conclusion

Arthur left Van Diemen's Land in 1836, the year after the publication of his *Defence of Transportation*. He remained interested in transportation and 'his' penal colony, but apart from his appearance before the Molesworth Committee, for the immediate future Arthur was obliged to direct his attention to the problems of rebellious Upper Canada. This chapter has examined the way in which religious means of reformation were incorporated into Arthur's penal system. Initially this amounted to strict and highly supervised management of the private assignment system. Eventually Arthur recommended the concentration of prisoners in the

[109] Ibid., 62.   [110] Ibid., 63.   [111] Ibid., 123.

'natural penitentiary' of Port Arthur and the Forestier Peninsula, which he regarded as a great imperial gaol. Like the penitentiaries proposed by penal reformers at home, Arthur's 'natural penitentiary' was supported and enhanced by religious personnel. Arthur's extensive correspondence with the Colonial Office and his Evangelical friends in England, as well as his collaboration with Archdeacons Scott and Broughton over the creation of an appropriate religious establishment for Van Diemen's Land, show how seriously he took the need for religious as well as physical means to ensure transportation was properly punitive and reformative. Working together with the leading churchmen of the colony, he provided a defence of transportation against the critique of Archbishop Whately, the blustering of Edward Gibbon Wakefield and the evidence marshalled by the SC on Secondary Punishments. He supported the appointment of Methodist ministers with a special duty to convicts in the toughest of the ultra-penal stations, such as Macquarie Harbour.

Unfortunately for Arthur's legacy with historians, the mood of commentators and government was shifting inexorably from the harsh view of human nature and criminality espoused by committed Evangelicals. Resources for reforming convicts were begrudged if they could be commandeered for the rising tide of free settlers. The advocates for penitentiaries at home, including utilitarian and Christian critics of the practice of transportation were to have their moment in the Molesworth SC of 1838. And the utilitarians had their own religious advocate to put their case: Archbishop Richard Whately, who duelled with Arthur over the efficacy of the transportation experiment. The secular and Christian tradition of utilitarian objections to penal reform will be considered in Chapter 6. First, however, we need to go back a little to examine the other significant religious voice on penal reform and the efficacy of convict transportation: the Quakers.

4   Quakers and Convict Concerns

> About this time I was first impressed with the belief that it was the will of the Lord that, at a future time, I should go on a Gospel errand into Australia.[1]
>
> (James Backhouse, c.1814)

> I was torn from endearments of country and home,
> And doomed to this far distant shore
> Where hopeless I suffer, or pensively roam,
> And sigh, and sigh, for the land I adore.[2]
>
> (Norfolk Island prisoner, c.1835)

Concern for convicts and penal reform was slow to burn as an issue among British Quakers. Yet by 1835, when James Backhouse (1794–1869) collected the poem quoted above during his visit to Norfolk Island, Quakers were poised to make a major impact on the operation of British penal policy in the Antipodes. This chapter will concentrate on three main themes: the emergence of penal reform as a 'concern' of Quakers, partly as an extension of the anti-slavery campaign; the penal reforms initiated by British Quakers, including Elizabeth Fry and her work for women convicts awaiting transportation; and the ministerial visitation to Australia conducted by Backhouse and George Washington Walker (1800–1859) in the 1830s. It will be argued that Quakers made a disproportionate contribution to penal reform, given their small numbers, but they hoped to ameliorate, not abolish transportation. Backhouse and Walker sought to encourage the colonial authorities to replace physical punishments such as flogging with a Christian regimen of productive work, silence and separation for dangerous offenders, based on the prospect of reformation. This work was complemented by Fry's determination to improve female convicts' conditions in British and Irish prisons and while

---

[1] Sarah Backhouse, *Memoir of James Backhouse, by His Sister* (York: William Sessions, 1870), p. 13.
[2] 'The Norfolk Island Exile by a Prisoner', in James Backhouse, 'Letters, 1831–1856', Library of the Religious Society of Friends MS 375: 29 [Hereafter 'Backhouse Letters'].

undergoing transportation. The Quaker view was also reflected in the Prison Discipline Society (PDS), which members helped found and which undergirded systematic reforms demanded by the Secondary Punishments Committee, a vehicle for the PDS and its friends.[3] In this chapter, however, we will examine the work of Quakers in the field, reporting, recommending and seeking just and Christian solutions to the problem of crime.

Anti-Slavery and Its Heirs

The abolition of the transatlantic slave trade in 1807 was the culmination of decades of agitation by a network of religious, humanitarian and libertarian groups and reflected a new idea – that the conduct of empire, so long the preserve of military and commercial interests, should reflect the highest moral principles of the British people. It represented an unprecedented mobilization of the moral middle class, nurtured in the writing of Hannah More and her circle, to a common cause.[4] But it did not stop there. By 1823, when William Wilberforce made his 'Appeal to the Religion, Justice and Humanity of the Inhabitants of the British Empire',[5] he made a much wider claim of responsibility for all those caught within the expanding web of British colonization. The subsequent outpouring of effort by Victorian churches on moral and social causes was not necessarily altruistic and might be explained in terms of Pierre Bourdieu's theory of unembodied capital (cultural and social), which can be transformed into economic capital over time.[6]

Without accepting the materialist implications of Bourdieu's theory, anti-slavery was foundational to other humanitarian campaigns in the nineteenth century, including penal reform.[7] By borrowing some of its premises about the innate value of free labour and the dignity of the human being, anti-slavery supplied the rhetorical frame for the three-stage campaign to mitigate the physical abuse of convict

---

[3] See Chapter 2.

[4] Christopher Leslie Brown, *Moral Capital* (Chapel Hill: University of North Carolina Press, 2006), p. 344.

[5] William Wilberforce, *An Appeal to the Religion, Justice, and Humanity of the Inhabitants of the British Empire in Behalf of the Negro Slaves in the West Indies* (London: J. Hatchard, 1823).

[6] Pierre Bourdieu, 'The Forms of Capital', in J. G. Richardson (ed.), *Handbook for Theory and Research for the Sociology of Education* (Westport, CT: Greenwood, 1985), 241–258, p. 25.

[7] For discussion of the multiple origins of humanitarianism, including anti-slavery, see Michael N. Barnett, *Empire of Humanity* (Ithaca, NY: Cornell University Press, 2010), p. 57.

bodies, end private assignment and abolish convict transportation.[8] By tethering religion to nationalism, Peter van der Veer argues that the evangelical revival created a profound shift in British politics, effectively producing a new moral state.[9] The 'evangelical project', he maintains, which engaged active Quakers, 'convert[ed] people to a morally inspired existence in which individual conscience of sins and atonement are catchwords, within a nation with a colonizing mission that is interpreted as liberating'.[10] Hence the moral empire expanded well beyond the established domains of the fused church and state of the old regime, providing significant opportunities for Dissenting Christians to make their mark. Among the first to do so were the Quakers.[11]

Quakers and Penal Reform

There was no natural path drawing Quakers to social activism. The movement founded by George Fox (1624–1691) was among the few radical sects to survive the persecution of nonconformity in the seventeenth and eighteenth centuries. By the nineteenth century, the Religious Society of Friends bore little resemblance to the wildly quaking men and women who had gathered around Fox, prophesying, missionizing the American colonies, or, when the spirit called on them, going naked 'for a sign'.[12] Their numbers had shrunk from an estimated 60,000 in Fox's time to about 16,227 in 1840. The Quaker mainstream was not socially activist but dominated by quietism, a theology stressing personal sanctity rather than good works in the world. It was Mrs Elizabeth Fry's singular achievement to be one of those who transformed Quakerism into a

---

[8] For the connections between the slave and convict labour trades in the late eighteenth century, see Emma Christopher, '"The Slave Trade Is Merciful Compared to [This]': Slave Traders, Convict Transportation and the Abolitionists', in Emma Christopher, Cassandra Pybus and Marcus Rediker (eds.), *Many Middle Passages* (Berkeley: University of California Press, 2007), pp. 109–128. For arguments comparing slavery and convicts, see Hamish Maxwell-Stewart, '"Like Poor Galley Slaves": Slavery and Convict Transportation', in Maria Suzette Fernandes Dias (ed.), *Legacies of Slavery* (Newcastle upon Tyne: Cambridge Scholars, 2007), pp. 48–61.
[9] Peter Van Der Veer, *Imperial Encounters* (Princeton, NJ: Princeton University Press, 2001), pp. 30–54.
[10] Ibid., 36.
[11] Timothy Larsen and Michael Ledger-Lomas (eds.), *The Oxford History of Protestant Dissenting Traditions, Vol. III* (Oxford: Oxford University Press, 2017), p. 80.
[12] Elizabeth Isichei, *Victorian Quakers* (Oxford: Oxford University Press, 1970), p. xxiv. For the interconnection between domestic and ecstatic experience for early Quakers, see Phyllis Mack, *Visionary Women* (Berkeley: University of California Press, 1989), pp. 212–235.

movement associated in the public mind with philanthropy, even though this rested more on a few wealthy families than the majority of ordinary Friends. The change from quietism to activism for some Quakers began in the early nineteenth century. Quakers were influential out of all proportion to their numbers in activities such as the Peace Society (founded 1816), which promoted pacifism, the anti-slavery movement, as well as temperance, the Anti-Corn Law League, Fry's prison visiting and opposition to capital punishment.[13]

American Quakers were the first to marry utilitarian and religious approaches for prison design and prisoner reform. In his study of Quaker prison reformers, Christopher Adamson suggests that the Quakers' call to penal reform arose from their conversion to a more evangelical interpretation of Christianity than had traditionally characterized the movement's mainstream.[14] Evangelicalism encouraged Quakers' rediscovery of Christianity's more active face and they sought to extend the redeeming power of the cross to suffering humanity, including slaves, poor families, wounded soldiers and those incarcerated in institutions.[15] Quaker activism was regulated and authorized by means of 'travelling under concern' (approval from Meeting for a visit on a particular social purpose). James Backhouse and George Washington Walker received such authorization for their visit to the penal colonies of Australia, South Africa and Mauritius, reporting on conditions for convicts, slaves and Aborigines.[16] On both sides of the Atlantic and, subsequently, across the globe, Friends were informed on events elsewhere through the visitation of ministers bearing 'concerns' with them, such as Stephen Grellet (1773–1855), who restlessly crossed Europe, then America and Britain pursuing the causes of anti-slavery, penal reform and hospitals. It was Grellet who introduced Elizabeth Fry and her sister to the needs of female prisoners, a work she was soon to make her own.[17]

---

[13] Isichei, *Victorian Quakers*, pp. 212–257.
[14] Christopher Adamson, 'Evangelical Quakerism and the Early American Penitentiary Revisited', *Quaker History*, 90.2 (2001), 35–58.
[15] Ibid., 36.
[16] For the Australian leg of this nine-year journey, see Penelope Edmonds, 'Travelling "under Concern": Quakers James Backhouse and George Washington Walker Tour the Antipodean Colonies, 1832–41', *Journal of Imperial and Commonwealth History*, 40.5 (2012), 769–788.
[17] For Grellet's contacts with his 'dear friends' Elizabeth J. Fry and her sister, see Benjamin Seebohm (ed.), *Memoirs of the Life and Gospel Labours of Stephen Grellet*, 2 vols., 3rd edn (London: Bennett, 1862), vol. II, pp. 99, 258, 333.

Quakers were also drawn to penal reform through their interest in experimental science and Rational Dissent.[18] This is reflected in the most significant monuments to Quaker prison theories, such as the New York State Prison at Auburn (1819), the reformatory prison in Pennsylvania, or the New York House of Refuge, the first reformatory specially built for children (1825).[19] Transforming recalcitrant human beings into pious and orderly citizens was an experiment on a grand scale, and one to which some Quakers gave their enthusiastic attention.

British Quakers were slower to become interested in penal reform than American Friends, influenced by the reluctance of mainstream Quakers to be engaged in social and political affairs. As reflected in the Epistles from the Yearly Meeting in London, British Friends were urged to live in the world, but seek to remain apart from its burdens: 'the pursuits of business, of intellect and of taste, will be subject to holy restraints'.[20] Some Quakers, especially younger ones, were attracted to the freer ways and opportunities for more ardent expression offered by other noncon- formist churches.[21] Pressure to reject the world slowly led some Quakers to leave the Society and enter the evangelical mainstream, which was not so hostile to practices such as marrying out or social activism. In Amer- ica, Quakerism split into evangelical, conservative and liberal branches. The evangelicals gave the highest priority to penal reform and social issues.[22]

These divisions between Friends are important for British penal reform. Indeed, most of the best-known 'Quakers' involved in penal reform became so after they had left the Society of Friends. The Buxtons were disowned for non-attendance in 1816 and 1817. William and Mary Howitt, two Friends who emigrated to Australia, resigned from the Society in 1847. Mary was frustrated by the Society's closed nature; 'They would not read books. They would not go into society.'[23]

---

[18] Anthony Page, 'Rational Dissent, Enlightenment and Abolition of the British Slave Trade', *The Historical Journal*, 54.3 (2011), 741–772.

[19] Jennifer Graber, *The Furnace of Affliction: Prisons & Religion in Antebellum America* (Chapel Hill: University of North Carolina Press): Graber considers Auburn, 1816–1827, and Sing Sing, 1828–1839; Adamson, 'Evangelical Quakerism', 38.

[20] *Epistles from the Yearly Meeting of Friends*, 2 vols. (London: Edward March, 1858), vol. II, p. 343.

[21] Isichei, *Victorian Quakers*, p. 127.

[22] Pink Dandelion, *The Quakers: A Very Short Introduction* (Oxford: Oxford University Press, 2008), pp. 106–118; Thomas D. Hamm, *The Transformation of American Quakerism: Orthodox Friends, 1800–1907* ; Bloomington: Indiana University Press, 1988); Pink Dandelion, *An Introduction to Quakerism* (Cambridge: Cambridge University Press, 2007).

[23] Cited by William Nicolle Oats, *A Question of Survival: Quakers in Australia in the Nineteenth Century* (St Lucia: University of Queensland Press, 1985), pp. 20–21.

William's commitment to radical politics, reflected in his denunciation of British imperial policy towards Aboriginal peoples in *Colonization and Christianity*, divided him from his Quaker roots.[24] The attachment of Quaker and former Quakers to humanitarian causes replaced, for some at least, the closeness of Quaker communal worship from which they were now excluded. By the 1850s, Friends were encouraged to work individually with their fellow countrymen towards easing the four great issues which concerned Quakers: capital punishment, temperance, slavery in the British colonies and penal reform: 'We have also earnestly desired that our Legislature may proceed in mitigating the severity of the criminal code of our beloved country, and thus make its laws more conformable to the spirit of the Christian religion.'[25] The challenge for Quakers was in balancing the demands for intervention in the affairs of the world with the need for religious quiet and peace independent of it. On the issue of penal reform, one woman made this concern uniquely her own: Elizabeth Fry.

Elizabeth Fry and Convict Women

After John Howard, Mrs Elizabeth Fry, née Gurney (1780–1845), is probably the best known of all the British penal reformers; her major contribution was in effecting change for women prisoners.[26] Like Florence Nightingale, Fry was celebrated in her lifetime as something of a living saint. While Nightingale, along with other 'eminent Victorians', was disparaged by Lytton Strachey in 1918, Fry's reputation has survived remarkably intact.[27] 'Everyone knows the popular conception of Florence Nightingale', wrote Strachey, 'But the truth was different.'[28] The truth is also different about Fry and she deserves recognition for her extraordinary persistence, powers of organization and effective delegation; her contribution to the cause of prison reform in Europe, the United States as well as in Britain and the convict colonies; and her total commitment to the work of women for women.[29]

---

[24] William Howitt, *Colonization and Christianity* (London: Longman, 1838).
[25] Epistles from the Yearly Meeting, vol. 2, p. 239.
[26] John Kent, *Elizabeth Fry* (London: B. T. Batsford, 1962), p. 12. For context, sources and discussion of Victorian reformers, see David M. Horton, *Pioneers in Penology*, 2 vols. (Lewiston, NY; Lampeter: Edwin Mellen Press, 2006).
[27] Giles Lytton Strachey, *Eminent Victorians* (London: Chatto & Windus, 1918).
[28] Ibid., 135.
[29] For biographical and critical studies of Fry, see Anne Isba, *The Excellent Mrs. Fry* (London: Continuum, 2010); Anne Summers, *Female Lives, Moral States: Women, Religion and Public Life in Britain, 1800–1930* (Newbury: Threshold, 2000); Janet Payne Whitney, *Elizabeth Fry, Quaker Heroine* (London: Harrap, 1937); Annemieke Van Drenth

Fry was born into a wealthy Quaker household of the merchant and banking family of John Gurney (later consolidated into Barclays Bank). By March 1811, she was recognized as a Quaker minister with authority to preach, frequently travelling with certificates of authorization from her own Monthly Meeting to attend meetings of Friends throughout the British Isles.[30] Her travels later extended to much of Europe. Fry's 'concern' for prison visitation had Friends' support but was initially a family affair. Inspired by Stephen Grellet's reports of the terrible conditions for women and children,[31] Fry began visiting London's Newgate Prison in 1813, where she established the first and most important of her Ladies' Committees. Other women had visited prisons, including female followers of John Wesley, who accompanied his public preaching to prisoners in Oxford, Cardiff, Bristol and elsewhere in England. These could be disruptive events, such as Wesley's visit to Newgate Prison in Bristol in April 1739, when 'all Newgate rang with the cries of those whom the word of God cut to the heart'.[32] This did not endear them to the authorities. What distinguished Fry's work was the extent to which she secured authorization for women's ministry in gaols, hulks and other sites of confinement. In securing this goal, Fry benefitted from the support of her respectable and politically active male relatives who initially collaborated in forming the Association for the Improvement of the Female Prisoners in Newgate.

Based on her work at Newgate, Fry and her Ladies' Committee provided her brother-in-law, the politician and anti-slavery campaigner, Thomas Fowell Buxton (1786–1845), with information about conditions for women in Newgate for his *Inquiry*, published in 1818.[33] Fry initiated basic improvements, such as providing clothing for the children and, with the women's consent, a school and paid employment. After consulting the women, she devised a set of rules which they agreed to follow, with a schedule of activities for the day. One of the ladies suggested that the women prisoners might supply Botany Bay with stockings and other articles of clothing, and this was negotiated with a local business. Fry's intervention was so effective that the night before the departure of a

and Francisca De Haan, *The Rise of Caring Power: Elizabeth Fry and Josephine Butler* (Amsterdam: Amsterdam University Press, 1999); June Rose, *Elizabeth Fry* (London: Macmillan, 1980); Francisca de Haan, 'Fry, Elizabeth (1780–1845)', ODNB.

[30] Thomas Timpson, *Memoirs of Mrs. Elizabeth Fry* (London: Aylott and Jones, 1847), p. 327.

[31] Seebohm (ed.), *Memoirs of Stephen Grellet*, vol. I, pp. 224–225.

[32] John Wesley, *The Works of the Rev. John Wesley*, 17 vols., 4th edn (London: Mason, 1837), vol. I, p. 129.

[33] Buxton, *An Inquiry*, pp. 20,110–136.

group of women for Botany Bay, instead of their usual practice, which had been to 'break every thing breakable', the women made their adieux with all the decorum of a funeral procession.[34] On Fry's intervention with the Governor of Newgate, the women were given secure transport and sorted into classes as recommended by the PDS. For the first time, women were given occupation for the voyage – quilt-making – the proceeds of which could be used to obtain accommodation in the colony.

When Buxton was elected to parliament, Fry made use of his connections to continue advocacy for better conditions for women in prison. She testified to the 1818 SC on London Prisons, the 1832 SC on Secondary Punishments and the 1835 HL SC on gaols in England and Wales to which she extolled the power of reading the Bible to 'poor Sinners': 'you there see how the Gospel is exactly adapted to the fallen Condition of Man'.[35] Her focus on women prisoners may have influenced Home Secretary Sir Robert Peel, whose Gaol Act (1823) ensured women prisoners were cared for by women wardens. Although the Gaol Act had many limitations, it was a step in the right direction, particularly in attempting to ensure there was classification of prisoners and efforts to provide them with employment.[36] Seeking more evidence to support the cause, in 1819 Fry accompanied her brother, Joseph John Gurney (1788–1847) on a tour of prisons in Scotland and Northern England.[37] By this stage Fry's witness had become sufficiently important for her name to be included in the title of their report and care was taken to focus on the conditions endured by female prisoners and children.

Other reforms followed. In her one published book, *Observations on the Visiting, Superintendence and Government of Female Prisoners* (1827), Fry described a range of 'humane regulations' which had been passed by the government at her behest.[38] These included provisions enabling women sentenced to transportation to take any child younger than seven with them on the voyage and preventing breastfeeding mothers from being forced to leave before their children were weaned. She lobbied authorities to prevent women from being placed in irons when transported from prison to ship. She urged the members of her Ladies' Committees to encourage women prisoners to behave well in the hope that, in the colony, they might secure employment with respectable families.[39] Fry was also an unstinting opponent of capital punishment which she

---

[34] Ibid., 132.
[35] *HL SC on Gaols and Houses of Correction* (First Report), BPP 1835 (438) XI.I, p. 522; *SC on Secondary Punishments* BPP 1831–1832 (547) VII.559, pp. 116–123.
[36] McConville, *English Prison Administration*, p. 249.
[37] Gurney, *Notes on a Visit to Prisons*.   [38] Fry, *Observations on Female Prisoners*, p. 63.
[39] Ibid., 65.

regarded as abhorrent to every Christian principle. Public execution removed the opportunity for true repentance, cheapening the privilege of God to determine 'the hour and the time' and, in her view, was not an effective deterrent on crime.[40] Instead of the threat of death, Fry placed her faith in the exercise of strict discipline, 'severe in proportion to the enormity of the crime', but mitigated with religious care and Christian kindness: '[L]et us ever aim at the diminution of crime, though the just and happy medium OF THE REFORMATION OF CRIMINALS.'[41] At Newgate, Fry made Bible reading a central feature of her visits to women prisoners, to the extent that it became one of the spectacles of London. Disturbed by her growing authority, in 1824 the authorities took steps to suppress it. Undeterred, her visitors became grander and grander and in 1842 she read the Bible to prisoners of Newgate in the presence of the King of Prussia.[42] In time the British Ladies' Society for Promoting the Reformation of Female Prisoners (1821), the national organization inspired by Fry, provided woman transportees with a kit of clothing and sewing materials; those who could read received a copy of the New Testament and the Psalms.[43] Fry's ladies were in touch with every female convict transport, and by 1829 reported on visitations to 106 ships containing 12,000 female convicts.[44] Initially supported by private charity boosted by royal patronage, the outfitting of female prisoners for the voyage was soon taken over by the government.[45]

Fry's major contribution to the practice of reformed transportation was to secure more effective surveillance of their conditions at every point of the journey from prison to penal colony. Her correspondence with Backhouse, in the period shortly before his departure for Australia, was focussed on securing this oversight. During the voyage, she hoped to reinforce the transformation of women's characters she had initiated at Newgate, by providing meaningful work, copies of the Bible and sincere, Christian sympathy for their condition. When a transport left for Van Diemen's Land before she had made arrangements for the employment of women, she was disappointed but undeterred. She asked Backhouse to follow up the errant vessel in the colony: 'we think that very great good would result from an exact report of these things being taken upon the

---

[40] Ibid., 74–75. [41] Ibid., 76.
[42] Timothy Larsen, *A People of One Book* (Oxford: Oxford University Press, 2011), p. 180.
[43] *A Concise View of the Origin and Progress of the British Ladies Society for Promoting the Reformation of Female Prisoners* (London: The Society, 1840), p. 18; Timpson, *Memoirs of Mrs Elizabeth Fry*, pp. 122–123.
[44] Timpson, *Memoirs of Mrs Elizabeth Fry*, p. 123. [45] Ibid., 19.

arrival of every ship and a copy of that report *always* forwarded to us'.[46] Fry urged that the surgeon superintendent and officers also follow her instructions, and that the Ladies' Association in New South Wales 'would more regularly correspond with us as we believe that much good would result from it'. She provided a list of questions for Backhouse, soliciting detailed information on the extent of the convict women's compliance with the rules of the Ladies' Committee, culminating with: 'Are they attentive at times of religious service, reading the Scriptures &c and do they attend to keeping the Sabbath holy?'[47] Fry wanted the jurisdiction of her ladies to extend beyond Newgate to include all women transported. Hers was a total vision of women ruled and reformed by other women. Nevertheless, Fry and her British Ladies' Society aimed to reform women's transportation, not abolish it.

Backhouse and Walker

While Fry continued her work with women prisoners and Thomas Buxton was galvanizing the PDS, the most important Quaker intervention in the penal colonies was already underway. On 17 May 1831, James Backhouse 'opened a concern to pay a visit to New Zealand and South Africa' at the Yearly Meeting of Ministers and Elders. He brought with him certificates of unity from the Monthly and Quarterly Meetings held at York in December 1830. The minutes state that Backhouse wished 'to perform a visit in the love of the Gospel to the Inhabitants of the British Colonies and settlements in New Holland, Van Dieman's Land [sic] and South Africa'.[48] Backhouse was advised to select a travel companion; he chose George Washington Walker, a young member of the same York Meeting. Together they would travel, apparently without any conflict, for the next ten years. While the two men were Friends in every sense, Backhouse, naturalist, nurseryman and missionary, was the leader with responsibility to report to the London Meeting. His memoirs relate his precocious belief that he was called to 'go on a Gospel errand into Australia' as early as 1814 when he was living in Norwich.[49] His interest in Australia was strengthened by contact with Fry who was by then visiting Newgate Prison, and did so with Backhouse. Fry was determined

---

[46] Fry to Backhouse, 23 June 1832, in Elizabeth Fry, 'Elizabeth Fry and Convict Ships [Letter from Elizabeth Fry to James Backhouse, 23 June 1832]', *The Journal of the Friends Historical Society*, 25 (1928), 22–24.

[47] Ibid., 23.

[48] 'Yearly Meeting of Ministers and Elders', 17 May 1831, vol. 6, p. 285, Library of the Religious Society of Friends, London [Hereafter 'Yearly Meeting'].

[49] Backhouse and Backhouse, *Memoir*, p. 13.

that her efforts in England and Ireland, where she had good connections and had established many Ladies' Committees, be matched by direct observation in Van Diemen's Land and New South Wales. As the senior partner and an accredited minister, Backhouse was formally entrusted by the London Yearly Meeting to undertake this concern. Financed by the Meeting, the duty was undertaken substantially on foot with the two missionaries often journeying twenty-five to thirty miles a day. In Cape Town, the botanist W. H. Harvey reported that Backhouse took four hours of exercise daily 'for health's sake'.[50]

The two Quaker travellers were following the path of many other Friends abroad, particularly those visiting America to investigate the practice of slavery. Friends were given certificates of leave to attend Meetings in their destination, which they were required to return when their duty was over. At the London Yearly Meeting, the certificate for James Backhouse caused little fuss, explaining: 'Our dear friend James Backhouse of the City of York a Minister of our religious Society has stated to this Meeting that an apprehension of religious duty had rested in his mind to visit, in the love of the Gospel, some of the Inhabitants of the British Colonies of New Holland, Van Diemen's Land, and South Africa.' He produced a certificate of York Monthly and Quarterly Meetings offering their support. In response, the Meeting solidly endorsed him.[51] Copious manuscript and printed records document Backhouse and Walker's long journey: extensive personal correspondence with their families; a shared journal maintained throughout their travels; and reports delivered to the colonial government on conditions in the Port Arthur and Norfolk Island penal settlements, and the Flinders Island Aboriginal settlement. Backhouse's *Journal*, originally published as a cheap ten-part serial covering all parts of his immense itinerary,[52] later appeared in a more handsome format complete with detailed maps and etchings, some of them based on Backhouse's sketches.[53] In this form, their travel narrative served as a guide to religious Friends and others who might be contemplating emigration or undertaking missionary service. It was also intended to reform and edify colonists and their administrators. Back home at last in York, Backhouse hoped that his Australian

---

[50] William Nicolle Oats, *Backhouse and Walker* (Sandy Bay: Blubber Head Press, 1981), p. 4.
[51] 'Yearly Meeting', 28 May 1831, pp. 28–29.
[52] James Backhouse, *Extracts from the Letters of James Backhouse, Now Engaged in a Religious Visit to Van Dieman's Land, and New South Wales, Accompanied by George Washington Walker*, 10 Parts (London: Harvey and Darton, 1837–1841).
[53] Backhouse, *Visit to the Australian Colonies; James Backhouse, A Narrative of a Visit to the Mauritius and South Africa* (London: Hamilton Adams, 1844).

volume 'may convey a measure of useful information, and excite some interest on behalf of the Aborigines, and the Emigrant and Prisoner Population of Australia';[54] and his second, African journal, would succeed in exciting 'christian [sic] interest for all classes of the inhabitants of the countries described; and he especially hopes, that it may promote the feeling of sympathy for the devoted individuals who are labouring amidst many privations, to spread the Redeemer's kingdom'.[55] To free settlers in both Australia and southern Africa, Backhouse addressed an open letter urging them to do justice to the native people, provide them with missions, and undertake moral reforms including temperance, religious assembly and family prayer.[56] White settlers in Africa he urged to recognize the evil of slavery, which was accepted by all the Protestant churches of Europe.

In New South Wales, Backhouse and Walker were engaged for two years by the colonial government to prepare a report 'with a view to promote the moral and religious welfare of its inhabitants.'[57] Travelling throughout the colony revealed a landscape whose natural beauty was blighted by the human degradation and misery inflicted on free and unfree colonists and Aborigines alike by the convict system. More hopefully, but with few illusions, Backhouse reported on signs of Christian progress in the colony. Journeying from Parramatta, then the second largest town in the colony, to the Church Missionary Society station located across the Blue Mountains on the frontier in Wellington Valley, the Quaker visitors attended about ten churches, chapels, schools and missions, and held profitable religious conversations with a variety of colonial residents. The largest religious gathering they encountered was in the Anglican church in Parramatta, whose Sunday service was swollen by a compulsory congregation of 500–600 soldiers and convicts. Even in the frontier town of Bathurst there were both an Anglican and a Scotch church, with Bible and temperance associations also springing up.[58] At the far limits of the British colonial empire, a budding religious infrastructure strained to keep pace with colonial settlement.[59]

---

[54] Backhouse, *Visit to the Australian Colonies*, p. xviii. Dated York, 15 December 1842.
[55] Backhouse, *Visit to the Mauritius and South Africa*, p. xvi. Dated York, 20 March 1844.
[56] Backhouse, *Visit to the Australian Colonies*, pp. cvi–cxxiii; Backhouse, *Visit to the Mauritius and South Africa*, pp. xxviii–xxxviii.
[57] Backhouse, *Visit to the Australian Colonies*, pp. cxxiv–cxxxiii (appendix N).
[58] Ibid., 300–342; George Mackanesss (ed.), *Fourteen Voyages over the Blue Mountains of New South Wales, 1813–1841* (Sydney: Horwitz-Grahame, 1965), p. 236.
[59] David A. Roberts, 'A "City on a Hill": Religion and Buildings on the Frontier Mission at Wellngton Valley, New South Wales', *Australian Religion Studies Review*, 23.1 (2010), 91–114.

Through their openly published letters and journals to Friends and reports for the government, Backhouse and Walker provided independent accounts of conditions for convicts, Aborigines and settlers in Van Diemen's Land and New South Wales, including special reports on the penal settlements at Port Macquarie, Moreton Bay and Norfolk Island, then part of New South Wales, and Macquarie Harbour and Port Arthur in Van Diemen's Land. In Van Diemen's Land they supported the efforts of Lt Governor George Arthur for ordinary convicts on assignment. Arthur himself was so impressed by their report on the Macquarie Harbour penal settlement he included it with his despatches, ensuring it was read by Lord Stanley, who says it was given close attention by the Cabinet, and printed with the parliamentary papers.[60] Initially Backhouse and Walker wanted to know everything. They were not there to judge but to observe and write accounts for Friends at home or for government officials requesting their advice. The need to know began with the convict voyage. Backhouse requested the Admiralty's permission to travel on a convict hulk – a request sufficiently startling for it to reach the colonial secretary, Viscount Goderich (1782–1859). Despite refusing to allow this boon, Goderich supplied the two Friends with letters of introduction to the secretaries of the Australian colonies.[61]

Arriving in Van Diemen's Land, Backhouse and Walker were warmly received by Governor Arthur, whom Backhouse privately described as 'a man of deep practical piety and is like a father to us'. Invited to dine at Government House, they were charmed by Arthur's wife, Eliza Orde (m. 1814), 'a very agreeable woman: the more I see of her, the more I esteem her', and their 'large and interesting family which they are endeavouring to train up in the fear of the Lord'.[62] Backhouse's good impressions extended to the behaviour of the convicts in the penal colony, to which he attributed the beneficent guiding hand of Arthur: 'The influence of the example of the Governor's unwearied labours to promote religion and morality are to be seen in all parts of the island.'[63] Arthur gave the two Friends open access to undertake inspections and 'express freely any thing we wished to say connected with the welfare of the Colony'.[64] This closeness to Arthur was to have

---

[60] Arthur to Hay, 25 July 1832, encl. James Backhouse and George Washington Walker, 'Report of a Visit to the Penal Settlement of Macquarie Harbour, Van Diemen's Land', 23 July 1832, *Correspondence on Secondary Punishments*, BPP 1834 (82) XLVII.121, pp. 9–13.

[61] Backhouse to Mary Backhouse [his mother], 2 July 1831, 'Backhouse Letters', 4.

[62] Backhouse to Elizabeth Backhouse [his sister], Hobart Town, 3 April 1832, 'Backhouse Letters', 6.

[63] Ibid.   [64] Backhouse, *Visit to the Australian Colonies*, p. 224.

unexpected consequences, when, following the publication of their Macquarie Harbour report, they were denounced as 'Government Spies' in the colonial press.[65]

The two Quakers were not spies, but neither were they hostile to the government or indeed to transportation. When Arthur requested them to visit the penal settlement on the Tasman Peninsula, they gave 'calm consideration' to this before concluding that it would not be incompatible with their duty.[66] This was to be the first of three separate visits to the penal complex that Arthur was developing on the Forestier Peninsula. Backhouse saw Van Diemen's Land and the system created by Arthur positively and even regretted that English women were not transported on a first offence so they could benefit from it.[67] He highlighted the evidence of reformation he found at every penal establishment visited. His conversation with prisoners confirmed his view that confinement in prisons and hulks caused corruption – not the regime they underwent in Van Diemen's Land. Inadvertently, Backhouse was lending his weight to transportation as a reformative solution in opposition to the penitentiary model of reform which American Friends were recommending to the PDS and the government at home.

Despite its grim reputation, the Quaker friends were welcomed at Macquarie Harbour and were impressed by the class meeting for prisoners established by the Methodist catechist, William Schofield (1793–1878).[68] They noted with approval that ten of the prisoners, including three recent escapees, 'awakened to a lively sense of their wickedness, by a variety of providential circumstances', were 'led to seek a change of heart through the grace afforded to mankind through Our Lord Jesus Christ'.[69] With the support of the commandant, Schofield arranged for the men in whom he observed signs of reformation to be isolated from the other prisoners in the schoolroom, 'spending their time of leisure in reading and meditation'.[70] These arrangements were greeted with howls of derision in the Van Diemen's Land and New South Wales press, with *The Tasmanian* decrying the Quaker emissaries' credentials and their extreme gullibility in making any positive reports of 'Gomorrah, the earthly hell'.[71] At Macquarie Harbour, the military officers appear to have sincerely welcomed the opportunity to

[65] Ibid., 225.   [66] Ibid.
[67] Backhouse to Elizabeth Backhouse, 22 May 1832, 'Backhouse Letters', 6.
[68] Arthur to Hay, 25 July 1832, encl. Backhouse and Walker to Arthur, 'Report of a Visit to the Penal Settlement of Macquarie Harbour, Van Diemen's Land', 23 July 1832, BPP 1834 (82) XLVII.121, pp. 9–13.
[69] *Sydney Herald*, 6 October 1834, p. 2; BPP 1834 (82) XLVII.121, pp. 10.   [70] Ibid.
[71] *The Tasmanian* (Hobart), 7 November 1834, p. 4; *The True Colonist* (Van Diemen's Land), 11 November 1834, p. 4.

meet with Backhouse and Walker. As Backhouse informed his sister, the Limerick-born commandant, Major Pery Baylee (1784–1845) provided them with statistics on punishment at Macquarie Harbour from 1826 to 1832, which revealed variation in the number of lashes inflicted under different administrations (see Table 4.1).

Under Captain Butler, from 1826 to 1829, almost no use had been made at Macquarie Harbour of solitary confinement on bread and water; instead the lash was heartily used and almost half the men (45 per cent) had been flogged. Since those times, Baylee could demonstrate a clear progression away from the lash and towards solitary confinement. In 1832, only nine men out of 180 in the settlement were flogged, with another sixteen sentenced to solitary confinement.[72] The officers were keen to appear to the Quaker visitors as advocates for religious and reformist discipline focussed on achieving something better for the prisoners than mere punishment. Baylee, a committed Irish Protestant, approved and supported the work of John Alan Manton (1807–1864), the Methodist catechist who succeeded Schofield at Macquarie Harbour.[73] The settlement clerk, John Douglas, provided the Quakers with the return of punishments, begging them to contact him with any queries and endorsing their whole enterprise: 'Gentlemen – You are embarked in one of the noblest undertakings that ever influenced the human breast ... the amelioration of a very considerable, but depraved, and lowly fallen portion of the Family of Man.'[74] These favourable impressions of the colony would change under the impact of the roasting the two Quakers received at the hands of an unsympathetic press, however on the whole they admired and supported Arthur's system and embraced its potential for reforming convicts during and on completion of their sentences.

Between 1833 and 1835, the Quaker missionaries produced eight reports for Lt Governor Arthur on settlements in Van Diemen's Land for Aborigines and convicts and Governor Bourke in New South Wales. In September 1833 Backhouse and Walker paid a brief visit to Port Arthur, shortly before it became a full penal industrial complex, on their way to Flinders Island.[75] In November 1834, at Governor Arthur's

---

[72] Note that the average punishment inflicted remained fairly constant and, if anything, went up slightly over time.

[73] E. R. Pretyman, 'Manton, John Allen (1807–1864)', *ADB*.

[74] John Douglas to Backhouse, 28 June 1832, 'Backhouse Letters', 8.

[75] A précis of this visit is provided in Backhouse, *Visit to the Australian Colonies*, pp. 71–72. A fuller manuscript version is Backhouse and Walker, 'Report of a Visit to the Penal Settlement of Port Arthur and to the Aboriginal Establishment on Flinders Island, 1833', Cambridge University Library RCS/ RCMS 278/3 (1) [Hereafter Backhouse and Walker, 'Port Arthur, September 1833'].

Table 4.1 Return of punishments at Macquarie Harbour, Van Diemen's Land, from 1 January 1826 to 21 June 1832

	Prisoners		Lashes			Solitary confinement on bread and water		
Year	No. in the settlement	No. sentenced	No. sentenced	No. inflicted	No. of prisoners sentenced	No. of days Sentenced	No. of Days remitted	
1826	250	170	7,303	6,012	1	2	0	Captain Butler's Command from 1 January 1826 to 11 June 1829
1827	328	198	7,989	7,272	1	14	0	Annual average no. of lashes per sentenced prisoner: 37
1828	358	197	5,879	5,558	0	0	0	Average inflicted: 33
1829	335	18	599	574	2	42	0	
1829	335	14	454	429	16	110	22	Captain Briggs Command from 11 June 1829 to 14 February 1831
1830	308	29	1,336	1,195	34	225	43	Annual average no. of lashes per sentenced prisoner: 40
1831	226	7	185	185	5	23	1	Average inflicted: 36
1831	226	24	967	917	13	206	76	Major Baylee's Command from 14 February 1831 to 21 June 1832
1832	180	9	235	194	16	256	51	Annual average no. of lashes per sentenced prisoner: 36
								Average inflicted: 34

Source: Backhouse to Elizabeth Backhouse, 22 May 1832, 'Backhouse Letters', 6.

request, they returned and produced a more substantial report.[76] From 1835 to 1877 they produced further reports for New South Wales Governor Richard Bourke (1777–1855), visiting Norfolk Island in March 1835.[77] In both penal colonies they attempted to persuade authorities to modify the punishment regime in the direction of the separate system, with solitary confinement in place of whipping and a programme of work tempered by religious and moral instruction. All their reports were suffused with Rational Dissent, with Christian principles healthily defended by statistics and their own direct observations.[78] At their first visit to Port Arthur, where they were received by Lt Gibbons, the Commandant, they recognized that the establishment was 'in its infancy' and hoped that a reformative regime would be put in place.[79] Their recommendations called for classification of prisoners and separate accommodation at night to safeguard the prisoners' morals. They regretted the absence of a missionary or catechist who might provide moral or religious instruction, and the lack of a place for public worship. They wanted secure cells for the 'disorderly', for without it there was no alternative to the lash. The Quakers favoured indulgences to positively reinforce good behaviour and were pleased that eighty individuals had secured an allowance of a little tea and sugar. The men were also allowed to cultivate a small plot of ground – not only an effective remedy against scurvy if fruit and vegetables were grown, but a defence against 'listlessness, or unprofitable discourse'. Perhaps their most important finding concerned Port Arthur, where good security and sufficient employment in productive labour made it not inferior to Macquarie Harbour, justifying Arthur's plan to concentrate prisoners on Tasman's Peninsula. The only thing missing was appropriate moral and religious instruction, the 'indispensable auxiliaries in the work of reformation'.[80]

Returning to Port Arthur in November 1834, they found the station 'greatly improved' in appearance.[81] This time they anticipated the

---

[76] Ibid., 226. Backhouse and Walker, 'Report of a Visit to the Penal Settlement on Tasman's Peninsula, November 1834', Tasmania Archives and Heritage Office (TAHO) CSOA 807–17244.

[77] Backhouse and Walker, 'Report of a Visit to the Penal Settlement of Norfolk Island, 4 March to 29 April 1835', Cambridge University Library RCMS 278/3 (2) [Hereafter Backhouse and Walker, 'Norfolk Island'].

[78] Idem, 'Report of a Visit to Norfolk Island, 4 March to 29 April 1835', Cambridge University Library RCMS 278/3/1.

[79] Backhouse and Walker, 'Port Arthur, September 1833'.   [80] Ibid., 3.

[81] Backhouse and Walker, 'Report of a Visit to the Penal Settlement on Tasman's Peninsula, November 1834', Tasmanian Archives and Heritage Office (TAHO) CSO1 807–17244. I thank David Roberts for providing me with a copy of this report. [Hereafter Backhouse and Walker, 'Tasman's Peninsula, November 1834'].

construction of a penitentiary and chapel, which would allow separation and isolation of disorderly prisoners, without resort to the lash, and a system of classification. Instead of rigid partitions of boards on platforms (designed to prevent vice), they expressed a preference for hammocks, which could be rolled away in the day and were easier to protect from vermin. They were concerned at the increasing confinement of the men, without access to gardens to provide fresh vegetables, which meant scurvy was becoming 'appallingly prevalent', leaving prisoners with debility for life, 'which is a dreadful aggravation of their punishment'.[82] They recommended the discontinuation of public flogging, which not only tended to 'harden their minds & to lessen their dread of punishment', but entailed some risk, since it occasioned the assembly of several hundred prisoners supervised by no more than forty guards. They were disappointed not to see any 'cases of reformation on Christian principles' that were so heartening a feature of Macquarie Harbour. They seem to have been more impressed by the juvenile establishment at Point Puer where 'the boys present a scene of lively industry when at labour'.[83] The report was not optimistic about reform, referring to the risks associated with the imposition of punishments, including solitary confinement on bread and water, which 'no man of a civilized mind could, were he witness to them, conscientiously impose upon his fellow man even as punishments for his crimes'.[84]

The Quakers' report on Norfolk Island was their most comprehensive effort, undertaken with the permission of Governor Richard Bourke and with sufficient time, from 4 March until 29 April 1835, to make a good job of it. Their mature analysis reflects the increasing unease which Backhouse and Walker seem to have felt about the lack of intrinsic reformatory design in any of the sites of punishment in the two penal colonies. The two Friends clearly found Norfolk Island a depressing place with a demoralizing effect on those sent there. They observed the impact of the policy of exemplary punishment, in place since the recommendations of the Bigge Reports in 1822: '[N]o-one can remain long at the settlement without being forcibly impressed with the conviction of the extremely depraved condition of this portion of our race.' Backhouse and Walker gave three reasons as evidence of the depraved condition of the Norfolk Island convicts: firstly, the 'dreadfully profane language', used even in the presence of visitors; secondly, the frequency of crime against their fellow convicts; and thirdly, the

---

[82] Ibid., 3.
[83] Ibid., 7; Cameron Nunn, 'Pure Minds, Pure Bodies, Pure Lips: Religious Ideology and the Juvenile Convict Institutions at Carter's Barracks and Point Puer', *Journal of Religious History* 40.2 (2016), 161–184.
[84] Ibid., 10

high incidence of homosexuality – delicately referred to as 'a crime most revolting to nature' which was rarely convicted owing to the reluctance of prisoners to give evidence about it, but 'by the acknowledgement of the prisoners themselves' was highly prevalent among them. To prevent this, the Quakers suggested that separate sleeping cells be constructed, while recognizing that 'the only effectual remedy for any of these evils is, the substitution of better principles'.[85]

Despite the grim reputation of Norfolk Island, Backhouse and Walker noted that solitary confinement was rarely used because of the absence of suitable accommodation. As at Macquarie Harbour, flagellation was decreasing, something of which they heartily approved, noting that 'the men are rendered callous by the frequency of the punishment.'[86] To replace the 'inefficient' punishment of flagellation, they recommended installing a treadmill and cells to allow 'solitude and silence'. The most pressing reform they recommended was a change to the work regime, replacing idle detention with productive employment. In addition to work, health and effective discipline, they approved of the religious pro-gramme put in place by Commandant Joseph Anderson (1790–1877).[87] In the absence of clergy willing to volunteer for service on Norfolk Island, Anderson had chosen a Catholic and a Protestant religious instructor from among the convicts. Backhouse and Walker recommended that essentials of books, pens and paper be provided for the convicts, noting arrangements made for a library at Port Arthur and Macquarie Harbour in Van Diemen's Land, 'without any inconvenience that we are aware of'.[88] In truth, religion was slow to come to Norfolk Island and the first attempt to create a place of worship was not until March 1839, when H. W. Lingard, lieutenant in the Royal Engineers, proposed alterations to the mess rooms at Longridge to provide a vestry, confessional, pulpit and benched seating.[89] The presence of the confessional indicates that the planned accommodation was intended to be shared between both Cath-olics and Protestants, an arrangement which soon caused difficulties.[90] There were also plans for a cottage for the Protestant chaplain.[91]

[85] Backhouse and Walker, 'Norfolk Island', 2. Quotations in this paragraph are from the same source.

[86] Ibid. 4   [87] John V. Barry, 'Anderson, Joseph (1790–1877)', *ADB*.

[88] Backhouse and Walker, 'Norfolk Island', 7,

[89] H. W. Lingard., 'Plans Shewing Proposed Alterations for Better Accommodation in Buildings used for Divine Service, Norfolk Island', March 1839, Tasmanian Archive and Heritage Office [TAHO] PWD266/1/1914.

[90] Rev. Thomas Sharpe, 'Journal on Norfolk Island', 1837–1840, SLNSW B217–B218, claimed this obliged Protestant prisoners to listen to Catholic error.

[91] John Ferguson, 'Plans of a Chaplain's Cottage Norfolk Island', 1838–39,' TAHO PWD266/1/1912; H. W. Lingard, 'Plan Section of the Protestant Clergyman's Quarters, Norfolk Island, 21 November 1838', TAHO PWD266/1/1913.

It is surprising that Backhouse and Walker were not more critical of the lack of appropriate religious instructors on Norfolk Island since they had decided views on this subject, reflected in the lengthy set of instructions to the catechist nominated for Port Arthur in 1834.[92] Backhouse urged him to maintain his enthusiasm, 'in season; out of season' (2 Timothy 4:2), not merely performing the duty of preaching and teaching. He recommended that prisoners 'who show signs of religious reformation' should be set aside, as Schofield had been doing at Macquarie Harbour. They also had forthright advice about the character required of prison officers. Norfolk Island was well staffed and included thirteen military, twenty-four civil officers and no fewer than thirty women and forty children to cater for some 850 prisoners.[93] The Quakers stipulated that the Commandant avoid bad language and the use of 'ardent spirits': 'they are the bane of discipline, and a frequent case of want of harmony among the officers'.[94] They wanted a spirit of reform and emulation to infiltrate the penal colony. They were especially anxious that all prisoners have some reason to behave well, which currently did not exist, with unfortunate consequences: 'they in general resign themselves to despair [and] become totally reckless of their conduct'.[95] This verdict on Norfolk Island constituted a call to abandon the purely punitive regime, unredeemed by other reformative efforts.

Later Travellers

Later Quaker visitors travelling under concern in the penal colonies supported transportation, in lieu of any practical, Christian alternative. Quaker fascination with the penal world continued after Backhouse and Walker completed their tour of duty. Indeed, young Walker was so impressed by Van Diemen's Land (and a young woman he met while visiting there), that in 1840 he returned there, marrying Sarah Benson Mather and making a home in Tasmania with her and their ten children.[96] At least three other Quaker parties travelled to the Australian penal colonies: Daniel Wheeler, who toured the Pacific in 1834,

---

[92] Backhouse, 'A Letter to the Catechist, at Port Arthur, Hobart Town, 27 November 1834', in Backhouse, *Visit to the Australian Colonies*, pp. lxxii–lxxv. Presumably this was to John Allen Manton, for whom see Chapter 3.

[93] According to their census of religious profession, there were 464 prisoners who professed to be Protestants, 380 Roman Catholics and six Jews.

[94] Backhouse and Walker, 'Norfolk Island', 9.   [95] Ibid., appendix, 4.

[96] Mary Bartram Trot, 'Walker, George Washington (1800–1859)', *ADB*.

including a brief visit to Van Diemen's Land;[97] the moral writer Charlotte Anley (1796–1893), who visited in 1836–1837;[98] and Robert Lindsey (1801–1863) and Frederick Mackie (1812–1893), who left England for a tour of the Australian colonies, New Zealand and South Africa in July 1852. Lindsey made three missionary journeys, the first in 1846 to North America, the second with Frederick Mackie to Australia and South Africa, and a final journey, in 1857, to North America, the Sandwich Islands (Hawaii) and back to the Australasian colonies.[99] His Australian concern, undertaken with Mackie, included a visit to the 'natural penitentiary' of Port Arthur,[100] after it had received its Pentonvillian makeover. Throughout this journey, Mackie made observations and drawings on the operation of the probation system with its chain of stations on the Tasman Peninsula. Lindsey, the senior partner, was a wealthy businessman who decided to retire in 1843 and devote himself to missionary duties. He provided the necessary financial support enabling him to invite his young friend to accompany him.

While lacking the high level of authorization granted Backhouse and Walker, Lindsey and Mackie provide valuable additional information about the convict system shortly before it ended. Like Backhouse, Mackie was trained as a nurseryman and naturalist and showed a keen interest in Australian native fauna and the horticultural potential of the colonies. Arriving in Hobart on 11 November 1852, he was delighted to encounter George Washington Walker and his growing family.[101] He was less pleased by convict society, noting that women did not attend Meetings in Hobart claiming they could not leave their children with convict servants. On 17 November his diary notes the murmuring in the colony about the convict question, that 'steady respectable house servants are not to be had' and, with some apparent disapproval, that Walker employed two convict servants in his household. He was unnerved by the evidence of convicts under sentence, including some in chains: 'I am quite struck with the numerous forbidding countenances

[97] Daniel Wheeler and Daniel Wheeler the Younger, *A Memoir of Daniel Wheeler, with an Account of His Gospel Labours in the Islands of the Pacific* (Philadelphia: Association of Friends for the Diffusion of Religious and Useful Knowledge, 1859), p. 146. Wheeler was lucky to have escaped shipwreck and reports very little about his time in Hobart, though he did meet up with Backhouse and Walker.

[98] Alan Atkinson, *The Europeans in Australia: A History, Vol. 2, Democracy* 2nd edn (Sydney: University of New South Wales Press, 2016), pp. 195–196, 267.

[99] Robert Lindsey Clark (ed.), *Travels of Robert and Sarah Lindsey* (London: Samuel Harris, 1886).

[100] The term was Colonel Arthur's. See Chapter 3.

[101] Clark (ed.), *Travels of Robert and Sarah Lindsey*, pp. 36–37.

that we meet with in the streets. Chain gangs are abolished, though chains are not, for we met yesterday a man in his party-coloured dress wearing chains which clanked at every step he took.'[102] Like his predecessors, Mackie was not inclined to take a stand against transportation and made pastoral visits to convicts who had served their terms and turned around their lives.

The progress of Fry's work with women convicts was investigated by Charlotte Anley, who stated that she had been commissioned 'to investigate the state of the female prisoners at Parramatta', for which she sought and received the permission of the Governor.[103] A cousin of Henry Dumaresq, Anley served as governess to his children during which time she met with James Backhouse.[104] In the colony, she contacted the Governor to promote her aim of forming 'a ladies' visiting committee, similar to that of the 'British Ladies' Society in England, for the reformation of female prisoners', but only if sufficient women might be found in Sydney and Parramatta to take up the cause.[105] Anley had been warned of what to expect of the women at the Female Factory but Fry's example inspired her to make the attempt.[106] In the company of the elderly Samuel Marsden, she visited the Factory where nearly 700 women were divided into three classes. In a somewhat unlikely scene, she claims to have moved the women of the worst class by an appeal to what she calls 'their maternal feelings', actually shameless moral blackmail: 'I reminded them of the double guilt they must incur, if [their] helpless infants were trained as partners of their own sin and shame. Many wept bitterly, and some answered me, that they would, indeed rather see their children die, than live to be what they themselves had been, and were!'[107] Like other Quaker travellers, Anley supported transportation within an overall framework aimed at ameliorating prisoners' conditions without challenging either the colonial authorities or the continuance of transportation for both women and men.

Conclusion

The Quaker stream of the penal reform movement takes a very different course to that of anti-slavery. In his history of abolition, Clarkson depicted anti-slavery as a 'map' consisting of a great river with 'so many

---

[102] Ibid., 43.
[103] Charlotte Anley, *The Prisoners of Australia: A Narrative* (London: Hatchard, 1841), p. 7.
[104] Nancy Grey, 'Dumaresq, Henry (1792–1838)', *ADB*; Backhouse, *Visit to the Australian Colonies*, p. 393.
[105] Anley, *Prisoners of Australia*, p. 8.   [106] Ibid.   [107] Ibid., 7.

springs or rivulets, which assisted in making and swelling the torrent which swept away the Slave-trade'.[108] In Clarkson's map, the Quaker impact was critical. Not so in relation to the abolition of convict transportation. Rather than challenging government policy in the British penal colonies, all the travellers under concern considered in this chapter supported amelioration rather than abolition of transportation. Backhouse and Walker worked closely with Arthur in Van Diemen's Land and Bourke in New South Wales to produce reports on the ultra-penal stations of Macquarie Harbour, Port Arthur and Norfolk Island and other sites for convict labour and punishment. In general, they found little to criticize in Arthur's arrangements. Instead of the abolition of transportation, their recommendations were generally concordant with the views of the PDS considered in Chapter 2. They hoped for more classification and separation of prisoners, especially at night, a wholesome regime of labour and consistent, strict discipline. They opposed – but did not proscribe – the lash, recognizing that it required the construction of appropriate, secure accommodation for solitary confinement as an alternative. At all sites they recommended the appointment of suitably qualified religious instructors to provide the essential moral training without which they saw no prospects for reformation. They recommended positive rewards, including tea, sugar, and leisure and space to grow gardens, to ensure prisoners were occupied during their free time rather than being drawn into vicious conversation and gambling.

The most radical of the Quaker critics of transportation and in many ways the most effective was Fry. Her Ladies' Committees made an immediate difference to the conditions of women under sentence of transportation. Her correspondence and strict instructions to Backhouse and the inspiration she provided to reformers in the colony and at home, including Charlotte Anley, ensured women convicts had advocates with an ear to authority. Women convicts had more physical security and opportunities to work while in prison because of these interventions. Fry was ultimately less successful in her goal of trying to ensure women were kept secure by other women, with ladies' committees attached to every female prison. These efforts ensured that women were not subject to the harshest rigours of the transportation system, were excluded from the ultra-penal stations and were not transported to sites such as Bermuda, Gibraltar or Western Australia.

---

[108] Thomas Clarkson, *The History of the Rise, Progress and Accomplishment of the Abolition of the African Slave-Trade by the British Parliament*, 2 vols. (London: Longman, 1808), vol. I, p. 84.

Quaker penal reformers aimed to end physical punishments such as flogging and replace them with a penitential system considered compatible with Christianity which incorporated silence, separation, productive labour and religious instruction. By the 1840s, based on the testimony of Quakers travelling under concern in the penal colonies, Quakers tended to continue support for transportation as the most likely to achieve the prisoner's reformation. Initially, Backhouse and Walker did not see private assignment or the employment of convict labour as the equivalent of slavery, though Captain Maconochie would later change their minds about this (see Chapter 7). In combination with a new reformatory emphasis on penitentiaries, they had reason to believe that exile to Australia was integral to the penitential journey which a prisoner undertook within the British penal system. While Backhouse and Walker revealed limitations and challenges in the system at work, they gave their approval to the methods implemented by Arthur in Van Diemen's Land and provided advice on how to reform those in place at Norfolk Island in a more Christian, reformatory direction. Prison officers, both military and civil, needed to be reformed as well as the prisoners, and all colonists had to share responsibility for the Christian management of their society.

Penal reform was adopted by evangelical Quakers who took up social activism at the risk of disrupting cherished Quaker principles of separation from the world and quietist pursuit of the Inner Light. In their engagement with penal reform in the convict colonies, they provided a service to government with exemplary, evidence-based assessments of a working system without judgement or challenge to just authority. This was the same method devised by John Howard which led eventually to a revolutionary change in prisoners' conditions, away from harsh physical punishment and towards internal, moral and psychological controls: solitary confinement, separate cells and the chapel at the heart of the prison. Unlike the extreme, Evangelical advocates of the separate system, Quakers showed their enlightened and utilitarian principles by also approving productive work and the efficient use of convict labour. At Port Arthur, Backhouse and Walker were pleased to see the full range of industrial opportunities being put in place. They believed that work as well as contemplation were essential for rehabilitation. Their close inspection of the penal stations in Australia led Backhouse and Walker to consider that reformation could occur in well-managed penal colonies as well as in home-based penitentiaries. The next chapter will consider the impact of Christian utilitarians much more decidedly antipathetic to transportation, who believed that it was without redeeming features and had to end.

5 Christian Utilitarianism and Archbishop Richard Whately

To the great bulk of those, therefore, who are sentenced to transportation the punishment amounts to this, that they are carried to a country whose climate is delightful, producing in profusion all the necessaries and most of the luxuries of life; that they have a certainty of maintenance, instead of an uncertainty; are better fed, clothed, and lodged, than (by *honest means*) ... Whatever other advantages this system may possess, it certainly does not look like a very terrific punishment.[1]
(Richard Whately, 1829)

'[L]iberal politics' may degrade an archbishop to a state of thought and feeling not higher than that of a hangman.[2]   (Wiliam Maginn, 1932)

The most original and startling voice in the anti-transportation debate was that of the archbishop of Dublin, Richard Whately (1787–1863). Before Whately, critics of transportation had been a marginal group, divided between utilitarians such as Bentham and his heirs (Chapter 1), or the humanitarian coalition of Evangelical Anglicans and Dissenting activists who supported the construction of penitentiaries at home (Chapter 2). It was Whately who effectively demolished the rational and moral pretensions of transportation; unlike the Evangelicals, including the Quakers (Chapter 4), he was unconvinced that religion could or should be used to reform criminals under sentence. Whately was a Liberal Anglican whose practical morality had its roots in the thinking of earlier Christian utilitarians and Scottish divines. His central importance was that he was a leader in a group of theologians who were admired by politicians and intellectuals, led by Lord John Russell (1792–1878), who succeeded in revitalizing the Whig party and bringing it to power in 1830. The Anglican and Evangelical ascendancy that had sustained the Tories and their penal polices was met with an incoming tide of Liberal Anglican and Dissenting reformers. This chapter traces the roots of

[1] Richard Whately, 'Transportation', *London Review*, 1.1 (1829), 122.
[2] [William Maginn], 'Archbishop Whately's Secondary Punishments Dissected', *Fraser's Magazine*, 6 (1832), 575.

Christian utilitarianism as it impacted on the anti-transportation movement. It has three sections: it examines the sources for Whately's Christian utilitarianism and how this relates to his critique of penal reform and
transportation. It then examines the different responses to Whately by
writers in both the colonies and the metropole. It concludes with the
deliberations of the Molesworth SC, the most significant of the numerous government inquiries into transportation and the one which provided
an effective platform for its utilitarian critics.

Christian Utilitarianism and Penal Reform

As a moral theory, utilitarianism attracted secular and religious thinkers
from across the denominational spectrum. In the form of Rational Dissent, it was espoused by Quakers and other Dissenters interested in penal
reform; it also claimed adherents from the established church in both
Scotland and England. Originating in the eighteenth-century Enlightenment, utilitarianism was embraced by Dissenters such as Joseph Priestley
(1733–1804), orthodox Anglicans such as William Paley (1743–1805),
archdeacon of Carlisle and Scottish moral philosophers such as Adam
Ferguson (1723–1816) and Dugald Stewart (1754–1828).[3] In politics, it
was a significant element in the alliance of Whiggish reformers, including
Liberal Anglicans, moderate Evangelicals, Dissenters and Catholics, who
combined to oppose Tory claims to a monopoly interest in the moral
state. Working together, they effectively isolated high church Anglican
defenders of the Protestant constitution and facilitated the sweeping
constitutional changes that included the repeal of the Test and Corporation Acts (1828), Catholic Emancipation (1829) and the First Reform
Act (1832).[4]

Many Christian utilitarians were attracted to issues of practical governance and eager to create a just society that was compatible with
Christian teaching. They were a significant force in causes such as the
abolition of the slave trade,[5] schemes for the creation of wealth to
ameliorate poverty and penal reform. Of those who wrote on the latter,
Paley has proven to be the most influential, not least through the lectures
of Richard Whately at Oxford, delivered fifty years after Paley's death.[6]

---

[3] Robert Hole, *Pulpits, Politics and Public Order in England, 1760–1832* (Cambridge:
Cambridge University Press, 1989), p. 72.
[4] J. C. D. Clark, *English Society, 1660–1832* 2nd edn (Cambridge: Cambridge University
Press, 2000), p. 515.
[5] Page, 'Rational Dissent', 741–772.
[6] William Paley and Richard Whately, *A View of the Evidences of Christianity* (London:
J. Parker, 1859).

Paley opposed slavery and argued for penal reform on rational, humanitarian and Christian grounds suggesting, in his celebrated argument from a flock of pigeons in a field of corn, that there was no moral justification in the poor having to work to hoard property for the rich or to be imprisoned and even executed for stealing from the necessity of hunger.[7] Paley's views are said to have had an important influence on the development of humanitarian modes of prison governance in the American colonies.[8] Paley argued that the purpose of the legal code was to support the poor, not protect the property and interests of the rich: 'The care of the poor ought to be the principal object of all laws, for this plain reason, that the rich are able to take care of themselves.'[9] Paley, citing Dr Samuel Johnson, saw nothing incompatible in the rule of law, Christian morality and rational reform. '[L]et the sanctions of Christianity never be forgotten; by which it will be shewn that they give strength and lustre to each other; religion will appear to be the voice of reason, and morality the will of God.'[10] Inequality of property he regarded as an evil that could only be justified by the motivation this gave to industry, which in turn created wealth in which the whole society could share. All forms of involuntary labour, including slavery, were repellent to Paley and he devoted a chapter of his most celebrated book, *The Principles of Moral and Political Philosophy*, to repudiating arguments in its favour, including those from scripture, and advocating the gradual emancipation of slaves.[11] In relation to penal reform Paley reflected his utilitarian roots by rejecting both the cry for vengeance of earlier ages and the metaphysical speculation that punishment should reform and purify the prisoner.[12] On the other hand, Paley was an influential advocate of capital punishment, which he saw as the most effective way to deter crime; he objected to transportation as a 'slight punishment' since it was inflicted on those with no property, who therefore had little to lose.[13]

Christian utilitarians were opposed to 'useless' punishment which failed in its primary function which, in their view, was the prevention of

---

[7] William Paley, *The Principles of Moral and Political Philosophy* (London: Faulder, 1785), pp. 91–92.
[8] Curt R. Blakely, *Prisons, Penology and Penal Reform* (New York: Peter Lang, 2007), p. 15.
[9] Paley, *The Principles of Moral and Political Philosophy*, p. 199.
[10] Ibid., iv. Samuel Johnson, 'Preface to the Preceptor', p. 240, in *The Works of Samuel Johnson*, edited by Arthur Murphy, vol. 2 (London: Rivington, 1823).
[11] Ibid., 195–198. Paley defines slaves as all those obliged to labour without their consent, including those enslaved from crimes, captivity and debt.
[12] For discussion of Paley's arguments about the function of punishment, see Austin Sarat, *Pain, Death, and the Law* (Ann Arbor: University of Michigan Press, 2001), p. 38.
[13] Leon Radzinowicz, *History of English Criminal Law*, 4 vols. (London: Stevens, 1948–1968), vol. I, p. 253.

crime. They opposed the Evangelical reformers, considered in the previous two chapters, who viewed prisons and penal colonies as an opportunity to save souls and reform and regenerate fallen humanity. Among
Scottish thinkers, Adam Ferguson (1723–1816), chaplain to the Black
Watch from 1745 to 1754, advocated a practical, rational theology as
professor of natural philosophy, then mental and moral philosophy, at
the University of Edinburgh. Ferguson saw a just and transparent legal
system, founded on habeas corpus, as essential for a free society. 'We
must admire, as the key stone (sic) of civil liberty, the statute which forces
the secrets of every prison to be revealed, the cause of every commitment
to be declared, and the person of the accused to be produced, that he
may claim his enlargement, or his trial, within a limited time. No wiser
form was ever opposed to the abuses of power.'[14] Yet he admitted that to
secure this freedom it required the whole constitutional apparatus of
Great Britain and effective restraints on the freedom of those who did
harm to society. It was criminal for a robber or an assassin to kill a man,
but acceptable, in Ferguson's view, to kill in self-defence and the inno-
cent duty of a judge who condemns a prisoner to death, or a soldier who
kills the enemy of his country.[15] Ferguson also approved a scale of
punishments, including exile or death, for the worst cases, 'to remove
the criminal from the Society whose peace he alarms'.[16] The alternative
was a reversion to the disorder and violence characterized by people in a
state of nature, such as the American Indians. Both secular and Christian
utilitarians were much more concerned with securing the freedom of civil
society by punishing and restraining prisoners than advocacy for their
humane treatment.

Liberal Anglicans

Liberal Anglicans emerged to prominence because of political changes
which flowed from granting full access to the public sphere to those
outside the established churches. According to Boyd Hilton, from
1828, a broad liberal coalition developed which began to absorb moderate Dissenters, Methodists keen to assert their loyalty and establishment
roots and Congregationalists, as well as the newly enfranchised middle
class including Jews, Catholics, Unitarians and Quakers who had

---

[14] Adam Ferguson, *An Essay on the History of Civil Society* 8th edn (Philadelphia: A. Finsley,
     1819), p. 302.
[15] Adam Ferguson, *Principles of Moral and Political Science*, 2 vols. (Edinburgh: A. Strachan,
     1792), vol. II, p. 139.
[16] Ibid., vol. II, p. 277.

outgrown their Radical tendencies.[17] For Anglicans there was the additional stress of the increasing tension between the low and high church wings of the Church of England, which marginalized those in the political mainstream who abhorred the scriptural dogmatism of the low church on the one hand, and the supernaturalism of the high church on the other.[18] Reforming Anglicans looked to German philosophy and French science to expand the intellectual foundation of Anglican theology and broaden its economic, social and political relevance. Liberal Anglicans could be found at Trinity College, Cambridge; others were attracted to the movement in Trinity College, Dublin and in Edinburgh, where Thomas Chalmers, as we will see, shared some of their views. In Oxford, the movement was centred on Oriel College and its group of 'Noetics', who included John Eveleigh (1748–1814), Edward Copleston (1776–1849), Richard Whately, Thomas Arnold (1795–1842), Renn Dickson Hampden (1793–1868), Edward Hawkins (1789–1882), Baden Powell (1796–1880) and José Blanco White (1775–1841), several of whom, including Whately, went on to become bishops.[19] Thomas Arnold, later headmaster of Rugby School, was something of a prophet for the movement, preaching an undogmatic Christianity engaged with society, as he wrote to his friend and former pupil William Greenhill: 'Surely the one thing needful for a Christian and an Englishman to study is Christian and moral and political philosophy.'[20]

While Whately was the only Noetic to interest himself in penal reform, they all argued that the moral society was one which was best for the national interest. The Noetics provided a theological reading of political and social issues which combined natural theology with political economy. It was their aspiration that the Church of England should be a national church which served the interest of the people and be saved from descent into doctrinal narrowness and party conflict. Whately was deeply interested throughout his life in the proper relationship of church and state particularly in areas relating to education and philanthropy. He used his position to oppose the reformatory model of transportation, preferring that it should be abolished altogether. In a letter to his friend Ernest Hawkins, written in about 1826, Whately imagined a debate over

---

[17] Boyd Hilton, *A Mad, Bad, and Dangerous People?: England, 1783–1846* (Oxford: Clarendon Press, 2006), p. clxxvii.

[18] For the later development of the movement towards the Broad Church, see Tod E. Jones, *The Broad Church: A Biography of a Movement* (New York: Lexington, 2003).

[19] W. Tuckwell, *Pre-Tractarian Oxford: A Reminiscence of the Oriel 'Noetics'* (London: Smith, Elder & Co, 1909), frontispiece.

[20] Arnold to Dr Greenhill, 9 May 1836, Arthur Penrhyn Stanley (ed.), *The Life and Correspondence of Thomas Arnold* 6th edn (London: B. Fellowes, 1846), p. 377.

the issue of church and state: 'The points proposed to be altered by each of you, are, I think, precisely the same & whether, if those alterations were made, the Church & State would still be in alliance or not, would be merely a question of words.'[21] Whately was a believer in the role the church had to play in the state, intellectually, morally and even politically. Very few agreed with him on the latter but he was happy to lead by example.

Thomas Chalmers, 1832

So far discussion has focussed on English (and Irish) moral philosophers, but Scotland was earlier the crucible for ideas about the moral philosophy of government, crime and social order. Political economy was promoted in Scotland through the work and writing of Thomas Chalmers (1780–1847), whose lectures on political economy were published in 1832 when he was Professor of Divinity at the University of Edinburgh.[22] For Chalmers, poverty was a moral issue which should be addressed by voluntarism and private charity, arguing that statutory intervention, such as the English Poor Law, led to 'general dependence' and the decline of virtue:

[T]he benevolence of the law holds out a wholesale bounty and temptation to improvidence. It has changed the timid supplications of want, into so many stout and resolute demands for justice. The cry of the distressed few for pity, has been strangely transformed by it, into the cry of the whole of a population for the redress and rectification of their grievances. All the tenderness of charity on the one hand, and all its delicacy on the other, have been put to flight, by this metamorphosis of a matter of love, into a matter of angry litigation.[23]

With his optimistic interpretation of the potentiality of human nature, Chalmer's views are closer to the moderate utilitarianism of the Scottish Enlightenment and diverge from the orthodox Calvinism of the Evangelical party in both England and Scotland considered in Chapter 2. Nevertheless, Chalmers has been criticized for seeking to solve nineteenth-century social problems with eighteenth-century tools and to some degree his vision was backward-looking.[24] Chalmers wanted to establish a voluntarist moral state that was permeated by principles of private benevolence and charity mobilized by the Church and focussed

---

[21] Whately to Hawkins, c.1826 [no date], Oriel College Oxford Library, 'Whately Letters', 1837–1852.
[22] Thomas Chalmers, *On Political Economy in Connection with the Moral State and Moral Prospects of Society* 2nd edn (Glasgow: Collins, 1832).
[23] Ibid., 403.
[24] S. Dow, A. Dow and A. Hutton, 'Thomas Chalmers and the Economics and Religion Debate', in Hum, D. (ed.), *Faith, Reason and Economics* (Winnipeg: St John's College Press, 2003), pp. 47–58.

on the parish. Significantly, Chalmers did not see prison reform as a work of charity, or at least he never discussed it. If precious taxes were to be spent on schools, prisons, churches and 'colleges of justice', it was done 'for the protection of society from crime and violence, and for the increase of national virtue'.[25] Direct expenditure on criminals was a dead loss in terms of Chalmers' political economy and a drain on the wealth of the country. These ideas are reflected in Presbyterian commentators on crime and transportation in the colonies, including John Dunmore Lang (1799–1878), considered shortly, and Frederick Maitland Innes, the Scottish critic of Colonel Arthur who had settled in Van Diemen's Land.[26]

One factor which united Paley, Chalmers and Whately was their direct encounter with profound poverty which radicalized their thinking on social issues. Whately's experience of Ireland, where he lived through the famine years, turned his attention to emigration, then assumed to be the great solution to British social challenges. Whately and his friend Samuel Hinds (1793–1872), who was chaplain to Whately in Dublin and later bishop of Norwich, were charmed by the theories of Edward Gibbon Wakefield, agreeing with his published and verbal testimony to the *SC on Secondary Punishments* that prisoners viewed transportation 'with delight' as an opportunity to change their lives for the better.[27] The next section will consider Whately's writing on penal reform and try to explain how his Christian political economy provided such an effective intervention on the issue of convict transportation.

Richard Whately

Political economy has been seen as the ultimate secular philosophy of the imperial age with its leading exponents either dead or indifferent to the claims of religion.[28] However, it had a significant religious character, which was entrenched through the appointment of moral theologians to the first chairs of political economy in Oxford and Dublin.[29] The debates about the corn laws raised up a keen interest in the discussion of

[25] Chalmers, *Political Economy*, p. 244.
[26] Innes, 'The Convict System of Van Diemen's Land', 431–449. For John Dunmore Lang's critique of Whately, see the next section in this chapter.
[27] 'Testimony of E. G. Wakefield', 12 August 1831, *SC on Secondary Punishments*, BPP 1831 (276) VII.519, p. 98.
[28] J. K. Ingram, *A History of Political Economy* (first published 1888) (Cambridge: Cambridge University Press, 2013), p. 104. Here Ingram is discussing Adam Smith.
[29] A. M. C. Waterman, 'The Ideological Alliance of Political Economy and Christian Theology 1793–1833', *Journal of Ecclesiastical History*, 34 (1983), 251–344; A. M. C. Waterman, *Revolution, Economics and Religion* (Cambridge: Cambridge University Press, 1991).

economic matters and gave popularity to the thought of Bentham, James Mill and David Ricardo. In 1825, the 'extreme evangelical' Henry Drummond endowed the Oxford Chair in Political Economy.[30] Whately became its second incumbent from 1830 to 1831 and stated that he would try to bring together religious truth with political economy because it was clearly a force so powerful that it could not be left to the anti-Christians.[31] Whately, who has been the subject of three biographies, is a central figure in the debates about political economy, the state of Ireland and the Christian political economics he helped to found.[32] As a leading figure in Oxford, and not even a bishop, he was an unlikely choice as archbishop of Dublin but accepted out of a sense of duty when offered the post by Earl Grey in March 1831, succeeding the ultra-Tory William Magee (1766–1831).[33] His main qualification was that he could work with the Whigs and had the capacity to accommodate the complexities of Ireland's religious landscape, something Magee lamentably failed to achieve. From this vantage, which included a seat in the House of Lords, he continued to write on an immense range of social, economic and political topics, sometimes spiced with Christian morality, sometimes infused with statistics.[34] In Dublin, Whately endowed a Chair in Political Economy at Trinity College and was active in debates in the House of Lords, one of a tiny number of bishops to support Grey's Reform Bill. It is this Christian utilitarianism that he brought to the discussion of convict transportation.[35]

According to his daughter Jane, Whately had been drawn to the issue of 'Secondary Punishments' at a time when the matter was of keen public interest, though by 1866, when *Life and Correspondence of Richard Whately* was published, it had all but disappeared.[36] Whately's intervention formed part of his creative refashioning of the Anglican tradition, bringing together utilitarianism, Liberal Anglican social theory and the new

[30] Hilton, *Age of Atonement*, p. 42.   [31] Ibid., 46.
[32] William John Fitzpatrick, *Memoirs of Richard Whately*, 2 vols. (London: Bentley, 1864); E. Jane Whately, *Life and Correspondence of Richard Whately*, 2 vols. (London: Longmans, 1866); Donald H. Akenson, *A Protestant in Purgatory* (Hamden, CT: Archon, 1981).
[33] David De Giustino, 'Finding an Archbishop: The Whigs and Richard Whately in 1831', *Church History*, 64.2 (1995), 221.
[34] Salim Rashid, 'Richard Whately and Christian Political Economy at Oxford and Dublin', *Journal of the History of Ideas*, 38.1 (1977), 147–155; Salim Rashid, 'Richard Whately and the Struggle for Rational Christianity in the Mid-Nineteenth Century', *Historical Magazine of the Protestant Episcopal Church*, 47 (1978), 293–311; Ray E. McKerrow, 'Archbishop Whately, Human Nature, and Christian Assistance', *Church History*, 50 (1981), 166–181.
[35] Rashid, 'Richard Whately and Christian Political Economy'.
[36] Whately, *Life*, vol. I, pp. 171–177.

political economy to create a Christian political economy for the times.[37] Those whom Richard Brent has labelled 'Liberal Anglicans' were few in number, but through Whately, and other Liberals appointed as governors in the penal colonies, they were to play a major role in voicing the moral and rational objections to transportation that ultimately brought about its demise. The Liberal Anglicans included many younger men concerned to implement a moral constitutionalism, without establishment or sectarianism, that would enable both national and moral progress.[38] They were also active in Ireland.[39]

Like Chalmers, Whately was a voluminous and untidy author and the list of his writing compiled by his daughter comes to over seventy items, though some were quite short.[40] Within this rambling corpus, his pieces on transportation and secondary punishments are not particularly prominent though they were critical to the evolution of the transportation debate. They were all written between 1829 and 1834, after which Whately seems to have moved on to other matters, with the exception of his fantasy satire *Account of an Expedition to the Interior of New Holland* (1837), written collectively with some of his friends in the style of Jonathan Swift's *Gulliver's Travels*, and which includes a subtle dig at the practice of transportation.[41] He provided a written submission to the Molesworth SC on Transportation stating that he had little to add to his earlier published letters to Earl Grey other than to quote from a friend that transportation was 'commenced in defiance of all reason, and persevered, in defiance of all experience'[42] He made explicit his view that the destruction of the Aborigines, not only in Australia but also New Zealand and Polynesia could be traced directly to the creation of British penal colonies.[43] Whately's speech to the House of Lords, delivered in 1840,[44] allowed him to return to his earlier arguments about transportation and rebut arguments by other correspondents and critics, not all of whom he deigned to acknowledge by name.

[37] For the Liberal Anglicans, see especially Richard Brent, *Liberal Anglican Politics* (Oxford: Clarendon, 1987).

[38] Boyd Hilton, 'Whiggery, Religion and Social Reform: The Case of Lord Morpeth', *The Historical Journal*, 37.4 (1994), 830.

[39] Jennifer Ridden, 'The Forgotten History of the Protestant Crusade: Religious Liberalism in Ireland', *Journal of Religious History*, 31.1 (2007), 78–102.

[40] E. Jane Whately, *Life and Correspondence of Richard Whately* 2nd edn (London: Longmans, 1868), pp. 472–744.

[41] Lady Mary Fox and Richard Whately (eds.), *Account of an Expedition to the Interior of New Holland* (London: Bentley, 1837), p. 31.

[42] Ibid., p. 299.

[43] *Molesworth SC on Transportation (Report)*, appendix L, BPP 1837–38 (669) XXII.1, p. 299.

[44] Richard Whately, *Substance of a Speech on Transportation* (London: B. Fellowes, 1840).

Transportation (1829)

Whately's first study of transportation appeared in the *London Review* in 1829.[45] This was published anonymously, in the usual way of reviews, and was not entirely written by Whately, as he explained when the piece was reprinted in 1832.[46] The works that Whately and his co-author (who from this point I will refer to simply as 'Whately') put under the Noetic microscope were the Report from the 1826–1827 SC on Criminal Commitments and Convictions;[47] Governor Macquarie's defence of his regime in New South Wales dated 1 May 1828;[48] and the naval surgeon Peter Miller Cunningham's memoir of New South Wales published in 1827.[49] As a systematic critique of convict transportation, Whately's review was limited in several ways, including its exclusive focus on New South Wales at a time when the transportation debate hung largely on Arthur's penal regime in Van Diemen's Land. It would be Arthur, and the archdeacon of New South Wales, William Grant Broughton, both writing from Hobart in Van Diemen's Land, who would be Whately's major antagonists. Before addressing the three works under review, Whately provided a brief account of the orthodox utilitarian theory of punishment much as this was promoted by Jeremy Bentham.[50] So long as crime existed, Whately proposed, there must be punishment, but this was only justified in three cases: firstly as retribution or vengeance defined as 'a desire to allot a proportionate suffering to each degree of moral guilt', independent of any other consideration; secondly as 'correction', that is the prevention of a repetition of an offence, and thirdly if it provided an incidental advantage, such as that derived from criminal employment on public works. In all cases, the great object should be the prevention of crime.[51] This was important because it was the only way to justify the practice of communal vengeance, explicitly forbidden by 'Our Saviour and His Apostles' (Romans 12:19), beyond the force necessary for individuals to defend themselves and their possessions. The argument about the secondary punishment of transportation,

---

[45] Whately, 'Transportation'.
[46] Richard Whately, *Thoughts on Secondary Punishments in a Letter to Earl Grey* (London: Fellowes, 1832), p. 2.
[47] *SC on Criminal Commitments and Convictions*, BPP 1826–27 (534) VI.5.
[48] *Report by Macquarie to Bathurst*, 27 July 1822, BPP 1828 (477) XXI.538.
[49] Peter Miller Cunningham, *Two Years in New South Wales*, 2 vols. (London: Henry Colburn, 1827).
[50] Tony Draper, 'An Introduction to Jeremy Bentham's Theory of Punishment', *Journal of Bentham Studies*, 5.1 (2002), 1–17.
[51] Whately, 'Transportation', 115–116.

therefore, in Whately's view, hung on whether or not it effectively deterred criminals.

In the first place he noted that the sentence of transportation was neither swift nor certain, since for many sentenced to seven years of transportation (i.e., those guilty of lesser offences), transportation was never executed, but replaced by confinement with hard labour in the hulks or the penitentiary.[52] This uncertainty was fatal to the principle that punishment should deter crime, because of the gambler's optimism which necessarily overcame fear of capture: 'Like a party of gamblers at rouge et noir, all buoyed up with hope ... convicts who have taken tickets in our penal lottery, flatter themselves with opposite hopes; he who dreads nothing so much as a penitentiary; that he shall *only* be trans-ported; and he who is most afraid (if there be any such) of expatriation, that he shall *not* be transported, but left in the penitentiary or the hulks.'[53] Whately suggested that if transportation alone were seen not as a punish-ment but as a reward, then it opened the door to hope, which effectively nullified the deterrent of all other possible secondary punishments. This, he went on to argue, was evidently the case both from his own experience at home and from the colonial reports of Cunningham and Macquarie. Whereas, for those gently brought up, the prospect of gaol and transpor-tation might be very terrible, for the majority who were sentenced to transportation, it was perceived as a boon: 'they are carried to a country whose climate is delightful, producing in profusion all the necessaries and most of the luxuries of life;– ... Whatever other advantages this system may possess, it certainly does not look like a very terrific punish-ment'.[54] He concluded that, although improvement might be made, the only effective solution was to abandon transportation altogether. This left unanswered the question of what should be done with convicts. Here Whately came up with what appears to be an entirely original proposal; namely that instead of serving a certain period of time, convicts should be required to perform a certain quantity of work, and that this should be performed at home.[55] Draining peat bogs in Ireland to create productive agricultural land, he believed, would serve this purpose.

Thoughts on Secondary Punishments (1832)

There Whately might have left his interest in this subject, neatly buried with the *London Review*, which turned up its toes in mid-1829. Whately seems to have regarded this study of the transportation question quite

---

[52] Ibid., 118.   [53] Ibid., 119.   [54] Ibid., 122.
[55] Ibid., 138; almost certainly this idea came originally from William Paley. See Chapter 7.

highly; enough so to have released it at least twice, once as an appendix to his *Letter to Earl Grey on Secondary Punishments* (1832) and again in 1861 as part of a collection of his letters and reviews.[56] In 1832, the spark for republishing was provided by the long-running, though ultimately ineffectual, SC on Secondary Punishments (1831–1832), which was raising questions about the perceived rise of crime and the adequacies of the available remedies.[57] The only clergy to testify were Whitworth Russell and Elizabeth Fry, Russell to defend Millbank and Fry to plead, with some success, on behalf of prisoners awaiting trial and for women prisoners.[58]

While the essay which appeared in the *London Review* appears to have been more or less ignored (there does not appear to have been a review of it), Whately secured a lively and informed audience for the same piece when it was refurbished in a new volume.[59] While reviewers rightly pointed to its slender credentials, since nearly all of it had already appeared elsewhere, Whately's piece was reviewed in the quarterlies. As Stefan Collini points out, whereas the eighteenth century had been the 'age of the pamphlet', in the first half of the nineteenth century literary and cultural debate was dominated by the review essay, carried by the weighty quarterlies such as the *Edinburgh Review* (founded 1802) and the *Quarterly Review* (founded 1809), each with their own politics, audience and style.[60] The essays they published were opinionated, political and even polemical, and they were meant to stimulate debate and drive public policy. A figure like Whately, who contributed to the reviews (and even tried to launch one of his own) is particularly challenging to categorize: liberal, though not in debt to any party, socially and political engaged with a seat in the House of Lords, but independent on many issues, and a Christian utilitarian in an age when these two things were sometimes seen as mutually contradictory. His main aim was to stir things up.

There are two sections to Whately's volume. The first, 'Thoughts on Secondary Punishments' is in the form of a letter to Earl Grey, and is the only original piece in the collection. To this are added an appendix made

---

[56] Whately, *Thoughts on Secondary Punishments*; Richard Whately, *Miscellaneous Lectures and Reviews* (London: Parker, 1861).

[57] *SC on Secondary Punishments* (Report) BPP (1831–1832) VII.559, p. 561; *SC on Secondary Punishments* (Minutes) BPP (1831) VII.519.

[58] 'Testimony of Whitworth Russell', 25 March 1831, BPP (1831) VII.519, p. 20; 'Testimony of Mrs Fry and Miss Caroline Neave', 23 March 1832, BPP (1831–1832) VII.559, 116–128.

[59] Whately, *Thoughts on Secondary Punishments*.

[60] Stefan Collini, *Public Moralists* (Oxford: Clarendon, 1991), p. 52.

up of the 1829 essay on transportation; a review, published in the *Law Magazine* for January 1832, of the *Report of the SC on Secondary Punishments* (1831), and Edward Gibbon Wakefield's *Facts Relating to the Punishment of Death in the Metropolis* (1831); and an article written by 'a friend', entitled 'Suggestions for the Improvement of our System of Colonization'. The author is not identified, but it is possible that it was by Samuel Hinds (1793–1872), later bishop of Norwich, who was preaching 'Christian colonization' on behalf of the Committee of the New Zealand Association at about this time.[61] It is reasonable to suggest that Hinds may also have assisted Whately's earlier critique of transportation.

By the time Whately's later critique of transportation appeared, the context of the debate had noticeably changed, transforming the work from a study of the efficacy of transportation as a punishment, to one which saw transportation as an impediment to systematic colonization by free settlers. This reflects the change of mood in the years since Whately's 1829 essay had appeared and the rise of vocal, well-connected and cross-party support for colonization under the leadership of Edward Gibbon Wakefield. Whately began by hanging his argument not just on the logic of the theory of punishment, as he had done in 1829, but on his own experience as minister of a London parish. There he found that transportation had become a subject of envy for the 'honest and industrious labourer struggling at home', that the government policy was rather that of 'terror to the good than to the evil'.[62] He repeated his earlier argument about the failure of transportation to deter and about it being not a single, efficient and focussed punishment, but several. To be effective, he argued that four things were needed, all lacking in the current system: it should be *formidable* (Whately was fond of italics); *humane*, not imposing suffering for its own sake; *corrective*, tending to lead to moral improvement rather than debasement; and finally it should be *cheap*.[63]

Whately considered transportation to be the abrogation of a duty to society because it provided an indulgent gesture of compassion to the culprit rather than the victim of crime.[64] In its place, he recommended a trial of different experiments, which might include penitentiaries and special arrangements for juveniles and first offenders. He then repeated his recommendation of the system proposed in the *London Review*, namely that of requiring sentences to consist of a 'certain amount of work' rather than a sentence of time.[65] Task work should be controlled by superintendents and not by the system of private assignment.[66] He

[61] Hilary M. Carey, *God's Empire* (Cambridge: Cambridge University Press, 2011), p. 314.
[62] Whately, *Thoughts on Secondary Punishments*, p. 2.   [63] Ibid., 6–7.   [64] Ibid., 14.
[65] Ibid., 35–36.   [66] Ibid., 40.

expressed his opposition to public executions, which he maintained did not produce terror, except in the minds of those unlikely to commit serious crimes, but instead created sympathy for the culprit.[67] Finally he concluded, very fairly, by pointing out the two striking problems created by the abolition of transportation: 'What shall we do with the convicts?' and 'What shall we do with the colonies?'[68]

Remarks on Transportation (1834)

Whately's most substantial work on the subject of transportation appeared two years later, in 1834. Written specifically to address the objections raised by Colonel Arthur and Bishop Broughton in their Hobart pamphlet considered in Chapter 3, it included a point-by-point rebuttal of their argument, together with an appendix including extracts from the *Report of the SC on Secondary Punishments* (1832) pointing to the evils of transportation, and newspaper accounts of criminals who expressed their delight at receiving the sentence.[69] A soldier, for instance, when sentenced, is said to announce: 'Thank you, my Lord; transportation is better than soldiering.'[70] There were also records relating to the treatment of female convicts on the *Amphitrite*, tragically wrecked off Boulogne on 31 August 1833, with the loss of most of the women and children on board,[71] with 'Remarks of the French Commissioners' that: 'The punishment of transportation intimidates no one, and emboldens many in the path of crime.'[72] All this was grist to the argument that transportation did not deter. In answer to the question: 'What is to be done for our colonies', Whately added the prospectus of the South Australian Association, the first attempt to found a colony without the use of convict labour.[73] The final appendix cites Francis Bacon on the moral case against transporting criminals for the purpose of founding colonies: 'To establish a colony ... in order to serve as a

---

[67] Ibid., 46.   [68] Ibid., 49.   [69] See Chapter 3.

[70] Whately, *Remarks on Transportation*, p. 148. The soldier's comment was cited by the *Examiner*, 8 September 1833.

[71] 'Facts relating to the Condition and Treatment of Female Convicts, on their Passage to Botany Bay, collected from the Mouth of John Owen, Boatswain of the Amphitrite Female Convict Vessel', Ibid., 156–161. For *Amphitrite* and other convict transport wrecks, see Charles Bateson, *The Convict Ships, 1787–1868* 2nd edn (Glasgow: Brown, 1969), pp. 246–248. and entries for *George III (1835)*, *Hive* (1835), *Neva* (1835) and *Waterloo* (1842). The wreck of the Amphitrite was the likely inspiration for J. M. W. Turner's unfinished, 'Disaster at Sea' (1835) in Tate Britain featured on the cover of this book. See also 'An Account, by an Eye-Witness, of the Wreck of the Amphitrite', *Fraser's Magazine* 8 (1833), 557–560.

[72] Whately, *Remarks on Transportation*, pp. 161–168.   [73] Ibid., 168–70.

drain for the impurities of the mother-country, is to do an act which no casuistry can defend.'[74]

The letter itself is divided into chapters which summarize Arthur and Broughton's attempt to defend the convict system, point out the discrepancy between what is anticipated by the system and its actual effects, note the demoralizing reality of the system, suggest the advantages – rather than disincentives – which many convicts receive from their sentences, and strongly recommended a commission of inquiry to establish the facts. Whately informed his readers that Arthur had accompanied his printed rebuttal with a manuscript letter in which he expressed hopes for the reformed system of transportation which he was then in the process of setting in place. Whately was simply unconvinced that any such improvements could be made and, in any case, had the effect of 'substituting sanguine anticipation for actual existences'.[75]

From the religious point of view, the most interesting chapter is the one devoted to the repudiation of the views of the senior Anglican cleric of the colony of New South Wales, Archdeacon Broughton.[76] Possibly this is because Whately felt personally rebuked by Broughton's suggestion that his arguments were neither moral nor religious in character and unbecoming to a bishop. In response to this slur, Whately denied that he overlooked 'the moral effect of religious principle in diminishing crime', or that, by proposing an alternative punishment to that of transportation that he was attempting to 'supersede the fear of God!'[77] In response, Whately expressed himself flabbergasted, pointing to his own efforts over a number of years on what he called (with more italics) 'the *application* of religion to *moral* conduct'.[78] For Whately, there was nothing so reprehensible as the inappropriate application of religious precepts to social issues. 'I have long been convinced', he stated, 'that nothing tends so much to bring Christianity into contempt, as the representations which some of its professors give both of its doctrines and of its application'.[79] Whately put Broughton's proposition, that religion tended to reduce crime, in the form of a syllogism, effectively demonstrating the preposterous nature of its fundamental tenets:

That men who fear God as they ought will not commit crimes, we knew before; but are you proposing an act of parliament to compel men to fear God? Or have you any plan for so promoting religious faith as to do away all need for punishment? Or do you hold that all kinds of punishment are equally efficacious, or equally inefficacious, in promoting or in discouraging such conduct as religion forbids? If all punishments are useless, let all be abolished;

[74] Ibid., 170.   [75] Ibid., 4.   [76] Ibid., 67–80.   [77] Ibid., 67.
[78] Ibid., 71. Italics in original.   [79] Ibid.

if all are equally proper, let things remain as they are; or if it is possible the system may be improved, let inquiries and suggestions be made with a view to improvement.[80]

What Whately proposed to Earl Grey, was that transportation was a system beyond reform, and that Broughton was much too sanguine on the effectiveness of chaplains and surgeons to ameliorate the moral dangers of the system. The reality, openly acknowledged by Broughton, was that, in the interior of New South Wales, road gangs of convicts rarely, if ever, encountered a clergyman.[81]

Responses to Whately

Responses to Whately came in the form of letters and articles published in the quarterlies and the colonial press; the former generally supported him (with one exception) while the latter did not.[82] Writing for the *The Law Review*, George Cornewall Lewis (1806–1863) regarded Whately's case as compelling: 'He must indeed be armed with triple mail who can resist the force of the arguments against transportation.'[83] The *Phrenological Journal* agreed that Whately demonstrated that transportation to New South Wales presented a 'lamentable picture of failure'.[84] Of the three substantial critiques, the most hostile appeared in *Fraser's Magazine*.[85] Asserting that 'God is nowhere in the archbishop's book', it concludes:

The work itself, catchpenny in form, grovelling in style, cruel in sentiment, godless in feeling, absurd in reasoning and, when the rank and order of its author is considered, revolting in choice of subject, calls only for attention as

---

[80] Ibid., 74–75.   [81] Ibid., 79.

[82] For UK responses to Whately, see [Wlliam Maginn], 'Archbishop Whately's Secondary Punishments Dissected', 566; [Earl Grey], 'Secondary Punishments – Transportation', *Edinburgh Review*, 58 (1834), 336–362; [George Cornewall Lewis], Secondary Punishments, *Law Magazine* 7 (1832), 1–32; For a sample of – generally hostile – colonial responses to Whately, see *Hobart Town Chronicle*, 23 April 1833, p. 2; *Sydney Herald*, 29 August 1833, p. 2; *Hobart Town Courier*, 23 January 1835, p. 4; *Colonial Times* (Hobart), 29 March 1836, p. 4; *Austral-Asiatic Review*, 22 May 1838, p. 4. The Molesworth SC on Transportation and the later stages of the anti-transportation debate prompted others, notably Charles Bowyer Adderley, *A Century of Experiments on Secondary Punishment* (London: Parker, Son and Bourn, 1863).

[83] Lewis, 'Secondary Punishments', p. 31.

[84] *The Phrenological Journal*, 8.34 (1832), 37. Whately was also reviewed by the *Quarterly Theological Review* 12 (1832), 470, which disapproved of total abolition of transportation.

[85] Maginn, 'Archbishop Whately's Secondary Punishments Dissected', 566–575.

affording a lamentable proof that 'liberal politics' may degrade an archbishop to a state of thought and feeling not higher than that of a hangman.[86]

This blistering attack needs to be seen in the context of Whately's principled intervention in Ireland, at the height of the Famine, where he cooperated with the Catholic archbishop of Dublin to create a national education system which threatened to overturn the monopoly of the established Church of Ireland. In Ireland, some of the more vitriolic attacks, which ran from 1832 to 1834, were made by John Nelson Darby (1800–1882), an Evangelical who later left the Church of Ireland to become one of the founders of the Plymouth Brethren. Donald Akenson has noted that Darby's attacks 'would be libellous in our own time' but that they differed from those of other Irish clergy, especially evangelicals, simply in their extreme form.[87] Darby could scarcely bring himself to refer to Whately by his title as archbishop of Dublin.[88]

Whately's Irish reforms enraged Evangelicals in the Church of Ireland who saw them as an assault on the Reformation, made, moreover, by an Englishman. As Akenson argues, these attacks were fuelled by a millennial crisis led by Evangelicals in the south of Ireland who correctly perceived that Whately represented an existential threat to their existence, even if not a literal harbinger of the last days.[89] As Houghton suggests,[90] Whately's reviewer was no doubt William McGinn (1794–1842), the brilliant, polemical editor of *Fraser's Magazine*, who wrote much of its copy and gave it its edgy, witty – and Tory – character.[91] A brilliant speaker of Irish, McGinn's sympathies were with the poor Irish while his religious and political loyalties were firmly Protestant and Tory. Like most critics of Whately, he found the idea of liberal, utilitarian Anglicanism simply incomprehensible and a Christian political economy a contradiction in terms. McGinn was probably right about the miserliness of the style and concepts promoted by Whately, but the archbishop had support. What the Liberal Anglicans recognized – Richard Bourke in Sydney as much as Whately in Dublin –

---

[86] Ibid., 575.
[87] Donald Harman Akenson, *Discovering the End of Time* (Montreal: McGill-Queens University Press, 2016), p. 309.
[88] Ibid., 312.
[89] The tithe war and the disestablishment of the Church of Ireland lie outside the remit of this book, but for the timeline, see Ibid.
[90] According to Walter E. Houghton (ed.), *The Wellesley Index to Victorian Periodicals, 1824–1900* (Toronto: University of Toronto Press, 1972), vol. II, p. 335, the author is probably William Maginn since Maginn wrote no. 434 attacking Whately 'in similar style'.
[91] D. E. Latané Jr, 'Maginn, William (1794–1842)', *ODNB*.

was that the continued privileges of Protestant establishment were as unsustainable in Ireland as they were in the British settler colonies. The polemics of the New Reformation in Ireland, like that of the so-called crime wave in New South Wales denounced by Judge Burton (Chapter 6), were driven by the will to maintain control of the public sphere by sections of the established, Protestant, episcopal church.

A rather more temperate reaction to Whately was provided by the veteran Presbyterian minister and immigration advocate, the Rev. John Dunmore Lang.[92] Against Whately's abolitionism Lang testified, at length, to the Molesworth SC on Transportation, that transportation and private assignment in New South Wales was effective in reforming criminals.[93] *Transportation and Colonization* was written in 1836 during a voyage to Britain to recruit clergy for the New South Wales Presbytery. He actively opposed the use of government funds to support other churches, notably the Roman Catholic error, and regarded convict labour as a resource for colonists. He respected Whately's utilitarian principles but provided a careful rebuttal of their logical force in light of his superior knowledge of the colonial penal system. Lang argued in favour of transportation, suggesting that it had not been tested sufficiently since it had been been grossly mismanaged. In relation to New South Wales, he argued persuasively that it was never intended that the colony should remain exclusively penal but that convicts should pave the way for free settlers. From his own experience, he confirmed that not only was convict reformation possible, but that that he had witnessed it 'in many instances'.[94] Lang also thought that transportation was a humane punishment which provided criminals with 'new scenes and new circumstances' to break the cycle of reoffending. This he considered better than the system of hard labour and penitentiaries recommended by Whately and implemented in the United States. He deplored the outcome of the latter which resulted in a cycle of repeated offending and perpetual servitude: 'till at last, in perfect recklessness, [the prisoner] comes to regard a prison as his home and his country; – and the hopeless condition of his existence, that of enmity towards the whole human race'.[95]

Lang provided a serviceable review of the literature on penal reform, citing Beccaria, Rousseau and also the experience of convicts transported to the former American colonies. He observed that trans-Atlantic

---

[92] Lang, *Transportation and Colonization.*
[93] 'Testimony of J. D. Lang', 30 May, 2 June and 6 June 1837, *Molesworth SC on Transportation (Minutes)*, BPP 1837 (518) XIX.1, p. 226.
[94] Lang, *Transportation and Colonization*, p. 23.   [95] Ibid., 26.

transportation, which involved their distribution across the continent and among a large body of free setters, had been so successful in reformation that all traces of convict origins had dissipated long ago.[96] He rebutted two of Whately's misconceptions about transportation, firstly that it had failed to reform convicts, and secondly that it could not be made profitable. On reform, he asserted that what was lacking was simply the effective implementation of a more punitive regime, focussed on using the resource of convict labour to benefit the colonization of new lands, especially in northern Australia. But the most important change needed was to switch to support for the arrival of a 'free emigrant and virtuous population, to afford the requisite stimulus to reformation, and to repress the general tendency to criminality'.[97] All convict labour should be devoted to clearing land with profits invested to support free emigrants, providing them at the same time with a clergyman and a schoolmaster for every one hundred families.[98]

A third substantial discussion of Whately's *Thoughts on Secondary Punishments* appeared in the *Edinburgh Review* in 1834.[99] The review was prepared by Henry George Grey (1802–1894), the third Earl Grey,[100] and it is an important milestone in the plans to change the character of transportation to penal colonies. The eldest of Charles Grey's sixteen children, Earl Grey was made Colonial Secretary in Lord John Russell's administration, and his lengthy defence of his own policy is the most significant contemporary reflection on the rise and fall of convict transportation to British penal colonies.[101] To the last, Earl Grey aspired to improve transportation and make it reformative – not abolish it.

For the *Edinburgh Review*, Grey chose to review three works: De Beaumont and de Tocqueville's study of the penitentiary system in the United States with its application to France and an appendix on penal

---

[96] Ibid., 41.   [97] Ibid., 56.   [98] Ibid., 176.   [99] Grey, 'Secondary Punishments'.
[100] For Earl Grey's authorship, see correspondence with Macvey Napier, editor of the *Edinburgh Review*: Napier to Grey, 18 January 1834; Grey to Napier, 20 January 1834, concerning Grey's article on transportation; also Grey's Journal GRE/V/C3/1A for 1 December 1833: Durham University Library, Archives and Special Collections, Papers of Henry George, 3rd Earl Grey, GB-0033-GRE-B.
[101] Earl Grey, *The Colonial Policy of Lord John Russell's Administration*, 2 vols, 2nd edn (London: Bentley, 1853); John M. Ward, 'Grey, Henry George (1802–1894)', *ADB*; John M. Ward, *Earl Grey and the Australian Colonies, 1846–1857* (Melbourne: Melbourne University Press, 1958); John M. Ward, 'The Colonial Policy of Lord John Russell's Administration', *Historical Studies, Australia and New Zealand*, 9.35 (1960), 244–262. Ward criticized Grey for infuriating the colonists by colluding, with Governor Denison, to 'improve' transportation instead of abolishing it.

colonies, including those of Britain (1833);[102] Whately's *Thoughts on Secondary* Punishments (1833); and the *Reports from the SC on Secondary Punishments* (1831 and 1832). Grey began by situating penal reforms as part of the triumphant achievements of the Whig reformist government. Both Catholic emancipation and parliamentary reform were stages in the 'one great struggle' which had progressively seen the transfer of power from the few to 'the people at large'.[103] Having achieved 'the ascendancy of the oligarchical principle', it remained to try and disentangle the grip on power of the established elite. This was achieved first in Ireland, with the Catholic Relief Bill, and then the expansion of the electorate. But for Grey, the next logical step was to look to improve the quality of life for everyone: 'how that power might best be used for the welfare of the whole community'.[104] The two areas that he singled out as most in need of reform were the poor laws and the legal system. In relation to transportation, Grey thought that the high price of labour in the colonies ensured that most prisoners benefitted from it, demonstrated by the fact that very few returned. However, while this was an advantage of the system to Britain, it was not a punishment.[105] Grey went on to suggest that convicts should be required to cover all the costs incurred by their incarceration. Opposing excessive rigour, he argued that in order to make transportation an effective remedy for the reformation of criminals it should become, 'an indulgence granted to them at their own desire'.[106]

Grey's lengthy rebuttal of Whately was soon overshadowed by the findings of the SC on Transportation, chaired by Sir William Molesworth, which brought down its report in 1837 and 1838 and is considered in more detail in Chapter 6.[107] Molesworth prepared a single-volume version of the report, dedicated to his constituents in Leeds.[108] In the preface to this version of the report, Molesworth explained that he had dedicated it to his constituents for two reasons: first, that they should recognize how 'inefficient, cruel and demoralizing' transportation was, that it failed to either prevent crime by terror or reform criminals and led to deplorable conditions in the colonies. Secondly, that they should exert themselves to lobby Parliament to abolish transportation, which he

---

[102] Gustave de Beaumont and Alexis de Tocqueville, *Système Pénitentaire aux États-Unis et de son Application en France suivi d'un Appendice sur les Colonies Pénales* (Paris: Charles Gosselin, 1833). Grey reviewed the French edition though an English translation by Francis Lieber appeared in an American edition the same year.
[103] Grey, 'Secondary Punishments', 337.   [104] Ibid.   [105] Ibid., 353.
[106] Ibid., 337.
[107] *SC on Transportation* (Minutes of Evidence) BPP 1837 (518) XIX.1; *SC on Transportation* (report and appendix) BPP 1837–8 (669) XXII.1.
[108] Molesworth, *Select Committee on Transportation*.

declared 'disgraceful to a civilized and Christian nation'.[109] From the beginning, therefore, Molesworth at least sought the authority of religion and morality to bolster the logical arguments which he considered provided overwhelming support for the abolition of convict transportation. His closest ally, one on whom he was prepared to draw for an appeal to his own Leodensian constituents, was none other than Richard Whately, to the extent that he attached a copy of Whately's *Letter to the Transportation Committee* as part of his report, describing him as the first of those who had brought public attention to the transportation question, 'and to whose admirable works on these subjects I have been most deeply indebted.'[110] As already noted, Whately's Letter introduced an important additional argument, largely ignored by Molesworth – though strongly advanced by the SC on Aborigines and the friends of Edward Gibbon Wakefield – namely the genocidal impact of convict colonization on indigenous people.[111]

Whately's direct engagement with the issue of transportation did not continue much beyond his exchange of views with Arthur and Broughton, considered in Chapters 3 and 5, but he did not abandon the case altogether. Whately never wavered from his view that the best solution was the immediate abolition of transportation; he even disapproved of the ticket-of-leave system.[112] After initial qualms, Whately's views were endorsed as the popular anti-transportation cause gathered momentum in the 1840s. The Registrar-General of South Australia, Robert Torrens, extolled Whately for liberating the Australian colonies from their compulsory burden of convicts, and also praised him for attending a meeting of the Statistical Society, in one of the last activities of Whately's life, in order to lend his support to a report on transportation.[113]

Conclusion

From 1829, when Richard Whately published his critical review of convict transportation, he succeeded in shifting the debate to a new level of intellectual seriousness. While his first thoughts on the subject appeared prior to his appointment as archbishop of Dublin in 1831, they were not an aberration but part of Whately's consistently expressed views as a Liberal Anglican who attempted, with like-minded colleagues at

---

[109] Ibid., 1v.   [110] Ibid.
[111] *Molesworth SC on Transportation (Report)*, appendix L, BPP 1837–38 (669) XXII.1, p. 299. For Edward Gibbon Wakefield's arguments about the moral obligation to protect indigenous people in settler colonization, see McKenzie, *Scandal*, p. 147.
[112] Fitzpatrick, *Memoirs of Richard Whately*, p. 13.
[113] Ibid. Whately died on 8 October 1863.

Oriel College, to find a pathway between the secular utilitarians on the one hand, and the birth of the Oxford movement and its radical swing to tradition on the other. Whately was a champion of rational solutions to social problems and his views on transportation were enthusiastically taken up by the Radical Whigs, such as Molesworth, for the much more strongly expressed condemnation of transportation by the Select Committee which he chaired. Molesworth skilfully manipulated witnesses to the Select Committee, including Anglican, Presbyterian and Catholic clergy, to bolster support for his move to abolish convict transportation to New South Wales. This was to continue a campaign which had been initiated by Jeremy Bentham but which had not succeeded, in part because of doubts by mainstream politicians about the religious implications of what seemed to be a godless solution to a moral problem.

Whately was not afraid to speak his mind and have his opinions appear in print, which he originally feared would hold back his career. In 1826, he wrote to Ernest Hawkins that he thought this was worth the risk: 'I have not put myself at the head of a school or party; I have proclaimed no new discovery; I have coveted neither wealth nor honor, but have, with my eyes open, shut myself out from both.'[114] In the case of transportation, his influence was substantial. He was the most distinguished intellectual to address the question of transportation since Bentham in 1812.[115] Whately's entry into the debate and his principled rebuttal of the arguments put in favour of transportation by Bishop Broughton and Colonel Arthur gave the opponents of transportation the opportunity to resume the moral high ground. Whately's arguments were internally convincing, however they were effectively combatted from three directions, by the home government represented by the third Earl Grey, from colonial authorities such as Colonel Arthur, and from those with experience of the practical reformation of convicts, including the Rev. John Dunmore Lang. Evidently there was still considerable life left in transportation, though the call for reform was now more strident than ever. If rational arguments could not overthrow transportation, another strategy was to appeal to the emotions and sympathies of the moral middle class. The next chapter considers the ways in which Catholic reformers, including Father Ullathorne and Bishop Willson, led a humanitarian and religious denunciation of the 'horrors of transportation', and how Catholic claims for entry into the moral realm were resisted by defenders of the Protestant establishment.

[114] Whately to Hawkins, 3 December 1826, Oriel College Library, Whateley Letters, vol. 4, p. 349.
[115] See Chapter 1.

6   Catholics, Protestants and the 'Horrors of Transportation'

> They look for death, as those who dig for treasure, and it cometh not; they are exceedingly rejoiced when they have found a grave.[1]
>   (Ullathorne, 1837)

> A cage of unclean birds, full of crimes against God and Man, of Murders, Blasphemies, and all Uncleanness.[2]   (Judge Burton, 1840)

The 'horrors of transportation' was a term that originated with the writing of the Rev. William Bernard Ullathorne (1806–1889) when serving as Roman Catholic (hereafter Catholic) Vicar General of New South Wales. It was given greater prominence through his testimony to the Molesworth SC on Transportation. Originally preached by Ullathorne to warn poor Irish Catholics of the dangers of courting conviction as a way out of poverty, 'the horrors of transportation' soon entered popular discourse in other forms. In England, the Molesworth SC provided a vehicle by which Gothic elaborations of convict demoralization were woven together with traditional Catholic teaching on the purgatorial suffering of the damned and conservative Protestant fears of Catholic incursion on the moral realm. In the penal colony, fears of a calamitous rise in crime were stoked by Judge William Westbrooke Burton (1794–1888) from his bully pulpit in the New South Wales Supreme Court. Burton and Ullathorne would go on to engage in a sparring match over the relative number and moral status of Catholics in the colony and who should receive funding to run schools, churches and provide religious instruction to convicts. In this proxy war, Burton emerged as the leading defendant of the older Anglican ascendancy, while Ullathorne and Governor Bourke supported the newly enfranchised Catholic and Dissenting

---

[1] William Bernard Ullathorne, *The Catholic Mission in Australasia* (Liverpool: Rockliff & Duckworth, 1837), p. 52.

[2] William Westbrooke Burton, *The State of Religion and Education in New South Wales* (London: J. Cross, 1840), p. 255; C. F. Pascoe, *Two Hundred Years of the S. P. G.*, 2 vols. (London: SPG, 1901), vol. I, pp. 390–391.

citizens of a rising liberal empire in which moral authority was shared between the leading Christian denominations.

This chapter provides a brief outline of Catholic teaching on penal reform and why this matters to the sectarian dispute which broke out between Ulltathorne and Burton. It considers how their polarized views were appropriated by Molesworth and his committee in the attempt to deliver a killer blow to the transportation system. It goes on to suggest that liberal, including Catholic, denunciation of the 'horrors of transportation' turned the tide of public opinion against transportation.

Catholics and Convicts

Despite a rich historiography concerning Irish convict transportation, less has been said about Catholic convicts, the great majority of them Irish, and their clergy in the penal colonies.[3] Stoked by civil and foreign war, anti-Catholicism was essential to Britain's Protestant identity and formed an aspect of the British imperial state.[4] This mattered in the first decades of the nineteenth century, when the pressure of high levels of Catholic emigration from Ireland challenged liberal initiatives to remove faith-based civil disabilities from British citizens. Based on the available data on religion, British and Irish Catholics were over represented in English, Scottish and Irish prisons, as they were in penal colonies and convict establishments with significant Irish flows.[5] According to parliamentary returns published in 1852–1853, Catholics made up 13.7 per cent of the English, 90 per cent of the Irish and 18.5 per cent of the Scottish prison population (see Tables 6.1 and 6.2); compared with the 1851 census of religious worship

---

[3] For Irish convicts, see Simon Devereaux, 'Irish Convict Transportation and the Reach of the State in Late Hannoverian Britain', *Journal of the Canadian Historical Association* 8.1 (1997), 61–85; Bob Reece, *The Origins of Irish Convict Transportation to New South Wales* (Houndmills: Palgrave, 2001) Hamish Maxwell-Stewart, '"And all my great hardships endured"?: Irish Convicts in Van Diemen's Land, in Nial Whelehan (ed.), *Transnational Perspectives in Modern Irish History* (London: Routledge, 2015), pp. 69–87.

[4] For imperial anti-Catholicism, see Géraldine Vaughan, '"Britishers and Protestants": Protestantism and Imperial British Identities in Britain, Canada and Australia from the 1880s to the 1920s', *Studies in Church History* 54 (2018), 359–373; Donald MacRaild, 'Transnationalizing "Anti-Popery": Militant Protestant Preachers in the Nineteenth-Century Anglo-World', *Journal of Religious History* 39 (2015), 224–243; John Wolffe, 'Change and Continuity in British Anti-Catholicism', in Frank Tallett and Nicholas Atkin (eds.), (London: Hambledon Press, 1996), pp. 67–83; John Wolffe, 'Anti-Catholicism and the British Empire, 1815–1914', in Hilary M. Carey (ed.), *Empires of Religion* (Basingstoke: Palgrave Macmillan, 2008), pp. 43–63.

[5] For Catholics in New South Wales, see Burton, *State of Religion*, p. 303. Burton thought the Catholics made up one-third of the convicts and about one-quarter of the free population in New South Wales. For religious censuses of convicts in Gibraltar (1863) and Bermuda (1858), see Tables 10.1 and 10.7.

Table 6.1 *Prisoners by denomination in English prisons on 25 September 1852, compared with 1851 census of religious worship for England and Wales*

	Church of England	Presbyterians	Dissenters (all)	Roman Catholics	Jews	Described as no religion	Not stated	Total
Prisoners	16,077	496	1,391	2,955	45	323	339	21,626
Percentage	74.3	2.3	6.4	13.7	0.1	0.2	1.6	100%
Percentage religious attendance 1851	48.7	0.7	46.9	3.5	0.05	–	–	100%

Source: Religion in Prison, 1852–1853; Census of Religious Worship, 1851: England and Wales. [a]

[a] *Return of Numbers of Prisoners of each Religious Denomination in Prisons in England, Scotland and Ireland, September 1852*, BPP 1852–1853 (908 908-I) LXXXI.317, 333, p. 331 [Hereafter *Religion in Prison, 1852–1853*]; Robert Currie, Alan D. Gilbert, and Lee Horsley, *Churches and Churchgoers* (Oxford: Clarendon Press, 1977), pp. 216–218.

Table 6.2 *Prisoners by denomination in Scottish prisons on 25 September 1852, compared with 1851 census of religious worship for Scotland*

	Number of prisoners in custody	Presbyterian	Episcopalian	Roman Catholic	Congregational	Baptist	Unknown	Total
Prisoners	2,828	1,698	179	522	4	4	328	2,828
Percentage		60	6.3	18.5	0.1	0.1	11.6	96.6%
Percentage religious attendance 1851		85	2.5	4.5	3.9	1.2	Other 2.7	100%

Source: Religion in Prison, 1852–1853; Census of Religious Worship 1851: Scotland.[a]
[a] *Religion in Prison, 1852–53*, pp. 335–337; Ibid., 219.

with 8 per cent and 4.5 per cent for England and Wales and Scotland respectively and 78 per cent in Ireland, according to the 1861 census (see Table 6.3). Despite the high numbers of Catholic convicts, religious provision per prisoner was below that provided for Protestants, particularly in Ireland (see Table 6.3),[6] and this became a matter of contention in the penal colonies.

Irish Catholics were already moving in considerable numbers to England, Scotland and Wales before the catastrophe of the Great Famine (1845–1850).[7] In England, they were concentrated in the industrial north and in ports, and they soon found their way into the gaols and courts and transports heading to Botany Bay. Both for demographic reasons, then, and because it coincided with liberal reforms to the imperial church and state, the anti-transportation debate was affected in important ways by religious sectarianism.

At first blush, Catholic clerics' assertive denunciation of the 'horrors of transportation' appears surprising. Throughout the nineteenth century, the Church of Rome displayed entrenched social and political conservatism and preached passive acceptance of poverty, the authority of secular rulers and the unequal distribution of goods and power. Yet penal reform had made strides in enlightened Catholic states, including the papacy itself. In 1703, Pope Clement XI founded Rome's first prison, the hospice of San Michele (Ospizio Apostolico di San Michele a Ripa), which provided delinquent boys with a work regime by day and private cells for rest and contemplation by night. Visiting in 1778, John Howard found San Michele 'sadly neglected', but approved the seminary founded by Pope Clement XII in 1735 for young women on the same principles.[8] The Catholic prison which most attracted the interest of British penal reformers was the Ghent Maison de Force (House of Correction) or Octagon in Catholic Belgium. Designed by Flemish magistrate Count Jean Philippe Vilain in 1773, it incorporated religious discipline, silence, classification and separation of prisoners and a work regime alongside training for a trade and education. In 1817 the Society for the Diffusion of Knowledge upon the Punishment of Death and the Improvement of Prison Discipline published a detailed report of it, noting some decline in conditions since Howard's day.[9] When Buxton visited, it was still one of

---

[6] Although Catholics made up 89.9 per cent of the prison population, only 48.8 per cent of salaries were paid to Catholic prison chaplains and religious instructors (Table 6.3).

[7] K. D. M. Snell and Paul S. Ell, *Rival Jerusalems* (Cambridge: Cambridge University Press, 2004), pp. 173–184.

[8] Howard, *Lazarettos*, p. 58.

[9] Society for Diffusing Information on the Subject of Capital Punishment and Prison Discipline, *An Account of the Maison de Force at Ghent from the Philanthropist, May 1817*.

Table 6.3 Prisoners by denomination in Irish gaols on 10 September 1853, compared with 1861 census of Ireland

	Prisoners				Salary of Chaplains			
	Number of prisoners in custody	Protestant (Church of England)	Dissenter	Roman Catholic	Total Salaries	Protestant	Dissenter	Roman Catholic
Government Prisons	3,902	222	44	3,636	£1245	£370	£60	£815
Irish Gaols	6,006	601	137	5,268	£2,000	£656	£576	£768
Total	9,908	823	181	8904	£3245	£1026	£636	£1,583
Percentage in Prison		8.3	1.8	89.9		31.6%	19.6%	48.8%
Percentage in 1861		12	Other 11	77.7				

Source: Religion in Prison, 1852–1853; Irish Census, 1861.[a]
[a] Religion in Prison, 1852–53, pp. 335–337; Ibid., 220–221.

the most admired and imitated prisons in the world, influencing many 'model' institutions in Britain, Europe and America. Buxton noted the classification system, the exercise yard and 'perfectly sweet and clean' rooms.[10]

There was a rich body of Catholic penal theory which would later inform Ullathorne's writing on conditions for convicts in Australia.[11] Christ's passion and suffering and his own words and sympathy for fellow condemned prisoners inspired Christians to see the prisoner as another Christ and a source of both charity and pious contemplation. According to Isaiah, God sought to bring not punishment but liberty to captives and release to prisoners (Is 61:1), a text recalled by Christ in his public mission (Lk 4:18). The suffering and imprisonment of the apostles and Christian martyrs provided further models for emulation.[12] As Ullathorne noted, both the penitentiary and the house of correction had Catholic origins and the first reformatory prisons were established by the papacy and Catholic Ghent, not in the United States.[13]

This political and theological context informed the steady advocacy of Catholic clergy appointed to the penal colonies for Catholic prisoners under sentence. From the beginning of their appointments to New South Wales, Vicar General Ullathorne and Vicar Apostolic Polding relished a mission to the convict population.[14] Ullathorne engaged defenders of the Protestant ascendancy in the colony, including the Rev. Henry Fulton, Archdeacon Broughton and Judge Burton of the Supreme Court.[15] Of those promoting colonial Protestantism, Burton had an appetite for controversy and wrote at the greatest length.[16] Before coming to New

---

[10] Buxton, *An Inquiry*, pp. 83–89.

[11] Andrew Scotnicki, *Criminal Justice and the Catholic Church* (Plymouth: Sheed & Ward, 2008). For Ullathorne's own account of the Catholic origins of reformatory prisons, see W. Ullathorne, *On the Management of Criminals* (London: Richardson, 1866).

[12] Edward Peters, 'Prison before the Prison', in Norval Morris and David Rothman (eds.), *The Oxford History of the Prison* (New York: Oxford University Press, 1998), pp. 17–21.

[13] Ullathorne, *On the Management of Criminals*, p. 23.

[14] Ullathorne, *Cabin-Boy to Archbishop*, p. 50.

[15] Controversial writing by Ullathorne included a response to anti-Catholic pamphlets by the Rev. Henry Fulton, *A Few Word to the Rev. Henry Fulton and His Readers* (Sydney: Stephens, 1833), to which Fulton replied with Henry Fulton, *A Letter to the Rev. W. B. Ullathorne* (Sydney: Stephens and Stokes, 1833). Against the British and Foreign School Society, Ullathorne wrote: *Observations on the Use and Abuse of the Sacred Scriptures* (Sydney: Jones, 1834), and the *Reply to Judge Burton*, first published in 1835 with other editions in 1840 and 1841. For detailed description of Ullathorne's writings, see Michael F. Glancey (ed.), *Characteristics from the Writings of Archbishop Ullathorne* (London: Burns & Oates, 1889).

[16] For Burton, see Kenneth G. Allars, 'William Westbrooke Burton', *Journal of the Royal Australian Historical Society*, 37.5 (1951), 257–294. Burton's most substantial work was Burton, *State of Religion*. With lengthy appendices it is just under 500 pages.

South Wales he had served in the navy and trained as a barrister, going out to the Cape as second puisne judge of the Supreme Court in 1827. In New South Wales, anti-Catholic and anti-liberal polemic never achieved the level of vitriol directed against liberals like Archbishop Whately on issues such as government support for a national system of non-sectarian education for Catholic children in Ireland.[17] However, the flames were fanned by the same ultra-Protestant world view in which Catholics were seen as agents of Anti-Christ, the papacy as the whore of Babylon and the defence of the British moral empire as the exclusive duty and privilege of the national, Protestant church. Underlying sectarianism ensured that the debate about transportation was fought with pugnacious intensity.

Judge Burton (1835)

In December 1835, Judge William Burton wrote to Governor Richard Bourke about the rise in crime and the 'overwhelming depravity and disregard of moral obligation' witnessed in the Supreme Court.[18] Burton had already delivered this rebuke, without consulting either Bourke or his fellow judges, as a 'charge' to the minor jury on the closing of the sittings of the Supreme Court in November 1835. It was printed in the colonial papers, reprinted by Burton's cronies and swooped on by the Molesworth SC, ensuring it had an impact on the transportation debate.[19] Witnesses were interrogated about Burton's claims for the rise in capital crime and the dearth of religious provision in the colony.[20] According to the Rev. John West, 'nothing so powerfully contributed to rouse the attention of the empire' to the evils of transportation and its impact on the colony as this speech.[21] Burton's 'charge' summarized the capital crimes from 1833 to 1835, including 399 capital convictions and 229 executions. He claimed, 'It would seem as if the main business of all the community were the commission of crime and the punishment of it – as if

---

[17] Akenson, *Protestant in Purgatory*; See Chapter 5.

[18] Burton to Bourke, 2 December 1835, Bourke Papers, Miscellaneous 1831–1838, SLNSW MLMSS 404–411. I thank David Roberts for providing me with a copy of this source.

[19] William Westbrooke Burton, 'Charge of Judge Burton to the Jury on Closing the Supreme Court, 18 November 1835', *Molesworth SC on Transportation (Minutes)*, BPP 1837 (518) XIX.1, appendix, pp. 289–293. [Herafter Burton, 'Charge']. It was also printed in the colony: *The Sydney Monitor*, 21 November 1835, p. 2; *The Australian*, 24 November 1835, p. 2.

[20] 'Testimony of Sir Francis Forbes', 28 April 1837, BPP 1837 (518) XIX.1, p. 70. Forbes agreed with Burton's general view of the colony, but not with the claimed rise in crime; 'Testimony of James Mudie', 9 May 1837, Ibid., p. 132, supported Burton and declared no confidence in any of the other judges.

[21] West, *History of Tasmania*, vol. 2, p. 220.

the whole colony were continually in motion towards the several courts of justice.' The reason for this, he argued, was 'an overwhelming defect of religious principle in this community'. Burton accused masters of failing to supervise their convict servants or require them to attend religious services, instead allowing them to spend the Lord's Day in drunken debauchery. Burton provided even grimmer testimony concerning the state of Norfolk Island. During his 1834 visit, he had tried 130 prisoners for involvement in a rebellion. One Norfolk Island prisoner who had come before Burton for sentencing stated: 'Let a man be what he will when he comes here, he is soon as bad as the rest; a man's heart is taken from him, and there is given to him the heart of a beast.'[22] He would later refer to Norfolk Island as: 'a cage of unclean birds, full of crimes against God and Man, of Murders, Blasphemies, and all Uncleanness'.[23] Burton's readers would have discerned the reference to the Book of Revelation.[24] Expressed in striking, scriptural language, neither Burton's 1835 charge to the jury nor his account of Norfolk Island provided an accurate reflection of the state of crime or morality in New South Wales.

No matter. Burton's depiction was approved by his serious-minded clerical supporters and colonial conservatives, such as James Macarthur and James Mudie.[25] The Rev. John Dunmore Lang acclaimed Burton's view in his own mouthpiece, *The Colonist*, as did the *Sydney Gazette* and the Rev. Samuel Marsden.[26] The Rev. Charles Frederick Pascoe (1844–1919) credited Burton with exposing the 'enormous moral evils of the colony'.[27] It also provided useful fodder for the 1838 SC on Transportation, given continued prominence when Molesworth repeated it in an 1840 speech to parliament.[28] To its credit, the Molesworth Committee printed both Burton's rant as well as Governor Bourke's response and those of Burton's fellow judges. The senior puisne judge, James Dowling (1787–1844), pointed out that he, rather

---

[22] Burton, 'Charge', p. 290.

[23] Burton, *State of Religion*, p. 255; Pascoe, *Two Hundred Years*, vol. I, pp. 390–391.

[24] Rev. 18:1–5: 'Babylon the great is fallen, is fallen, and is become the habitation of devils, and the hold of every foul spirit, and a cage of every unclean and hateful birds.'

[25] James Macarthur, *New South Wales, Its Present State and Future Prospects* (London, 1837), appendix, p. 35. James Mudie, *The Felonry of New South Wales* (London: Whaley, 1837), pp. 251–264.

[26] *The Colonist*, 15 December 1835; Marsden to Burton, SLNSW, Marsden Papers, vol. I: 590; Allars, 'William Westbrooke Burton', 269. It was a mutual admiration society and Lang's call for support for Presbyterians in the colony is included as an appendix in Burton, *State of Religion*, pp. cxxix–cxxxv.

[27] Pascoe, *Two Hundred Years*, vol. I, pp. 390–391.

[28] Sir William Molesworth, *Speech on Transportation* (London: Hooper, 1840), p. 17.

than Burton, had tried more criminal cases in the Supreme Court and without dwelling unduly on the most heinous cases, it was evident that crime had decreased in recent years.[29] Bourke confirmed that Burton's views were simply 'indecisive questionings and vague aspersions'.[30] Nevertheless, the damage was done; the image of the colony mired in a morass of moral filth chimed with the dismal Evangelical view of convict society, which had changed little since Wilberforce's denunciations prior to the Bigge Commission.[31] It effectively countermanded the rising demands of Dissenting and Catholic colonists for a say in the governance of the colony as a free, moral state without an established church.[32]

Liberals like Bourke were optimistic about the colony, though concerned about the need for greater religious provision, distinguishing themselves by believing that this should be distributed according to need to Anglicans, Dissenters and Catholics alike. Meanwhile, Ullathorne had both the ear of the Governor and the sympathetic support of the Colonial Office. Writing to Lord Glenelg in June 1836, Ullathorne argued that the moral standing of the penal colony of Van Diemen's Land would only improve with more resident Catholic clergy, paid for by the government, to cater for the 5,000 Catholics in Van Diemen's Land, many of them convicts. Requesting an additional five clergymen, Ullathorne blamed the 'crimes and disorders' of the Catholics of Van Diemen's Land on their religious deprivation, which, when remedied, might be expected to work a marvellous change, promising:

Property would become more secure; habitual concubinage would give place to marriage and domestic order; drunkenness, that paralysis of the colony, would be diminished in its causes; the sanctity of an oath would be better understood and observed; and the children, on whose education the reformation of the colony mainly depends, would have better guides and instructors than the bad example of vicious parents.[33]

Lt Governor Arthur supported this request, though suggested that only three additional clergy were 'absolutely necessary'.[34] Ullathorne also successfully secured the appointment of a salaried Catholic chaplain, to

[29] Dowling to Bourke, 9 April 1836, BPP 1837 (518) XIX.1, p. 296.
[30] Bourke to Glenelg, 10 June 1836, Ibid.   [31] See Chapter 2.
[32] For Burton's role, see Brian H. Fletcher, 'Christianity and Free Society in New South Wales 1788–1840', *Journal of the Royal Australian Historical Society*, 86.2 (2000), 86.
[33] Ullathorne to Glenelg, 4 June 1836, *Correspondence on Religion in Australia*, BPP 1837–1838 (75) XL.115, p. 28.
[34] Arthur to Glenelg, 2 October 1836, Ibid., p. 27.

be stationed on Norfolk Island, where 450 of the 1,175 prisoners were professed Catholics in 1836.[35]

Burton, on the other hand, believed that more Anglican churches, clergy and schools were the only way to counter the terrible evils of the colony reflected in atrocities such as the massacre on the Liverpool Plains, 'far out of the reach of the laws, and uninfluenced by Religion'.[36] Addressing those accused of the 1838 Myall Creek massacre, who included both convicts and former convicts, Burton stated: 'I do not think that Christian men, men speaking the English language, could have brought themselves to the commission of this crime.'[37] As Gipps noted, all eleven of those hanged for the massacre arrived in the colony as convicts, reflecting the compromised morality of a penal colony.[38] Using the language of anti-slavery, the SC on Aborigines condemned violence and dispossession along the ever-expanding British settler frontier. It recommended legal sanctions be provided to 'protect' Aborigines and constrain convicts, paradoxically entrenching Aboriginal disenfranchisement while doing little to address its underlying cause.[39] Burton wanted a union of the laws of God and man to prevent any recurrence of the atrocity. For the convicts, he suggested appointing equal numbers of itinerating clergy and police magistrates and the provision of public worship and religious instruction for 'every Gaol, Factory, Ironed gang, and Road party'.[40] To pay for it, he proposed directing the substantial funds released by the dissolution of the [Anglican] Clergy and School Estates Corporation, under Governor Bourke's Church Act of 1836. He opposed provision for the Catholic Church, arguing that it was already too successful, securing converts through its ministry to male prisoners, including those counselled prior to executions or, in the case of the women convicts supported by the Sisters of Charity, who chose to baptize their 'numerous illegitimate children' as Catholics.[41] Burton was especially galled by Bishop Polding's laying of the foundation for a new Catholic church at Windsor, dressed

---

[35] Ullathorne to Glenelg, 8 February 1837, Ibid., p. 17. Father John Brady was selected for this position.

[36] Burton, *State of Religion*, p. 279. Burton cites his own address to the prisoners, in *The Colonist*, 12 December 1838.

[37] Ibid., 282.

[38] Gipps to Glenelg, 19 December 1838, *Despatches Relative to the Massacre of Aborigines in 1838*, BPP 1838 (526) XXXIV.391, p. 427. Jane Lydon, 'Anti-Slavery in Australia: Picturing the 1838 Myall Creek Massacre', *History Compass* 15.5 (2017): doi.org/10.1111/hic3.12330.

[39] Lisa Ford, *Settler Sovereignty: Jurisdiction and Indigenous People in America and Australia, 1788–1836* (Cambridge, MA: Harvard University Press, 2010), p. 123.

[40] Burton, *State of Religion*, p. 282.   [41] Ibid.

'in his full Canonicals', accompanied by a military band.[42] Burton had greater tolerance for the Presbyterian Church, established in Scotland, but none for Dissenters whom he derided as flourishing largely because of the absence of a sufficiently endowed 'National Church'. This had left the colony a 'great Moral Wilderness' where both Catholics and Dissenters rose up like weeds.[43] 'In this', Burton opined, 'an injury was done to the National Church, and to the common cause of True Religion'.[44] On these points, Burton was promoting a cause that had been swept away by the New South Wales and Van Diemen's Land Church Acts.

Ullathorne challenged the exclusivist premises of Burton's *State of Religion and Education in New South Wales* (1840) as '[s]ix hundred pages of hot-pressed octavo', bound in green for jealousy, a receptacle for the grievances of 'one of those *ultra* parties of men who become discontented because from the nature of things they can no longer be dominant'.[45] Ullathorne also attacked the reputation of Protestant clerical magistrates, including Samuel Marsden and Henry Fulton, who in four well-attested cases in 1822 and 1823 had ordered prisoners be regularly flogged, and kept on bread and water until they confessed to minor crimes.[46] 'I would not have touched upon such things', Ullathorne notes, 'had not those persons been exalted as models of the apostolic life, whilst the poor Catholic and his priest are covered with all revilings'.[47] While Burton was an unreconstructed Protestant, his *ultra* party and denunciation of the moral state of the colony provided a useful prop for the Molesworth SC on Transportation.

Molesworth SC on Transportation, 1836

On 14 July 1837, the Select Committee of the House of Commons appointed 'to inquire into the System of Transportation, its efficacy as a Punishment, its influence on the Moral State in the Penal Colonies,

---

[42] Ibid.   [43] Ibid.   [44] Ibid.

[45] William Bernard Ullathorne, *A Reply to Judge Burton, of the Supreme Court of New South Wales, on 'the State of Religion' in the Colony* (Sydney: A. W. Duncan, 1840), p. vii.

[46] Ibid., 9–10. For the 1825 Grand Jury and Executive Council inquiry into 'acts of magisterial authority beyond the law' including those of the Parramatta clerical magistrates, see Lisa Ford and David Andrew Roberts, 'Legal Change, Convict Activism and the Reform of Penal Relocation in Colonial New South Wales', *Australian Historical Studies*, 46.2 (2015), 184.

[47] Ullathorne, *Reply to Judge Burton*, pp. 9–10. For defenders of Marsden, see Allen, 'The Myth of the Flogging Parson', 486–501; Gladwin, 'Flogging Parsons?', 386–403.

and how far it is susceptible of Improvement', tabled its evidence, and then, on 3 August 1838, its full report.[48] The committee of fifteen members of parliament chaired by Molesworth was the most senior and significant of all the parliamentary inquiries into transportation and among the most important legal initiatives of the reformist Whig regimes in power from 1830 to 1841. Besides Molesworth, it had an exceptional membership, including the home secretary, Lord John Russell, Sir Henry George Grey, Sir Robert Peel (1788–1850) and other leading politicians from across the political spectrum.[49] In his first despatch on receiving the Report, Governor Gipps observed that it had produced 'a very consider-able sensation in this colony'.[50] Reaction to the report in Van Diemen's Land was no less hostile and was led by churchmen. Franklin reported on a public meeting which called on the 'clergy of all denominations' to report on the 'morality, decency of conduct, and attention to religious duties' of the free community.[51]

Australian historians have generally judged Molesworth harshly for manipulating evidence to support his view that transportation, which he equated with slavery, should be abolished.[52] A. G. L. Shaw asserted that the SC's condemnation of assignment and its recommendations 'bore little relation to the evidence presented to it, and rest largely on the preconceptions of Molesworth and his disciples'.[53] Norma Townsend credited the quality of the committee's deliberation of the evidence.[54] Isobelle Barrett Meyering has suggested that the case against Molesworth is unproven in relation to flogging, but that he has generally been seen as a prejudicial figure in league with metropolitan and anti-colonial forces.[55] The greatest criticism concerns his role in intensifying homo-phobic panic, a claim first raised by John Ritchie, elaborated by Kirsty Reid and argued with particular vehemence by Babette Smith.[56] Reid has

---

[48] *Molesworth SC on Transportation (Minutes)*, BPP 1837 (518) XIX.1; *Molesworth SC on Transportation (Report)*, BPP 1837–1838 (669) XXII.1 (Hereafter *Molesworth SC on Transportation (Minutes)* and *Molesworth SC on Transportation (Report)*).

[49] L. Radzinowicz, *A History of English Criminal Law and Its Administration from 1750*, 4 vols. (London: Stevens, 1948–1968), vol. IV, p. 334.

[50] Gipps to Glenelg, 18 July 1838, *Transportation and the Assignment of Convicts*, BPP 1839 (76), XXXIV.551, p. 553.

[51] Franklin to Glenelg, 6 October 1838; W. Wood to Franklin, 7 September 1838, Ibid., pp. 556–557.

[52] McKenzie, *Scandal in the Colonies*, p. 146.   [53] Shaw, *Convicts and the Colonies*, p. 272.

[54] Norma Townsend, 'The Molesworth Enquiry: Does the Report Fit the Evidence?', *Journal of Australian Studies*, 1.1 (1977), 33–51.

[55] Isobelle Barrett Meyering, 'Abolitionism, Settler Violence and the Case against Flogging', *History Australia*, 7.1 (2010), 6.1–6.18.

[56] John Ritchie, 'Towards Ending an Unclean Thing', *Australian Historical Studies*, 17 (1976), 144–164; Reid, *Gender, Crime and Empire*.

also argued that the claimed 'horrors' of convict life were adopted by radical politicians, including Chartists transported to Van Diemen's Land, to validate their own vision of a better life for working people at home.[57] Most agree that on many points, including allegations of rampant crime in New South Wales and the prevalence of 'unnatural crime' (the most common euphemism for homosexuality and bestiality), the Molesworth Report was both wrong and intentionally provocative.[58] It promoted a particularly harsh view of the assignment system, equating it with slavery, insisting that this led to demoralization of the settlers who employed convict labour.

Overall the Molesworth Committee recommended abolishing the existing system of transportation on the utilitarian principles that it failed to fulfil its central purposes. It concluded: 'the two main characteristics of Transportation, as a punishment, are, inefficiency in deterring from crime, and remarkable efficiency, not in reforming, but in still further corrupting those who undergo the punishment'.[59] The Committee conceded that an immediate alternative to transportation was not available, since investment was needed to create suitable forms of secondary punishment. They suggested that British convicts be subject to forced labour in penitentiaries of the kind pioneered in America on the 'separate system', which they perceived as a humane alternative to physical punishments, while inflicting a satisfactory yield of psychological pain sufficient to 'inspire terror'.[60] The expense of constructing such prisons prompted the tabling of two alternatives in the colonies: the separate system, and the radical innovation of Captain Maconochie's mark system. The ever-increasing cost of transportation – estimated at between £400,000 and £500,000 annually, not including the hulks in both Bermuda and at home – lent urgency to these deliberations.[61] The final recommendations were that transportation, if maintained, should not continue in settled areas, but be reformed in new penal colonies with long-term prisoners sent to the existing penal establishments of Tasman's Peninsula and Norfolk Island, 'provided the system of punishment now pursued there was completely altered'.[62] This led to the abolition of private assignment, a halt to transportation to New South Wales and the implementation of the probation system in Van Diemen's Land, considered in Chapter 9. The Committee recommended that Captain

[57] Kirsty Reid, 'The Horrors of Convict Life', *Cultural & Social History*, 5.4 (2008), 481–495.
[58] Brian Fletcher, 'Australia's Convict Origins', *History Today*, 42.10 (1992), pp. 39–43.
[59] *Molesworth SC on Transportation (Report)*, p. xii.   [60] Ibid.   [61] Ibid., p. xliii.
[62] Ibid.

Maconochie's mark system be given a trial (Chapter 7), at least until well-constructed penitentiaries were erected in Britain. It further recommended, following Maconochie, that no one be sent to a penitentiary for life, 'as such punishment destroys all hope, and renders the culprit reckless'.[63] In order to make Maconochie's system more effective it was proposed that it be married to the hardy nostrum of greater religious instruction. Apart from the latter aspiration, none of the six final recommendations were religious in nature, but the Committee supported Evangelical models of penal reform, including separation, classification and religious instruction.[64] This was a more secular inquiry than previous committees and most witnesses who testified were laypeople, including former colonial administrators such as Colonel Arthur.[65] The three clergy who provided evidence were the Rev. Henry Bishop (c.1800–1857), a commissioner of the Poor Law Inquiry, John Dunmore Lang, Presbyterian minister and emigration advocate and Ullathorne, Catholic Vicar General of New South Wales. There was considerable attention given to religion in the voluminous appendix to the report, including a letter from Richard Whately, which was put into evidence by Bishop.[66]

In the colonies, the immediate popular reaction to the Molesworth Report was one of outrage.[67] As the metropolitan press published the salacious details of witness testimony,[68] the colonists were incredulous at the implication that all sections of society, from the basest convict to substantial convict employers, were complicit in crime and immorality. There were public meetings held throughout 1838 and 1839 in the course of which clerical opinion was invoked to defend the reputation of the colonists. In Launceston, a report in the *Times* prompted a lengthy rebuttal following a meeting on 1 September 1838, chaired by William Wood, a former regimental paymaster who would later lead petitions for the continuation of transportation to Van Diemen's Land.[69] The meeting protested about the statements in the British papers, 'calculated to inflict the deepest wounds on their own feelings'. To dress the wounds, statements were prepared from clerical and governing authorities,

---

[63] Ibid., xlvi.   [64] Ibid., p. xlvii.   [65] Chapter 3.

[66] *Molesworth SC on Transportation (Report)*, appendix A, pp. 145–171; 'Letter from the Archbishop of Dublin to the Rev. H. Bishop'; appendix L, Ibid., p. 299. For Whately see Chapter 5.

[67] McKenzie, *Scandal in the Colonies*, pp. 146, 150–151.

[68] *Leeds Times*, 23 December 1837; *Spectator*, 25 August 1838, p. 11; *The Atlas*, 17 December 1837.

[69] Anonymous, *An Answer to the Calumnies of the English Press* (Launceston VDL: Dowling, 1839).

including Lt Governor John Franklin, Mr Joseph Orton (1795–1842), superintendent of the Wesleyan Mission, John Lillie (1806–1866), moderator of the Van Diemen's Land Presbytery, William Hutchins (1792–1841), first Anglican archdeacon of Van Diemen's Land and Frederick Miller (1806–62) and Charles Price (1807–1891) on behalf of the Congregational Union. 'We readily attest', Miller and Price affirmed, 'that as regards social order and decorum, and a disposition to sanction and support the institutions of religion, the free population of this colony will not suffer from comparison ... [with] any part of the mother country'.[70] There was one significant omission from this list; there was no Catholic representative. Ullathorne could not join in the outrage of the colonists because he had testified to the Molesworth SC and was held to be complicit in its findings.

William Bernard Ullathorne

Ullathorne was not the only Catholic priest who campaigned against transportation, however he did so with such eloquence that his writings achieved impact well beyond the original intended audience.[71] Born into a large Catholic gentry family of diminished circumstances in Yorkshire, Ullathorne spent four years at sea as a midshipman before entering the English Benedictine school at Downside where he came under Polding's influence, later stating: 'In him I found all that my soul needed.'[72] Volunteering for the Benedictines' Australian mission, Ullathorne, like Polding, benefitted from Governor Bourke's liberal reforms. Still only twenty-six, Ullathorne was appointed vicar general under the authority of Vicar Apostolic William Placid Morris, whose diocese covered all of Australia, the Cape of Good Hope and Mauritius. This territory was so vast that Ullathorne was effectively on his own when he arrived in Sydney in February 1833. The following year, working together with leading Catholic lawyer, Roger Therry (1800–1874) and the Rev. John McEncroe (1794–1868), the colony's senior priest, Ullathorne secured Polding's appointment as vicar apostolic, a missionary appointment with the status of a bishop for New South Wales.

Almost immediately, Ullathorne and Polding launched an energetic ministry to a Catholic population made up of a substantial minority of Irish convicts and former convicts – just how substantial provoked

---

[70] Ibid., 15.
[71] See, for instance, Whately, *Substance of a Speech on Transportation*, pp. 41, 55, 79, 80.
[72] Ullathorne, *Cabin-Boy to Archbishop*, p. 31.

dispute, but it was between a third (Ullathorne) and a quarter (Burton).[73] This was a radicalizing experience for Ullathorne who was strongly affected by his experiences on Norfolk Island, which he first visited after the 1834 convict rebellion at the same time as Judge Burton.[74] Burton was chosen, by lot, from his fellow judges to travel to Norfolk Island and conduct the trials, which saw thirty convicts sentenced to execution.[75] After sentencing them to death, Burton gave the convicted men a sermon on forgiveness and the mercy of the Lamb:

Forgive all men their trespasses, as you hope your trespasses shall be forgiven you. Take advantage of all that charitable assistance, which pious and devout persons may tender you. Apply yourselves to the book of life, and look up to the Lamb of God ... Show by your penitence, a deep and contrite sense of your awful situation, return in your hearts to that state of childhood in which you had parents, or beloved relatives, who instructed you to the God whom they taught you to worship, and to the prayers they taught you.[76]

Back in Sydney, Burton's claims for expenses were considered excessive, as were the number of capital convictions. The governor and Executive Council reprieved twenty-two of them, leaving thirteen to be hanged over two days in the presence of all the officers and men.[77]

These executions were delayed, enabling a Protestant and a Catholic chaplain, the Rev. Henry Tarlton Stiles (1808–1867) and Ullathorne, to travel to Norfolk Island and supply the 'consolation of religion'.[78] On arrival, Ullathorne describes a 'heart-rending scene' where he announced which of the men had received the Governor's mercy and which had not. Those who were reprieved wept to hear they were going to remain on Norfolk Island, whereas those condemned: 'with dry eyes, thanked God they were to be delivered from this horrid place'.[79] Ullathorne later had a

---

[73] For comparison with the Catholic population of Britain and Ireland, and their respective prisons, see Tables 6.1–6.3.

[74] Judith F. Champ, *William Bernard Ullathorne* (Leominster: Gracewing, 2006), p. 54.

[75] *Australian*, 22 August 1834. For newspaper accounts of the trials, see R. v Douglas and others [1834] Supreme Court of New South Wales, *Sydney Gazette*, 13 September 1834, 'Decisions of the Superior Courts of New South Wales, 1788–1899' (Macquarie University, www.law.mq.edu.au/).

[76] 'J. Burton, 22 July 1834', *Sydney Gazette*, 27 September 1834.

[77] Bourke to T. Spring Rice, 15 January 1835, *Molesworth SC on Transportation (Minutes)*, appendix 7, p. 202.

[78] *The Australian*, 5 September 1834.

[79] Ullathorne, *Cabin-Boy to Archbishop*, pp. 84–85. Note that Causer contests the view that any men participated in the 'suicide lotteries', but Ullathorne's account makes clear that many were happier to die than remain under the discipline they endured on the island. See Tim Causer, '"The Worst Types of Sub-Human Beings"? The Myth and Reality of the Convicts of the Second Penal Settlement at Norfolk Island, 1825–1855', *Islands of History (Sydney)*, n.v. (2011), 8–31.

distinguished career as Catholic bishop of Birmingham (1850–1888), with highlights including attendance at the First Vatican Council in 1870 where he supported the moderates on papal infallibility.[80] However, it was his experiences on Norfolk Island that most moved him. In his autobiography, Ullathorne gave an account of the execution of the 1834 rebels, including his passionate address to those permitted to follow the executed men's coffins to their graves.[81] On the scaffold, he had trained the Catholic prisoners to mentally rehearse the words of the psalm (and some of the last words of Christ on the cross): 'Into thy hands I commend my spirit. Lord Jesus receive my soul!' (Luke 23:46). To his surprise, they said the words aloud, 'repeating it until the fall and the ropes stopped their voices forever'.[82] These theatrical details were omitted from both the accounts of Commandant Joseph Anderson (1790–1877), who served from 1834 to 1839, and Governor Bourke's dry recitation of the facts in his despatch to the colonial secretary.[83] The breathless hush during the executions may have been enhanced by Anderson's instruction to the convicts that his men had orders to open fire at any sign of resistance.[84]

Religious services to the second convict settlement on Norfolk Island had a curious beginning.[85] In his memoirs, written some fifty years after the events, Anderson recalled his efforts to improve religious provision by making use of a convict called Robert Atcherley (or Ackerley) Taylor (b. 1784), 'the swindling parson of Botany Bay' who had been convicted of forgery,[86] and an educated Catholic called Sheahan, also a prisoner.[87] They were in place when Backhouse and Walker visited in March

---

[80] Ullathorne to Thomas Joseph Brown, 28 October 1869; Champ, *William Bernard Ullathorne*, p. 364.

[81] Ullathorne, *Cabin-Boy to Archbishop*, pp. 81–86. Remarkably a number of these men were provided with their own headstones and respectful memorials.

[82] Ibid., 84.

[83] Bourke to T. Spring Rice, 15 January 1835. *Molesworth SC on Transportation (Minutes)*, appendix 7, p. 202. Rice, an Irish Whig, was briefly Secretary of State for War and the Colonies, from 5 June to 14 November 1834.

[84] Joseph Jocelyn Anderson, *Recollections of a Peninsular Veteran* (London: E. Arnold, 1913), p. 137.

[85] See Chapter 7 and Table 7.1 for Norfolk Island's resident clergy.

[86] 'Church and State, Swindling and Botany Bay', *The Reformists' Register*, 1 (8 September 1811), p. 45. Taylor was not in any kind of ministerial orders, but in the course of a busy career as a fraud, had pretended to be a vicar of Hertford as well as a naval chaplain; 'Clerkenwell Sessions – The Sham Parson', *Edinburgh Annual Register*, 4.2 (1811), p. 167.

[87] Anderson, *Recollections*, pp. 158–161. Sheehan appears to have been 'authorised to instruct the prisoners in the rudiments of religion' following correspondence with the Rev. John Joseph Therry (1790–1864) in Sydney. See John Cullen, 'Norfolk Island: Its Catholic Story', *Advocate (Melbourne)*, 13 September 1928, p. 9.

1835 and commented quizzically on the peculiar status of convict ministers of the gospel who, 'appear to be well acquainted with the principles of religion, at least theoretically'.[88] Anderson accepted the executions as part of his duty and essential to restoring security on the island. Although not the harshest Norfolk Island commandant,[89] Anderson's benign representation of his regime was challenged by the Anglican chaplain, the Rev. Thomas Atkins (1808–1860), who accused him of cruelty and financial abuses and being unfit to command.[90] As with other denunciations of the 'horrors of transportation', many testimonies were embroidered to fit the compelling 'hell on earth' stereotype, with clerics particularly vulnerable to grandstanding in the aftermath of clashes with both church and penal authorities.[91]

As for Ullathorne, he determinedly preached the evils of transportation through his publications,[92] but even more in 'the two most eventful years of my life' he spent 'always on the move' in England, Ireland and Rome, delivering lectures on the Australian Mission.[93] He persuaded the government to fund the travel of fifteen Catholic priests, seminarians, Sisters of Charity, schoolmasters and an editor of a Catholic newspaper. In a missionary sermon preached in Canterbury Cathedral in September 1835, Archdeacon Broughton objected to these arrivals for 'promoting the Spread of Popish idolatry and delusion in the various districts of the interior'.[94]

---

[88] James Backhouse and George Washington Walker, 'Report of a Visit to the Penal Settlement of Norfolk Island, 4 March to 29 April 1835', Cambridge University Library RCMS 278/3/2: 6. They were repelled by the 'dreadfully profane language' of the convicts, particularly when unaware of their presence, Ibid.: 2.

[89] For a forensic examination of all twenty-one commandants, see Reg Wright, 'The Trial of the Twenty-One: A Reassessment of the Commandants of Norfolk Island, 1788–1814 and 1825–1855', (PhD thesis, Macquarie University, 2001).

[90] K. J. Cable, 'Atkins, Thomas (1808–1860)', *ADB*. For Atkins's quarrels with Anderson, Thomas Atkins, *Reminiscences of Twelve Years' Residence in Tasmania and New South Wales* (Malvern: Advertiser Office, 1869), pp. 21–57.

[91] For other examples see Chapter 8.

[92] Ullathorne's publications relating to transportation comprise: *The Catholic Mission in Australasia* (1837); *The Horrors of Transportation* (1838); *Substance of a Sermon against Drunkenness* (1838); *A Reply to Judge Burton* (1840); and *On the Management of Criminals* (1866). Posthumous publications include William Bernard Ullathorne, *The Autobiography of Archbishop Ullathorne*, 2 vols. (London: Burns & Oates, 1891–1892); Ullathorne, *Cabin-Boy to Archbishop*. There are two biographies of Ullathorne: *Cuthbert Butler, The Life and Times of Bishop Ullathorne, 1806–1889* (London: Burns, 1926); Champ, *Different Kind of Monk*.

[93] Ullathorne, *Cabin-Boy to Archbishop*, pp. 99–107.

[94] Broughton, 'Sermon preached in Canterbury Cathedral, 17 September 1835', Burton, *State of Religion*, p. 301.

The Catholic Mission in Australasia (1837)

The Catholic Mission in Australasia (1837) was the most dramatic of Ullathorne's writings on transportation and its horrors, written to raise money for the Catholic mission and warn others of the 'lot of the transported convict'.[95] Quickly running to four editions, Ullathorne admitted it 'produced quite a sensation'.[96] According to Michael Glancey, the origins of this paper 'long ago ceased to exist', but Ullathorne explains that he wrote a 'long paper for the publication of the Society for the Propagation of the Faith'.[97] This was published in the first English issue of the *Annals of the Propagation of the Faith*, the official organ of the Oeuvre de la Propagation de la Foi, the Catholic charity founded in Lyons in 1822 to support missions worldwide; it was also translated into Italian. Ullathorne's essay was a masterly piece of expository writing, drawing on scripture, Irish and Catholic nationalist grievances against the British and sympathy for convicts for its emotive charge. Dublin and Edinburgh reviewers recognized its literary qualities and Ullathorne claimed that it inspired several English ladies into convents.[98] What made it so effective?

Sympathy for convicts was not entirely absent in secular or Protestant writing about penal reform. For example, in Charles Dickens's *Great Expectations* (1861) Pip's act of sympathy for Abel Magwitch is the unwitting source of his good fortune. It was also part of the discourse supporting the transportation of exiles and experiments in reformist transportation in Western Australia, and on the convict ships from the same era. But it was rare. As Daniel Ritchie notes, 'Alas! Sympathy and condolence are less seldom found in a prison than their disagreeable and galling contraries.'[99] What was truly exceptional about Ullathorne's *Catholic Mission* was the absence of the parodic moralizing or contempt for the culprit more typical of penitential reflections on crime and the prisoner.[100] In missionary mode, Ullathorne demanded that the convict be imagined not as a social outcast but as a penitent whose physical

---

[95] Ullathorne, *Catholic Mission*.   [96] Glancey (ed.), *Characteristics*, p. xi.

[97] Ullathorne, *Cabin-Boy to Archbishop*, p. 99. Possibly the same as the 'Report to the Holy See on the Mission of Australia', trans. into Italian by Dr Collier, revised by Abbate Peschiatelli (Rome, 1837); Glancey (ed.), *Characteristics*, p. xiii.

[98] *Dublin Review*, 5 (1838), p. 274; *Edinburgh Catholic Magazine*, 2 (1838), p. 28; Glancey (ed.), *Characteristics*, p. xi; For the English lady converts, Ullathorne, *Cabin-Boy to Archbishop*, p. 99.

[99] Daniel Ritchie (ed.), *The Voice of Our Exiles* (Edinburgh: John Menzies, 1854), p. 271. Comment comes from the *Pentonjee Bomanjee Journal*, one of a number of convict newspapers produced by exiles.

[100] For example, as discussed in Chapter 2, Holford, *The Convict's Complaint in 1815*.

torments recalled the suffering body of Christ: 'Oh, remember the human lot, and have pity! The presence of Christ is amongst them: his wounds and his agonies bleed anew: he calls on you for help. Will you refuse him: No: for you are also a child of his sorrows.'[101] To add weight to his argument, Ullathorne inserted descriptions of a series of flagellations in a pamphlet written by 'An Unpaid Magistrate', well known to be the Catholic lawyer Roger Therry.[102] The apposition was a powerful indictment of penal discipline, suggesting that young people, including a disproportionate number of poor Irish Catholics, were flogged, just as Christ was scourged and humiliated.

Sensitive to his Catholic and mostly Irish audience, Ullathorne evoked a penal time, equivalent to the persecution of the early Christian martyrs, the English Catholics during the Reformation or in Ireland under British occupation, when the Catholic population was denied the comforts of true religion. He denounced the physical torments inflicted by Protestant clergy in the penal colonies: 'Clerical magistrates, of another creed, awarded him the scourge and darksome imprisonment for refusing to enter the protestant churches, and to mingle in a worship which his conscience disowned.'[103] Arthur's regime in Van Diemen's Land was depicted as 'a scene of absolute destitution' for Catholics: 'The Governor was a man of a pious turn of mind, who thought religion and education of the utmost value to everyone but a Catholic.'[104] Perhaps this remark prompted Arthur to provide his minute iteration of religious services for different denominations, which included more provision for Catholics than Ullathorne alleged.[105] To back his case, Ullathorne implied that the proportion of Catholics was systematically understated by the government, something strongly disputed by Judge Burton.[106] Using skills honed as a missionary preacher, Ullathorne invoked the cadences of penitential prayer familiar to his Catholic readers and listeners. As the natural climax of the pamphlet, Ullathorne included twenty-two convict

---

[101] Ullathorne, *Catholic Mission*, p. 55.

[102] Ibid., 56–57. An Unpaid Magistrate (Roger Therry), *Observations on the 'Hole and Corner Petition'* (Sydney, 1834); Brian Walsh, 'The Politics of Convict Control in Colonial New South Wales: —"the Notorious OPQ" and the Clandestine Press', *Journal of the Royal Australian Historical Society*. December (2010), 149–167. The appendix to Ullathorne's pamphlet with its list of floggings is omitted in the version printed in *Annals*.

[103] Ullathorne, *Catholic Mission*, p. 9.   [104] Ibid., 11.

[105] Arthur to Glenelg, 26 January 1836, *Religious Instruction, Australia*, BPP 1837 (112) XLIII.21, pp. 68–72.

[106] Burton, *State of Religion*, p. 303. Using the census returns, Burton suggests that the Catholics made up about one-fourth of the free population in 1836, and up to one-third of the convicts.

'inspirations of sorrow' which closely paraphrased the psalms and Old Testament books of Ezekiel, Job and Jeremiah in the Catholic Douai bible.[107] 'The iron has entered their souls – the scourge devours them', he lamented:[108] 'They look for death, as those who dig for treasure, and it cometh not; they are exceedingly rejoiced when they have found a grave.'[109] Ullathorne's portrait of the convict mission invoked tropes of Irish and Catholic suffering which have continued to resonate with many Australians of Irish descent to this day.[110]

Ullathorne's *Catholic Mission* helped bring new recruits to the mission. But this work was also used to fuel tales of the moral depravity of convicts of New South Wales and Van Diemen's Land. Incorporated into the 1838 SC Report, Ullathorne's words were mined for their sensational content. Reproduced almost in its entirety by the Evangelical physician Michael Ryan in his admonitory *Prostitution in London* (1839), Ullathorne's testimony was redacted to parade colonial sexual aberration: 'the immorality of the convicts', 'the natives schooled in horror by English prisoners', 'their horrible treatment', 'account of female convicts … almost all drunken and abandoned prostitutes', 'married women the common property of male convict servants', 'the penal settlement of Norfolk Island worse than Sodom and Gomorrah'.[111] Ryan aimed to demonstrate the horror of 'moral depravity', with cautionary examples of how unregulated sex produces personal and social misery.[112] This was polemical and admonitory writing, not factual. Just like Burton's 'cage of unclean birds', Ullathorne's rhetorical vision of the fate of convicts and the Catholic people in New South Wales was hardly accurate. James Waldersee demonstrated that by 1829 two-thirds of Catholics in the colony were either emancipists or had arrived free, and there was a substantial respectable middle class.[113] While Ullathorne's motives were excellent, his portrait of the colony met a storm of

---

[107] The Douai is an English Bible revised by Bishop Richard Challoner and Bernard MacMahon and published in Dublin from 1783 to 1810.

[108] Ullathorne, *Catholic Mission*, p. 51.   [109] Ibid., 52.

[110] For a review of modern nationalist identification with the convict past, which enjoyed a resurgence at the time of the Australian Bicentenary of 1988, see Greg Jackman, 'From Stain to Saint: Ancestry, Archaeology, and Agendas in Tasmania's Convict Heritage – a View from Port Arthur', *Historical Archaeology*, 43.3 (2009), 101–112. Jackman notes (p. 103) that in a 1999 survey, 49 per cent of Tasmanians claimed a convict ancestor, which was almost as high as in 1847 when transportation was at its peak.

[111] Harling, 'The Trouble with Convicts', 80–110.

[112] Catie Gilchrist, 'Male Convict Sexuality in the Penal Colonies of Australia, 1820–1850', (PhD thesis, University of Sydney, 2004b) at 33: 'These authors presented themselves as brave explorers into the social abyss.'

[113] James Waldersee, *Catholic Society in New South Wales, 1788–1860* (Sydney: Sydney University Press, 1974), p. 103.

opposition, undermining the cause of both Catholics and convicts. It was something he never regretted, particularly when the colonists came to embrace his point of view as their own.[114]

The Horrors of Transportation 1838

Following a request from the under secretary of Ireland, Thomas Drummond (1797–1840), Ullathorne wrote a second pamphlet entitled 'The Horrors of Transportation'. Read and approved by Lord Morpeth (1802–1864), chief secretary of Ireland (1835–1841), twenty thousand copies were printed and sent to all the prisons and gaols in Ireland and all parish clergy.[115] Morpeth's support was important, representing one of those liberal Anglican politicians who became active in the 1830s, seeking to moderate the harsher features of both Radical politics and extreme Evangelicalism.[116] Addressed to 'The People', Ullathorne's pamphlet aimed to destroy the 'terrible delusion' that transportation was not a punishment.[117] Unlike his missionary tract, it was not primarily religious but admonitory and informative and focussed on two themes: the subject condition of the convict under assignment and conditions in the ultra-penal settlements of Norfolk Island and Port Arthur.

Transported convicts, Ullathorne confirmed, were slaves who received no earnings and endured the tyranny of magistrates empowered to extend sentences indefinitely.[118] As in his previous pamphlet, Ullathorne described floggings, using accounts collected following Governor Bourke's legislation to better regulate magistrates' summary powers in New South Wales.[119] Ullathorne referred to reports from ten magistrates, describing in grim detail 247 floggings all inflicted in September 1833.[120] Few magistrates expressed any distaste for their duty,[121] though at Campbelltown, George Kenyon Holden protested that he personally felt every blow: 'I do not profess to have yet acquired the power of

---

[114] Ullathorne, 'On the Management of Criminals', p. 12.
[115] Ullathorne, *Cabin-Boy to Archbishop*, p. 107.
[116] Hilton, 'Whiggery, Religion and Social Reform', 829–859.
[117] William Bernard Ullathorne, *The Horrors of Transportation Briefly Unfolded* (Dublin: Richard Coyne, 1838). Another edition was printed in Birmingham by R. P. Stone.
[118] Ibid., 4–7.
[119] David Andrew Roberts, 'The "Illegal Sentences Which Magistrates Were Daily Passing": The Backstory to Governor Richard Bourke's 1832 Punishment and Summary Jurisdiction Act in Convict New South Wales', *The Journal of Legal History*, 38.3 (2017), 231–253.
[120] Ullathorne, *Horrors*, p. 14.
[121] For the Magistrates' descriptions, *Secondary Punishments*, BPP 1834 (614), appendix E, pp. 17–33.

witnessing the infliction of pain with such unmoved nerves, as may be, perhaps, justly considered to be as necessary in a magistrate dealing with this subject, as in a surgeon when inflicting pain for the beneficial purposes of his art.'[122] Other magistrates suggested that army service inflicted greater punishment and coolly recommended ways to ensure the 'instrument' was sufficiently heavy, powerful and consistent. Rarely was there overt sympathy for the flagellator's victim. Ullathorne provided an eye-opening account of conditions at Port Arthur and Norfolk Island, where he claimed men preferred death to returning. While prisoners were generally better fed than the starving poor of Ireland, Ullathorne reminded listeners of the words of scripture: '"Their bread is loathsome to their eyes, and their meat unto their soul" (Ezechiel 12:19). Oh! Say not, then, that the convict is happy, because he has bread and meat.'[123] Back in the colony, reactions to Ullathorne's testimony to the Molesworth SC and pamphlets on transportation were reported in the *Sydney Herald*. 'Crimes unmentionable were declared to be so frequent, so much so that this Colony is worse than the ancient city of Sodom.'[124] In retaliation for spreading scandal, Ullathorne's superior was urged to discipline him. A settler who met Ullathorne on his return to the colony made clear why he had aroused such vituperation: 'Sir, we can never forgive you. For what you said was the truth. They will take away our convict labour, and we shall all be ruined.'[125] Thirteen years later, those same colonists were using the evidence of the Molesworth SC to bring down transportation.

For rather different reasons, Judge Burton also alerted the colony to what he saw as its runaway culture of crime. In a scripture-laden address to the Bathurst Circuit Court jury in May 1841, he denounced those who regarded reform rather than punishment as the duty of the magistrate:

I deny that convicts should be treated as sick patients, morally sick, whose reformation is the only object, and who are to be petted, and flattered, and beguiled into reformation, or an appearance of reformation. I deny that the sole end of punishment is the reformation of the criminal; this is mistaken, and, in my opinion, a mischievous theory. Another object of punishment is to be a 'terror to evil doers'.[126]

---

[122] Kenyon to McLeay, 1 October 1833, Ibid., p. 25.   [123] Ullathorne, *Horrors*, p. 21.
[124] *Sydney Morning Herald*, 13 July 1838, p. 2.
[125] Ullathorne, *On the Management of Criminals*, p. 12.
[126] 'Bathurst Circuit Court', *Sydney Morning Herald*, 1 May 1841, p. 2. Bruce Kersher, 'Perish or Prosper: The Law and Convict Transportation in the British Empire, 1700–1850', *Law and History Review*, 21.3 (2003), 558.

On this occasion, Burton's charge was delivered following his attendance at Anglican Divine Service in the presence of Archdeacon Broughton. Burton presented himself as a Christian judge, authorized by the church and armed by the law to defend the nation against 'drunkards, blasphemers, and those who commit lewdness'.[127] Burton's jurors would have immediately recognized the scriptural origin of his suggestion that the law be overall a 'terror to evil doers'. Texts from both the Old and New Testaments were regularly cited to defend a draconian law code, but the most important and frequently cited was Romans 13:3–4:

For rulers are not a terror to good works, but to the evil. Wilt thou then not be afraid of the power? Do that which is good, and thou shalt have praise of the same: For he is the minister of God to thee for good. But if thou do that which is evil, be afraid; for he beareth not the sword in vain: for he is the minister of God, a revenger to execute wrath upon him that doeth evil. (Romans 13:3–4)

British Protestants who accepted the Westminster Confession of Faith (1646), including Presbyterians, Congregationalists and Baptists, were assured that condemning evildoers to death and exile was no offence in God's eyes. Civil magistrates were ordained by God, who 'armed them with the power of the sword, for the defence and encouragement of them that are good, and for the punishment of evildoers'.[128] Because it justified their role in judicially sanctioned violence, Romans 13, 3–4 continued to resonate with agents of criminal justice. As Randall McGowen has been eloquent in arguing, the old draconian criminal law had been justified on the grounds of these texts.[129] Underneath the reformist rhetoric, the lion of greater severity in punishment was still lying in wait.

Horrors of Transportation

One paradox of the anti-transportation campaign was the perennial belief that it held no terror for criminals yet plunged the convict into a personal moral abyss. The Molesworth Report noted the proposal by Sir George Arthur to '[d]iffuse a knowledge of the hapless lot of some offenders, by

---

[127] 'Bathurst Circuit Court', *Sydney Morning Herald*, 1 May 1841, p. 2.
[128] 'The Westminster Confession of Faith, 1646', chapter 23, Tudor Jones (ed.), *Protestant Nonconformist Texts*, 4 vols. (Aldershot: Ashgate, 2006), vol. I, p. 183.
[129] Randall McGowen, '"He Beareth Not the Sword in Vain": Religion and the Criminal Law in Eighteenth-Century England', *Eighteenth-Century Studies*, 21.2 (1987), 192–211; Randall McGowen, 'A Powerful Sympathy: Terror, the Prison, and Humanitarian Reform in Early Nineteenth-Century Britain', *Journal of British Studies*, 25 (1986), 312–334; Randall McGowen, 'The Problem of Punishment in Eighteenth-Century England', in Simon Devereaux and Paul Griffiths (eds.), *Penal Practice and Culture, 1500–1900* (Houndmills: Palgrave Macmillan, 2004), 210–231.

means of pamphlets, tracts, pictures of convicts in irons and others under other punishments, to be published by the Government'.[130] The under secretary of Ireland circulated Ullathorne's pamphlet on 'The Horrors of Transportation' for just this purpose. Following the Molesworth Report, a body of quasi-officially sanctioned literature appeared, warning and deterring those who might assume that transportation was an easy option. Initially, warnings were written by judges and religious ministers and might be delivered from the bench or the pulpit. But the genre acquired a life of its own, feeding into popular melodramas of aristocratic brutality, libertine excess and contempt for the poor printed in chapbooks, attacked by preachers and dramatized in the theatre.[131] Kirsty Reid has shown that the 'the horrors of transportation' were promoted by the radical left, who represented penal colonies as a socialist dystopia.[132] Frost delivered lectures under this title, based on the experience of the Dorchester labourers transported for agrarian violence in 1834.[133] James Loveless and his fellow swing rioters provided their own accounts of their wrongs and suffering in Van Diemen's Land.[134] Most of these accounts display varying degrees of contempt for their fellow prisoners; the horror was their own unjust imprisonment, not that of the criminals they shared it with.

Rare though they are, fresher and sometimes more subversive unpublished convict narratives have the virtue of occasionally slipping the straitjacket provided by ghostwriters with moralizing, demoralizing or money-making agendas.[135] Published narratives more often fall into a common genre in which the convict is said to have been born of humble but honest parents, led astray by women, drink and companions, suffers under transportation (while retaining his moral values) and – like the Prodigal Son (Luke 15:11–32) – returns home, at which point readers are urged to mend their lives. *The Life of John Broxup* (1850) is a good example. Broxup was a former soldier who was repeatedly flogged, both in the army and following his transportation to Van Diemen's Land for receiving stolen goods in 1835. Broxup was born in York and met James

---

[130] *Molesworth SC on Transportation (Report)*, p. xx.
[131] Anna Clark, *The Struggle for the Breeches: Gender and the Making of the British Working Class* (London: Rivers Oram Press, 1995), p. 169.
[132] Reid, 'The Horrors of Convict Life'.
[133] John Frost, *The Horrors of Convict Life, Two Lectures, 31 August 1856* (London: Holyoake, 1856).
[134] James Loveless et al., *A Narrative of the Sufferings of J. Loveless, J. Brine, and T. & J. Standfield, Four of the Dorchester Labourers; Displaying the Horrors of Transportation* (London, 1838).
[135] For nine manuscript autobiographies of convicts see 'Norfolk Island Convict Papers', c.1842–1867, SLNSW MLMSS 102, Q168 [Reel CY 2754].

Backhouse and George Washington Walker during his time in a Launceston chain gang. He recalled their discourse to the convicts in the barracks and seems to have retained his religious commitment up to the time he returned to York and his wife and four children:

Readers, you who are placed in independent circumstances and wish to obtain a reward hereafter, adopt the humane and philanthropic conduct of Messrs. Backhouse, Walker and Kershaw, Members of the Society of Friends, who through disinterested motives, took a tour through the penal Settlements and pryed into the hardships of poor abject fellow-creatures who suffered with myself.[136]

Christian narratives of the return of the reformed sinner were a recurrent theme of religious chapbooks circulated to prisoners. More didactic in character, they lacked the grisly sensationalism of the confessions of executed prisoners, sold for a profit by the Ordinary of Newgate.[137] Protestants were familiar with thrilling stories of suffering under Catholic tyranny through Fox's *Book of Martyrs*, a book which enjoyed renewed popularity in the 1830s as part of the 'Protestant Crusade'.[138] Similar tales of Christian suffering and reform (or death) remained at the core of religious revivals and life-writing practised by Methodists and other Dissenters, as well as temperance meetings and hymns. All echo the early Christian confessional autobiographies and accounts of the sufferings of the first martyrs.

The saturation of meaning in these earlier texts works against convict life-writing providing a simple conduit to prisoner experience. Meaning therefore must be gleaned by intertextual reference to a relatively small number of mostly Christian narrative forms. More flexibly, convict authors deployed a wide range of media to present their message, adopting conventions of popular religion and entertainment and choosing to reveal or hide different layers of their embodied experiences.[139] Although allegedly true, the narrative of 'Henry Easy', who was supposedly wrongly convicted before suffering all the horrors of Van

---

[136] John Broxup, *Life of John Broxup Late Convict at Van Diemen's Land* (Leeds: J. Cook (for the author), 1850), p. 9.

[137] These began to decline in popularity around 1800 when tales of transportation partly replace them. McKenzie, 'True Confessions', 55–70.

[138] Vivienne Westwood, 'Mid-Victorian Foxe', *The Unabridged (Foxe's) Acts and Monuments Online* or TAMO (1576 edn) (HRI Online, www.johnfoxe.orgs, 2011); John Wolffe, *The Protestant Crusade in Great Britain, 1829–1860* (Oxford: Clarendon, 1991).

[139] Kay Walsh and Joy W. Hooton, *Australian Autobiographical Narratives: An Annotated Bibliography* (Canberra: Australian Scholarly Editions Centre, 1993); Anne Conlon, '"Mine Is a Sad Yet True Story": Convict Narratives 1818–1850', *Royal Australian Historical Society Journal*, 55 (1969), 43–82.

Diemen's Land, reads like a melodramatic novel compiled by someone with first-hand knowledge of the penal system.[140] Alison Alexander suggests it 'may or may not be true', which was possibly its attraction.[141]

A more entrepreneurial attitude to the horrors of transportation was demonstrated by Charles Adolphus King (1818–?), the 'returned Norfolk Island convict',[142] who Conlon identifies as Charles Dolphus, transported for fourteen years in 1836.[143] In 1839, King's arrest in Liverpool after he was recognized by two former wardens was widely reported.[144] King appears to have published the first account of his experiences under the title, 'A Warning Voice from a Penitent Convict' the following year.[145] In a speech supposedly delivered to the jury, King acknowledged his erroneous view of transportation: 'He was anxious to go, because he thought it would better his circumstances, but he soon found he was mistaken.' King's alleged adventures included a dramatic escape with a native woman whom he assisted, with some friendly missionaries, to build a church before returning home (having left the woman with the missionary).[146] After enduring a term in the Millbank penitentiary, King emerged to present a lecture series around the country which included a dramatic appearance in the dress and double chains of his supposed Norfolk Island years.[147] A surviving brochure publicizing his Liverpool performance in 1847 exclaims, 'Positively for one night only … A returned convict will deliver his highly-popular and national lecture on the horrors of transportation!!'[148] Unlike the large number of 'true-ish' convict fictions,[149]

---

[140] Henry Easy, *Horrors of Transportation: Or the Danger of Keeping Bad Company, or Being Careless in the Choice of Companions* (Bristol: John Wright, 1847).

[141] Alexander, *Tasmania's Convicts*, p. 64.

[142] According to Ann Conlon, 'Mine Is a Sad Yet True Story', *Journal of the Royal Australian Historical Society*.

[143] Conlon, 'Mine Is a Sad Yet True Story', 43–82. Tim Causer (personal communication, 22 October 2018) notes that neither 'King' nor 'Dolphus' ever went to Norfolk Island.

[144] *Reading Mercury*, 30 November 1839, p. 4; *Perthshire Advertiser*, 5 December 1839, p. 4; *Falmouth Express and Colonial Journal*, 30 November 1838, p. 3.

[145] Charles Adolphus King, *A Warning Voice from a Penitent Convict* (London: Birt's Wholesale Song & Book Warehouse, 1840).

[146] Ibid., 7.

[147] King appears to have begun lecturing in 1847: *Liverpool Mail*, 24 April 1847, p. 3, and continued until at least 1857: *Leicester Journal*, 8 May 1857, p. 6.

[148] Charles Adolphus King, *By Authority!!! V. R. … Positively for One Night Only, in the [Blank] … A Returned Convict Will Deliver His Highly-Popular and National Lecture on the Horrors of Transportation!! … The Lecturer Will Appear in the Character of a Norfolk Island Convict, in Full Costume! Wearing the Convict Dress in Double Chains* (Hull: John Howe, 1847 [?]).

[149] Laurie Hergenhan, *Unnatural Lives; Studies in Australian Convict Fiction* (St Lucia: University of Queensland Press, 1993).

King's theatrics were based on genuine experiences, or at least they were accepted as true by papers which reported them.[150]

Of the dozens of surviving convict memoirs, George Benson, Thomas Page and Joseph Platt all borrowed Ullathorne's title.[151] Benson provided little personal information other than the date of his transportation and the usual story of disgrace, following birth to respectable parents, suffering, repentance and homecoming. It contained egregious errors, such as labouring in Australia's non-existent mercury mines, before his happy return to his family.[152] Platt's was the most successful and widely published of this series, perhaps because it included pictures.[153] Sentenced to fourteen years' transportation for theft, Platt arrived in *The Hooghley* in November 1834. He self-published his pamphlet in Birmingham in 1850 with an image of black slaves and well-dressed white owners – irrelevant to Platt's story but possibly all the printer had. A second edition (1862) featured a black and white illustration of the author (clothed) being flogged for trying to escape from his master, a pastry chef with a taste for the macabre. Born in Manchester and transported at eighteen, one week after he had been assigned, Platt was ordered by his master to accompany him to The Rocks. There he saw a notice that seven men were sentenced to hang, to which his master said: 'Let this be a warning to you, for each of these men is hanged, and not one of them for murder.'[154] Apparently left at liberty to do so, Platt chose to watch all twenty-one executions over the following week. Platt's life was a catalogue of pain and punishment; in the space of thirty months he received 550 lashes, fourteen days of solitary confinement, and four months on the treadmill. He absconded and served time in three penal settlements: 'Sidney' (sic), Norfolk Island, and Port Arthur, living in conditions of filth and hunger: 'A clean pigstye in any part of England is preferable to a Norfolk Island bunk … it was truly an earthly hell.'[155] Throughout his three years at Norfolk Island, Platt's only exposure to

[150] For example, 'The Horrors of Transportation', *Liverpool Mercury*, 20 April 1847, p. 4.
[151] George Benson, *The Horrors of Transportation* (Bristol: Author, 1843); Thomas Page, *The Horrors of Transportation* (London?: n.p., 1846); Joseph Platt, *The Horrors of Transportation* (Birmingham: Pratt, 1850).
[152] Benson, *Horrors of Transportation*. It is possible this is George Benson (b. 1807) of Fermanagh, convicted of stealing a watch, sentenced to seven (not fourteen) years and is listed with 187 convicts transported on the *Sophia* in 1828; 'British Convict Transportation Register', convictrecords.com.au/ships/sophia/1828) (Accessed 22 August 2018).
[153] William Ross, *The Fell Tyrant, or, the Suffering Convict* (London: Ward, 1836).
[154] Joseph Platt, *The Horrors of Transportation* (London: The author, 1862), p. 4.
[155] Ibid., 7–8.

religion were the hasty recital of prayers as part of a day's labour and when mustered for Sunday service.

These 'horror' narratives haunted British memories of transportation into the decades following the Molesworth Report. The 'horrors' tag was invoked by the anti-transportation movement in the 1840s and in the report of the 1856 SC on Transportation. Although transportation was already declining, witnesses were attentively questioned on whether criminals feared transportation or penal servitude more.[156] By 1864, the Bristol reformer Mary Carpenter (1807–1877) cited evidence given by Police Sergeant Loome to demonstrate that all the old horrors of transportation had disappeared and that it was frequently, according to one judge, a 'matter of hope'.[157] Nevertheless, the genre of convict narratives did not die with transportation and continuing horrors were reported, with official sanction, about conditions of penal servitude in Newgate, Millbank and Dartmoor.[158] Through his anonymous persona 'One Who Has Endured It', Edward Bannister Callow (1825–1900), a company secretary convicted in July 1868 for forging cheques and embezzling thousands of pounds from the Elham Railway Company (destroying the livelihoods of many when it collapsed), provides a useful reminder of the casuistry of most prison memoirs.[159] Like other gentleman convicts, 'One Who Has Endured It' reports critically and appreciatively on religious services, such as those of the chaplain at Newgate who provided 'prayers really prayed, without suspicion of intoning'.[160] His overall tone is that of dismal fortitude. As in most prison memoirs, religion appears primarily as a break from labour and institutional routine, and the true horror of transportation and the Victorian prison system overall resides in

---

[156] 'The Horrors of Transportation', *The Goulburn Herald*, 17 March 1849 p. 2; 'Testimony of Police Serjeant M. Loome', 12 June 1856; 'Mr E. Shepherd', 16 June 1856, 'Police Inspector James Brennon', 16 June 1856, *SC on Transportation* (First Report) BPP 1856 (244) XVII.1, pp. 79, 113, 123.

[157] Mary Carpenter, *Our Convicts*, 2 vols. (London: Longman, 1864), p. 238.

[158] Edward Callow, *Five Years' Penal Servitude: By One Who Has Endured It* (London: R. Bentley & son, 1877). For other memoirs of penal servitude: Ben Bethell, 'An Exception Too Far: "Gentleman" Convicts and the 1878–9 Penal Servitude Acts Commission', *Prison Service Journal*, 232.39 (2017), 40–45. Callow's authorship was only revealed after his death. Callow was declared bankrupt on 18 May 1868, *London Gazette*, 26 June 1868, p. 3634.

[159] Callow, *Five Years' Penal Servitude*, p. 2. 'Many a quiet smile have I had over the perusal of convicts' confessions, chaplains' reminiscences, and other similar articles I have met with in magazines, journals, and newspapers.'

[160] Ibid., 20.

how rarely it moved prisoners to contrition, self-knowledge, or 'reformation' by either civil or ecclesiastical authority.[161]

Conclusion

In the first decades of the nineteenth century, the relatively high numbers of Catholic prisoners in British and Irish penal institutions reflected their history of social and economic deprivation and exclusion from political power and administrative authority. Their increasing visibility and spiritual, economic and political needs attracted the attention of missionaries and benefactors in the course of which the convict system represented a frontier in centuries of religious hostilities. While sectarianism was part of the anti-transportation campaign from the beginning, it was most evident in the tussles over the liberal expansion of provision to Irish Catholic convicts in New South Wales and later, as discussed in Chapter 10, the hulks of Bermuda. Catholic theology of punishment and retribution, as much as innovations in prison and penal theory, provided ample grounds for the development of an alternative, Catholic discourse of the 'horrors of transportation', outlined in this chapter.

Ullathorne's motivation in condemning the horrors of transportation was the simple one of seeking to educate those who had been misled about the reality of a punishment that, in his view, was harsh, degrading and removed all respect and dignity from the human person. His other objective was to encourage candidates to the Catholic mission in New South Wales. For this purpose, it was important that the situation of the convicts be seen to arise as much from the iniquities of the British penal system as from any fault of the Irish prisoners. Ullathorne was not Irish but he seems to have been adept in adapting narratives of Irish resistance to British oppression to the particular purpose of the mission to New South Wales. This adaptation was to have a power far beyond what Ullathorne might have anticipated. His narrative would be embraced by free and unfree Irish and denounced by the Protestant colonists as deceitful and degrading to their own view of their role in building a moral colony in the southern seas. At a time when there were limited avenues to express a liberal Catholic interpretation of penal reform, Ullathorne's preaching underpinned resistance to the religious and political establishment.

---

[161] Monica Fludernik, 'Stone Walles Do (Not) a Prison Make', in Jason W. Haslam and Julia M. Wright (eds.), *Captivating Subjects* (Toronto: University of Toronto Press, 2005), p. 169.

The 'horrors of transportation' were critical to a political moment in the anti-transportation campaign, shortly before, during and after the bringing down of the Molesworth Report with which it is intimately connected. For very different reasons, humanitarian and sectarian advocates, including Catholic and ultra-Protestant Evangelicals in the colonies, found it convenient to exaggerate the moral challenges created by convict transportation. The polemical and popular narratives they deployed fed into long-standing scriptural narratives, reflecting Catholic and Protestant theologies of penance and suffering, as well as popular tropes of the returning penitent. Judge Burton's charge to the jury, which represented New South Wales as sinking in a pit of crime and vice, was inaccurate but explicable in the light of Evangelical assertions for the established church to dominate the moral realm, including its courts, prisons, schools and other public institutions. For Burton it provided grounds to oppose the efforts of the liberal government committed to dismantling the exclusive privileges of the Church of England. From very different premises, Ullathorne's depiction of the 'horrors of transportation' was an indictment of the treatment of Irish Catholic prisoners by British authorities whom he represented as indifferent to their spiritual and physical wellbeing. For this reason, Catholic writers, following in the footsteps of Ullathorne, as well as McEncroe and Willson on Norfolk Island,[162] have tended to embrace the convict experience, with all its horrors, as part of their own national story.

Harder questions arise when we ask what the 'horrors of transportation' meant to those who endured it, reflected in the various fictionalized and factual narratives written by political prisoners, returning convicts and occasionally, convict diaries written while under sentence. While it is tempting to seize on these as conveying the convict's voice, they are nearly all compromised by the circumstances of their creation and the conventions of existing Christian narratives of suffering, penitence and homecoming. What is clear is that the 'horrors of transportation' provided a powerful vehicle to advance arguments for abolishing transportation. Yet despite its real and imagined horrors, transportation continued in new formats. The next chapter will examine one of the most hopeful and innovative: Captain Maconochie's experiment on Norfolk Island.

---

[162] See Chapter 7.

7   'Ocean Hell': Captain Maconochie and Norfolk Island, 1837–1855

> No prospect being afforded them of ever again being blest with the enjoyment of Woman's love, without hope of Heaven or fear of Hell, their already darkened reason became more clouded, their lax morals gave way and they indulged with apparent delight in every filthy and unnatural propensity.[1]   (Thomas Cook, 1841–1843)

> I found the Island a turbulent brutal hell, and I left it a peaceful well-ordered community.[2]   (Captain Maconochie, 1848)

In 1848, the penal reformer Captain Alexander Maconochie (1787–1860) published a defence of the system he had implemented for the reform of prisoners on Norfolk Island, the most infamous penal settlement in the empire, claiming: 'I found the Island a turbulent brutal hell, and I left it a peaceful, well-ordered community.'[3] While claims for demonic conditions and heroic agency are common in tales of penal reform, Maconochie's contribution has been more controversial than most, more so even than Colonel Arthur's, considered in Chapter 3. Maconochie attracted both admirers and detractors in the course of his career, including many religious-minded supporters. Yet Maconochie's own motivation for engagement in penal reform remains somewhat opaque. He denounced those Evangelicals who attempted to use religion and physical suffering to secure the reformation of the criminal. However, he was not a secular Benthamite whose faith in a rational system of rewards and penalties served the sole purpose of reducing the burden of crime to the state. Rather he was heir to the Christian utilitarianism espoused by Paley and Whately, though transmitted through Scottish Presbyterian rather than English Anglican liberalism.

Maconochie's cause has not been helped by his biographies, including the most substantial study by John Vincent Barry, a judge of the Supreme Court of Victoria, who also wrote the entry on Maconochie in the

[1] Thomas Cook, *The Exile's Lamentations* (North Sydney: Library of Australian History, 1978), p. 69.
[2] Captain Maconochie, *Norfolk Island* (London: John Ollivier, 1848), p. 13.   [3] Ibid.

Australian Dictionary of Biography.[4] Subsequent studies by John Clay and Norval Morris, depend on Barry.[5] Robert Hughes sanctified him as 'a prophetic reformer, a noble anomaly in the theater of antipodean terror and punishment', and the 'one and only inspired penal reformer to work in Australia throughout the whole history of transportation',[6] but this is overly sanguine about his methods. A more modern perspective is reflected in the *Oxford Dictionary of National Biography*,[7] but even this has missed important contemporary evidence, especially his character assassination of Colonel Arthur which has only recently been printed (though readily accessible in the UK National Archives).[8] The full extent of Maconochie's originality has only recently been discerned in studies of his use of music for moral improvement,[9] or the practical working of the mark system as it was implemented in other institutional settings such as Ireland,[10] as well as many sites around the British Empire, including the Andaman Islands.[11]

This chapter will consider Maconochie's term as Commandant of Norfolk Island, from 1840 to 1844 whose contested history in many ways lies at the heart of the convict transportation debate. It will examine the religious sources for the 'social system' that Maconochie first attempted to implement on Norfolk Island, the most original and daring experiment in the long history of British convict transportation. It will examine Maconochie's radical disagreement with Colonel Arthur and other defenders of Evangelical modes of penal governance and why the mark system secured the support of other clerical writers on penal reform. With the abrupt cancellation of Maconochie's experiment, Norfolk Island became an essential stage in Lord Stanley's probation system. This chapter will go on to assess the role of religion on Norfolk Island where it failed to shake off its reputation as the island for the repose of the

---

[4] J. V. Barry, *Alexander Maconochie of Norfolk Island: A Study of a Pioneer in Penal Reform* (Melbourne: Oxford University Press, 1958); John Vincent Barry, 'Pioneers in Criminology Xii–Alexander Maconochie (1787–1860)', *Journal of Criminal Law and Criminology*, 47.2 (1956), 145–161.

[5] John Clay, *Maconochie's Experiment* (London: John Murray, 2001); Norval Morris, *Maconochie's Gentlemen* (Oxford University Press, 2002).

[6] Hughes, *Fatal Shore*, pp. 484, 488–489.

[7] M. F. G. Selby and Felix Driver, 'Maconochie, Alexander (1787–1860)', *ODNB*.

[8] Alexander Maconochie, *On Colonel Arthur's General Character and Government* [1837–38] (Adelaide: Sullivan's Cover, 1989).

[9] Alan Maddox, 'On the Machinery of Moral Improvement: Music and Prison Reform in the Penal Colony of Norfolk Island', *Musicology Australia*, 34.2 (2012), 185–205.

[10] John Moore, 'Alexander Maconochie's "Mark System"', *Prison Service Journal*, 198 (2011), 38–46. For a critique of the mark system in Ireland, see Chris B. Gibson, *Irish Convict Reform: The Intermediate Prisons, a Mistake* (Dublin: McGlashan & Gill, 1863).

[11] Anderson, 'Transnational Histories of Penal Transportation', 396.

'vilest of the vile'.[12] It will consider the views of the many clerical visitors for whom Norfolk Island was represented as a place of suffering and redemption, but also as the 'Ocean Hell', where pious hopes and the best-laid plans ended, as they did for Maconochie, in dashed expectations and shattered illusions.

Norfolk Island

Norfolk Island has been the site of a series of human occupations,[13] including two British convict settlements: the first, which lasted from 1788 to 1814, was not a penal establishment and included both free settlers and men and women convicts. Among the convicts were three clergy convicted for their involvement in the 1798 United Irishmen Rebellion.[14] The second penal settlement, which ran from 1824 to 1855, was initiated when New South Wales Governor Sir Thomas Brisbane was ordered to abandon Moreton Bay and reoccupy Norfolk Island as a site for the 'worst description of Convicts'.[15] Like other ultra-penal settlements created in the wake of the Bigge Reports, such as Macquarie Harbour in Van Diemen's Land, the object was to make transportation an object of terror and to increase the severity of penal discipline. Advised by Bishop Polding and the Rev. Henry Tarlton-Stiles about Norfolk Island, Governor Bourke reported to Bathurst that 'no real reformation of heart' took place there, banishment extinguished hope and a moral sense and there was a dearth of religious instruction.[16] There were repeated efforts to secure religious instructors by Darling, Bourke and higher clergy.[17] However, as Tim Causer has demonstrated from an exhaustive study of the records relating to all the convicts sent to Norfolk Island during its second settlement phase, the overall profile of these men

[12] William Howitt, *Land, Labour, and Gold*, 2 vols, 2nd edn (London: Longman, 1858), vol. II, p. 6.

[13] For the Polynesian settlement of Norfolk Island, which appears to have been abandoned in the fifteenth century, see Atholl Anderson and Peter White, 'Prehistoric Settlement on Norfolk Island and Its Oceanic Context', *Records of the Australian Museum*, Supplement 27 (2001), 139. In 1856, the island was given to the Pitcairn Islander descendants of the Bligh mutineers.

[14] The clergy included two Catholic priests, the Rev. James Harold and the Rev. Peter O'Neil, and a Protestant minister, the Rev. Henry Fulton, who served as colonial chaplain on Norfolk from 1801 to 1805 after which he received a full pardon.

[15] Bathurst to Brisbane, 21 May 1825, *Historical Records of Australia, ser. 1* (Sydney: Government Printer, 1917), vol. 11, p. 321.

[16] Bourke to Glenelg, 5 November 1837, encl. 'Observations on the State of Norfolk Island by the Right Rev. Dr Polding', *Molesworth SC on Transportation (Minutes)*, pp. 265–266.

[17] Darling to Goderich, 12 November 1831; Bourke to Goderich, 28 February 1832, encl. Archdeacon Broughton's Report, 29 September 1831; Bourke to Glenelg, 26 December 1835, *Molesworth SC on Transportation (Minutes)*, pp. 180–181.

(no women were sent) differed little from those sent to convict stations on the mainland; they had mostly committed property offences.[18] It is the second phase of the settlement which has attracted the greatest infamy and tended to obscure all other occupations of the island, including the Maconochie experiment from 1840 to 1844, and its final repurposing as a stage in Lord Stanley's probation system. All phases of its history have been attentively studied by historians.[19] The remarkable contrast between the exquisite loveliness of the island setting and its historic use as a site of extreme punishment was not lost on contemporaries. McEncroe described it to a friend as 'both a Paradise and a Purgatory'.[20] Even the academic historian L. L. Robson succumbed in his foreword to Margaret Hazzard's standard history, encapsulating the vision of Norfolk Island as 'a paradise turned into hell'.[21]

In terms of numbers, Causer identified 6,458 convicts who served time on Norfolk Island, including 2,590 transported from New South Wales, 1,270 from Van Diemen's Land, 730 transported direct from England and Ireland to form part of Captain Maconochie's experiment, 1,703 transported from Millbank Prison under the probation system and 165 men who were locally convicted in Australia.[22] Despite its small size, Norfolk Island generated a remarkable number of more or less reliable memoirs and eye-witness accounts from its highly mobile population of prisoners and officers, including many visiting and resident clergy and religious instructors. Those by resident clergy are summarized in Table 7.1.[23] The clergy ranged from the unfortunate convict

---

[18] Causer, '"The Worst Types of Sub-Human Beings"', 8–31; Timothy Causer, '"Only a Place Fit for Angels and Eagles": The Norfolk Island Penal Settlement', (PhD thesis, University College London, 2010).

[19] Frank Clune, *The Norfolk Island Story* (Sydney: Angus and Robertson, 1967). Hazzard, *Punishment Short of Death*; Merval Hoare, *Norfolk Island* (Rockhampton: Central Queensland University Press, 1999). The most scholarly history was edited by Raymond Nobbs for the 1988 Bicentenary: Raymond Nobbs, *Norfolk Island and Its Second Settlement, 1825–1855* (Sydney: Library of Australian History, 1991). An additional volume covered the third settlement. An updated version of Nobbs's first volume, including a new chapter by Merval Hoare on religion on Norfolk Island, was published in 1999: Merval Hoare, 'A Religious Presence', in Raymond Nobbs (ed.), *Norfolk Island and Its Second Settlement, 1825–1855* (Sydney: Library of Australian History, 1991), pp. 138–157. To date, this is the only account of religion on Norfolk Island.

[20] McEncroe to Vicar Apostolic at Calcutta, n.d.; Delia Birchley, *John McEncroe: Colonial Democrat* (Melbourne: Collins Dove, 1986), p. 68.

[21] Hazzard, *Punishment Short of Death*, p. v.

[22] Figures from Tim Causer, 'Norfolk Island: A Tiny Fist of Volcanic Rock', *Convict Voyages, A Global History of Convicts and Penal Colonies*, convictvoyages.org/expert-essays/norfolk-island (Accessed 23 August 2018); Causer, 'Only a Place Fit for Angels and Eagles'.

[23] See also Hoare, 'A Religious Presence', pp. 138–157.

Table 7.1 *Resident clergy on Norfolk Island, 1836–1850*

Protestant	Catholic
Rev. Thomas Sharpe (1797–1877), chaplain, 1836–1841. Dismissed by Maconochie.[a]	Rev. Henry Gregory OSB (1813–1877), assistant chaplain, October 1838–1839. Resigned.
	Lewis Harding (1807–1893), catechist, 1837–1842. Dismissed by Maconochie.
Rev. Thomas Beagly Naylor (1805–1849), chaplain, 1841–1845. Resigned, calling Norfolk Island a 'plague spot'.[b]	Rev. John McEncroe (1794–1868), chaplain, 1838–1842. Recalled.[c]
Rev. John Leverack Ison (1808–1867), chaplain, May 1844. Dismissed by Price.[d]	Rev. Richard Walshe, chaplain, 1842–1845. Recalled.
Rev. Thomas Rogers (1806–1903), chaplain, 1845–1847. Dismissed by Price.[e]	
Rev. Henry Elliott (1814–1858), religious instructor, 1847–1850. Dismissed.	Rev. Thomas Joseph Malachy Murray OSB (d. 1852), religious instructor, 1848.
Rev. Frederick S. Batchelor (c.1817–1892), chaplain, 1850.	

[a] Rev. Thomas Sharpe, 'Journal on Norfolk Island', 1837–1840, SLNSW B217–B218.

[b] Rev. T. B. Naylor to Lord Stanley, written before 22 September 1846, Confidential Print, TNA CO 885/2/9.

[c] R. A. Daly, 'Archdeacon McEncroe on Norfolk Island, 1838–42', *Australasian Catholic Record*, 36.4 (1959), 285–305.

[d] John L. Ison, *Appeal to the Secretary of State Relative to the Dismissal of the Rev. John L. Ison, from His Chaplaincy at Norfolk Island* (Oatlands, Van Diemen's Land: Private, 1850).

[e] Thomas Rogers, *Review of Dr. Hampton's First Report on Norfolk Island* (Hobart: Henry Dowling, 1849b).

Sources: Merval Hoare, 'A Religious Presence', in *Norfolk Island and Its Second Settlement, 1825–1855*, edited by Raymond Nobbs (Sydney: Library of Australian History, 1991), pp. 138–157; Cullen, 'Norfolk Island: Its Catholic Story', *Advocate* 13 September 1928.

clergy, who formed part of the first penal settlement, to a stream of high-profile visitors encountered in previous chapters, including Broughton, Ullathorne, Backhouse and Walker, along with Robert Willson (1794–1866), first Catholic bishop of Hobart.[24] Two important changes to the condition of the island occurred in the wake of the Molesworth Report. First, Captain Maconochie was engaged to make a trial of his social system of convict management. At more or less the same time, permanent Protestant and Catholic chaplains arrived

[24] For the Quakers on Norfolk Island, see Chapter 4; For Ullathorne, Chapter 6.

on the island, though not without considerable difficulty in persuading them to commit to their appointments. Of the Catholic chaplains, the unstable John Brady (1800–1871) had his passage paid by the government but refused to proceed to Norfolk Island on arrival in Sydney,[25] as did Christopher Vincent Dowling (1789–1873), calling it the 'hell of the double-damned' in a letter to Bishop Polding.[26] Polding eventually sent two priests: his fellow Benedictine, Henry Gregory and John McEncroe, who heroically committed himself to an isolated convict ministry and conquering his personal addiction to alcohol,[27] with a lay catechist, Lewis Harding (1807–1893).[28] The clash of clergy and commandants created a combustible situation in the course of which five of the six Protestant chaplains were dismissed, as was Harding, while McEncroe became one of the leaders of the anti-transportation movement. This chapter will consider the religious elements of Maconochie's scheme and the many complaints of the island's resident clergy about the administration of the island.

Captain Maconochie

Maconochie was more than a 'lawyer's son', as Hughes puts it;[29] he descended from the Olympian heights of Scotland's intellectual and professional elite and addressed governors and cabinet ministers as social equals. An independent spirit may have prompted him to take a commission in the Royal Navy in 1803. He had an active career, if not one of good fortune, spending two years, from 1812 to 1814, as a prisoner of war. M'Konochie (who did not modernize the spelling of his name until 1832) was placed on the naval reserve on half-pay in 1815 and looked for a new career. While living with his mother in Edinburgh, he wrote a 'memoir' which recommended to the Secretary of State for War

---

[25] Gipps to Glenelg, 7 April 1838, encl. Polding to Gipps, 15 March 1833, *Correspondence on Religion in Australia*, BPP 1837–38 (75) XL.115, p. 21. According to Birchley, *John McEncroe*, pp. 61–63, Brady had been educated in France and, at Polding's request, he served the fifty-seven French Canadian prisoners transported for their involvement in the 1837 Rebellion in Lower Canada, who arrived in 1840. Polding's intervention saved the *patriotes* from transportation to Norfolk Island.

[26] J. A. Morley, 'Dowling, Christopher Vincent (1789–1873), *ADB*. He retired to Maitland instead.

[27] Gipps to Glenelg, 28 November 1838, *Correspondence on Religion in Australia*, BPP 1837–1838 (75) XL.115, p. 25; Birchley, *John McEncroe*, p. 68.

[28] Gipps assured Glenelg, 28 November 1838, Ibid., p. 25, that all three men would share a stipend of £150.

[29] Hughes, *Fatal Shore*, p. 489.

and Colonies and the Lords Commissioner of the Admiralty that they establish a colony in the Sandwich Islands (Hawaii).[30] This was interesting speculation, though not backed up by any great research or data since M'Konochie had never been to the Sandwich Islands. In 1818, he published another speculative study of the potential for commerce and colonization of the Pacific.[31] M'Konochie may have had no greater impact on society if over the next ten years he had not failed, first as a farmer and then as a schoolmaster in Fife. Seeking to recover his fortunes, he moved his family to London.

Maconochie made new intellectual connections in the south, building on his interest in geography, colonization and exploration. In 1830, he became founding secretary of the Royal Geographical Society, editing its journal and helping to secure funding for expeditions to the Arctic, Southern Africa and British Guiana.[32] This experience was sufficient for him to be warmly recommended for the inaugural Professorship of Geography at the newly fledged University College London, the brainchild of Jeremy Bentham and his utilitarian followers, as well as Dissenters and Jews excluded by religious tests from the established universities. Maconochie himself was careful to distance himself from too close an identification with Bentham, and in 1847 published a paper pointing out the differences between their views on penal reform.[33] John Gascoigne has noted that Maconochie's intellectual connections to the Scottish enlightenment were as strong as the English, Benthamite ones.[34] It was his practical Christianity which was to define his views of penal reform. The opportunity to make his mark came in 1837. Having been an armchair explorer for long enough, Maconochie seized the opportunity to travel to Van Diemen's Land as personal secretary to his friend, Sir John Franklin (1786–1847), when he was appointed Lt Governor. At the same time, he accepted a commission from the Society for the Improvement of Prison Discipline to report on the convict system.

---

[30] Alexander Maconochie, *Considerations on the Propriety of Establishing a Colony in One of the Sandwich Islands* (London: Richardson, 1816).
[31] Alexander Maconochie, *A Summary View of the Statistics and Existing Commerce of the Principal Shores of the Pacific Ocean* (London: pr. James R. Richardson, 1818).
[32] Rev. Felix Driver M. F. G. Selby, 'Maconochie (Formerly M'Konochie), Alexander', *ODNB*; Hugh Clout, 'Alexander Maconochie: Britain's First Professor of Geography', *Bloomsbury Project*, www.ucl.ac.uk/bloomsbury-project/ (London: University College London, 2009).
[33] Alexander Maconochie, *Comparison between Mr Bentham's Views on Punishment and Those Advocated in Connexion with the Mark System* (Marylebone: Compton, 1847).
[34] Gascoigne, *The Enlightenment*, p. 141.

Report on the State of Prison Discipline, 1838

Maconochie's report was designed to cause the maximum disruption to the existing system of convict transportation and replace it with one of his own devising. By rather devious means, he contrived to send a summary to the home secretary, Lord John Russell, who published it in the parliamentary papers before it had been processed by the Lt Governor.[35] In Van Diemen's Land, this was perceived as a personal affront to Franklin, who asked for Maconochie's resignation. Since it was based on no more than four months' experience of the colony, Maconochie was open to criticism by long-established members of the Van Diemen's Land administration, the much derided 'Arthur faction'.[36] Back in Hobart, Maconochie wrote a lengthy defence of his breach of trust, claiming he had no intention of 'blaming the masters' or any administration individually, but simply the ramshackle transportation system itself.[37] Yet both the summary report, published by Russell, and the longer report, published with Sir John Franklin's despatch, clearly did blame the masters, and in no uncertain terms:

The servants being made slaves, the masters are made slave-holders ... Being made slave-owners, they are subjected to all the demoralization incident to such a position, and to more also. They are charged to punish and reform their country's criminals; and they neither know nor care about either operation, for naturally and necessarily their dominant object is to make the most of the labour which thus passes through their hands.[38]

Even more severe strictures were directed against Colonel Arthur's complex system of private assignment, controlled by Arthur's friends and family, which Maconochie declared to be innately corrupting. In its place he made a radical plea for sentencing based not on time but on work and the self-interested reform of the convicts. Such a system would be 'in harmony with, and not in direct opposition to, the acknowledged

---

[35] Maconochie to Russell, 30 September 1837, *Report on Prison Discipline in Van Diemen's Land*, BPP 1837–1838 (121) XL.237, p. 239 [Hereafter *Maconochie's Report*].

[36] For a detailed critique of Maconochie's report by John Montagu, colonial secretary, Matthew Forster, chief police magistrate and head of the convict establishment, John Gregory, colonial secretary and Sir John Franklin, *Despatch from Lieutenant Governor Sir J. Franklin to Lord Glenelg, 7 October 1837, Relative to Present System of Convict Discipline in Van Diemen's Land*, BPP 1827–1838 (309) XLII.15, encl. nos. 1–14 [Hereafter *Franklin's Despatch*]. For a local reaction, see *Hobart Town Courier*, 4 January 1839, p. 3.

[37] Maconochie to Alfred Stephen, *The Australian*, 8 November 1838, p. 3.

[38] *Maconochie's Report*, pp. 6, 8.

impulses of the human mind, the constitution bestowed on it by its great Creator'.[39] He recommended raising the 'tone of public character' by multiplying churches, chapels and schools and improving the qualifications of public officers administering the convict system.[40] To oversee his vision, he asked that 'some nobleman or gentleman of high rank, talent, and estimation' be invited to come out and lead the system.[41] His first suggestion was William Crawford (1788–1847), author of the parliamentary report on American prisons,[42] or he may have been thinking of himself for this role; if so, he would be disappointed.

Maconochie asserted that he had no existing views on the subject of transportation prior to his arrival in the colony and that his proposals were based not on 'strong feelings of compassion for the convicts' but rather the need to modernize a system which had outlived its purpose.[43] This was a utilitarian flourish, and somewhat specious, for Maconochie's covering letter to Franklin recalled their conversations 'regarding the controversy between Archbishop Whately and Colonel Arthur', indicating that he was already deeply engaged in the transportation debate before his arrival.[44] Having resolutely supported Whately in his initial discussions with Franklin, Maconochie claimed to have settled on a position somewhere between the two protagonists, driven 'solely by facts and principles'. He presented his proposals to the government as a break with the past which moreover held 'high moral and religious as well as political interest'.[45]

Maconochie's Report outlined in a nutshell the principles of what he would later call the mark system, including the abolition of private assignment, the separation of punishment and reform and the replacement of physical punishment with 'moral training' which would be employment, such as public works on roads, conducted in social groups.[46] In support of his vision for a new form of penal discipline, Maconochie attached letters from eminent authorities, including the outgoing Governor of New South Wales, Sir Richard Bourke, who stated that he fully agreed with the evils of the system 'under its present form'.[47] At the same time it is significant that Bourke advised Maconochie that he would not be recommending him, as he had requested, to the position of

---

[39] Franklin to Glenelg, 7 October 1837, encl. 1, Maconochie to Franklin, 20 May 1837, 'Report on Convict Discipline', *Franklin's Despatch*, p. 12.
[40] *Franklin's Despatch*, p. 11.   [41] *Maconochie's Report*, p. 4.
[42] *W. Crawford on Penitentiaries in USA*, BPP 1834 (593) XLVI.349.
[43] Maconochie to Russell, 30 September 1837, *Maconochie's Report*, p. 3.
[44] Maconochie to Franklin, 20 May 1837, *Franklin's Despatch*, p. 5.   [45] Ibid.
[46] *Maconochie's Report*, p. 10.
[47] Sir Richard Bourke to Maconochie, 6 July 1837, *Maconochie's Report*, p. 12.

superintendent of the Port Phillip District. Rather stronger endorsement came from the veteran Quaker penal reformers Backhouse and Walker, who were so enthused by Maconochie's brave new ideas that they provided three separate responses to it. In the first they fully endorsed the replacement of physical with moral coercion, which they knew was already operating successfully in schools and lunatic establishments.[48] They agreed that assignment was equivalent to domestic slavery, a principle they had earlier dismissed.[49] What caused them to change their minds about private assignment was the attraction of Maconochie's system, 'bringing moral principles to bear on the prison population for the promotion of their own reform'.[50] In their reports for the New South Wales and Van Diemen's Land governments, Backhouse and Walker consistently recommended that prisoners be separated by sex and age and allowed to attempt reformation – by this was usually meant Bible reading and literacy. They were excited that Maconochie proposed a new, moral system contiguous with Christian principles to govern prison labour.

There was less enthusiasm for Maconochie's Report in Van Diemen's Land, where it aroused a chorus of disapproval from the colonial administration. On the Executive Council, Archdeacon Hutchins approved of the plan to place convicts in gangs, on the grounds that this would make it easier to provide them with religious instruction, without feeling any enthusiasm for delegating this to Wesleyans or educated convicts in preference to colonial chaplains.[51] Sir John Franklin pointed out that most of Maconochie's recommendations, including one calling for the appointment of a 'superintendent-general' or 'convict protector' to police and patrol the conditions of convicts, conflicted with the central responsibilities of the chief police magistrate (namely Matthew Forster), and, of course, himself.[52] Maconochie's real target was not Sir John Franklin, whom he liked and admired, but rather the system designed by Arthur and his clique who continued to manage it. The level of Maconochie's distance from the administration is indicated best by a document which never made it into the public domain. This was a savagely personal denunciation of Arthur, marked 'private', which Maconochie included in the papers he sent to the Colonial Office in

---

[48] Backhouse and Walker to Maconochie, 10th of 8th month [August] 1837, *Maconochie's Report*, p. 13.
[49] Backhouse and Walker to Maconochie, 5th of 9th month [September] 1837, *Maconochie's Report*, p. 14.
[50] Ibid.   [51] 'Archdeacon Hutchins' Minute', *Franklin's Despatch*, pp. 87, 89.
[52] 'Sir John Franklin's Minute to the Executive Council', *Franklin's Despatch*, p. 107.

1837 and 1838.[53] On receiving notice of this, the under secretary for the colonies, James Stephen, provided a hostile comment on the means by which Maconochie had put his Report on the official record. Stephen recommended that the summary 'should be communicated to Lord John Russell, and the Transportation Committee', but he thought the private paper should never leave the Colonial Office. Maconochie's extreme charges against General Arthur were vague, unanswerable and, in his view, 'drawn up for no one purpose, but to exhibit the cleverness of the accuser'.[54] There is some justice in this. Although he had never met Arthur and had spent no more than a few months in the colony, Maconochie felt free to declare Arthur's system rotten to the core:

His system of convict discipline must be entirely subverted. It cannot be improved. It is essentially vicious – a detestable upas-tree[55] rooted in a false and degrading estimate of human nature – deteriorating, consequently, everything within its influence – a disgrace to England, to science, to humanity – and a lamentable example of how closely political mistake may in its effects ... resemble intense wickedness.[56]

There are various interpretations one might hazard to account for Maconochie's actions. The view in the colony was that he had been captured by the anti-Arthur faction by whom he was persuaded that Franklin had been overly placatory to the rival, pro-Arthur clique. Possibly he chose to wildly exceed, or failed to understand, the brief given to him by the Prison Discipline Society. He may have felt a Christian duty to denounce the evil he saw perpetuated in the assignment system. For whatever reason or combination of reasons, Maconochie did a brave thing because it must have been clear to him, as it certainly was to his wife, that he would be unlikely to secure another colonial appointment without the patronage of Sir John Franklin (though ultimately Franklin did him more harm in this respect when he was lost in the course of the 1847 Expedition to find the North-West Passage). Maconochie did something few had dared to do, which was to suggest a positive alternative to the physical cruelties of convict discipline, one designed to 'punish, train and eventually restore criminals to society'.[57] He was realistic, not claiming to work a 'magical change', but simply a change for the better, 'compassed by patience, perseverance, and *religious*

[53] Maconochie, *On Colonel Arthur*.
[54] For the original, see TNA CO 280/103, as noted Ibid., 8–9.
[55] In travellers' tales, the most poisonous tree in the world, which caused men to die simply by breathing its scent.
[56] Maconochie, *On Colonel Arthur*, p. 21.
[57] Alexander Maconochie, *Australiana: Thoughts on Convict Management* (London: John W. Parker, 1839), p. 56.

and *moral culture*.[58] It is only fair to add that even Maconochie felt that he had less to offer women convicts other than to suggest that they were more sinned against than sinning, and that since a return to society was the ultimate goal, they should be 'seen at church', encouraged to dress respectably and to be sought as wives and household servants.[59]

To win the approval of the colonists in Van Diemen's Land where he hoped to be allowed to make a trial of his system, Maconochie made a direct appeal to them, publishing fuller accounts of what he called the social system of convict management, as opposed to the separate system promoted by the Evangelicals. In 1838, he published his *Thoughts on Convict Management* in London, and a *Supplement to Thoughts on Convict Management* in Hobart, directly addressed to those most affected by any change to the transportation system.[60] To the people of Hobart, he invoked the example of the greatest reformers in Christian history, Martin Luther, Wilberforce, Clarkson, Macaulay, Stephen and Sharpe, and their struggle against slavery. *They* were not deterred, and neither should those he called 'the friends of religion and humanity' from the challenge of penal reform.[61] Maconochie envisioned himself as a Protestant hero leading a moral reformation. Where Crawford and Russell regarded any contact with the world beyond the penitentiary as objectionable,[62] Maconochie sought to enhance social bonds and validate self-expression, removing as much as possible artificial and external disciplinary levers, including religious instruction, with those based on self-interest and social connections. He also sought to control the many hours that convicts spent working, rather than the few snatched for religious instruction, prayer and worship.

Maconochie on Norfolk Island, 1840–1844

Remarkably, given its reception in the colony, Maconochie was not cashiered. On the contrary, his recommendations so inspired the government that he was given every chance to make a success of his scheme. To Maconochie's disappointment, the setting chosen for this was not the primary and well-developed penal settlement of Van Diemen's Land, but the isolated penal outpost of Norfolk Island. Accordingly, in March 1840 he arrived with his wife and six children to take up residence in the elegant house and garden that had been built on the island by his

---

[58] Ibid.   [59] Ibid., 131.
[60] Ibid.; Captain Maconochie, *Supplement to Thoughts on Convict Management* (Hobart Town: MacDougall, 1839).
[61] Maconochie, *Supplement to Convict Management*, p. 13.   [62] Ibid.

predecessors. Maconochie was given considerable licence to creatively introduce new elements into the disciplinary regime on Norfolk Island, though he was directed to make his trial of the mark system only with the men sent to Norfolk Island direct from Britain, not the old hands. Alan Maddox has pointed to the deep investment that Maconochie made in providing 'moral machinery' for the prisoners on Norfolk Island, especially music. Maconochie took with him to the island instruments for prisoner bands, both for secular music and church services. He acquired two seraphines (keyed wind instruments which were probably intended as a low-cost alternative to pipe organs) to furnish the two churches he planned to construct. He purchased the entire set of scores from a Sydney music supplier and a large supply of blank sheet music to enable prisoners to make copies of music. Famously, this included the complete score of a comic opera, which was performed for the Queen's birthday.[63]

Maconochie gave particular attention to building the prisoners' religious sensibilities, with the important distinction from earlier regimes that he was religiously tolerant and demanded the same tolerance of chaplains serving on the island. In this, Maconochie was marching very much to the hymn sheet of the outgoing Governor, Sir Richard Bourke, who had implemented the New South Wales Church Act providing parity of state support to the four largest religious denominations in the colony. Norfolk Island acquired a Protestant and a Catholic chapel, which Fr McEncroe would dedicate to St Vincent, apostle of the French galley slaves.[64] Neither chapel was approved by the government, but Maconochie built them anyway. A detailed description of the Catholic chapel indicates that it was richly decorated, almost certainly with Maconochie's subvention: the windows were filled with transparencies, 'perfect imitations of stained glass' depicting scenes from the life of Christ and Joshua Reynolds' figures of Faith and Hope (originally designed for windows in New College Chapel, Oxford).[65] There were over twenty large pictures taken from 'our national gallery', including reproductions of works by masters such as Gentileschi, Rubens, Van Dyck, Titian, Guercino, Raphael and Eustache Le Sueur. One of the more modern pieces was Jean-Baptiste Regnault's *Le Déluge* (1789), now in the Louvre, an eerie masterpiece depicting a man carrying his aged parent on his back and a woman desperately lifting up a child in a vain attempt to escape the

[63] Maddox, 'On the Machinery of Moral Improvement'.
[64] Cullen, 'Norfolk Island: Its Catholic Story'.
[65] Alumnus, 'Catholic Church Norfolk Island', *Australasian Chronicle*, 10 (12 August 1841), p. 2. 'Alumnus' is possibly the Rev. Henry Gregory, OSB, who served as chaplain with McEncroe from 1838 to 1839.

rising flood.[66] There was also a convict choir and devout congregation of officers and prisoners, with full credit given to Maconochie, 'indefatigable in carrying out his views of reform, and at the same time showing a wise regard for the equal claims and rights of conscience of the several denominations'.[67] Maconochie says he attended services at both Protestant and Catholic chapels. The Norfolk Island diary of the Rev. Thomas Sharpe suggests the hostility created by this even-handed approach for Protestants with strongly held anti-Catholic views.[68]

Was there a religious basis to Maconochie's system? The direct answer to this is both yes and no. Although it could accommodate religious principles and instruction (and attracted many religious supporters),[69] it was based on utilitarian rather than Evangelical expectations of reform, though to Gipps he acknowledged that religion and moral instruction were critical to 'genuine Reform' and that they should be provided for generously.[70] Like Whately, Maconochie saw no justification for the belief that religious indoctrination led to correct moral behaviour – indeed, rather the opposite appeared to be the case. The jaundiced former chaplain of Norfolk Island, the Rev. Thomas Atkins (1808–1860), who was expelled from his position as a result of quarrelling with Commandant Anderson, had no direct experience of Maconochie's regime at Norfolk Island. However, he rejected it as a frivolous experiment without religious foundation because it did not assume the 'radical corruption of human nature' assumed by a strict Calvinist. For Atkins, this was proof that Maconochie's system was 'not based on religious principles' but was 'a mere philanthropic experiment made on depraved human nature, more on the principles of the late Robert Owen than on Christian principles'.[71] As such, he felt it deserved to fail. In denouncing the mark system as deployed in Dublin's Mountjoy Prison, Chris Gibson felt that marks were a gadget that undermined the operation of religious training, particularly since there were no marks for school or church.[72]

Despite these objections, Maconochie clearly did perceive his system as having religious foundations superior to those of its Evangelical rival.

[66] Ibid., 2.   [67] Ibid.
[68] Rev. Thomas Sharpe, 'Journal on Norfolk Island', 1837–1840, SLNSW B217, B218. See Chapter 8.
[69] For example, Anonymous, *Benevolence in Punishment, or Transportation Made Reformatory* (London: Seeley, Burnside, and Seeley, 1845); the title bears scripture quotations including 'Overcome evil with good' (Romans xii.21).
[70] Gipps to Stanley, 1 April 1843, encl. 18, Maconochie to Gipps, BPP 1846, House of Lords (40 & 94) VII.425, 599, p. 157.
[71] Atkins, *Reminiscences*, pp. 50–51.   [72] Gibson, *Irish Convict Reform*, p. 18.

With Atkins's successor, the Rev. Thomas Beagly Naylor (1805–1849), he formed a close and mutually productive working partnership reflected in Beagly's Norfolk Island diary.[73] Together Naylor and Maconochie achieved a kind of spiritual liberation for some of the men which may have generated a unique group of unpublished convict autobiographies.[74] Now in the National Library of Australia, the Norfolk Island diary of John Ward was written between 1841 and 1844 and, although ostensibly a contemporary record, it follows the model of Christian narratives of the return of the penitent discussed in Chapter 6.[75] A wild and dangerous criminal, Ward was reformed under Naylor's influence, 'who suddenly aroused me to new and more serious thought'.[76] Ward records retrieving a book sent to him by his mother called 'James's Anxious Inquirer', a work he had never cared to read since it was 'all about Religion'.[77] But, after two years, he turned to it 'it was ordained by my heavenly Father to bring me to his footstool at last; which gave me great comfort, something I never in my life experienced before'.[78] Possibly he read the chapter on 'Encouragements': 'God will not, and Satan and the world cannot hinder our salvation.'[79] He began attending divine service and reading his Bible. Although the diary ends with Ward leaving Norfolk Island, it ends not with despair, but a quotation from Genesis about the animals leaving the Ark to inherit the post-diluvial world and a new future.

The pencil sketches Naylor left behind of his garden on Norfolk Island suggests his time there was fruitful artistically as well as spiritually.[80] Like other ordained ministers engaged as religious instructors under the probation system, he felt strongly the loss of status and autonomy by his subordination to the Comptroller General of Convicts rather than the appropriate ecclesiastical authority, discussed in Chapter 8. He felt forced to resign, but did not let the matter rest. As with other Norfolk Island chaplains, Naylor took his revenge by writing a denunciation of

---

[73] Rev. T. B. Naylor Papers, May 1829–30 June 1849, SLNSW DLMS 134, DLMSQ 363.

[74] 'Norfolk Island Convict Papers, c.1842–1867', SLNSW MS 102, MS Q168.

[75] Partly transcribed in June Slee and John Ward, *Crime, Punishment and Redemption: A Convict's Story* (Canberra: National Library of Australia, 2014). For a perceptive review, see Tim Causer, 'Crime, Punishment and Redemption: A Convict's Story by June Slee', *The Mariner's Mirror*, 101.3 (2015), n.p.

[76] 'Diary of John Ward, convict', 1841–1844, NLA MS 3275; Slee, *Crime, Punishment and Redemption*, p. 140.

[77] John Angell James, *The Anxious Inquirer after Salvation: Directed and Encouraged* (London: Religious Tract Society, 1835).

[78] 'Diary of John Ward, convict', 1841–1844, NLA MS 3275; Slee, *Crime, Punishment and Redemption*, p. 156.

[79] James, *Anxious Inquirer*, p. 163.

[80] 'Summer house in Mr Naylor's garden' c.1842; 'The Valley of Ferns', National Library of Australia, PIC Drawer 6025.

conditions on the island. Naylor's wife brought this to London with instructions to publish it in the form of a letter to Earl Grey, but when she showed it to Maconochie he discreetly forwarded it to the Colonial Office instead. It was not the most hostile account of the Island, but it does describe Norfolk Island as 'a plague-spot' which was 'as wrong as it can be' in every sphere of its operations and that it should be closed.[81] In compelling detail (and his own illustration) Naylor dwelt on the moral danger created by herding prisoners into confined barracks, the crushing of all hope and the scanty fare: 'My Lord, the men cannot live upon this.'[82] Galvanized into action, Earl Grey enclosed Naylor's letter in a despatch to Denison and instructed him to break up the establishment on Norfolk Island immediately and move the prisoners to Tasman's Peninsula.[83]

It is true that Maconochie rarely spoke or wrote about religion. However, the exception to this comes in the form of a report which he prepared in 1843 for the Statistical Society of London. The Society was formed in 1834 with a view to providing data beneficial to society and for the deliberations of parliament.[84] In regard to religion, Maconochie observed that moral issues were almost entirely neglected by prisoners on Norfolk Island. Their lives were short and they had little to live for: 'In general the men die here very quietly and composedly ... even the worst of them [receive] the consolations of religion with little apparent doubt or hesitation.' There were exceptions, men who died 'utterly obdurate and impenitent', but generally they lacked a sense of moral guilt, which Maconochie blamed on a system which measured sentences by time, instead of labour and conduct. Though the men listened respectfully in church, Maconochie felt that the soil was barren: 'The wheat is sown among so many tares, that it is unable to yield a crop.'[85] Maconochie found more to admire in the apparent faith and despair of the older criminals than those who came to Norfolk Island with the benefit of penitentiary training.[86] Despite their condition, Maconochie was aware of considerable religious conservatism among the older generation and

---

[81] Rev. T. B. Naylor to Lord Stanley, written before 22 September 1846, Confidential Print, TNA CO 885/2/9; For the redacted printed version, *Convict Discipline and Transportation*, BPP 1847 (785) XLVIII.93, pp. 67–70.

[82] Ibid., p. 530.

[83] Grey to Denison, 30 September 1846, *Convict Discipline and Transportation*, BPP 1847 (785) XLVIII.93, p. 66.

[84] Founders included Adolphe Quetelet, the Belgian statistician, as well as Richard Jones, Thomas Malthus and Charles Babbage.

[85] Alexander Maconochie, 'Criminal Statistics and Movement of the Bond Population of Norfolk Island, to December, 1843', *Journal of the Statistical Society*, 8.1 (1845), 30.

[86] Ibid., 39.

apparent dislike for Owenite secularism. It would be interesting to know
how they responded to the arrival of the former Chartist, the Rev. Henry
Elliott, when he came to the island in 1847.[87]

Norfolk Island (1847)

By the time Maconochie's article for the Statistical Society was published, he had been relieved of his command. He was to spend much of
the rest of his life attempting to maintain his reputation as an effective
manager of penal systems. The shattering of Maconochie's hopes is
reflected in the defence of his regime on Norfolk Island, which he
published in 1847.[88] The most personal of Maconochie's publications,
it is full of brassy testimony about the success of his methods. In this
retrospective, he describes his arrival on the island where he found things
were, if anything, worse than he had expected. He was given charge of
1,400 doubly convicted prisoners, 'the refuse of both penal colonies'.[89]
Among many enlightened and innovative experiments he introduced a
revival of religious attendance by prisoners and officers. Having constructed two churches, he attended himself almost every Sunday during
the full four years of his term as Commandant, often reading the service
and delivering a sermon at one or other of the outstations. He established
schools and gave prizes for those who performed well. He encouraged
celebrations and national feeling, granting a half-holiday for St George's,
St David's, St Patrick's and St Andrew's Days, as well as for the anniver-
saries of the Battles of Trafalgar and Waterloo. Most controversially, on
one occasion he 'gave a glass of rum-punch to all hands to drink the
Queen's health'. The same day he had two plays performed, 'one of the
wisest and best considered acts of my whole administration, and which
was been the most pertinaciously censured'.[90]

While encouraging his social system and building moral improvement,
through music, theatre, self-expression (he also encouraged convicts to
write their memoirs) and religion, Maconochie denounced the principles
of the 'separate system', especially its reliance on pain, suffering and
social isolation. This he dismissed as a fundamental flaw: 'Men are
utterly helpless in its grasp; – they thus make excellent prisoners; – and
those who manage, and those who view, them in this position, are thus

[87] E. Strickland, *The Australian Pastor: A Record of the Remarkable Changes in Mind and Outward State of Henry Elliott* (London: Wertheim, Macintosh & Hunt, 1862).

[88] Captain Maconochie, *Norfolk Island*.

[89] Alexander Maconochie, *Norfolk Island* (London: J. Hatchard, 1847), p. 3.

[90] Ibid., 6.

enamoured of their success with them.'[91] But such a system, based on bondage, could not prepare men for liberty in contrast to his 'social system' which was based on the social nature of men who were born social beings, 'so fashioned by the hand of the Creator'. *Norfolk Island* (1847) reflects both Maconochie's bitter disappointment and what he felt to be his legacy and achievement.[92]

The Mark System, 1847

Maconochie provided an outline of the mark system in a second pamphlet published in 1847.[93] It contained four principles: firstly, sentences were measured by labour and good conduct combined, with a minimum of time, but no maximum. Secondly, labour was represented by marks, a certain number of which had to be earned 'in a penal condition' before discharge. Thirdly, prisoners worked and lived together in small parties with common interests. And finally, the system was voluntary. By 'voluntary' Maconochie meant that prisoners could choose to engage or not – but it was in their own interest to do so since without it they could not progress through their sentences. They were charged for their own keep and were issued 'moderate' fines for misconduct, with only the surplus counting towards liberation. Its major distinction from the 'separate system' was that prisoners were required to cooperate, building social skills. Its overall purpose was 'to train up manly, industrious, self-regulated men, capable of guiding themselves, and not requiring incessant control for their direction'.[94]

Although Maconochie took exclusive credit for devising the mark system, it bore more than a passing resemblance to the system of punishment and rewards in place in schools for poor children, particularly the influential Madras system of education devised by the Scottish Episcopalian minister, the Rev. Andrew Bell (1753–1832), promoted by the 'National' (i.e., Anglican) Society, or the rival 'Lancasterian' system devised by the English Quaker Joseph Lancaster (1778–1838), of the British and Foreign School Society, which was more popular with Evangelicals and Dissenters. Backhouse and Walker probably had the Lancasterian system in mind when they observed that Maconochie's mark system was 'the same that has been successfully brought into

---

[91] Ibid., 10.   [92] Captain Maconochie, *Norfolk Island*, p. 13.
[93] Alexander Maconochie, *The Mark System of Prison Discipline* (London, 1847c), pp. 1–2; Tim Causer, 'Alexander Maconochie's "Mark System"', *Prison Service Journal*, 198 (2011), 38–46.
[94] Maconochie, *The Mark System*, p. 6.

operation in schools, lunatic establishments, etc.'[95] Bell's system was devised in India but particularly celebrated in his home city of St Andrews in Fife, about forty miles from North Queensferry where Maconochie had once set up a school for local children.[96] Under the Madras system, children earned pecuniary rewards by accumulating 'tickets' for maintaining a particular rank in class.[97] Tickets could also be lost for poor conduct and there were punishments, some quite humiliating, but the aim was to eliminate the rod and replace it with what Bell called 'an engine ... giving motion to the moral world'.[98] Lancaster's 'British system' also deployed emulation, ranking and tickets for rewards to encourage performance.[99] Modes of punishment were grim and illegal by modern standards, including shackles, tying the left hand behind the back or tying the feet together: 'This is an excellent punishment for boys who offend by leaving their seats', Lancaster chortled.[100] The object of Lancaster's system was to provide a Christian education to teach the poor how to read Scripture, and, as Thomas Clarkson noted, 'to improve their moral condition, and to make them more useful and respectable members of the community in which they live'.[101] Like Maconochie, both Bell and Lancaster aimed to reduce the reliance on physical punishment in education and replace them with positive, moral alternatives.

Both the Lancasterian and the Bell system of education worked on similar principles to those of Maconochie's mark system. As for the marks themselves, in his account of the system, the Rev. Walter Clay explained that convicts were treated as labourers, with marks for wages, a certain number of which had to be earned prior to discharge. A fair wage for completing a day's tasks was fixed at ten marks and food could be purchased for three, four or five marks per day, according to quality, with extra marks available for earning more than the day's quota and penalties deducted for misconduct.[102] Maconochie outlined how the penalties worked in practice in a letter to New South Wales Governor George Gipps on 4 April 1832, when, much against his judgement, he was required to identify twelve of the 'least deserving' men from among the

[95] Backhouse and Walker to Maconochie, 13 August 1837, *Maconochie's Report*, p. 13.
[96] On his death in 1832, Bell donated his fortune for a school in St Andrews, the present Madras College, founded 1833.
[97] Andrew Bell, *An Abridged Edition of the Work of the Rev. Andrew Bell* (Edinburgh: Oliver & Boyd, 1833), p. 379.
[98] Ibid., 158.
[99] Joseph Lancaster, *The British System of Education* (London: Longman, 1810).
[100] Ibid., 34.
[101] 'Resolution of a Meeting at Bury St Edmund's, 27 March 1810', Ibid., xiv.
[102] W. L. Clay, *Our Convict Systems* (London: Macmillan, 1862), p. 22.

Norfolk Islanders.[103] In an attempt to comply he provided a table for 104 prisoners, listing the marks earned and the particular offences for which they had been fined. It was part of the regime that there were no marks awarded for education or religious pursuits, which were regarded as a benefit to prisoners, though being absent from prayers would cost twenty-five marks and a 'violent tempered, insubordinate young man' was fined twenty-five marks for 'sleeping during Divine Service in chapel, and impertinence under examination'.[104] At the lower end of the scale were fines for misbehaviour or breaches of hygiene such as refusing to bathe (twelve marks), misbehaviour at the night muster (twelve marks), nuisance in rear of his hut (twelve marks), being absent from muster on Sunday (twelve marks) or stealing clothes (nine marks). More serious were offences such as neglect of work (twenty-five marks), malingering (twenty-five marks), careless field-labour (eighty-four marks) or refusing to work (one hundred marks). The most serious penalties were reserved for threats to Maconochie himself, damage to property and sexual offences. For 'insolence and threatening language to Captain Macono-chie', a man described as 'very bad and very insubordinate' was fined 1,000 marks and served a month in gaol. For falsehood to the Rev. Mr Naylor, 1,000 marks, and for stealing shirt and trousers, 1,000 marks and two months in gaol. A man described as 'partly silly, but very trouble-some', received a fine of 1,000 marks for 'making a false confession of murder at home' and fifty marks for 'riotous conduct in the stockade'. Another received 1,000 marks for stealing a fellow prisoner's clothes and selling them, with one month in gaol. For unnatural crime, 'a poor lad, weak and much ashamed' was fined 1,000 marks and twice received fifty lashes. Since sodomy was a felony, this was a lenient sentence and opened Maconochie up to accusations that his system failed to control unnatural crime. What should be evident is that the mark system did not replace physical punishments but was used in addition to them. Another flaw in the system was that Maconochie never succeeded in his wish to be able to reduce sentences based on marks received on the island. By every account, once prisoners were aware of this there was considerable change from the almost miraculous improvement reported by Maconochie when the system was first introduced.

The mark system was a significant challenge to the religious principles of the Evangelical penitentiary, where moral training was directed exter-nally by the chaplain or religious instructor, and physical pain by the

[103] Gipps to Stanley, 29 May 1842, encl. Maconochie to Gipps, 4 April 1842, BPP 1843 (158) XLII.353, pp. 16–22.
[104] Ibid., p. 21.

infliction of physical punishments, such as flogging and chaining, or less violent (but equally repressive) measures such as solitary confinement, hard and scanty fare, loss of light and forced, hard labour (all parts of the system Maconochie inherited). However, Maconochie was equally committed to religious principles, indeed he describes his system as 'exclusively a mental, or rather moral, process', which aimed not to crush the will, but to elevate it: 'The exercise of will', Maconochie argues, 'sustained by self-interest is in the hands of Divine Providence the great spring and stimulant to improvement in society. Combined with social and kindly feeling, which it is also a special object of the Mark System to cultivate, it is the fruitful parent of every social virtue'.[105] Earlier religious regimes in prison had made the Calvinist assumption of man's fallen nature and depravity; Maconochie stressed individuals' moral discernment, capacity for rational self-interest and the virtue of labour, while acknowledging they remained equally dependent on God for its reformative effects.

Although Maconochie stated that the mark system and his proposals for penal reform were completely original, almost all the elements of his system had precedents in the work of earlier Christian utilitarian reformers and educators, especially Paley, Bentham and Whately on penal reform. This was recognized by contemporaries such as Walter Clay, who thought Maconochie derived his best ideas from Sir John Franklin.[106] Maconochie himself credited Whately with outlining the principle of labour-based rather than time-based sentences:[107] 'It would be difficult to express the direct primary effect of the system in happier or terser terms.'[108] Yet Whately was mistaken in thinking the labour-based sentence was original to him.[109] Without doubt, the notion derived from Paley's chapter on crime in his *Principles on Moral and Political Philosophy* (1795), a book well known to Whately.[110] Despite the lack of originality on key points, it is fair to recognize that Maconochie's promotion of labour-based sentencing coupled to the mark system, as well as his

---

[105] Maconochie, *The Mark System*, p. 7.
[106] Clay, *Our Convict Systems*, p. 21. For Maconochie's debt to Whately, see *The North American Review*, vol. 102, no. 210 (1866), p. 213.
[107] Whately, *Thoughts on Secondary Punishments.*   [108] Maconochie, *Mark System*, p. 42
[109] Whately, *Life and Correspondence of Richard Whately, D. D. Late Archbishop of Dublin*, pp. vol. I, p. 172. Whately himself believed it to be one of his most original proposals and the source for both Maconochie and Crofton's subsequent use of it. See Ibid., vol. II, p. 394.
[110] Thorsten Sellin, 'Paley on the Time Sentence', *Journal of Criminal Law and Criminology*, 22.2 (1931–1951), 264–266; Paley, *The Principles of Moral and Political Philosophy*. vol. II, pp. 292–293: 'I would measure the confinement, not by the duration of time, but by the quantity of work.'

dynamism in carrying through an effective trial of the system, was responsible for a significant shift in the practice of secondary punishments away from negative and towards positive reinforcement for good behaviour.

Verdict on Maconochie

While Maconochie provided an eloquent defence of his methods supported by testimony from convicts and the sympathetic religious and humanitarian reformers who took up his cause, the experiment was deemed a failure by most of his superiors. The most important reports were those of George Gipps, Governor of New South Wales from 1840 to 1843.[111] In Sydney, Gipps had been too far away to provide effective supervision for Maconochie's experiment on Norfolk Island, about which he was initially very sceptical.[112] However he made two visits and provided full and detailed accounts of Maconochie's progress. Following his first visit, he was cautiously positive.[113] By the time of his second report, completed after a second personal examination of the island, he recommended that the experiment should end.[114] In the Colonial Office, a dispassionate assessment of Captain Maconochie's experiment is reflected in the lengthy confidential memorandum compiled for the Colonial Office by Thomas William Clinton Murdoch (1809–1891) in 1837.[115] Murdoch provided a précis of all the correspondence relating to Captain Maconochie on Norfolk Island, including Maconochie's own reports, which were invariably effusive and positive. There were numerous letters from hostile and yet generally well-informed sources, who accused Maconochie of leniency and inconsistency. His regime was notable for his radical departure from the policy agreed when he undertook his office, especially the intermingling of the old and new prisoners under his charge which was promptly disallowed by Gipps.[116] While the experiment continued, Gipps communicated his reservations to the Colonial Office, calling it 'a system of extreme indulgence':

[111] S. C. McCulloch, 'Sir George Gipps and Captain Alexander Maconochie: The Attempted Penal Reforms at Norfolk Island, 1840–44', *Historical Studies Australia and New Zealand*, 7 (1957), 387–406. For the reports on Maconochie, see *Convict System (Norfolk Island)*, BPP House of Lords 1846 (40, 94) VII.425, 599 [Hereafter *Convict System (Norfolk Island)*.]

[112] Gipps to Russell, 29 September 1840, *Convict System (Norfolk Island)*, p. 1.

[113] Gipps to Stanley, 15 August 1842, *Convict System (Norfolk Island)*, p. 63.

[114] Gipps to Stanley, 1 April 1843, *Convict System (Norfolk Island)*, p. 137.

[115] T. W. C. Murdoch, 'The Transportation System', 15 August 1846, TNA Confidential Print CO 885/2/11. Subsequent quotations are from this report.

[116] Ibid., 11.

Captain Maconochie avows his opinion that the first object of all convict discipline should be the reformation of the criminal. This opinion, however agreeable it may be to the dictates of humanity, is not, I believe the received one of legislators, who rather require as the first object of convict discipline, that it should be a terror to evil-doers.[117]

In February 1842, continuing to feel anxious about the progress of Maconochie's experiment, Governor Gipps returned to the island. Reporting to Gipps, Maconochie was as positive as ever: 'In no case', he stated, 'have I failed to realize all, or even more than all, that I had ventured to expect'. In August 1842, Gipps prepared his own account of the mark system, arguing that it was prohibitively expensive and could not be extended beyond the initial trial.[118] For Maconochie, this elicited even more extravagant claims for success: 'I have almost made black white. With scarcely any change in the externals of a system long known for its deteriorating effects, I have yet converted many previously very bad men into good.'

While Gipps admired what Maconochie was doing, he astutely observed that it relied on the personal attachment of the men to Maconochie himself: 'He has much influence over them, and they greatly desire to please him.'[119] Worryingly, the economic viability of the island was being compromised by the scheme, with less effective labour and depredations of the timber and firewood; there was also an outbreak of dysentery. Maconochie was also inconsistent and inclined to striking effects, especially on 'the worst men'.[120] Gipps's final report was written after a second visit to the island in March 1843. This is particularly interesting in the support it provided to Maconochie's methods, the good order that prevailed and the quiet and respectful demeanour of the prisoners. Gipps was particularly glowing in his approval of the system as it impacted on the older hands: 'These Men had suffered, and suffered severely, before Captain Maconochie assumed the Management of them, and their Minds had consequently been brought to a State in which the Manifestation of Kindness on the part of their ruler, was likely to make the best impression on them.'[121] This had led to no evil consequences. This did not mean it could go on. The end for Maconochie came when the government of Lord John Russell launched the probation system, with Norfolk Island serving as the first stage in the reception of prisoners

---

[117] Sir George Gipps, February 1841. Commons Paper, No. 412 of 1841, p. 64; Murdoch, 'The Transportation System', TNA Confidential Print CO 885/2/11: 12.
[118] Gipps to Stanley, 15 August 1842, *Convict System (Norfolk Island)*, p. 61
[119] Ibid., p. 63   [120] Ibid., p. 63.
[121] Gipps to Stanley, 1 April 1843, *Convict System (Norfolk Island)*, p. 144.

in the scheme devised by the home secretary, Lord Stanley, discussed in the next chapter.

The clergy who worked with Maconochie on Norfolk Island had a range of views about his experiment. Most Protestant convict chaplains were strongly anti-Catholic and those who offered themselves for Norfolk Island seem to have been so intensely. The Rev. Thomas Sharpe was unable to tolerate Maconochie's liberal regime and was dismissed in 1840.[122] In his diary Sharpe accused the Catholic chaplains of a 'mania' for inflating their numbers, aided by the Commandant: 'I am sorry to see how highly favoured the priests of Rome are by the present Government.'[123] Sharpe blamed Maconochie's social system for offences against the Sabbath and a tide of antinomian excess among the prisoners: 'As liberalism has advanced among them, the fear of doing wrong has vanished, and, the dread of punishment being taken away, they exult in their evil deeds without restraint.'[124] He was horrified when Maconochie attended a Roman Catholic service, appalled that a Protestant would sanction 'the awful apostacy of their fallen Church'.[125] Although Captain Maconochie also attended his services with his wife and ensured the construction of an attractive Protestant church, Sharpe remained implacably hostile to his methods: 'Religion has little to do with the boasted new System, but amusements much.'[126] Also finding sectarian solace in writing, the Catholic chaplain, John McEncroe, enlivened his sojourn on the island by completing a popular guide to heresies, including those of Protestant apostates such as Martin Luther, Thomas Müntzer and John Calvin: 'If these men were sent by our blessed Saviour to reform his church, founded by the Apostles, there must have been a most extraordinary change in the ways of Providence.'[127]

Maconochie's strongest supporter was the Rev. Thomas Beagly Naylor (1805–1849).[128] Naylor's long letter to Lord Stanley laid most of the burden of blame for the collapse of discipline on Maconochie's successor, but the lack of effective moral supervision and the excessive power of the older men on new arrivals were systemic problems. Naylor's most severe strictures concerned unnatural crime: 'As a clergyman and a magistrate, I feel bound to tell your Lordship, that the curse of Almighty

[122] Rev. Thomas Sharpe, 'Journal on Norfolk Island', 1837–1840, SLNSW B217-B218.
[123] Sharpe 'Journal', 4 January 1839, Ibid., p. 346,
[124] Sharpe 'Journal', 1 October 1840, Ibid., p. 595.
[125] Sharpe 'Journal', 20 April 1840, Ibid., p. 647.
[126] Sharpe 'Journal', 20 April 1840, Ibid., p. 678.
[127] John McEncroe, *The Wanderings of the Human Mind* (Sydney: Duncan, 1841), p. iv.
[128] Earl Grey to Denison, 30 September 1846, encl. Rev. T. B. Naylor to Lord Stanley, n.d., TNA Confidential Print CO 885/2/9.

God must sooner or later fall in scorching anger upon a nation which can tolerate the continuance of a state of things so demoniacal and unnatural.'[129] A rather more detached review of the administration of Maconochie comes from the Rev. John McEncroe, longest-serving chaplain on Norfolk Island, who observed Commandants Anderson, Bunbury, Ryan and Maconochie. McEncroe provided his report in a series of letters to Governor Gipps, the first dated 31 March 1842, a year after McEncroe left the island, while Maconochie was still in command.[130] According to McEncroe, Anderson was 'over-rigid' and Bunbury unwise, but he initially had high hopes for Maconochie, exclaiming 'a new era has commenced; a mild, considerate and reformatory form of prison discipline' had been introduced and with 'good results'.[131] In retrospect, McEncroe felt that Maconochie's system worked well on first offenders, but that he was imposed on by the older hands: 'As Major Anderson had too low an opinion of human nature, so Captain Maconochie seems to have fallen into the opposite extreme. Two hundred old hands under Major Ryan's management, would do as much work as is done now by the whole six hundred new hands.'[132] McEncroe believed there were significant problems with 'detestable and horrible abominations' practised by the 'flashmen' and that Maconochie was negligent in providing effective discipline to prevent abuses, something echoed by Naylor. McEncroe concluded that Maconochie was 'a gentleman of kind and amiable dispositions, of extensive literary acquirements and of benevolent views', but he would not succeed unless he addressed the problems in his administration.[133] This assessment carried the weight of experience of a man who was a consistent advocate for convicts, while recognizing their fallen nature. According to Ullathorne's testimony to the Molesworth SC, McEncroe attended seventy-four executions in four years, where he found 'that the greater number of criminals had, on their way to the scaffold, thanked God that they were not going to Norfolk Island'.[134]

Maconochie's administration clearly had numerous problems, but the most tragic feature of his story is what happened on his departure.

---

[129] Naylor to Lord Stanley, Ibid., p. 24.
[130] Daly, 'Archdeacon McEncroe on Norfolk Island, 1838–42'; The originals are in the Sydney Diocesan Archives with the title, 'Norfolk Island Past and present in six letters on the Penal Administration of four successive Commandants inscribed to His Excellency Sir George Gipps Knight Governor of New South Wales etc. With an Appendix on the prevention of revolting offences among prisoners and practical reflection on prison discipline'; See Birchley, *John McEncroe*, pp. 71–74.
[131] McEncroe to Gipps, 31 March 1842; Birchley, *John McEncroe*, p. 73.
[132] McEncroe to Gipps, 31 March 1842; Ibid., 74.
[133] McEncroe to Gipps, 31 March 1842; Ibid., 75.
[134] Ullathorne, *Autobiography of Archbishop Ullathorne*, p. 100.

He did what he could to secure the future of 'his gentlemen', but he was succeeded in rapid succession by two very different officers. Major Joseph Childs (1787–1870) served as Commandant from 8 February 1844 to 5 August 1846. Although Mortlock regarded him as an able administrator who continued Maconochie's reforms,[135] he was not able to maintain his authority over either the convicts or his officers. A convict rebellion on 1 July 1846 resulted in the deaths of four officials, and in the reprisals that followed seventeen convicts were executed. Child's successor was the infamous John Giles Price (1808–1857), commandant from 1846 to 1853, reports of whose repressive regime finally shocked the government into action.

The most telling critique of Maconochie's successors was provided by clerical observers, including the Rev. Beagly Naylor and Bishop Robert Willson of Van Diemen's Land, beginning with Willson's testimony to the HLSC in 1847 following his first visit to Norfolk Island in May 1846.[136] Willson made two further visits to Norfolk Island in 1849 and 1852, each time reporting on his findings to the appropriate authorities.[137] After his first visit he told Denison: 'Gloom, sullen despondency, despair of leaving the Island, seemed to be the general condition of the men's minds.'[138] In contrast to Van Diemen's Land, where the task system (a modified version of Maconochie's marks) gave purpose to penal activity, the men on Norfolk Island were without hope, burdened with heavy punishments on the word of convict informers for minor breaches of discipline. This, he acknowledged, could only be confirmed by checking the records of the convict comptroller. Yet, there were some things which Willson witnessed directly, including the use of heavy irons and the aftermath of excessive flogging. Willson's description of the scene in Norfolk Island, when forty-three men were flogged over two days, still has the power to shock.[139] He described the use of a tube gag for speech offences and the chaining of men spread-eagled so they could not relax or sleep. Willson expressed his deep concern with the pattern of extending convict sentences for trivial offences so that their time under the harsh regime of Norfolk Island might be indefinitely extended,

---

[135] G. A. Wilkes and A. G. Mitchell (eds.), *Experiences of a Convict Transported for Twenty-One Years by J. A. Mortlock* (Sydney: Sydney University Press, 1965).

[136] 'Testimony of Bishop Willson', *HL SC on Criminal Laws*, BPP 1847 (447 & 534) VII.1,637.

[137] J. H. Cullen, 'Bishop Willson and Norfolk Island', *Tasmanian Historical Research Association Papers and Proceedings*, 1.2 (1952), 4–10; J. H. Cullen, 'Bishop Willson', *Australasian Catholic Record*, 29.1, 2, 3 (1952), 20–27, 117–124, 205–214.

[138] Thomas Kelsh, *Personal Recollections' of the Right Reverend Robert William Willson* (Hobart: Davies, 1882), p. 40.

[139] Ibid., 41.

regardless of their original offences: 'What I deprecate is not the punishing men for disobedience, but for making the penalties disproportionate, both in kind and intensity to the offence.'[140] The Rev. Thomas Rogers's account of the criminal informing and brutal punishments meted out for minor breaches of discipline, especially using tobacco, corroborated Willson's.[141]

There was an official response to Willson's report of humanitarian abuses. With some condescension, Denison noted that as 'a really good and earnest man', Willson was entitled to 'every consideration', but recommended no change.[142] In his response to Willson's accusations, including the practice of cumulative sentences for minor breaches of discipline, John Hampton, Van Diemen's Land comptroller general of convicts, was concerned purely with the consequence of closing Norfolk Island and having to transfer the men to Port Arthur, or some other secure location.[143] Hampton commended all its rigours, which were 'well calculated to render Norfolk Island, as it is now, a terror to evil doers of the worst class'.[144] Nevertheless, the cumulative effect of the reports of articulate clerical informants, including Naylor, Willson and Rogers, finally had an impact. Following Grey's instruction, Governor Denison ordered that the second settlement of Norfolk Island be wound down. By 1855 all the convicts had been transferred to Van Diemen's Land, two years after the ending of transportation to eastern Australia.

Conclusion

The immediate impact of Maconochie's experiment was felt widely throughout the penal colonies. In 1846, Earl Grey instructed Colonel Denison to introduce a form of reformatory transportation that included elements of the Maconochie system.[145] Denison was less impressed, claiming it was neither original nor effective and 'in effect an inferior system of task work'.[146] Perhaps the most significant change to prison discipline which followed in Maconochie's wake was the appointment of more religious instructors and resident convict chaplains. Having been largely invisible in the earliest days of the ultra-penal settlements, they became a fixture in those which continued to run in the 1840s and 1850s.

---

[140] Ibid., 48.
[141] W. Foster Rogers and Thomas George Rogers, 'Man's Inhumanity', SLNSW MS C214.
[142] Denison to Grey, 27 July 1850, BPP 1851 (1361 & 1418) XLV.1, 265, p. 21.
[143] J. G. Hampton to Denison, 'Report', 10 July 1850, Ibid., p. 26.   [144] Ibid., p. 27.
[145] Grey to Denison, 30 September 1846, TNA Confidential Print CO 885/2/9: 5.
[146] Denison to Grey, 12 September 1846, TNA Confidential Print CO 885/2/9: 3.

One effect of this was that clerical observers provided a continuous stream of commentary, often with a direct channel to the latest parliamentary committee. Followng Governor Gipps' cautiously positive reports, the mark system was implemented at Port Arthur, Bermuda and elsewhere and generally served to regulate penal discipline and moderate resort to physical punishments.

Maconochie was given another opportunity when he was appointed governor of the new prison at Birmingham at the initiative of Matthew Davenport Hill (1792–1872), the 'Recorder of Birmingham'.[147] If Norfolk Island was an experiment which was not given an effective trial, then Birmingham should probably be seen as a reasonable test of Maconochie's methods. Like other Victorian heroes, Maconochie had feet of clay, revealed by the abuse of young boys and women under his management and that of his successor at Birmingham.[148] The press of the day tended to exonerate Maconochie and blame Austin for abuse, as did Robert Hughes.[149] In his careful assessment of Maconochie at Birmingham, John Moore notes that Maconochie's belief in his system and the absolute necessity of 'breaking' prisoners to it – male and female – led him to coercive methods which were far from benevolent.[150] Maconochie's originality lay in proposing 'moral methods', including religion, the arts and promoting social engagement and reintegration with society, rather than isolation and religious indoctrination, and this represented a major leap forward for prisoners. But it was deemed insufficiently punitive and it was expensive. Nevertheless, the appetite for reform and experiments in transportation had not yet been extinguished, and Maconochie demonstrated that utilitarian penal principles need not be incompatible with practical Christianity. His was the first attempt to implement liberal and non-sectarian regimes of penal discipline in the penal colonies, a challenge to the harsher values of the Evangelical penitentiary and the separate system. The next chapter examines the ways in which religion was woven into the rules and processes of the probation system, the ambitious reformative experiment devised to counter the ever-growing demand for an end to transportation and the closure of the 'Ocean Hell'.

---

[147] Rosamond Davenport-Hill, Florence Davenport Hill, *A Memoir of Matthew Davenport Hill, the Recorder of Birmingham* (London: Macmillan, 1878), pp. 241–242.
[148] *RC into Condition and Treatment of Prisoners in Birmingham Borough Prison*, BPP 1854 (1809) XXXI.1.
[149] *The Spectator*, 5 August 1854, p. 10; Hughes, *Fatal Shore*, p. 521.
[150] Moore, 'Alexander Maconochie's "Mark System"'.

For the first time in the history of mankind reformation has been adopted as the principle of penal discipline.[1]   (*Herald of Tasmania*, 1845)

I regret to state my impression that after all the stress laid upon the necessity of providing adequately for the religious and moral instruction of the Convict under the New System, in no particular has the difficulty of attaining the object been more glaringly apparent.[2]   (La Trobe, 1847)

After the abolition of private assignment under transportation, religious engagement intensified for most prisoners, from silence and separation in Britain's penitentiaries to religious instruction and work in the probation stations abroad. In the penal colonies a period of experimentation in reformative transportation began, through which convicts would work, pray and be guided to better lives, at least in theory. Recent historians are sceptical about this process; Philip Harling, for one, notes that from 1840, the probation system constituted an attempt to 'moralize' the convicts to make them acceptable to the colonists.[3] The protracted end to convict transportation is thus considered a largely hypocritical attempt to avoid the expense of alternatives such as penal servitude in modern penitentiaries for British prisoners at home. This was the view of Radicals and utilitarians, Christian and secular, who believed the argument about transportation had been won and lost by Whately, Molesworth and his SC on Transportation. Yet this ignores the religious commitment and integrity of reformers in government and colonial administration, who continued to see merit in reformative schemes of penal exile.

This chapter traces the religious aspects of Lord Stanley's probation system and its impact on the anti-transportation campaign. After

---

[1] 'The Probation System', *Herald of Tasmania*, 1 August 1845, BPP 1847 (785) XLVIII.93, p. 191.

[2] 'La Trobe's Report', 31 May 1847, in Ian Brand, *The Convict Probation System: Van Diemen's Land 1839–1854*, edited by M. N. Sprod (Hobart: Blubber Head Press, 1990), p. 109.

[3] Harling, 'The Trouble with Convicts', 80–110.

examining regulations devised for Pentonville, which established the probation system and connected it to reform in the penal colonies, it considers the staffing and implementation of probation's religious provisions by the new class of religious prison officers, many of them pious laymen attracted to the system's reformative principles (and the relatively generous salaries). The system's ultimate failure provided powerful ammunition for the closure of penal colonies and fuelled the emergence of a settler lobby demanding an end to all transportation. The campaign would take almost twenty years to succeed and involved an extraordinary effort to bring religion to the dark places of the penal system: on board the 'floating hell' of the hulks and transports and in places of secondary punishment, from the 'hell on earth' of Port Arthur to the 'ocean hell' of Norfolk Island, and the naval dockyards of Bermuda and Gibraltar.

Pentonville, 1842

Probation was intimately connected with Pentonville. Opened in 1842 as a national prison, Pentonville emerged as part of a raft of social, legal and religious reforms promoted by the Whig administration of Lord John Russell, which continued the shift away from death or exile and towards reform and incarceration in punishment.[4] Designed by military engineer Major Joshua Jebb and set behind massive walls on its own six-acre site, Pentonville was among the most significant investments in social capital of the Victorian age. Lauded by reformers, ridiculed by satirists such as Thomas Carlisle (1795–1881) and Dickens, endlessly visited and commented on by contemporaries, in the 1970s radical historians, including Michael Ignatieff, represented it as the emblem of the repressive, perverted religiosity of the penitentiary movement.[5] Even its labour was designed to be cruelly pointless. Whatever the justice of this representation, and it has been subject to considerable revision by historians disagreeing with Ignatieff and Michel Foucault,[6] Pentonville, together with Parkhurst, was the most highly regulated prison ever built in England. By

---

[4] Clive Emsley, *Crime and Society in England, 1750–1900* 5th edn (Harlow: Longman, 2018), pp. 284–285; Radzinowicz, *English Criminal Law*, vol. 4, pp. 316–326.

[5] For the most extreme condemnation of Pentonville, see Ignatieff, *Just Measure*, pp. 3–11; Alternatively, McConville, *English Prison Administration*, pp. 204–217.

[6] Bill Forsythe, 'Foucault's Carceral and Ignatieff's Pentonville – English Prisons and the Revisionist Analysis of Control and Penality', *Policing and Society*, 1.2 (1990), 141–158. For alternative studies of the penitentiary, see Randall McGowen, 'The Well-Ordered Prison: England, 1780–1985', in Norval Morris and David J. Rothman (eds.), *The Oxford History of the Prison: The Practice of Punishment in Western Society* (Oxford: Oxford University Press, 1995), pp. 71–99; Norval Morris and David J. Rothman, 'Perfecting the Prison', Ibid.

1850, Jebb reported there were at least fifty-five British and Irish prisons 'erected or improved on the Pentonville Plan' and it was becoming the template for all prisons in the empire.[7] While prison building proceeded, Pentonville was not intended to be effective in isolation, but rather as a link in chains of morality and religion, encouraging the prisoner's repentance and reform at home, followed by transportation, public labour and release to a new life in the penal colonies. Vast though it was, in 1842 Pentonville could accommodate only 520 prisoners under the separate system, a year in which 4,656 men and 678 women were transported to Van Diemen's Land (transportation to New South Wales having ended).[8] After more unsuccessful attempts to find alternative locations for detention, including Corfu, the Falkland Islands, St Helena and Cape Town, more hardened offenders were consigned to the hulks, Bermuda, and Millbank, which handed over its penitentiary functions to Pentonville and Parkhurst to become a depot for convicts awaiting transportation.[9]

Though modified by the more utilitarian principles of Sir Joshua Jebb, Pentonville was infused with an Evangelical religious ethos. Just as Howard had recommended, a chapel lay at its heart, though its separate chapel (what Ignatieff called the 'brain of the penitentiary machine') bore little resemblance to Howard's design.[10] From early in the morning, when prisoners donned masks to attend the first service of the day, religion regulated their regime.[11] More important than the chapel's physical constraints, which were undermined by prisoners and disliked by serving chaplains,[12] was the chaplain's authority. At Pentonville, the chaplain was the prison's second-ranking officer, with an assistant chaplain and subordinate officers, including the schoolmasters, under his control and power to choose every book in the prison library. The Pentonville Rules approved by the Home Office Secretary Sir James

---

[7] 'Testimony of Joshua Jebb', 5 March 1850, *Select Committee on Prison Discipline*, BPP 1850 (632) XVII.1, p. 4.

[8] Shaw, *Convicts and the Colonies*, p. 367.

[9] Under the Millbank Prison Act (1843), the 'General Penitentiary at Millbank' became Millbank Prison. See McConville, *English Prison Administration*, p. 168.

[10] Ignatieff, *Just Measure*, p. 5.

[11] For a melodramatic summary, see Ibid. For another view, see Arthur Burns, 'The Authority of the Church', in Peter Mandler (ed.), *Liberty and Authority in Victorian Britain* (Oxford: Oxford University Press, 2006), pp. 179–200. Prisoners spent no more than half an hour per day in the separate chapel.

[12] *Reports of the Directors of Convict Prisons, 1851*, BPP 1852 (1524) XXIV.197, pp. 17–19, notes, as offences, fifty-one attempts to communicate in the Pentonville chapel; nine for disfiguring the chapel by obscene drawings, boring holes in stalls etc. and seven for 'indecorous conduct' in school and chapel.

Graham (1792–1861) in December 1842,[13] required the chaplain to be an ordained member of the Church of England, licensed by the bishop of London for the purpose.[14] At 400 pounds, his salary was substantially higher than that of gaol chaplains received elsewhere in England and Wales in 1835.[15] Like Millbank before it, Pentonville was a moral Panopticon (Bentham's term for the all-seeing supervisory chamber of his prison machine),[16] with the chaplain, in partnership with the governor, at its apex. While from the start objections were made concerning Pentonville's authoritarian character, one of its leading principles was the replacement of all other forms of physical punishment with labour, religious instruction and solitude. The social commentator Henry Mayhew (1812–1887), who was well aware of the objections to the regime at Pentonville, including the high risk of psychiatric damage posed by total silence and separation, nevertheless preferred it to the alternatives, including Maconochie's mark system.[17]

Although inspired by American models, Pentonville's separate system, which was followed by transportation and probation in the penal colonies, was distinct from systems of penal discipline tried elsewhere.[18] The various American models were essentially buildings designed for forced labour by long-term prisoners, with staff dedicated to maintaining discipline – not reform. Innovations such as the appointment of full-time salaried prison chaplains, schools, libraries and more inclusive religious provision, did not reach American prisoners until after the Civil War.[19] William Crawford (1788–1847), the great advocate of the separate

---

[13] Graham served as both a (Peelite) Tory and Whig and is regarded as a founder of the modern Liberal Party. He was succeeded by Sir George Grey as Home Secretary.

[14] 'Rules for the Government of the Pentonville Prison', TNA HO 43/335: 46.

[15] *Gaol Chaplains: Return of Salaries Paid to Chaplains in Gaols, Hours of Attendance, Emoluments from Other Sources*, BPP 1835 (200), XLV.187. Salaries ranged widely from as little as fifty pounds for part-time duty. Two hundred pounds was common for a full-time position, though chaplains complained they had to pay for a house. Fewer than ten chaplains received £300 per annum. The highest salary was £400 paid to Whitworth Russell at the General Penitentiary, Milbank (sic). Ibid., p. 205.

[16] Bentham's Panopticon was based on a design for a Russian factory and was suggested by his younger brother, Samuel. For links to the original drawings, prepared by the architect Willey Reveley (1760–1799), see 'Panopticon drawings and manuscripts', UCL Library Special Collections, Box 119, www.ucl.ac.uk/bentham-project/who/panopticon (Accessed 3 August 2018).

[17] Henry Mayhew and John Binny, *The Criminal Prisons of London and Scenes of Prison Life* (New York: Kelley, 1851), pp. 168–169.

[18] Bill Forsythe, 'The Aims and Methods of the Separate System', *Social Policy and Administration*, 14.3 (1980), 249–256; U. R. Q. Henriques, 'The Rise and Decline of the Separate System of Prison Discipline', *Past & Present*, 54 (1972), 61–93.

[19] Henry Kamerling, *Capital and Convict* (Charlottesville: University of Virginia Press, 2017). Race has continued to be a major determinant of punishment in many American states into living memory. Convict leasing, including forced labour for

system, noted these deficiencies in his report to parliament on American penitentiaries.[20] Auburn originally had neither chaplain nor religious instruction and the present chaplain admitted to Crawford that he could see the 680 prisoners in their cells only once in three months.[21] While British prisons were clearly grim and terrible places, they were nevertheless benign by comparison with many in America or Europe. Advocates of the superiority of the Pentonville model included Joseph Adshead (1800–1861), the Manchester penal and social reformer.[22] In contrast to Pentonville's separate system, the French inspectors De Beaumont and De Tocqueville found Auburn's silent system, where the prisoners 'see without knowing each other' to be both eerie and inhumane.[23] Objecting to the system of enforced silence and solitary confinement at Sing Sing, broken only by the visitation of the chaplain, the politician Sir Peter Laurie (1778–1861) expostulated: 'Can it be possible, that men, living in a Christian country, and under the dispensation of the gospel of mercy, should dare to propose this as a fitting mode of punishment? To immure a prisoner in a solitary cell, from which he is never to emerge, mocked with a bible which, perhaps he cannot read.'[24] In every case he preferred transportation to long sentences in American-style penitentiaries. Despite such objections, Pentonville's designers were confident that their system, which included reformatory transportation, was the most rational, salutary and moral ever constructed.

'Portal to the Penal Colony'

Having been introduced under the Whig regime of Lord John Russell, which was particularly supportive of the separate system and the dominant role of the chaplain, Russell's Tory successors continued to support both Pentonville and its extension to the penal colonies. More or less at the same time as Pentonville was opening its doors, Sir James Graham, home secretary in Robert Peel's administration from 1841 to 1846,

---

private enterprise coal mines and other debilitating labour, was a feature of post-Civil War southern states, with deployment of savage whipping for inmates.

[20] *Report of William Crawford on the Penitentiaries of the United States*, BPP 1834 (593), XLVI.349.

[21] Ibid., p. 18.

[22] 'Mr Adshead's Lecture on Prison Discipline', *Manchester Guardian*, 27 December 1843, p. 3 and 10 January 1844, n.p. From newspaper cuttings In TNA HO 45/335b.

[23] Gustave de Beaumont and Alexis de Tocqueville, *On the Penitentiary System in the United States and Its Application in France*, trans. Francis Lieber (Philadelphia: Carey, Lea & Blanchard, 1833), p. 24.

[24] P. Laurie, *Prison Discipline and Secondary Punishments: Remarks on the First Report of the Inspectors of Prisons* (London: Whittaker, 1837), p. 36.

advised the Pentonville commissioners of the connection between the new model prison, the penal colonies and the new probation system.[25] Graham demanded that every prisoner should understand that Pentonville 'is the portal to the penal colony' and the start of a new life, either on ticket-of-leave or on probation, in a new world.[26] This injunction suggests how committed the penal authorities remained to transportation as essential to the penal regime, no longer principally as a source of terror and preventive for crime, but as a permanent break with past associations and practices.

In theory, Pentonville and all its imitators were not factories of despair, but machines of utilitarian hope. As Graham explained, the system was intended to motivate prisoners to behave well and to work their way, in stages, to freedom and a new life in Van Diemen's Land, now transformed into the only colony receiving convicts direct from Britain. Every prisoner should be informed that imprisonment is a 'period of probation' of about eighteen months. After that, his fate would be decided. If he had behaved well, he would be sent to Van Diemen's Land and receive a ticket of leave, 'equivalent to freedom'; if he behaved badly, 'he will be transported to Tasman's Peninsula, there to work in a probationary gang, without wages, deprived of liberty, an abject convict'.[27] Juveniles, who were also subject to transportation, were given a similar message. Graham informed Parkhurst's Committee of Visitors in 1842 that: 'Every boy who enters Parkhurst, is doomed to be transported ... He must bid a long farewell to the hopes of revisiting his native home, of seeing his parents, or of rejoining his companions.' His future in the colony depended on his behaviour, whether to be pardoned and find a new life, or face the rigours of Point Puer, 'where every hardship and degradation awaits him, and where his sufferings will be severe'.[28]

Prison chaplains' reports on Pentonville (like the earliest reports on the Millbank penitentiary) were initially positive.[29] Five years later, the warning signs of the psychological damage to vulnerable prisoners were all too obvious, prompting three commissioners to resign. In their letter

[25] Graham's letter to the Commissioners of Pentonville, 16 December 1842 and Stanley's two despatches to Sir John Franklin, November 1842, were included as an appendix to the *Report of the Commissioners for the Government of the Pentonville Prison*, BPP 1843 (449), XXIX.377, pp. 381–390, hereafter Pentonville Report, 1843.

[26] Sir James Graham to Pentonville Commissioners, 16 December 1842, *Pentonville Report*, 1843, p. 5.

[27] Ibid., p. 448.

[28] Sir James Graham to Committee of Visitors of Parkhurst Prison, 20 December 1842, *Convict Discipline*, BPP 1843 (171) XLII.447, pp. 447–448.

[29] *Pentonville Report*, 1843, p. 4; 'Second Report of the Commissioners for the Government of the Pentonville Prison', 10 March 1844, TNA HO 45/335b.

of resignation Sir B. Brodie and Dr Ferguson (both of whom had approved the first, overly sanguine, reports on Pentonville) noted that 'there are some individuals who, either from original imbecility of mind, or from the nature of their previous habits, are not fitted for this kind of discipline'.[30] Debating the Prisons Bill (1847), Sir George Grey, who had succeeded Graham as home secretary in 1846, attempted to deprecate the seriousness of the resignations, asserting that medical authorities continued to support the separate system which, properly administered, might be 'a great instrument of good'. Promises were made to alleviate conditions of solitary confinement.[31] The *Quarterly Review* backed Earl Grey, arguing for a resumption of reformative transportation, which had been 'too hastily abandoned', and providing a rhapsodic account of Pentonville's order, silence and even its controversial chapel, which the prisoners attended in two rotas and where loud and enthusiastic hymn singing was strongly encouraged.[32]

In his publications, the Rev. Joseph Kingsmill (1805/1806–1865), Pentonville's first chaplain, defended the separate system, including its relationship to transportation and probation.[33] He was more moderate when directly confronted with evidence of cases of psychological disturbance, such as that from the Lt Governor of Van Diemen's Land, Sir John Eardley Wilmot (1783–1847), who claimed that on their arrival the Pentonville men were 'depressed in spirits, and appear as if their minds and energies still felt that weight which their peculiar treatment at home appears to have produced'.[34] Kingsmill admitted to the SC on Prison Discipline, that fifteen out of 3,000 prisoners had become insane and that many found it almost impossible to hear the chaplain in the stifling separate chapel; he agreed that it was 'dangerous and cruel' to subject prisoners to separate confinement for longer than twelve months.[35] Support for transportation's capacity to remove the convict from his previous associations and facilitate reform was also provided by the Rev. John Clay, chaplain of the Preston House of Correction.[36]

---

[30] Sir B. Brodie and Dr. Ferguson to Home Office, 27 January 1847, TNA HO 45/335b.

[31] Sir George Grey, Hansard, HC Deb, vol. 93, col. 41, 3 June 1847.

[32] 'Pentonville Prisoners', *Quarterly Review*, 82 (1847/48), 204.

[33] Joseph Kingsmill, *Chapters on Prisons and Prisoners* 2nd edn (London: Longmans, 1852). Kingsmill wrote extensively on the role of the prison chaplain; chapter 4 of *Prisons and Prisoners* relates to transportation.

[34] Sir George Grey quoting from a letter of Sir Eardley Wilmot, 'Testimony of the Rev. Joseph Kingsmill', 19 March 1850, *Select Committee on Prison Discipline*, BPP 1850 (632), XVII.1, p. 139.

[35] 'Testimony of the Rev. Joseph Kingsmill', 15 March 1850, Ibid., p. 109.

[36] The Rev. John Clay's views are discussed by Lord Mahon in the debate on the Prisons Bill (1847), Hansard, HC Deb, vol. 93, col. 41, 3 June 1847, citing a convict who stated

Kingsmill's role and influence were undermined by Pentonville's growing band of critics, including Charles Pennell Measor, the deputy governor of Chatham convict prison and a correspondent of Charles Dickens, who promoted penal servitude and derided the separate system.[37] Measor sent a copy of his critique of Kingsmill to Dickens who enthusiastically agreed with his views on the gullibility of prison chaplains generally and Kingsmill in particular. He shared his horror at the cost of the new model prison: 'I have often tried hard to attract attention to the enormous absurdity of the separate solitary system, and to the great harm done to society by the proceedings of injudicious chaplains.'[38] Measor continued to attack Kingsmill, accusing him of naivety towards prisoners, and bemoaning the use of religious inducements to create 'pet prisoners' as well as the unjustifiable costs of cellular penitentiaries. Dickens responded by publishing more damning accounts of credulous chaplains, high costs at home and hell holes abroad in the surviving sites of convict transportation.[39]

Probation and Lord John Russell

As colonial secretary in Lord Melbourne's Whig administration, Russell was chiefly responsible for the launch of the probation system and its distinctive religious format. Educated at the University of Edinburgh, Russell's utilitarian sympathies and latitudinarian religious convictions favouring the established Church of England found expression in his approach to legal and prison reform.[40] Sitting on the Molesworth Committee, he was moved by those who testified before him, further convinced that social problems could be addressed by tackling underlying economic constraints on trade. Russell has been called, after Gladstone,

---

that, in the absence of transportation, 'It's no use trying to repent here.' For Clay's views of the mark system, see Chapter 7.

[37] C. P. Measor, *The Convict Service* (London: Hardwicke, 1861). Measor's penal credentials were deflated following the Chatham prison riots which forced his resignation, though he continued to pose as a penal expert. See Alyson Brown, 'Challenging Discipline and Control: A Comparative Analysis of Prison Riots at Chatham (1861) and Dartmoor (1932)', in Helen Johnston (ed.), *Punishment and Control in Historical Perspective* (London: Palgrave Macmillan, 2008), p. 204.

[38] Charles Dickens, *The Letters of Charles Dickens*, vol. 9, 1859–1861, edited by Graham Storey (Oxford: Clarendon Press, 1997), p. 396.

[39] Thomas Beard and Charles Dickens, 'A Dialogue Concerning Convicts', *All the Year Round*, 5 (1861), 156–159.

[40] As summarized by John Prest, *ODNB*, these included the creation of a prison inspectorate, the abolition of the death penalty for forgery and most other offences, the creation of Parkhurst for young offenders, the phasing out of the hulks and the construction of the new penitentiaries, beginning with Pentonville.

'the most fervent and religious prime minister of the Victorian age'.[41] In his *Essays on the Christian Religion*, completed when he had left public life, Russell opposed Calvinists and Puritans and the errors of Rome, declaring: 'of all the churches which may be called established, or which count among their adherents a great national community, the Church of England is that which follows with the most fidelity the spirit of the Gospel'.[42] But he also conceded that theological purity was unnecessary: 'We are not directed to pray that they may hold the faith in unity of doctrine, but in unity of spirit, which may be the same in a Roman Catholic and a Unitarian.'[43] For Russell, the Church should be given the means to deliver its moral and charitable duties for the nation and other believers should be tolerated. In essence, this was the formula provided for both British penitentiaries and the probation system of Van Diemen's Land.

First mooted by Russell in January 1839, elements of the probation system were sketched by Lt Governor Franklin to Glenelg as early as October 1837.[44] The plan entailed working convicts in gangs away from settled districts but designing their accommodation and discipline on the separate system, including provision for religious instruction.[45] In 1842, Stanley finally outlined the probation system for Franklin's benefit, stressing that 'the most important of all the general principles underlying the system', was 'a systematic course of moral and religious instruction'.[46] After penitentiary detention at home, then transportation, the probation system for all serious offenders consisted of five stages: 1st detention in Norfolk Island; 2nd probationary gangs in Van Diemen's Land; 3rd probationary passes; 4th tickets of leave and 5th pardons. All convicts sentenced to life or transported for serious offences were sent to Norfolk Island for two years, minimum. The governor's discretion for the mitigation of sentences was removed. Only the Queen herself could shorten the detention at Norfolk Island. This would be a new system and

---

[41] Owen Chadwick, *The Victorian Church, Part 1* (New York: Oxford University Press, 1966), p. 233; Stefan Andersson, 'Religion in the Russell Family', *Russell: The Journal of Bertrand Russell Studies*, 13.2 (1993), 119. Andersson notes that Lady 'Fanny' Russell (Frances Anna Maria née Elliot) was more fervently religious than her husband, originally Church of Scotland, then Unitarian. Ibid. pp. 120–123.

[42] John Russell [Earl Russell], *Essays on the Rise and Progress of the Christian Religion in the West of Europe* (London: Longmans, 1873), p. 280.

[43] Ibid., 281.

[44] Franklin to Glenelg, 7 October 1837, BPP 1837–1838 (309) XLII.15, p. 17. Brand, *Convict Probation*, pp. 13–14.

[45] Ibid.

[46] Lord Stanley to Lt Governor Sir John Franklin, November 1842, *Pentonville Report*, 1843, p. 7.

the old guard would be moved on, including Maconochie whose experiment made way for the probation scheme on Norfolk Island.

Stanley proposed that religious teachers could be Anglicans, Wesleyan Methodists, or Roman Catholic priests, but they would all be subject to supervision and immediate suspension at the discretion of the convict comptroller.[47] Religious instructors' duties within the probation system were detailed by Matthew Forster (1796–1846), appointed by Stanley to the new role of comptroller-general of convicts and director of the probation system.[48] A Peninsular War veteran, Forster was a competent administrator who was married to Colonel Arthur's niece.[49] According to A. G. L. Shaw, Forster was largely responsible for the failure of the probation system since he neither anticipated the likely problems nor devised an effective system to replace private assignment.[50] Nevertheless, Forster's guidance for religious instructors indicate his conviction that delivering on the high ideals of the probation system required more effective implementation of the duties of the different prison officers. In the first stage of convict probation, discipline should be rigorous but fair, 'tempered with judicious advice, and instruction religious and moral'.[51] In his 'Regulations for the Religious and Moral Instruction of Convicts in Van Diemen's Land', Forster wrote that 'A change in moral character is the only solid ground upon which the restoration of the convict to society can be advantageous; and this result depends very considerably upon the zealous and persevering exertions that are made for his reformation, and for bringing him under the influence of religion.'[52] The guidelines guaranteed freedom of worship for the prisoners, and access to secular and religious instruction. By the time of his second report to Franklin in January 1845, Forster regretted these liberal arrangements, noting that 'much that might be done' if only all the religious instructors had been ordained ministers of the Church of England was in disarray. There was no unity among the religious instructors because they had such different educational and theological attainments.[53]

Religious instructors' duties in the probation system were not dissimilar to those traditionally performed by chaplains of gaols and prisons in

---

[47] Stanley to Franklin, November 1832, *Pentonville Report*, 1842, p. 8.

[48] Eardley Wilmot to Stanley, 4 December 1843, encl. no. 5, 'Regulations for the Religious and Moral Instruction of Convicts in Van Diemen's Land', BPP 1845 (659) XXXVII.329 [Hereafter *Forster's Regulations*], pp. 21–22.

[49] A. G. L. Shaw, 'Forster, Matthew (1796–1846)', *ADB*.   [50] Ibid.

[51] *Forster's Regulations*, p. 12.   [52] Ibid.

[53] Eardley Wilmot to Stanley, 31 January 1845, encl. Forster to Franklin, 27 January 1845, *Forster's Regulations*, p. 68.

England and Wales,[54] but they were onerous.[55] They celebrated Divine Service (twice) on Sundays, augmented by Sunday School, assembled the gangs for morning and evening prayers before and after work, and visited the hospital, the separate apartments and solitary cells daily. In addition, they conducted day schools, which prisoners attended on a rota amounting to three days' instruction per week. There was also a voluntary evening school and a library, from which books could be borrowed by prisoners and prison officers. These were combined with burdensome record-keeping and duties of surveillance which required them to: 'assiduously study the disposition and character' of every prisoner and, for reports which made up the first stage of probation, provide a monthly return for the comptroller-general on the state of the schools, detailing daily attendance of the convicts, their rate of advancement and any suggestions for improvement. Unsurprisingly, in 1847, the report prepared by Charles Joseph La Trobe (1801–1875) on the probation stations shows that of the twenty-one stations he visited, only eight could be considered 'satisfactory' or 'good', with defects in every sphere of their administration, religious instruction and medical provision.[56]

Probation failed not because of the deficiencies of its religious instructors, though this did not help, but primarily for economic reasons, including the sheer press of numbers. The Whig government prohibited private assignment and gave a pledge to New South Wales 'that it should no longer be dealt with as a convict colony'.[57] The Tories then dramatically increased the number of those sentenced to transportation, all of whom were channelled through Van Diemen's Land and Norfolk Island. Besides the over-abundant supply of convicts in Van Diemen's Land, which rose from under 20,000 in 1840 to nearly 30,000 in 1844, as indicated in Tables 8.1 and 8.2, demand from free settlers for convict labour (which they had previously received for next to nothing) evaporated. Previous regimes had been right to assume that on the expiry of their sentences former convicts would have little difficulty finding private employment. This was no longer the case as the Van Diemen's Land economy contracted, partly because of the impact of the probation system and the abolition of private assignment.

---

[54] *Return of Salaries to Chaplains of Prisons in England and Wales*, BPP 1831–1832 (622) XXXIII.533; *Gaol Chaplains: Return of Salaries*, BPP 1835 (200) XLV.187.

[55] *Forster's Regulations*, pp. 21–22.

[56] La Trobe to Grey, 31 May 1847, encl. 7, BPP 1847–1848 (941) LVIII.7; Brand, *Convict Probation*, pp. 167–207. For the libraries, see Keith Adkins, 'Convict Probation Station Libraries in Colonial Tasmania', *Script & Print* 34.2 (2010), 87–92.

[57] Lord Stanley, 'Memorandum on Transportation', 3 February 1845, TNA Confidential Print CO 885/2/8: 1.

Table 8.1 *Number of convicts annually transported from 1830 to 1844*

Year	New South Wales		Van Diemen's Land		Total
	Males	Females	Males	Females	
1830	1,751	337	1,737	308	4,133
1831	1,605	250	1,965	151	3,971
1832	1,992	206	1,782	249	4,229
1833	2,310	420	1,576	245	4,551
1834	2,336	144	2,124	316	4,920
1835	2,146	298	1,689	266	4,399
1836	2,029	259	1,800	185	4,273
1837	1,734	140	1,929	264	4,067
1838	1,716	344	1,489	256	3,805
1839	1096	143	1,130	363	2,732
1840	575	213	1,605	180	2,573
1841	0	0	2,375	551	2,926
1842	0	0	3,615	551	4,166
1843	199	0	2,420	374	2,993
1844	0	0	2,917	362	3,279
Total	19,489	2,754	30,153	4,621	57,017

Source: *Relgious Instruction in Colonies*, BPP 1845 (356) XXXV.171, p. 256.

Given the moral panic around 'unnatural crime' featured in the Molesworth Report,[58] it was particularly regrettable that the probation gang was thought to provide ideal conditions for it to flourish.[59] Despite the alarm bells, the incoming Lt Governor of Van Diemen's Land, Sir William Denison (1804–1871), who arrived in 1847, supported transportation; indeed Denison would become its last, leading advocate. In Stanley's original vision, the overall effect of his proposals was, by his own admission, to create a great prison out of Van Diemen's Land, albeit a model one: 'I see no mode so hopeful, both as to the relief of this country, and the reformation of a portion at least of the offenders, as an adherence to the present system in the main, by which Van Diemen's Land is constituted a great reformatory prison.'[60] This required further capital investment by the Government in people and penitentiaries, which was only partially forthcoming. The overall result was a rapid

---

[58] Molesworth returns to this in his lengthy intervention in the debate on the Prisons Bill, Hansard, HC Deb, vol. 93, col. 63–92, 3 June 1847.

[59] Catie Gilchrist, 'Space, Sexuality and Convict Resistance in Van Diemen's Land: The Limits of Repression?', *Eras Journal*, 6 November (2004), n.p.

[60] Lord Stanley, 'Memorandum on Transportation', 3 February 1845, TNA CO 885/2/8.

Table 8.2 *Return of the convict population in New South Wales and Van Diemen's Land, 1830–1844*

	New South Wales			Van Diemen's Land		
Year	Males	Females	TOTALS	Males	Females	TOTALS
1830	18,067	2,189	20,256	8,877	1,318	10,195
1831		No census		10,391	1,627	12,018
1832		No census		8,579	1,305	9,884
1833	21,845	2,698	24,543	10,758	1,500	12,258
1834		No census		13,664	1,874	15,538
1835		No census		14,914	2,054	16,968
1836	25,254	2,577	27,831	15,590	2,071	17,661
1837		No census		15,674	1,919	17,593
1838		No census		15,825	2,064	17,880
1839		No census		15,386	1,691	17,077
1840		No census		17,200	2,359	19,439
1841	23,844	3,153	26,977		No return	
1842		No census			No return	
1843		No census		21,359	3,537	24,926
1844		No return		24,824	4,367	29,191

Source: *Religious Instruction in Colonies*, BPP 1845 (356) XXXV.171, p. 257.

escalation of costs, indicated in Tables 8.3 and 8.4. In 1838, the total paid out for religious instruction to New South Wales's approximately 27,000 convicts was £1,100; £850 for the Church of England including £300 'for the instruction of convicts in the remote parts of the colony distributed at the discretion of the bishop of Australia', and £250 for Roman Catholics, including two chaplains on Norfolk Island, who shared £150 between them.[61]

In 1840, payment for the 'spiritual instruction of the convict population' in New South Wales and Van Diemen's Land was £2,609; in 1845, it had reached £3,959 in Van Diemen's Land alone. By 1846, the probation system in Van Diemen's Land required payment to over thirty chaplains, catechists, religious instructors, schoolmasters and schoolmistresses at a cost of £4,837 (see Table 8.5). While the amounts are relatively small, this was an unprecedented increase for a system which had previously been largely self-supporting.

Besides inadequate planning, a factor in the failure of probation was Eardley Wilmot's inept and unresponsive administration in Van

---

[61] Gipps to Glenelg, 9 November 1838, encl. 3, *Correspondence on Advancement of Religion in Australia*, BPP 1840 (243) XXXIII.239, p. 25. See Table 8.3.

Table 8.3 *Sums paid out of the military chest to clergymen in New South Wales, 1838*

		£	£
Church of England			
	Goat Island	50	
	Female Factory	50	
	For the instruction of convicts in the remote parts of the colony distributed at the discretion of the Bishop of Australia	300	
	Moreton Bay	50	
	Norfolk Island	200	
	Sydney (new)	200	
	Total Church of England		850
Roman Catholic			
	Female Factory	50	
	Sydney	50	
	Norfolk Island	150	
	Total Roman Catholic		250
		Total	1,100

Source: Dispatch from Gipps to Glenelg, 9 November 1838, encl. 3, *Correspondence on Advancement of Religion in Australia*, BPP 1840 (243) XXXIII.239, p. 25.

Diemen's Land.[62] Having succeeded Franklin in 1843, on 30 April 1846 Eardley Wilmot was dismissed by the rising William Ewart Gladstone (1809–1898), who had succeeded Stanley as colonial secretary in December 1845, for incompetence and unspecified moral failings.[63] Gladstone accused him of neglecting his core duty of 'impressing deeply a moral and reformatory character upon convict management'.[64] His informants are likely to have been Bishop Nixon and Archdeacon Marriott, who was then in England.[65] Defending

---

[62] For the Eardley Wilmot dismissal, see accounts by K. Fitzpatrick, 'Mr Gladstone and the Governor: The Recall of Sir John Eardley Wilmot from Van Diemen's Land', *Historical Studies*, 1.1 (1940), 31–45; A. G. L. Shaw, 'Sir John Eardley-Wilmot and the Probation System in Tasmania', *Papers and Proceedings (Tasmanian Historical Research Association)*, 11.1 (1963), 5–19; Peter Chapman, 'Wilmot, Sir John Eardley Eardley-, First Baronet (1783–1847)', ODNB; Leonie C. Mickleborough, 'Victim of an "Extraordinary Conspiracy"? Sir John Eardley Eardley-Wilmot Lieutenant Governor of Van Diemen's Land 1843–46', (PhD thesis, University of Tasmania, 2011).

[63] Gladstone to Sir E. Eardley Wilmot, 30 April 1846, *Correspondence Relative to Recall of Sir Eardley Wilmot*, BPP 1847 (262, 400) XXXVIII.513, 527, p. 527.

[64] Ibid., p. 528.

[65] G. R. Lennox, 'A Private and Confidential Despatch of Eardley-Wilmot', *Tasmanian Historical Research Association Papers and Proceedings*, 29 (1982), 80–92.

Table 8.4 *Payments for spiritual instruction of convicts in New South Wales and Van Diemen's Land 1840, 1840 and 1842; and estimate for 31 March 1846 for Van Diemen's Land*

		£
	NEW SOUTH WALES	
1840	Payments made for the spiritual instruction of the convict population in New South Wales	1,631
1841	Ditto	1,799
1842	Ditto	1,718
	VAN DIEMEN'S LAND	
1840	Payments made for the spiritual instruction of the convict population in Van Diemen's Land	978
1841	Ditto	1,124
1842	Ditto	2,239
1845–46	Ditto (estimate)	3,959
	TOTAL	
1840	Payments made for the spiritual instruction of the convict population in Van Diemen's Land and New South Wales	2,609
1841	Ditto	2,923
1842	Ditto	3,957
1845–46	Ditto (estimate)	3,959

Source: Home Office, 6 May 1845, *Religious Instruction in Colonies*, BPP 1845 (356) XXXV.171, p. 258.

himself, Eardley Wilmot obtained testimonials from respectable citizens, including clergy (though no one from the bishop's circle), and noted that he chaired meetings of religious societies which testified to his unblemished reputation.[66] The consensus in the colony was that Gladstone acted unreasonably; to Gladstone, the grounds were only too evident. John West expressed the view of colonial contemporaries that Eardley Wilmot was blamed for implementing a policy that he had informed the government was unworkable and had warned them against by 'incessant communications'.[67] Damning them all, Molesworth blamed Stanley, declaring him 'as guilty of negligence, and as deserving of being dismissed' as Eardley Wilmot or Major Joseph Childs (1787–1870), dismissed as commandant following the convict revolt on Norfolk Island.[68]

[66] Eardley Wilmot to Gladstone, 9 November 1846, *Recall of Sir Eardley Wilmot*, p. 534.
[67] West, *History of Tasmania*, vol. 2, p. 316.
[68] Sir William Molesworth, Hansard, HC Deb, vol. 93, col. 3, June 1847.

Table 8.5 *Estimate of the expenditure to be defrayed from the commissariat chest at Van Diemen's Land, from 1 April 1845 to 31 March 1846, for the spiritual instruction of the convict population in that colony*

	£
Clergymen	
1. One Religious Instructor at Hobart Town, and Lodging Allowance	250
2. Ditto for the Hospital at Hobart Town	100
3. Ditto for the Hospital at Launceston, and Lodging Allowance	250
4. One Religious Instructor, Coal Mines	200
5. Ditto Maria Island	200
6. Ditto Jerusalem	200
7. Ditto Jerico	200
8. One Catechist, Broadmarch	150
9. Ditto Rocky Hills	150
10. Ditto Fingal and St Mary's Pass, and Forage for a Horse	177
11. Ditto Westbury and Deloraine, and Forage	177
12. Ditto Southport	150
13. Ditto Victoria Valley and Seven-Mile Creek, and Forage	177
14. Allowance to District Clergyman for attending Lunatic Hospital at New Norfolk	50
15. Chaplain of Female Probation Establishment, Her Majesty's Ship 'Anson'	150
16. One Chaplain, Queen's Orphan Schools	100
17. One Roman Catholic Religious Instructor to Queen's Orphan Schools	50
18. One Chaplain, Penal Settlement, Port Arthur	200
19. One Catechist, Point Puer	150
20. Ditto Roman Catholic, Port Arthur	100
21. One Roman Catholic Religious Instructor, Port Arthur, and Forage	227
22. One Protestant ... Ditto ... Norfolk Island	200
23. Two Roman Catholic... Ditto... Ditto at £100 Each	200
24. One Protestant Catechist	100
25. One Roman Catholic Catechist	50
Total Clergymen	3,959
Schoolmasters	
26. One Schoolmaster, Brown's River	150
27. Ditto ... Impression Bay	100
28. Ditto ... Wedge Bay	100
29. Ditto ... Queen's Orphan School, Male	150
30. One Schoolmistress ... Ditto	60
31. One Assistant Schoolmistress, Queen's Orphan School	50
32. One ... Ditto ... Ditto ... for Infants	18
33. One Schoolmaster at Port Arthur	100
34. Two Assistant Teachers @ £75 each	150
Total Schoolmasters	878
Clergymen	3,959
Schoolmasters	878
Grand Total	4,837

Source: Religious Instruction in Colonies, BPP 1845 (356) XXXV.171, p. 258.

Probation in Van Diemen's Land

Eardley Wilmot's replacement, Sir William Denison (1804–1871), became the main defender of transportation against the rising tide of settler resistance to both the probation gangs and transportation in any form. The religious instructors and other penal officers appointed to serve in the probation system proved to be some of its most devastating assailants. Clerical critics included those who had served under Sir George Arthur's assignment-based progressive penal system, such as the Rev. J. Youl who gave evidence to the Bigge Commission, Henry Fry, Rector of St. George's Church, Hobart or the Rev. John West, leader of the Anti-Transportation League.[69] Yet, as Thompson notes, the probation system required significant investment to enable religious instruction, schooling and moral training. Chapels were incorporated into the designs for probation and punishment stations, for example the Plan of Impression Bay Probation Station, Tasman's Peninsula, 1842.[70] By mid-1845, staff for this station included a Protestant religious instructor-cum-schoolmaster, with about a dozen other officers. Protestant and Catholic catechists, religious instructors and school teachers were provided to every probation station, though as La Trobe's report would soon make clear, not to very great effect.

Under probation, the convict voyage became another site for religious intervention, with surgeons and religious instructors assigned to run schools, arrange lectures, maintain order and discipline, distribute tracts and testaments and sometimes produce an edifying shipboard newspaper.[71] Colin Arrott Browning (1791–1856), was the most assiduous of these pious naval surgeons. Between 1831 and 1850 he was engaged as surgeon superintendent on convict voyages which he conducted as a kind of floating mission. His published accounts were intended not just to inspire confidence in the probation system but also to encourage others to take up the call to convicts and emigrants.[72] Shaw calls him 'a strange man', though one whose style was approved of by Lt Governor Arthur

---

[69] John Thompson, *Probation in Paradise: The Story of Convict Probationers in Tasman's and Forestier's Peninsulas, Van Diemen's Land, 1841–1857* (Hobart: Artemis, 2007), pp. 14–15.

[70] Ibid., p. 120. See also Thompson's reproductions of plans for the Probation Station, Cascade, on p. 130, which shows a chapel, and Major Victor's plan for a boys' penitentiary, July 1845, which shows both a Roman Catholic and a Protestant chapel.

[71] For a list of these, see Bateson, *Convict Ships*, pp. 309–310.

[72] Colin Arrott Browning, *The Convict Ship* (London: Smith, Elder 1844); Colin Arrott Browning, *The Convict Ship and England's Exiles* 3rd edn (London: Hamilton, Adams, 1848).

and others in authority.[73] Bateson thought him 'earnest but narrow minded', but Browning's dedication to the convicts was unequalled among surgeon superintendents. He seems to have made the voyage at least six times, on every occasion dedicating himself to reforming the lives of his charges.[74] Browning is credited with observation of the psychiatric effects of solitary confinement on Pentonville prisoners which produced a sequence of alarming symptoms or 'epidemic hysteria' on the voyage to Van Diemen's Land.[75] It is intriguing to consider whether Browning's faith and sympathetic interest in the prisoners may have facilitated their exhibition of these symptoms; 'These prisoners', he states, 'are "prisoners of hope." They form a portion of that family whom Christ came to redeem by His blood, and by His gospel to call to Himself, – for He came not to call the righteous but sinners.'[76] To reinforce this message, Browning provided a series of dramatic confession narratives by prisoners, all presumably drafted by Browning himself.

Roman Catholic clergy were appointed to serve on convict ships leaving Ireland from 1848 to 1852, but they encountered significant problems.[77] Following a report from the Catholic Vicar General of the Melbourne diocese, Patrick Geoghehan (1805–1864), who had himself travelled out to the colony on the *London* in December 1850, attempts to 'assimilate the Irish and English convict service' in this manner were discontinued.[78] Like Bishop Nixon, Geoghehan objected to the loss of status suffered by ordained clergy from being designated 'religious instructors' rather than 'chaplains' and the effective secularization this entailed. It was hoped that the appointment of Catholic instructors would compensate Irish prisoners for the absence of penitentiary training in Ireland, but priests had neither the will nor capacity to effect the required transformation on the voyage. A memo complained that

---

[73] Shaw, *Convicts and the Colonies*, p. 123.
[74] Beth Palmer and Adelene Buckland, *A Return to the Common Reader: Print Culture and the Novel, 1850–1900* (Farnham: Ashgate, 2011), p. 112. Palmer states that Browning undertook nine voyages, Bateson, *Convict Ships*, p. 410 notes seven, two to New South Wales: *Margaret* three in 1840, *Hashemy* in 1849; and five to Van Diemen's Land: *Arab* I in 1833, *Elphinstone* I in 1836, *Earl Grey* three in 1843, and *Mount Stewart Elphinstone* I in 1845, and *Hashemy* I in 1849 (which went to New South Wales not Port Philip).
[75] Malcolm Kinnear, 'Epidemic Hysteria Aboard Ship in 1848', *British Journal of Psychiatry*, 197.2 (2010), 90.
[76] Browning, *The Convict Ship*, p. 10. Scriptural citations are to Luke xiv and Matt. xxii.
[77] 'List of religious and moral instructors appointed to convict shops from Ireland', National Library of Ireland (NLI) Mayo Papers, MS 11,183 (item 1).
[78] 'Extract from the Rev. Dr Geoghegan's Report', 1852, NLI Mayo Papers, MS 11,183 (item 2).

regardless of their respectability, which was not in doubt, Catholic clergy were 'liable to gross imposition' by the prisoners.[79]

A significant additional complication was the elevation of the first Anglican bishop of Tasmania, Francis Russell Nixon (1803–1879), one of five colonial bishops consecrated in Westminster on 25 August 1842. Bishop Nixon arrived in Hobart in July 1843, accompanied by his wife and family, Fitzherbert Adams Marriott (1811–1890), who became archdeacon of Hobart, and other clergy.[80] Nixon was well endowed with funding from the Colonial Bishoprics' Fund (1841), the Society for the Propagation of the Gospel and, within two years, a gift of £5,000 specifically for missions to convicts.[81] Like the late Archdeacon Hutchins, Nixon was strongly opposed to the continued reliance of Methodists to serve penal establishments in Van Diemen's Land and made intemperate claims for the extent of his episcopal authority. In confidential correspondence with Stanley, Eardley Wilmot explained his difficulty with Bishop Nixon's demand for ecclesiastical nomination of all chaplains to gaols.[82] Nixon informed Stanley that he would not licence or ordain any chaplains to convicts since they were under civil authority.[83] In a compromise that satisfied no one, Stanley appointed Marriott, 'superintendent of convict chaplains', which Nixon regarded as further undermining his episcopal authority. In a letter which may not have sent but reflected his thinking, Nixon accused Eardley Wilmot of giving admittance to Government House to ladies 'provided they are young & pretty and have no objection to the philandering attentions of an elderly Gentleman'.[84] Mrs Nixon confided to her journal in September 1844 that 'Sir Eardley is no friend of the Church' and that 'Everyone agreed that the probation system will be the entire ruin of the Colony'.[85] Nixon resolutely signed a mass petition for the abolition of the probation system presented to Eardley Wilmot,[86] while the Rev. Henry Phibbs Fry (1807?–1874),

---

[79] 'Minute as to the grounds on which the sending out R. Catholic clergymen as instructors on Convict Ships has been discontinued', 13 September 1852, NLI Mayo Papers, MS 11,183 (item 3).

[80] W. R. Barrett, *History of the Church of England in Tasmania* (Hobart: Mercury, 1942); W. R. Barrett, 'Nixon, Francis Russell (1803–1879)', ADB; Norah Nixon (ed.), *The Pioneer Bishop in Van Diemen's Land, 1843–1863* (Hobart: s.n., 1853).

[81] Barrett, *History*, p. 7.

[82] Eardley Wilmot to Stanley, 4 November 1843, TNA CO 280/160: 301–304; Mickleborough, 'Victim', p. 209.

[83] Nixon to Stanley, 29 May 1844; Barrett, 'Nixon', ADB.

[84] Nixon, no addressee, 20 December 1844, TAHO NS3/1/1; Mickleborough, 'Victim', p. 210.

[85] Anna Nixon, 30 September 1844, *Pioneer Bishop*, p. 32.

[86] Eardley Wilmot to Gladstone, 10 August 1846, BPP 1847 (785) XLVII.93, p. 107.

chaplain of St George's Hobart, who had earlier defended transportation as a 'blessing to thousands', informed Gladstone of his horror at conditions in the probation gangs.[87]

While colonial authorities were well aware of problems with probation, including the serious deficiency in the provision of both Protestant and Catholic religious instructors,[88] the Colonial Office first acknowledged the scale of the problem after receiving a series of irrefutable reports from well-placed settlers and religious authorities, led by Bishop Nixon and Archdeacon Marriott in Van Diemen's Land. Referring to the collapse in demand for convict labour as well as the 'moral condition of the convict population', Lord Stanley warned in February 1845 that transportation was becoming a 'very serious embarrassment'.[89] In August 1846, Earl Grey provided Cabinet with a detailed history by Thomas Murdoch which was more explicit, reporting of 'facts of so alarming and horrible a character', that immediate action was essential.[90] At issue were the mass congregation of men in gangs with little effective supervision and few signs of reformation in response to the all-important religious or moral instruction. These fed on longstanding anxieties about male and female convict (and slave) sexuality, including promiscuity, cross-racial pollution and the threat of unions between free and unfree settlers.[91]

Negative reports on the moral condition of the probation gangs and women convicts mostly came from sources outside the government, but those from higher clergy had particular weight. Just before leaving the colony, Franklin expressed alarm at the 'deplorable effects' of confinement of women in the factories, including their 'moral degradation and their addiction to unnatural practices'.[92] This was confirmed, but not augmented (with his usual laziness) by Eardley Wilmot on arriving in Hobart, attaching reports from local officers. The most severe strictures came from Archdeacon Marriott who, when visiting England, 'repeatedly denounced in very strong language' the new probation system.[93] As with

---

[87] Eardley Wilmot to Gladstone, 4 September 1846, encl. Fry to Colonial Secretary, 17 August 1846, Ibid., p. 188.

[88] Comptroller General to Eardley Wilmot, 1 August 1846, Ibid., pp. 127–128.

[89] Lord Stanley, 'Memorandum on Transportation', 3 February 1845, TNA Confidential Print CO 885/2/8: 1.

[90] Earl Grey, 'Transportation', 19 August 1846, TNA Confidential Print CO 885/2/11: 1.

[91] Reid, *Gender, Crime and Empire*; McKenzie, *Scandal in the Colonies*, p. 109, noting the promotion of marriage among former slaves in the Cape.

[92] T. W. C. Murdoch, 'Transportation', 15 August 1846, TNA Confidential Print, CO 885/2/12: 26. For the accusations of homosexuality among convict women, see Causer, 'Anti-Transportation', 230–240; Brand, Probation System, p. 23.

[93] Murdoch, 'Transportation', p. 26.

many accounts of unnatural crime among the convicts, Marriott's accusations were couched in colourful but rather vague terms. Then came the petitions. In February, a petition signed by 1,750 people claimed that land value in Van Diemen's Land had slumped since the introduction of the probation gangs, immigration had stalled and that should the planned transfer of the hardened criminals from Norfolk Island occur, then Van Diemen's Land would soon 'exhibit a spectacle of vice and infamy such as the history of the world cannot parallel'.[94] More private denunciations of unnatural crime followed. One resident declared that with the departure of the free settlers and the arrival of ever more convicts the colony had become 'a hell upon earth to the free people of property who are obliged by that property to remain there'.[95] A Mr James Smith provided a report from his father, a resident in Van Diemen's Land, claiming that 'At all the gangs, particularly at Port Arthur, sodomy is committed continually, and cases are numerous of venereal in the rectum.'[96] This potentially questionable testimony, cited uncritically by Murdoch, was solidified by evidence from surgeons working with the probation gangs. A verbal account given to Sir James Stephen claimed that over two-thirds of the gangs 'were living in the systematic and habitual practice of unnatural crimes, that people were actually paired together, and understood as having that revolting relation to each other'.[97] While apparently damning, the evidence has not been borne out by more careful review of the evidence. Tim Causer, for example, notes that all Norfolk Island convicts were examined for disease and, despite assaulting the dignity of every man, not a single case was found.[98] Eardley Wilmot consistently maintained that the issue was grossly exaggerated and despite pressure to find perpetrators, the number of prosecutions remained very small.[99] Ten days after his dismissal by Gladstone, Eardley Wilmot's disgrace is likely to have contributed to the shameful haste with which Michael Lyons, an Irish youth of eighteen from the Port Cygnet Probation Station, was tried and executed for unnatural crime (bestiality with a goat), largely it would seem to excite terror for what few regarded as a hanging matter.[100]

[94] Ibid., p. 27.   [95] Ibid.   [96] Ibid.
[97] La Trobe to Earl Grey, encl. no. 5 (Unnatural Crime), in Brand, *Convict Probation System*, pp. 147–160.
[98] Causer, 'Anti-Transportation', 2.   [99] Murdoch, 'Transportation', p. 26.
[100] Reid, *Gender, Crime and Empire*, p. 205. For press reports, *The Courier* (Hobart) 24 October 1846, p. 3; *The Port Philip Gazette*, 21 November 1846, p. 2; *Colonial Times* (Hobart), 23 October 1846, p. 3.

Religious Instructors

The religious element of the probation system required a significant number of newly appointed religious instructors and other clerical personnel. Given the longstanding shortage of clergy willing to work with convicts, this was always going to present a challenge. Even with the passing of the Church Acts, religious provision was focussed on tendering to free colonists rather than convicts. In 1837 a parliamentary return listed just two colonial inquiries relating to clergy for convicts in New South Wales, namely Ullathorne's request of a Catholic chaplain for Norfolk Island and Broughton's that colonial chaplains receive free passage in return for providing religious services to convicts on the voyage.[101] Convict religious need was recognized by the Church Act (1836) which allowed masters to include their convict servants when making a case for an officiating minister.[102] Once in the colony, few qualified ministers showed interest in working in convict establishments. The situation in Van Diemen's Land was slightly better than in New South Wales. Franklin reported to Normanby that there was a rural dean and three Episcopal chaplains who received a small stipend of £50 annually to attend convicts in gaols and hospitals; there was one Presbyterian minister for the same work, but no provision for Catholic convicts.[103] In 1839, Franklin was sufficiently concerned to ask Russell whether any of the clergy appointed to ecclesiastical establishments in Van Diemen's Land could be required to visit gaols, houses of correction and road gangs. Russell referred this to Charles Blomfield (1786–1857), bishop of London from 1828 to 1856, who observed that the new Church Acts imposed no such duties on them. It would therefore depend entirely on the bishop of the diocese, which, until Nixon's arrival in 1842, meant Broughton in faraway Sydney.[104] In April 1841, Franklin referred again to the 'great want of religious instruction for the large bodies of convicts arriving in the colony, asking for 'two pious and practical ministers whose hearts are in the cause'.[105] The Chief Police Magistrate wanted a Protestant clergyman attached to at least every two gangs who would be

---

[101] Broughton to Bourke, 26 November 1836; Grey to Ullathorne, 10 March 1837, *Correspondence on Religion in Australia*, BPP 1837–1838 (75), XL.111, pp. 10, 17.

[102] 'An Act to Promote the Building of Church and Chapels, and to provide for the Maintenance of Ministers of Religion in New South Wales (1836)', clause 2, Ibid, p. 4.

[103] Franklin to Normanby, 26 October 1839, 'Return of the Religious Establishments of Van Diemen's Land', Ibid., p. 63.

[104] Russell to Franklin, 24 February 1840, C. J. London (Blomfield) to Russell, 15 February 1840, Ibid., p. 64.

[105] Franklin to Russell, 15 April 1841, BPP 1843 (158) XLII.353, p. 384.

devoted entirely to the work of reformation, and another for the Roman Catholic convicts.[106]

For the Protestant chaplains and religious instructors, the Anglican Society for the Propagation of the Gospel (SPG) was the only organization with resources to respond to the call for a substantial increase in religious provision for convicts following the decision to implement the probation system. Their correspondence provides an important insight into the working clergy in these remote penal outposts. Names and terms of service can be gleaned from the records of the United Society for the Propagation of the Gospel, which includes the correspondence from missionaries sent to all the Australian convict establishments in New South Wales, Van Diemen's Land, Norfolk Island and Western Australia;[107] others can be identified from the Cable Index of Australian Anglican clergy.[108] According to the SPG missionary roll,[109] between 1835 and 1859 some seventeen missionaries were stationed in what became the Diocese of Tasmania (founded in 1842),[110] most of whom served in some capacity as missionaries, religious instructors, schoolmasters or chaplains to convicts. Including these SPG missionaries, the Cable Index identifies twenty-five convict chaplains or religious instructors; others left little record of their ministry. Anglicans, Catholics and Dissenters were engaged to work as religious instructors, catechists and school teachers at the height of the probation scheme (Table 8.5), though only the Anglicans are reviewed here. As Bishop Willson testified, there was no real attempt to provide for the needs of Roman Catholic prisoners under probation.[111] In 1845, Willson requested five Catholic priests for Van Diemen's Land; Stanley approved two, neither specified for convict pastoral duties.[112]

Traditionally the Church of England considered the work of SPG missionaries to convicts in Australia an antidote to 'ungodly colonisation

---

[106] 'Minutes of an Executive Council Meeting, Hobart, 29 March 1841', encl. 1, Ibid., p. 389.

[107] Oxford, Bodleian Library, United Society for the Propagation of the Gospel Archive C/AUS/TAS/2 [Hereafter BodL USPG].

[108] Michael Blain, Leonie Cable and K. J. Cable (eds.), Cable Clerical Index (Project Canterbury, anglicanhistory.org, c.2011).

[109] Pascoe, Two Hundred Years, vol. 2, cols. 849–931. For the Australian missionaries, see 'Missionary Roll, SPG', Ibid., vol. 2, cols. 900–908. Note that the SPG Missionary Roll does not include those paid from endowments.

[110] Prior to 1842, Van Diemen's Land formed part of Broughton's undivided diocese of Australia.

[111] 'Testimony of Bishop R. W. Willson', 7 June 1847, HL SC on Execution of the Criminal Laws, BPP 1847 (534) VII.1, p. 538.

[112] 'Roman Catholic Establishment in Van Diemen's Land', 8 February 1845, TNA CO 280/188; Mickleborough, 'Victim', p. 217.

in its worst form', which combined efforts to 'save the convicts from a state more pitiful than that of the heathen' and the free settlers from 'lapsing into heathenism'.[113] Convict support included funds to pay for schoolmasters or schoolmistresses chosen by the chaplains, including two, from 1797 to 1826, on Norfolk Island.[114] Three kinds of problems were negotiated by SPG missionaries posted to government appointments with responsibility for religious education or chaplaincy to convicts in the new, reformative transportation system. First, there were clashes of authority, specifically the authority of the government which managed the convict system as opposed to the ecclesiastical authority which Bishop Nixon claimed to exert over all clergy in his diocese. Secondly, there was friction with other clergy, especially those outside the established church. Thirdly, there was friction over clerical denunciation of physical and psychological abuse of convicts. The correspondence of religious instructors to the SPG provides extensive evidence of all three.

The arrival of so many new and untried personnel into the penal establishments was probably bound to cause friction. One of the more unfortunate was the clash between the Methodist catechist of Port Arthur, John Allen Manton (1807–1864), and his Anglican successor, the Rev. Edward Durham, who had been recommended by the SPG and understood he would have the standing of chaplain of a major penal establishment.[115] Manton, who had been popular with the men,[116] lost his post. Durham began (unwisely) by clashing with the Commandant of Port Arthur, Captain Charles O'Hara Booth (1800–1851) on a number of issues, including the use of the church, which he wished to dedicate for the exclusive use of his own denomination. This led to all the Catholic convicts refusing to attend until given their own place of worship. Durham also wanted to pay boys from Point Puer to sing at Divine Service and bring the men immured in solitary confinement to attend morning prayers and Divine Service in church, rather than in the prison yard. Booth reported that Durham hoped to enliven the library which consisted of 391 volumes, more than two-thirds of which were 'strictly

---

[113] Pascoe, *Two Hundred Years*, vol. I, p. xxii.   [114] Ibid., vol. I, cols. 387–389.

[115] For Durham's dispute with Commandant Booth, see TSA (now TAHO Tasmanian Archives and Heritage Office), Misc. 62/1/A 1087/1 128; transcription at 'Port Arthur Investigations' http://keyportarthur.org.au/ (Accessed 4 August 2018), to which page citations refer [Hereafter 'Durham Correspondence'].

[116] See Chapter 3 for Manton at Macquarie Harbour. For a warm appraisal of Manton by the Canadian exile Linus Miller, whom Manton asked to serve as his clerk and schoolmaster, see Linus W. Miller, *Notes of an Exile to Van Dieman's Land* (Fredonia, NY: McKinstry, 1846), p. 345.

religious', and 'better suited for a Methodist preacher's library' than for prisoners.[117] In fact, Port Arthur had one of the most diverse of all the prisoners' libraries, according to Linus Miller, who said it contained 'religious, historical and miscellaneous works'.[118] The greatest friction was created by Durham's attempt to take charge of the school, which was in the hands of a Dissenting (Independent) schoolmaster rather than being, as he had reason to expect, under his supervision. The schoolmaster wrote to Eardley Wilmot, who in his usual fashion did as little as possible simply asking the comptroller-general, Matthew Forster, to 'report'.[119] Given the support of the Commandant for the status quo, there was very little redress available to Durham, notwithstanding the divergence from Forster's printed regulations.

From an almost invisible base, the investment in religious instruction to convicts as part of the probation system markedly improved, as revealed by a return to Parliament in 1845 accounting for payments for the spiritual instruction of the convict population in British colonies (see Table 8.4). One of the more accomplished of the new arrivals was the Rev. Frederick Shum Batchelor (c.1817–1892), who travelled to the colony with Bishop Nixon. A former Methodist lay preacher, educated at King's College, London, and Cambridge, Batchelor served as a religious instructor on Norfolk Island from July 1838, then as chaplain to the coal mines on the Tasman Peninsula. He accepted a second term on Norfolk Island in 1850 before returning to Britain where for over thirty years he served in prisons, including Dartmoor, Millbank and Brixton.[120] In 1844, Batchelor wrote to Ernest Hawkins at the SPG that things were not as he had anticipated.[121] 'When I first accepted the appointment as Chaplain to the convicts in this place, I formed the idea that Mr Durham and myself should have the spiritual charge of all the prisoners; and that catechists would act under us, as is the case in other colonies; but I have found out that I was mistaken.'[122] Instead, prisoners were distributed all over the Tasman Peninsula, religious instructors could be Anglicans or Methodists and they had no ecclesiastical superior. Batchelor offered a perceptive analysis of a major failing of the probation system, which was the lack of institutional support for its programme of

---

[117] Commandant (Captain Booth) to Rev. Edward Durham, 29 March 1844; Durham to comptroller general, 2 April 1844, 'Durham Correspondence', p. 1.

[118] Miller, *Notes of an Exile*, p. 345.

[119] Schoolmaster (White) to Eardley Wilmot, 27 April 1844, 'Durham Correspondence', p. 30.

[120] 'Batchelor, Frederick Shum', *Alumni Cantabrigienses*, vol. 2: From 1752 to 1900, edited by John Venn and J. A. Venn (Cambridge: Cambridge University Press, 1940), p. 181.

[121] Batchelor to Hawkins, 17 February 1844, BodL USPG C/AUS/TAS/2.   [122] Ibid.

religious instruction. Two of the religious instructors appointed by the SPG, Wiliiam Bennett (1818–1865) and George Eastman (1818–1870), wrote to Hawkins asking that he enable them to return to England.[123] The SPG had no resources for this, but the extreme insecurity of the convict chaplains concerned Anna Nixon, who thought they would resign one after another and return to England.[124] Nevertheless, both men remained in the colony and did well. Originally a Wesleyan lay preacher, Bennett served as religious instructor at Jerusalem Probation Station in 1844 and Impression Bay before his ordination in 1850. Eastman, also a former Wesleyan, served on probation stations as religious instructor before his ordination; from 1857 to 1865 he was chaplain of Port Arthur.

With greater isolation and even less support than Van Diemen's Land, Norfolk Island represented a cauldron of lost hopes. Maconochie's clash with the Rev Thomas Sharpe is discussed in Chapter 7; conflict continued under Maconochie's successors tasked with implementing the probation scheme. Maconochie's friend, the Rev. Beagly Naylor was unable to adjust to his new status as 'religious instructor' in the probation system in which he had no autonomy as chaplain and was placed under the comptroller general of convicts, a layman.[125] He resigned in September 1845 and compiled a heartfelt and detailed charge against the regime on Norfolk Island, discussed in Chapter 7. Commandant Price dismissed the Rev. J. L. Ison (1808–1867) following a protracted dispute outlined for the press by his friend Rev. W. H. Browne of Launceston.[126] Like Durham at Port Arthur, Ison claimed to have been assured by the SPG that he would have complete religious oversight of the prisoners on Norfolk Island, delegated authority from the bishop and a team of subordinate clergy under him, 'being a kind of archdeacon without the designation'.[127] Not only was Nixon not involved, the bishop was locked in an elaborate standoff with Eardley Wilmot over the appointment of convict religious instructors whom he refused to either ordain or licence to preach.[128] Bullied, overworked and, no doubt, demoralized, Ison left

[123] W. R. Bennett and George Eastman (1818–1870) to Hawkins, 22 July 1844, BodL USPG C/AUS/TAS/2. Eastman was made chaplain at Ross in 1857 and chaplain of convicts in Hobart and Port Arthur. See *Hobart Mercury*, 26 April 1870; *Guardian* 13 July 1870.

[124] Anna Nixon to C. Woodstock (her father), 3 April 1844, 30 December 1844, *Pioneer Bishop*, pp. 24, 41. Bishop Nixon's solution was to send Marriott to England.

[125] 'The Respectful Protest of Thomas Beagly Naylor', Thomas Rogers Letterbook, SLNSW A323: 4a.

[126] Ison, *Appeal*, pp. 42–48.   [127] Ibid.   [128] Gladwin, *Anglican Clergy*, pp. 183–185.

Norfolk island in January 1848 accused of having 'neither moral nor physical qualifications for the post'.[129]

The most celebrated of the religious instructors associated with Norfolk Island was Thomas Rogers (1806–1903), dismissed by Price in circumstances which inspired the fictional character of the Rev. James North in Marcus Clarke's convict melodrama *For the Term of His Natural Life*, originally published in serial form in the *Australian Journal* between 1870 and 1872. There are significant differences between the fictional North and the real Rogers, as his son, W. Foster Rogers, was keen to point out in his edition of his father's journal.[130] Where 'North' was slovenly in his appearance as well as 'a brandy drunkard, an inveterate smoker, and almost a human derelict', Rogers was abstemious, a non-smoker, a natty dresser, physically robust and possessed of a remarkable constitution which secured him a long life.[131] While vividly expressed, North's denunciation of humanitarian abuses in his unpublished Journal was based on very little experience of Price's regime and lacks authenticating detail.[132] His published correspondence is largely concerned with indiscreet attempts to recover his position.[133] His view of the failings of the deficiencies of the probation system chimes with that of other observers. While still in post he wrote to Archdeacon Marriott that the prisoners' barracks was 'an excellent device of the devil to people the regions of eternal woe with ruined beings' (a point made with equal force by the Naylor) and that religion was regarded as 'the grand imposture': 'There is a great fuss on paper about Religion and Schools but in actual operation things are very low indeed.'[134] Having fought with Commandant Childs and Commandant Price, North left the island in February 1847. Denison removed him from the convict department soon afterwards.[135]

Other religious instructors appointed to serve in the probation system were not as troubled and troubling as Durham, Ison or Rogers. Richard Alderson (1821–1895) was ordained in York in 1846 and served for over twenty years as chaplain of the Fremantle convict establishment. For men in lower-status roles, who may have been schoolmasters in workhouses or prisons in Britain, a short posting as a religious instructor in Van Diemen's Land or Norfolk Island was the prelude to Anglican

---

[129] Ison, *Appeal*, p. 45.
[130] W. Foster Rogers and Thomas George Rogers, 'Man's Inhumanity, Being a Chaplain's Chronicles of Norfolk Island in the Forties', [ca 1912–1914], SLNSW MS C214.
[131] Ibid., 4.   [132] Ibid.
[133] Thomas Rogers, *Correspondence Relating to the Dismissal of the Rev. T. Rogers from His Chaplaincy at Norfolk Island* (Launceston: Dowling, 1849).
[134] Rogers to Marriott, 24 May 1846, SLNSW A 323: 4v–5.
[135] 'Rogers, Thomas George (1806–1903)', ADB.

ordination, usually in Tasmania, and a higher-paid chaplaincy, either in the prison system or elsewhere in the colony. The remarkable Henry Elliott (1814–1884), was a Chartist and Deist who converted under the instruction of the Rev. E. Strickland, serving effectively as religious instructor on Norfolk Island from 1847 to 1850.[136] Although delayed by Bishop Nixon's scruples, Elliott was ordained in Sydney in 1856. Like the former Methodist lay preachers, Bennett and Eastman, the probation system provided a number of devout men with a path to ordination and a career as prison chaplains. Others did less well. The Rev. T. H. Forster (1818–1881) travelled out to Van Diemen's Land with Bishop Nixon, writing a vivid account of his voyage on the convict ship; his correspondence suggests a sad decline into madness and he died in a lunatic asylum.[137] Other Anglican, Catholic, Methodist and Dissenting religious instructors were, like the prisoners, anxious for escape while resigned to serving out their sentences.

La Trobe's Verdict on Probation

Probation was widely regarded as a total failure that exacerbated the very moral and administrative problems it was intended to reform. In his testimony to the 1847 HL SC on the Execution of the Criminal Laws, Bishop Nixon stated that the presence of large numbers of prisoners under the probation system had been 'injurious in a moral, financial, social, and religious sense'.[138] The fairest assessment of it – delivered on the spot in 1847 by Charles La Trobe (1801–1875), and by historians chronologically removed such as A. G. L. Shaw – was that it was not given a chance to succeed given the surge in convict numbers in 1843 and 1844 (Table 8.1).[139] La Trobe's Report, written during his several months as administrator of the colony of Van Diemen's Land following the dismissal and untimely death of Eardley Wilmot, is the fullest and most careful appraisal of the system.[140] Unlike the great

---

[136] Strickland, *The Australian Pastor*.
[137] For the voyage, see Thomas Hay Forster, *Account of a Voyage in a Convict Ship with Notes of the First Itinerating Missionary in Tasmania* (London: SPCK, 1850).
[138] 'Testimony of Bishop of Tasmania (Nixon)', 23 March 1847, *HL SC on Execution of the Laws*, (BPP 1847 (534) VII.1, p. 233.
[139] Shaw, *Convicts and the Colonies*, pp. 310–311.
[140] C. J. La Trobe to Earl Grey, 'The present state of the convicts in Van Diemen's Land', 31 May 1847; James Boyd, 'Darlington Probation Station, Maria Island', 31 December 1845, TNA CO 33/60: 1311 and CO 280/206/551. I refer to the editions by Brand, *Convict Probation System* as 'La Trobe's Report', and 'Boyd's Report'. For the published reports (which lack the enclosures on unnatural crime), see BPP 1847–1848 (941) LII.7, pp. 39–52

majority of his predecessors, La Trobe lacked military or administrative experience and had initially been educated, like his father, for the Moravian ministry. He was a gifted musician, active in the anti-slavery movement and known to both Haydn and Wilberforce.[141] In terms of his outlook on penal reform, his views align with the rational Dissent of Backhouse and Walker (Chapter 4), rather than Arthur's Evangelical authoritarianism (Chapter 3) or Maconochie's liberalism (Chapter 7).[142]

La Trobe observed that the quality of the religious instructors was among the most problematic aspects of the entire probation system. While stoically avoiding naming any individuals, he suggested that many of those appointed were unfit for the task and were found wanting by some astute critics – the convicts themselves:

> I regret to state my impression that after all the stress laid upon the necessity of providing adequately for the religious and moral instruction of the Convict under the New System, in no particular has the difficulty of attaining the object been more glaringly apparent. Both in number and in general character and qualifications, the class of men whose services were at command, were not of the stamp that must be employed, if a reasonable hope of success were to be indulged.[143]

A more positive outcome was reflected in the schools conducted on the probation stations. As indicated in Table 8.6, of the more than 8,000 convicts distributed among twenty probation stations, 1,949 had learned to read, 1,310 to write and 1,222 to cipher since arriving in the colony; 7,875 could repeat the Lord's Prayer and 4,725 were attending school.[144] If nothing else, the probation gang system proved an effective vehicle for improving convict literacy. For more tangible progress, much more investment was required. This was not forthcoming.

Yet, even if it had wanted to, the government lacked the political capital to provide adequate resources for the moral regime of the probation system. The House of Commons' debate on the cost of penal institutions in June 1852 – one of the most extensive on transportation since the Molesworth Report – occurred on the very day that news of the death of the disgraced Eardley Wilmot reached the colonial secretary.[145] In addition to increased costs from the abolition of private assignment, Sir

---

[141] Jill Eastwood, 'La Trobe, Charles Joseph (1801–1875)', *ADB*.   [142] See Chapter 4.
[143] 'La Trobe's Report', 31 May 1847; Brand, *Convict Probation System*, p. 109.
[144] 'Return of the State of the Schools of Probation Gang Stations for the half year ending 31 December 1844', *Return of Colonial Bishops and Archdeacons; and of Grants, Endowments and Appropriation for Religious Instruction or Education in Colonies, 1840–42*, BPP 1845 (356) XXX.171, p. 241. [Hereafter *Religious Instruction in Colonies*].
[145] Hansard, HC Deb, vol. 121, col. 1409–1410, 3 June 1852.

Table 8.6 *State of the schools at probation gang stations in Van Diemen's Land, 31 December 1844*

Station	Number of convicts at the station on 31 December 1844	Of whom can			Of whom have learned since arrival in this colony			Number who can repeat the Lord's Prayer	Total number attending school at station on 31 December 1844
		Read	Write	Cipher	To read	To write	To cipher		
Brown's River	481	302	182	112	115	52	10	469	350
Jerusalem	342	247	230	204	45	53	16	342	144
Broad Marsh	309	226	197	83	55	40	20	296	138
Buckland	248	142	112	51	4	1	0	228	174
Rocky Hills	505	245	151	58	15	17	10	501	484
Victoria Valley	307	203	104	25	35	39	11	307	275
Seven-Mile Creek	224	224	105	40	95	73	30	224	119
Fingal	455	200	200	200	126	96	46	455	159
St Mary's Pass	330	227	152	75	66	44	22	330	82
Westbury	409	275	137	32	31	13	4	409	202
Deleraine	323	180	134	104	40	47	56	320	157
Oyster Cove	194	143	143	143	0	0	0	192	150
South Port	571	384	293	61	46	45	5	512	298
Salt-Water Creek	424	324	228	90	114	84	32	418	210
Cascades	397	322	162	66	85	92	34	396	234

Impression Bay	487	214	190	109	113	103	85	420	309
Wedge Bay	189	125	35	12	7	6	0	186	130
Coal Mines	583	347	354	73	108	87	62	582	311
Maria Island	627	347	267	101	79	106	26	625	360
Point Puer	634	310	310	310	136	245	84	663*	439
TOTAL	8,039	3,686	1,949	1,310	1,222	721	1,111	7,875	4,725
[ACTUAL TOTAL]	8,039	4,987	3,686	1,949	1,315	1,243	563	7,875	4,725

*A number higher than the total convicts at Point Puer and presumably incorrect.
Source: *Religious Instruction in Colonies*, BPP 1845 (356) XXXV.171, p. 241.

William Joliffe (1800–1876) reported on the higher costs provoked by the decision to adopt a disciplinary system focussed on reform, which included the expenses attached to constructing new prisons, such as Dartmoor and Portsmouth.[146] The usual claims were then made: that prisoners were better treated and fed than paupers, resulting in an 'injustice to the honest and industrious poor'; that Reading Gaol, a model prison, was offering 'a premium for the commission of crime'; and that, according to Chisholm Anstey, transportation was so easy that 'it was looked upon as leading to a life of comfort, if not of affluence, in another land'. Anstey claimed that chaplains' reports encouraged prisoners to escape the consequences of their actions, and objected to payments for religious instructors where beneficed clergy were available to do the job more economically. Concern was also expressed about the likely expense of religious instruction at the new convict establishment in Western Australia. While the vote for supply was grudgingly approved, there was no support for more generous provision for convict reform and religious literacy. In defence of reformatory methods, Mr Slaney argued that only 'by improving the condition of the youth of the country, and by giving them a religious education' could crime be prevented.[147] Nevertheless, financial support for reformation programmes was clearly waning, along with any expectation that educating criminals would reduce crime. Once the decision had been made to break up convict establishments in Van Diemen's Land and Norfolk Island, FitzRoy wasted no time in eliminating allowances to clergy from convict funds in New South Wales. Only the intervention of Bishop Broughton ensured a little continuity for clergy once regarded as lying at the heart of a reformative system.[148]

After Probation

For all its evident deficiencies, the failure of the probation system did not bring the empire much closer to a complete end to transportation for British and Irish prisoners. Clerical observers were understandably reluctant to attribute blame for its deficiencies on the weakness of religious instruction. Chaplains of gaols and penitentiaries, as well as Bishop Willson and Bishop Nixon, firmly opposed to transportation in other contexts, testified to the 1847 SC on Criminal Law that if properly

---

[146] Sir William Jolliffe, Hansard, HC Deb, vol. 121, col. 1410, 3 June 1852.
[147] Mr Slaney, Hansard, HC Deb, vol. 121 col. 1412, 3 June 1852.
[148] FitzRoy to Grey, 20 December 1847, 12 February 1843, BPP 1849 (1022 and 1121) XLIII.61, p. 90.

carried out, with sufficient well-supported religious instructors, the system was still better than the alternatives.[149] Only six of the twenty-four witnesses regarded transportation as an ineffective deterrent, and even the liberal reformer M. D. Hill did not recommend an end to the practice.[150] The SC endorsed 'sound moral and religious training' together with industrial training for the young as the best means to reduce crime, just as provided for by the probation system.[151]

That the probation scheme was not fundamentally flawed is strongly suggested by the success of the convict system devised by John Montagu (1797–1853), colonial secretary to Van Diemen's Land under Arthur, for the Cape Colony, which included provision for religious instruction to mobile gangs.[152] Under Montagu's system, rewards were provided to the gangs which 'laboured best' and also individuals who 'improved most in religious and secular instruction'.[153] This was tracked by a monthly report from the superintendent which listed attendance and progress at school and chapel; those who did best earned a monetary reward of six shillings which was placed in the savings bank on their behalf. To provide skilled religious instruction, ordained missionaries were sourced from the Rhenish Missionary Society and the Wesleyan Methodist Missionary Society, which also avoided clashes with the Anglican bishop. Montagu's scheme involved neither large numbers,[154] nor the transport of British or Irish convicts to the Cape Colony and was implemented without the moral panic aroused by gang-based labour for public works under probation in Van Diemen's Land. Until Britain built new penitentiaries, transportation still beckoned as the most convenient solution.

Probation continued despite the over-supply of convicts having driven Van Diemen's Land almost to the point of economic collapse, the dismissal of a governor and escalating costs, which had increased by two-thirds.[155] The key problem was under-resourcing, as evidenced by reports from Port Arthur following the closure of the probation stations

---

[149] *HL SC on Execution of Criminal Laws BPP* (534) VII.1, p. 3
[150] Noted by Shaw, *Convicts and the Colonies*, p. 312.
[151] *HL SC on Execution of Criminal Laws*, BPP (534) VII.1, p. 8.
[152] Nigel Penn, 'Close and Merciful Watchfulness': John Montagu's Convict System in the Mid-Nineteenth-Century Cape Colony', *Cultural and Social History*, 5 4 (2008), 465–480.
[153] Maitland to Stanley, 3 March 1845, encl. 1, Montagu's Report 20 January 1845, BPP 1850 (104) XXXVIII.387, p. 1.
[154] Maitland to Stanley, 26 February 1836, enc. 2, Montagu's Report, 19 February 1846, Ibid., p. 17, notes that the number received at four stations by 1 January 1845 was 716 with the greatest number at any one time, 452. For numbers under probation in Van Diemen's Land, see Table 8.1.
[155] Shaw, *Convicts and the Colonies*, p. 311.

on Norfolk Island and throughout the Tasman Peninsula in 1856.[156] This process was overseen by James Boyd, Civil Commandant from 1853 to 1871, who had implemented the Pentonville system at Port Arthur and managed the construction of the separate, model prison and associated labour system. Ian Brand calls Boyd 'without doubt, the top officer in the Convict Service at the time of this appointment as Commandant at Port Arthur'.[157] A reformer, Boyd believed in the separate system and used it to expedite the abolition of draconian, physical measures and replace them with the tools of enlightened penal management. Boyd's report for July 1856, the year that all remaining intractable prisoners were moved to Port Arthur from Norfolk Island, provided a return on the average population, free and establishment, of over 1,000 people.[158] Four deaths were recorded, one of them the child of a soldier. No punishments other than solitary confinement were noted and no prisoners were in heavy chains. No prisoner had been flogged – although still legally in force, this punishment had in effect been abolished, Boyd commented, since there had been no floggings at Port Arthur for eight years.[159] Even attempts to abscond had declined by over half, possibly because prisoners were given more varied and interesting work. The atmosphere had changed, almost literally, with the report noting: 'The climate of Port Arthur is very salubrious; the health of the convicts excellent.'[160]

Displaying true Pentonvillian assurance, Boyd attributed this change to the salutary effects of separate confinement, the replacement of corporal punishment by solitary confinement and continued attention to moral and religious instruction. More realistically, the change can be attributed to the drastic reduction in the prison population. In one year, the number had almost halved, as no new convict transports were arriving. Other than Port Arthur, the probation stations were closed and the army of prison officers de-mobbed, with no fewer than five chaplains let go, along with paid magistrates, superintendents, medical officers, clerks and 142 other subordinate officers. The abandonment of the probation gangs, the construction of modern, well-designed buildings and a leading penal reformer in the role at Port Arthur had changed the system. The most salient reminder of the probation system and the penal status of

---

[156] Boyd, 'Report of the Civil Commandant at Port Arthur', 15 July 1856, BPP 1857 (2197) XIV.543, pp. 161–180.

[157] Ian Brand, *Penal Peninsula: Port Arthur and Its Outstations, 1827–1898* (West Moonah: Jason Publications, 1978), p. 109.

[158] Boyd, 'Report', 15 July 1856, BPP 1857 (2197) XIV.543, pp. 163.   [159] Ibid.

[160] Governor H. E. F. Young to Hon H. Labouchere, 16 August 1856, BPP 1857 (2197) XIV.543, p. 708.

Van Diemen's Land, its parties of 'gang after gang of chained con-victs',[161] had gone forever. Visitors to Port Arthur approved these changes, including Frederick Mackie, a Quaker travelling 'under con-cern' in the footsteps of Backhouse and Walker who recognized the need for officers to take care, 'that their hearts do not become callous and unfeeling'.[162] At Port Arthur, the visitors' book was full of positive assessments of the convicts and their treatment. Edward MacDonnell, the crown solicitor, commended the men's behaviour in church. He praised the separate system for achieving 'at least the temporary reforma-tion of these men', and for having apparently succeeded where the lash and the gallows had failed.[163]

Conclusion

By the time Boyd handed down his 1856 report on Port Arthur, the horrors of transportation would appear to have dissolved in the Tasman-ian mist along with the gangs, religious instructors, chapels and schools of the failed probation system. La Trobe lamented that the religious instructors appointed to manage the probation system lacked commit-ment and energy to reform and educate the convicts, as they were required to do. This is not true in all cases, but it was true enough – though more for lack of resources than religious zeal. Appointed to provide ministry to settlers and religious instruction to convicts, a number of those who arrived as religious instructors went on to report on what they perceived as the humanitarian, moral and administrative failures of transportation in all its forms.

Stanley's probation system was a liberal attempt to reform transporta-tion and to implement the religious ideals of the leaders of the penal reform movement in the colonies. It had the support of leading British statesmen of the day, including Lord John Russell and Sir James Graham, and was implemented by a stream of newly appointed religious instructors. While never adequate for the task they were asked to under-take – nothing less than the reform of Britain and Ireland's most hardened criminals, armed only with the Rules devised for Pentonville, the Bible and a little theological training – the religious elements of the scheme were not entirely unsuccessful. Many prisoners learnt to read,

---

[161] H. Butler-Stoney, *A Year in Tasmania* (based on a journey undertaken in 1853), cited by Brand, *Penal Peninsula*, p. 109.

[162] See Chapter 4; Mary Nicholls (ed.), *Traveller under Concern: The Quaker Journals of Frederick Mackie* (Hobart: University of Tasmania, 1973), p. 170.

[163] Edward MacDonnell, 29 January 1855, 'Copies of Entries Made in the [Port Arthur] Visitors' Register, 1 January 1855–30 June 1856', in BPP 1857 (2197) XIV.543, p. 722.

write and learn the catechism, tools which were useful in negotiating a return to civil society. Despite its reputation, the probation system was an innovative experiment that might have enjoyed more success had it been conceived with a little more realism and implemented with a great deal more money. That it was a workable scheme was demonstrated by Montagu's success in the Cape Colony, where he had the support of the settlers.

For the religious instructors, a fundamental issue was their subordination to the convict comptroller general, which ensured probation was never embraced by the ecclesiastical hierarchy. This was felt more deeply by ordained priests and ministers and colonial chaplains, both Anglican and Catholic, though Methodists and former Methodists with experience of lay preaching seem to have managed rather better. The removal of private assignment more or less ensured that the colonists would abandon their support for convict transportation, since it brought few economic benefits to them while burdening them with the presence of former criminals, whom they believed to be responsible for rising crime, and tainted them with moral failures which they vehemently denied. The failure of the religious instructors to reform and uplift prisoners under the probation system was a personal indictment for many conscientious men and their families. It made them much more likely to join the ranks of those who considered the only future for the colony to consist in bringing an end to transportation. Anglican, Catholic, Methodist and other Dissenting clergy were therefore well represented, as we will see in the next chapter, in the anti-transportation movement led by the Rev. John West.

9   'Political Parsons' and the Anti-Transportation Movement, 1847–1854

We are no admirers of political parsons, but the transportation question is a social one, and not a political.[1]   (*Argus*, 1851)

Ours is no mercenary aim,
And nought shall save from scorn and shame
The man who yields this land to be
The home of crime or slavery.[2]
('A Song for the Australasian League', 1851)

The creation of the Launceston Anti-Transportation League in 1847,[3] the Cape's Anti-Convict Association in 1849 and the Australasian Anti-Transportation League in 1851 marked a new, more intensive and political phase for the anti-transportation movement. Despite traditional distaste for 'political parsons',[4] religious threads run through the different colonial campaigns at many levels: in the rhetoric of moral crisis and redemption deployed by all participants, in the participation by clergy in the activities of the different anti-transportation organizations, in the clerical leadership of the innumerable meetings, petitions to government and letters to newspapers which made up the campaigns. In Australia, the Rev. John West (1809–1873), a Congregationalist minister and journalist, helped give the movement much of its loyalist, non-sectarian political character. In the Cape, clergy wrote petitions and alternately inflamed and moderated the more radical elements of the rumbustious 'convict crisis' of 1848–1849. Bishops and higher clergy led

---

[1] *The Argus* (Melbourne), 12 May 1851, p. 2.
[2] 'A Song for the Australasian League, July 1851', Rev. John West Newspaper Cuttings, 1850–1851, SLNSW 365/W.
[3] Dan Huon, 'By Moral Means Only: The Origins of the Launceston Anti-Transportation Leagues, 1847–1849', *Papers and Proceedings: Tasmanian Historical Research Association*, 44.2 (1997), 92–119.
[4] For British rebukes of the 'political parson', see William Benbow, *The Crimes of the Clergy, or the Pillars of Priest-Craft Shaken* (London: Benbow, 1823), pp. 179–187; *Cobbett's Weekly Political Register*, 16.1 (3 July 1809), pp. 2–4; *Quarterly Review*, 68 (1841), p. 504. For Australian instances, see this chapter.

denominational interventions with government and wrote theological tracts attacking convict transportation. Archdeacon Marriot argued that it was immoral and irreconcilable with God's plan for human society to devise purely penal colonies.[5] This undercut schemes for reformative transportation and marked the end of the alliance between established church and state which had sustained Arthur's regime in Van Diemen's Land, the last of the fully penal colonies. This chapter will assess the significance of the religious interventions in this phase of the campaign to end convict transportation. It will consider why arguments about the reformative power of transportation, and the influence of religion within the penal system, failed to convince either the colonists or the government that it should continue.

Since the eighteenth century, secular and religious critics had opposed the practice of penal transportation for British and Irish criminals. What happened in the 1840s is that views previously restricted to a minority of penal reformers, with divergent theological, political and intellectual roots in Britain and Ireland, became much more widely diffused, vocal and organized as they were taken up by a liberal coalition mostly located in the colonies.[6] The restrained exchanges between Archbishop Whately

---

[5] Fitzherbert Adams Marriott, *Is a Penal Colony Reconcileable with God's Constitution of Human Society and the Laws of Christ's Kingdom?* (Hobart Town: s.n., 1847). For a colonial response, see *Launceston Examiner* (19 June 1847), p. 2.

[6] Pioneering accounts of the Australasian League include Charles Stuart Blackton, 'The Australasian League 1851–1854', *Pacific Historical Review*, 8.4 (1939), 385–400; C. S. Blackton, 'New Zealand and the Australian Anti-Transportation Movement', *Historical Studies: Australia and New Zealand*, 1 (1940), 116–122 and, for Victoria, Ernest Scott, 'The Resistance to Convict Transportation in Victoria, 1844–53', *Victorian Historical Magazine*, 1 (1911), 101–142. The most illuminating account is now Christopher Arthur Holdridge, 'Liberty Unchained: Anti-Convict Lobbying, Popular Politics and Settler Self-Government in the Australian Colonies and Cape of Good Hope, 1846–1856', (PhD thesis, University of Sydney, 2015). For John West and the movement in particular colonies, see Ann Mclaughlin, 'Against the League: Fighting the "Hated Stain"', *Tasmanian Historical Studies*, 5.1 (1995), 76–104; Gregory Picker, 'A State of Infancy: The Anti-Transportation Movement in New Zealand, 1848–1852', *New Zealand Journal of History*, 34.2 (2000), 226–240; Alan F. Hattersley, *The Convict Crisis and the Growth of Unity: Resistance to Transportation in South Africa and Australia 1848–1853* (Pietermaritzburg: University of Natal Press, 1965); Patricia Fitzgerald Ratcliffe, *The Usefulness of John West* (Launceston: Albernian, 2003); Barbara Richmond, 'John West and the Anti-Transportation Movement', *Papers and Proceedings (Tasmanian Historical Research Association)*, 2 (1951–1952). For comparison of the campaigns in New South Wales and Cape Colony, Chris Holdridge, 'Putting the Global Back into the Colonial Politics of Antitransportation', *Journal of Australian Colonial History*, 14 (2012), 272–279; Chris Holdridge, 'The Pageantry of the Anti-Convict Cause: Colonial Loyalism and Settler Celebrations in Van Diemen's Land and the Cape Colony', *History Australia*, 12.1 (2015), 141–164. For the historical reception of the anti-transportation movement, see David A. Roberts, 'Remembering "Australia's Glorious League": The Historiography of Anti-Transportation', *Journal of Australian*

and Lt Governor Arthur, the sectarian spat between Judge Burton and Father Ullathorne, or the outpourings of Captain Maconochie and his critics and supporters, were drowned out by a noisy, trans-colonial hue and cry. Abolitionists opposed the government view, promoted by Earl Grey, secretary of state for war and the colonies from 1846 to 1852, that transportation was a benefit to the colonies. Colonists and colonial administrators disagreed, pointing not only to the moral damage inflicted by convicts on penal colonies, but the miasma diffused to nearby regions with vulnerable native populations. Race was central to imperial arguments about convicts given the complex racial and religious dynamic of the Cape Colony and missionary claims of convict depredations on New Zealand and the Pacific.[7] In Australia, Archbishop Whately and the Aborigines Protection Society condemned the convict impact on Aborigines, with awareness heighted by the 1838 Myall Creek massacre.[8] The capacity of colonists to make their views heard increased as liberal reforms widened access to parliament, opened up political opportunities for Dissenters and fostered a vigorous, free and commercial press.

Debates about convicts and penal reform, as well as Aborigines and slaves and former slaves, burst into the new public sphere, which Jürgen Habermas argued was transformed through the rise of the bourgeois middle class and articulated, in part, through the 'moral weeklies' founded in the late eighteenth century, such as the *Guardian* and the *Spectator* and the various monthlies.[9] This was enhanced by the emergence of a liberal press in the colonies. Having taken eight chapters to consider these earlier phases of debate about convict transportation, we now turn to a particular political moment in New South Wales, Van Diemen's Land and the Cape Colony, when attempts were made to resume convict transportation in the late 1840s culminating in 1854 with abolition to all eastern colonies of Australia.

Colonial History, 14 (2012), 205–215; Henry Reynolds, '"That Hated Stain": The Aftermath of Transportation in Tasmania', *Historical Studies*, 14.53 (1969), pp. 19–33.

[7] On fears of convicts in New Zealand, Tony Ballantyne, *Entanglements of Empire: Missionaries, Māori, and the Question of the Body* (Durham, NC: Duke University Press, 2014), pp. 38–40, 42, 101–102; For racial and religious entanglement at the Cape Colony, Elizabeth Elbourne, *Blood Ground: Colonialism, Missions and the Contest for Christianity in the Cape Colony and Britain, 1799–1853* (Montreal: McGill-Queen's University Press, 2002); Alan Lester, 'Colonial Settlers and the Metropole: Racial Discourse in the Early 19th Century Cape Colony, Australia and New Zealand', *Landscape Research*, 27 (2002), 39–49.

[8] Jane Lydon, 'Anti-Slavery in Australia: Picturing the 1838 Myall Creek Massacre', *History Compass* (15 May 2017) doi.org/10.1111/hic3.12330.

[9] For the *Spectator* as an emblem of the moral middle class, see Jürgen Habermas, *The Structural Transformation of the Public Sphere: An Inquiry into a Category of Bourgeois Society* (Cambridge: Polity, 1989), p. 42.

Last Convicts to New South Wales

Convict transportation to New South Wales was ended, following the Molesworth SC, by an Order-in-Council of 22 May 1840, though, as subsequent events made clear, it could potentially have been revived at any time. In New South Wales, the last convict ship to arrive under the old system was the *Eden*, which berthed in Sydney on 18 November 1840. The problem for those who had no wish to see convicts return was the ongoing labour shortage affecting rural districts. In 1840 New South Wales was a vast colony which, even after the separation of South Australia in 1836, covered more than half a continent with settlers advancing in Moreton Bay (Queensland, 1859), the Port Phillip region (Victoria, 1859) and, until 1844 when it was transferred to Van Diemen's Land, Norfolk Island. Across this territory, squatters were driving their sheep, forcibly displacing traditional indigenous landowners, and resisting attempts to contain settlement within the bounds set by government. In Sydney in 1839, a meeting chaired by the explorer and landowner Gregory Blaxland (1778–1853) and addressed by William Charles Wentworth (1790–1872), completing his transition from young liberal to the reactionary of his middle years, petitioned for a renewal of transportation.[10] The resulting petition was signed by sixty-seven magistrates and 500 colonists, reflecting continued support for convict labour which had been maintained throughout the 1830s and 1840s.[11]

Where the Whigs had recommended reform and religion for convicts and ended private assignment, the Tories under Lord Stanley were sensitive to the needs of capital. In 1842 Stanley suggested that 'Exiles', that is, convicts who had been trained at Pentonville and were eligible for a ticket of leave, might be sent to New South Wales. Exiles, who included juveniles graduating from Parkhurst, were also sent to Western Australia and Van Diemen's Land, and despite some grumbling their initial reception was positive.[12] In 1844, a public meeting in Port Phillip (Melbourne) voted to receive exiles, so long as certain conditions were met.[13] Many landowners were happy to admit that, given a choice between free emigrants and convicts, they preferred convicts, who were more reliable, did not desert their posts (or not without facing the consequences), and who could be trusted to mind flocks of up to

---

[10] *Sydney Herald*, 11 February 1839, p. 2; Michael Persse, 'Wentworth, William Charles (1790–1872)', *ADB*.
[11] On factors behind this, Reid, *Gender, Crime and Empire*, p. 41.
[12] Shaw, *Convicts and the Colonies*, p. 314.   [13] Bateson, *Convict Ships*, p. 7.

500 sheep on the vast runs of the inland.[14] In the next five years, 1,739 exiles were transported to the Port Phillip District in eight ships.[15] Then, in 1849, four more convict transports arrived in New South Wales, namely the *Hashemy*, the *Randolph*, the *Havering* and the *Adelaide*; this time to significant protests.[16]

In political terms, public opinion in New South Wales was divided between the 'squatting interest' of large landholders, who wished to retain access to cheap convict labour, and the rising free population who, increasingly, opposed it. In the resultant standoff, the clergy of the different churches were squeezed between the urban middle classes, who opposed transportation, and their patrons among the colonial elites, including the governors, who supported it and whose wealth came from pastoralism. Somewhat similar conflicts of interest were evident in the Cape Colony where attempts were made to deliver convict exiles in 1849. Unlike New South Wales and Van Diemen's Land, the Cape was subject to the series of frontier wars with the amaXhosa which continued from 1779 to 1879 with intense outbreaks from 1846 to 1847 and from December 1850 to 1853.[17] Warfare led to the abandonment of mission stations in affected areas and white farmers faced threats to their lives and livelihoods; there was little toleration of arguments perceived to undermine the solidarity of the fragile settler state. As Bonk has argued, the liberal humanitarian consensus sustained since the abolition of the slave trade was undone in the Cape earlier than in other settler colonies.[18] Rather than advance a common humanity, the Bible was used to promote settler rights and mobilize rural communities against convicts and other perceived threats.[19] The church of the settler majority was the Dutch Reformed Church or NGK (*Nederduitse Gereformeerde Kerk*) and it was not 'established', though in 1847 the Colony had been endowed with an Anglican bishop, Robert Gray (1809–1834), one of four colonial bishops consecrated in a single ceremony in Westminster Abbey on St Peter's Day, 1847.[20] The replacement of the colonial chaplaincy with an

---

[14] Stephen H. Roberts, *The Squatting Age in Australia, 1835–1847* (Melbourne: Melbourne University Press, 1964), p. 320.

[15] Colleen Ruth Wood, 'Great Britain's Exiles Sent to Port Phillip, Australia, 1844–1849: Lord Stanley's Experiment', (PhD thesis, University of Melbourne, 2014).

[16] Bateson, *Convict Ships*, pp. 356–357.

[17] For the Kat River Anti-Convict Association, Ross, *The Borders of Race in Colonial South Africa*, p. 187.

[18] Andrew Bonk, 'Losing Faith in the Civilizing Mission: The Premature Decline of Humanitarian Liberalism at the Cape, 1840–60', in M. Daunton and R. Halpern (eds.), *Empire and Others* (London: UCL Press, 1999), pp. 364–383.

[19] Holdridge, 'Liberty Unchained', 266–271, 92–97.

[20] For a report of the service, see *Launceston Examiner*, 3 November 1847, p. 5.

Anglican episcopal hierarchy was not without its complications with most Anglican clergy on low stipends and lacking influence and status.[21] There were vigorous missions with rising numbers of adherents among different tribal and urban communities, some of which mobilized to oppose the convict arrivals.[22] Gray aligned himself with the anti-convict cause in the Cape, going so far as to come on board the *Neptune* in its infamous attempt to land convicts at the Cape, where he had the pleasure of meeting John Mitchel.[23] In New South Wales and the Cape, clergy who participated in the anti-transportation movement did so for rather different reasons, but to the same eventual outcome – a total rejection of the continued deployment of convict labour in British colonies.

Popular protest against convict transportation was ignited by the attempt to reintroduce convict labour to British colonies, including New South Wales. In 1846 Gladstone, who served as secretary of state for war and the colonies in the conservative ministry of Sir Robert Peel (despite not having a seat in either house), requested that the incoming New South Wales governor, Sir Charles FitzRoy (1796–1858), consider the resumption of transportation to New South Wales in a limited form.[24] The despatch is a good example of Gladstone's most convoluted style, but it gave FitzRoy the option of making a wide survey of public opinion, or simply getting the consent of the Legislative Council before proceeding. Although it was by no means an imperial edict, this has not prevented Gladstone being vilified as the politician who wanted to bring back the convicts. The third Earl Grey, who served as secretary of state for the colonies under Russell's Whig administration,[25] earned similar acrimony on the grounds that he was simply 'biding his time' before re-opening the convict sewer line between Britain and the southern colonies. When Gladstone's despatch was made public, editors denounced

---

[21] Hattersley, *The Convict Crisis*, p. 33.
[22] At the time of the convict crisis, major missionary societies active in the Cape included the Moravians, London Missionary Society (Congregationalist), Church Missionary Society (Anglican), Berlin Missionary Society (Lutheran), Rhenish Missionary Society (Lutheran), Glasgow Missionary Society (Presbyterian) and the Methodist Missionary Society; Elizabeth Elbourne and Robert Ross, 'Combating Spiritual and Social Bondage: Early Missions in the Cape Colony', in Richard Elphick and Rodney Davenport (eds.), *Christianity in South Africa* (Cape Town: Maskew Miller Longman, 1997), 31–50.
[23] See Chapter 1.
[24] The full text of Gladstone's despatch was published in the *Geelong Advertiser and Squatters' Advocate*, 21 October 1846, p. 1; Shaw, *Convicts and the Colonies*, pp. 318–319.
[25] Earl Grey served from 1846 to 1852. He had been under secretary for the colonies in 1830 when his father was Prime Minister.

the government for contemplating actions which were so much to the detriment of the ordinary colonists.[26]

In New South Wales, there was anger that the 1840 agreement to end the transport of convicts was not being honoured.[27] Having initially rejected the renewal of transportation, a select committee of the New South Wales Legislative Council chaired by veteran politician William Charles Wentworth recommended its return, largely on economic grounds. This apparent capitulation was challenged by a public meeting in Sydney at the City Theatre in October 1846 presided over by Charles Cowper (1807–1875), son of the Anglican colonial chaplain, and opposing the return of convicts on the grounds of economics, morality and justice.[28] Against the spectre of the return of the convicts, an unlikely clerical alliance formed including Archdeacon John McEncroe, the venerable, highly visible, former Catholic chaplain of Norfolk Island, the Rev. John Dunmore Lang, the vehemently anti-Catholic democrat who served as a member of the new Legislative Council as a member for Port Phillip, and the Rev. John Saunders (1806–1859),[29] minister of the Particular Baptist Chapel in Bathurst Street. All three attended the City Theatre meeting where they were among the leading speakers against any renewal of transportation.[30] McEncroe asserted that he had seen the practice of slavery in the West Indies and the convict system over many years and was certain that the West Indian slave was in a better position than the assigned servant in New South Wales. He opposed forced labour in all its forms, especially since there was now an abundance of free labour to provide for the needs of the colony instead. Indeed, 'convictism could not co-exist with free institutions'.[31] Saunders condemned the 'mischief and contamination' that would result if Britain did not manage its convict problem at home. Lang denounced Wentworth's pro-transportation petition as an abject and servile baying to the authorities: 'it reminded me of the speech of the prophet's ass to Balaam, "Am not I thine ass?" as if they had said, "Treat us, dispose of us, and belabour us as you please, are not we thine ass?"'[32] The one conspicuous clerical

---

[26] See the editorial in the *Geelong Advertiser and Squatters' Advocate*, 21 October 1846, p. 1.
[27] For a crisp narrative of these events, drawing on newspaper reports of the time, see 'Notable Australian Events No 12: The Abolition of Transportation', *Sunday Times* (Sydney), 17 July 1898, p. 9.
[28] *The Australian*, 24 October 1846, p. 3.
[29] B. G. Wright, 'Saunders, John (1806–1859)', ADB; Nicole Starling, 'Apostle of Temperance': John Saunders and the Early History of the Temperance Movement in New South Wales (Master of Research, Macquarie University, 2017).
[30] *The Australian*, 24 October 1846, p. 3   [31] Ibid.
[32] John Dunmore Lang, *Brief Sketch of My Parliamentary Life and Times: From 1st August 1843 Till the Late Dissolution of Parliament* (Sydney: Sherriff, 1870), p. 17.

absentee from the anti-transportation uproar was the Anglican bishop of Sydney, William Grant Broughton, whose principled support of Lt Governor Arthur's penal system, and childhood friendship with New South Wales Governor Sir George Gipps,[33] as much as a natural conservatism, made him a reluctant participant in this anti-government campaign, concerning a policy he had no real qualms accepting.[34]

Meanwhile, other events were overtaking the affairs of the penal colonies. The Great Famine of 1845–1849 caused the death of one million people from starvation and epidemic disease in Ireland and forced another two million to emigrate. In the Scottish Highlands and Islands, outright starvation was less common, but the clearances destroyed the livelihood of crofting communities, many of whom found emigration was the only solution to their distress. Of the many consequences of the famine, human, sociological, economic and demographic, one was a rise in crime.[35] A certain number of Irish pauper criminals were transported to Bermuda, where they became the concern of the governor, Sir Charles Elliott (1846–1852) and are discussed in Chapter 10. Another, less direct, consequence was the rise of Irish political radicalism, culminating in the trial and sentencing of the leaders of the Young Ireland Movement, including John Mitchel, who blamed the English government directly for the catastrophe.[36] Transported to Bermuda in 1848, he was now poised to be the most scathing witness to the collapsing transportation system, the 'empire of hell'.[37]

Issues of anti-Irish and anti-Catholic sectarianism became embroiled in the anti-transportation debate. Although it was unusual for convicts to be transferred between colonies either at the end of their sentences or, under probation, when eligible for ticket of leave, Governor Elliot arranged for Mitchel and other Irish ticket-of-leave holders to be transported to the Cape Colony as part of Earl Grey's exile scheme.[38] Here they would be released without undergoing any form of penitentiary or probationary training. The voyage of the *Neptune*, with its cargo of Irish pauper and political prisoners, became the catalyst for an outpouring of

---

[33] They were both educated at the King's School, Canterbury. Gipps was governor of New South Wales from 1838 to 1846.
[34] See Chapter 3.
[35] Nicholas Woodward, 'Transportation Convictions during the Great Irish Famine', *The Journal of Interdisciplinary History*, 37.1 (2006), 59–87. Woodward warns that the increase was relatively modest.
[36] Mitchel, *The Last Conquest of Ireland (Perhaps)*; for the quotation, see the 'Author's Edition' (Glasgow: Washourne, 1882), p. 219 and Chapter 1.
[37] Mitchel, *Jail Journal*, p. 187, entry for 12 September 1849.
[38] See Chapter 10 for Elliot's Irish prisoners.

cross-colonial, anti-convict agitation that was qualitatively different to the earlier phases of the anti-transportation movement.

Earl Grey's Exiles

As the subsistence crisis erupted in Ireland and Scotland, Earl Grey convinced himself that the colonies were receptive to a much-increased flow of more or less reformed convicts and Irish paupers. The scheme of ticket-of-leave release was largely Earl Grey's initiative, one of a number of attempts to mitigate the disaster. At roughly the same time, Earl Grey transported some 4,000 impoverished Irish girls to Sydney, Melbourne and Adelaide.[39] Other groups were settled in Cape Town under the patronage of a number of Catholic priests, such as the Rev. Arthur McCarthy.[40] In 1847, Earl Grey sent a circular despatch (no. 68 of 5 August) to the governors of New South Wales, New Zealand, Western Australia, the Cape, Ceylon and Mauritius, enquiring whether they would welcome convicts who had undergone 'preliminary punishment and training'. Most responded in the negative, but not all. Settlers in the Port Phillip District (in present-day Victoria) initially showed the greatest interest.[41] There was a series of editorials in the *Sydney Morning Herald* which praised the new scheme, noting that the men would be accompanied by wives and children, and would not be tied to government gangs but available for hire by the colonists.[42] The *Herald* admired not just the exiles but also the reformatory penal system: 'Our ticket-of-leave men have generally been found an orderly and useful class of labourers ... Our emancipists ... have constituted some of our most respectable and prosperous tradesmen and yeomanry.'[43] A third editorial, published a week later, was even more positive, declaring, with the support of Edward Curr, that the exile scheme differed from the workings of a penal colony: 'A convict colony is where convicts are punished. This is the

---

[39] Trevor McLaughlin, *Barefoot & Pregnant? Irish Famine Orphans in Australia* (Melbourne: Genealogical Society of Victoria, 2001).

[40] *Freeman's Journal* (Dublin), 10 March 1849; Ciarán Reilly, 'An Inhospitable Welcome? Emigration to the Cape of Good Hope during the Great Irish Famine', *Breac: A Digital Journal of Irish Studies* (28 January 2018) breac.nd.edu/articles, Footnote 30.

[41] *Port Phillip Patriot and Morning Advertiser*, 11 January 1847. The offer was accepted due to what was called 'the utter hopelessness of supplying the present demand for labor' (sic).

[42] 'The Exiles II', *Sydney Morning Herald* [SMH], 17 January 1845, p. 2; 'The Exiles III', *SMH*, 20 January 1845, p. 2.

[43] 'The Exiles II', *SMH*, 17 January 1845, p. 2.

great distinction ... Port Phillip was a place where convicts were rewarded.'[44] Strong promotion of the scheme was provided through the shipboard newspapers, a number which were edited by the religious instructor or chaplain on board.[45] In April 1845, the *South Australian* published extracts from the *Neptune Herald*, calling it 'a creditable production' carrying both religious and humorous pieces written by the exiles.[46] The general enthusiasm for the experiment is reflected in the *Geelong Advertiser and Squatters' Advocate*, which grandly announced, 'a better lot of men than the Pentonville Exiles never yet entered the District'.[47] There was competition to receive these paragons, and the *Herald* reported that a meeting held in Portland Bay resolved to request that some of the exiles be sent to that district.[48] Others were less sure. The *Maitland Mercury* noted that the supply of labour had to be weighed against the risks of a constant influx of criminals, even partially reformed.[49] A year later, accounts of poor behaviour by the exiles, including selling the books given them by the authorities at Pentonville, getting drunk, refusing wages offered in one place with hopes of getting better elsewhere or – worse – preferring to live in idleness, were all reported not just in the colonial press but in the London *Times*.[50]

For free colonies with indigenous populations, convicts were perceived to pose particular hazards. This would have important consequences in the Cape Colony, where missionaries were some of the most active in opposing convict overtures from the Colonial Office. In New Zealand, Sir George Grey (1812–1898) led the way in turning down Earl Grey's offer, declaring that New Zealand was the worst place for exiles to be sent since it would hold an 'irresistible temptation' to criminals to 'retire into the interior of the country, there to live amongst the native population and to cohabit with their women'.[51] Hostile responses were also received from settlers at New Plymouth, a site founded on the theories of Edward Gibbon Wakefield and subject to fighting over disputed Maori land purchases.[52] Maori opposition was voiced through a letter from 'the chiefs of New Zealand', translated by John Grant Johnson, interpreter

[44] 'The Exiles III', *SMH*, 20 January 1845, p. 2.
[45] For another example, see Ritchie (ed.), *The Voice of Our Exiles*.
[46] *South Australian*, 1 April 1845, p. 3.
[47] *Geelong Advertiser and Squatters' Advocate*, 28 May 1845, p. 5.
[48] *SMH*, 1 February 1845, p. 4.   [49] *Maitland Mercury*, 15 February 1845, p. 2.
[50] 'The Exiles and "The Times"', *The Geelong and Squatters' Advocate*, 16 April 1847 p. 1.
[51] Sir George Grey to Lord Grey, 8 May 1849, BPP 1850 (1153) XLV,11, p. 120
[52] 'Petition of Josiah Flight, New Plymouth', 7 May 1849, Ibid., p. 121. The Plymouth Company was a subsidiary of the New Zealand Company.

to the civil secretary, with 376 signatures. While the archaic language is the creation of the translator, it sets out clear objections to any additional convict arrivals:

> O Lady, we shall be perplexed if the convicts are allowed to come here. They would steal the property of the Europeans, and the natives would be accused of the theft ... [they] would come to our villages and annoy us; they would demoralize our women, and teach their evil ways to the men.[53]

The chiefs then called for other European settlers, 'rather let gentlemen, men of peaceful life, come here. We like such men. Let them be numerous, for our country in large'.[54] The Maori petition with its invitation to free settlers, is similar to anti-convict petitions curated by missionaries in the Cape Colony in response to the arrival of the *Neptune*. They embody the theories of Edward Gibbon Wakefield on systematic colonization which aimed to 'improve' the moral status of settler colonies by incorporating compensation to indigenous land owners, who would then be civilized, and avoiding all forms of unfree labour.[55] For the New Zealand Association, the untrammelled arrival of escaped convicts and those like them represented a fatal contagion of men of 'brutal appetites' willing to live as savages themselves.[56]

Undeterred, it was the early and positive reaction to exiles in Australia which led to Earl Grey's decision to attempt to revive transportation on a more comprehensive basis.[57] In 1848, Grey revoked the Order-in-Council that had ended transportation and opened it up, potentially, to any colony in the empire. 'Any colony' was not just a form of words, and over the next ten years attempts were made to consider the merits of sending convicts to all parts of the empire, from the Falkland Islands to Nova Scotia, with additional efforts to send probationers or those on tickets of leave direct from Bermuda to the Cape Colony, with particularly disastrous results.[58] In practical terms, Grey unilaterally changed the status of the Cape Colony so that it could receive ticket-of-leave convicts, widely interpreted as transforming the Cape into a penal colony; continued the

---

[53] '376 Chiefs of New Zealand to the Queen', trans. John Grant Johnson, Ibid., p. 122.
[54] Ibid.
[55] Jack Harrington, 'Edward Gibbon Wakefield, the Liberal Political Subject and the Settler State', *Journal of Political Ideologies*, 20.3 (2015), 333–351. Note that indigenous rights were always subsidiary to those of settlers.
[56] New Zealand Association, *The British Colonization of New Zealand* (London: Parker, 1837) p. 70.
[57] Shaw, *Convicts and the Colonies*, pp. 312–334.
[58] For Grey's attempts to persuade the governors of Ceylon, Mauritius, New Zealand and the Canadas, see Ibid., 330.

status of Van Diemen's Land as the major penal colony of the Empire; and recommenced the transport of ticket-of-leave convicts to New South Wales.

The factor which precipitated the change from support to outright opposition to convict arrivals, however reformed, was less the high-handedness of Earl Grey than the changing economic value of convicts to colonial employers and the rise in free emigrants coming to both New South Wales and Port Phillip Bay. In 1849, three convict transports were opposed when they attempted to land ticket-of-leave prisoner in Sydney.[59] An energetic petition-signing movement was weighted heavily in favour of the anti-transportation side, with forty petitions seeking the end of transportation in New South Wales, and eight seeking its continuance.[60] This had the desired effect, both in the Legislative Council in New South Wales and in Britain, and Governor FitzRoy belatedly recommended no further convicts be sent anywhere in New South Wales. While Grey was busily scouring the empire for potential hosts to the convict plague, the main focus of protest was the penal colonies of New South Wales and Van Diemen's Land. The rise of the anti-transportation movement is a tale of two transports: the *Hashemy* which arrived in Port Jackson in 1849, and the *Neptune*, repelled from the Cape Colony and driven to Van Diemen's Land in 1850. Both protests involved principled interventions by the scorned 'political parsons'.

The *Hashemy*: 1849

The *Hashemy* was the first convict transport to arrive in Sydney since the suspension of transportation in 1840;[61] unsurprisingly, it was met with strong protests, spearheaded by the politicians Henry Parkes (1815–1896) and Robert Lowe (1811–1892). On 3 February 1849 a public meeting was held, addressed by Lowe and the Rev. John McEncroe. On 8 March another was held in the Victoria Theatre. The largest meeting was that assembled at Circular Quay on Monday 11 June 1849, at which the *Sydney Morning Herald* estimated between 4,000 and 5,000

---

[59] Bateson, *Convict Ships*, p. 372: *Hashemy* (May), *Randolph* (8 August) and *Adelaide* (13 December). All disembarked in Sydney.

[60] For petitions relating to this phase of the anti-transportation movement, see BPP 1847 (169 692 741) XXXIX.281, 453, 539; BPP 1851 (130 and 280) XLV.437, 527; PP 1851 (262) XLV.471; BPP 1854 (3357).

[61] The *Hashemy* was never turned aside or met with protests in Port Phillip. See Douglas Wilkie, 'The Convict Ship *Hashemy* at Port Phillip: A Case Study in Historical Error', *Victorian Historical Journal*, 85.1 (2014), 31–53.

people (a figure contested by Governor Fitzroy),[62] listened to speeches and protested the 'first convict ship to arrive since New South Wales was pronounced free from the brand of a penal settlement'.[63] A deputation of twenty-two people nominated to wait upon the governor included McEncroe as the only representative of the clergy. In confronting the arrival of the *Hashemy* on the docks of Circular Quay, John Lamb (1790–1862), a wool broker and member of the Legislative Council, condemned the government's breach of faith, while acknowledging that the felons on board 'would perhaps cause but little evil: "[F]or the love we bear our families – in the strength of our loyalty to Great Britain, and from the depth of our reverence to Almighty God, we protest against the landing of British convicts on these shores"'.[64] In the event, the exiles were quickly picked up by employers, with 72 per cent finding positions in Sydney and the rest welcomed in Moreton Bay.[65] Fitzroy duly despatched the anti- transportation petitions but added two addresses supporting the government and objecting to misrepresentations in the *Sydney Morning Herald*.[66]

Not everyone opposed the arrival of the *Hashemy*'s reformed prisoners, who had been carefully prepared on the voyage by the pious surgeon superintendent, Dr Colin Arrott Browning.[67] Support for the new arrivals came from Edward Smith Hall (1786–1860), the veteran colonist and former newspaper editor who had been imprisoned under Governor Darling for libel. In a letter written to Earl Grey, Hall defended the reformed transportation system and the opportunities it provided convicts to build a new life in the colony.[68] He opposed the do-gooders who had ended private assignment: 'The religious and party cry of this colony against transportation ended in making Van Diemen's Land a second Sodom. There was no true benevolence, no justice, and consequently no true religion.'[69] To those who called the *Hashemy* 'a floating hell', he recalled for them the examples of Christ's forgiveness of the penitent

[62] Fitzroy to Grey, 30 June 1849, BPP 1850 (1153 1285) XLV.11, p. 39, 'A great proportion were mere idlers . . . attracted by curiosity.'
[63] *Sydney Morning Herald*, 12 June 1849, p. 2   [64] Ibid.
[65] Shaw, *Convicts and the Colonies*, p. 325. Bateson lists five convict ships: *Hashemy*, *Randolph*, *Mount Steward Elphinstone*, *Havering* and *Adelaide*, which transported 1,405 exiles, most of whom found ready employment.
[66] Fitzroy to Grey, 30 June 1849, BPP 1850 (1153, 1285) XLV.11, p. 30 and enclosures.
[67] See Browning's commendation, Fitzroy to Grey, 27 June 1849, BPP 1850 (1153, 1285) XLV.11, p. 26. Browning's voyage on the *Elphinstone* (1836) was the basis for *England's Exiles* (1842); his voyage on the Earl Grey (1843) for the *Convict Ship* (1844), subsequently published together in many editions, Browning, *Convict Ship*.
[68] E. S. Hall to Earl Grey, 1 August 1849, *Letter from E. S. Hall on Transportation*, BPP 1850 (40) XLV.397, p. 5.
[69] Ibid., p. 6.

thief and the woman taken in adultery calling them Pharisees and hypocrites, rejecting their fellow-countrymen: 'If a single convict ship, just arrived from the best-conducted penitentiaries in the world, "be a floating hell", what will be a convict barrack in a new penal settlement? What was Norfolk Island? What Moreton Bay?'[70] His testimony to the 1846 SC Colonial Committee on Transportation supported the reformative impact of private assignment and payment to itinerating missionaries, querying: 'If you pay turnkeys and floggers, why not pay preachers?'[71] Despite mavericks such as Hall, the numbers were against the pastoralists and supporters of the convicts, with most of the leaders of the New South Wales anti-transportation movement made up of metropolitan professionals, rising lawyers, politicians and journalists, as well as many clergy.

The *Neptune*, 1851

While resistance to the landing of the *Hashemy* sparked protest, it was the voyage of the *Neptune*, similarly carrying a cargo of ticket-of-leave prisoners but having sailed initially from Bermuda, that created a transcolonial furore. The *Neptune* left Bermuda on 22 April 1849 bearing 282 convicts for the long voyage to Cape Colony.[72] Elliot had asked to select some of the Irish paupers for immediate ticket of leave, however the list of the Neptune's prisoners who eventually landed in Hobart, suggest that many ordinary criminals made the voyage as well.[73] The average sentence was ten years; five convicts had been sentenced to life and over a third were not convicted in Ireland. It was a hard journey during which seven died 'of the scurvy' and the unfortunate surgeon-superintendent, Deas, passed away while the ship was at anchor at Simon's Bay.[74] The plan to transfer ticket-of-leave convicts from Bermuda to the Cape had been known since at least March and followed

---

[70] Hall to *Sydney Morning Herald*, 1 August 1849, Letter from E. S. Hall, p. 15.

[71] 'Testimony of E.S. Hall to the Colonial Committee on Transportation', 19 October 1846, *Letter from E. S. Hall*, p 16.

[72] For the prisoners, see 'Neptune Voyage to Van Diemen's Land, 18 April 1849', British Convict Transportation Register, convictrecords.com.au/ships/neptune/1849 (Accessed 22 August 2018).

[73] *Cape Town Advertiser*, 30 January 1850. The convict crisis was covered by the Dutch *De Zuid Afrikaan* and the two major English daily newspapers, the *South African Commercial Advertiser* and the *Cape Town Mail* and other smaller papers. I have made use of the extracts transcribed by Sue Mackay from copies at the UK National Archives, 'South African Commercial Advertiser', www.eggsa.org/newspapers/index.php/south-african-commercial-advertiser (Accessed 31 July 2018).

[74] In his *Jail Journal* [*Tasmanian Colonist*, 6 May 1852, p. 4], Mitchel describes how the 'poor sick old doctor' was finally taken off the *Neptune* after a grim period of illness on the

from the Order in Council of 4 September 1848 which had declared the
Cape a penal station. There were several months of preparation following
the meeting on 31 May 1849 at which an 'Anti-Convict Association' was
formed, with subsequent activity coordinated through newspapers,
churches, social clubs, cigar divans and coffee houses.[75]

Following the tactic of 'exclusive dealing' adopted by the Anti-Corn
Law League,[76] the Cape colonists pledged to boycott not just the use of
convict labour but any who refused to sign the anti-convict pledge
resulting in the ruin of some businesses. They also made extensive use
of the churches – another Anti-Corn Law League strategy.[77] As soon as
the *Neptune* was sighted, the bells of the three major Protestant churches,
English, Dutch and Lutheran, were rung to spread the alarm and gather
forces.[78] The *South African Commercial Advertiser* printed denunciations
of the convict menace and support for the editor, John Fairbairn
(1824–1864): 'nothing will satisfy the great bulk of the people of the
colony but the departure of the *Neptune*, with her cargo of criminals'.[79]
Of the lengthy list of signatories, there appear to have been no members
of the clergy, reluctant at this stage to be part of a new colonial public
sphere.[80] By 31 May, when 5,000 people are said to have attended a mass
meeting of the Anti-Convict Association headed by John Bardwell Ebden
(1787–1873), the colony was unanimous in its opposition to the convicts.
Another 7,000 attended a meeting on 4 July with the threat of violence
becoming real to Governor Harry Smith (1787–1860), who pledged to
resign before adopting any measure permitting the convicts to land.[81]
The agitation reached all the way to the top of colonial society: justices of
the peace and four members of the Legislative Council, including Ebden,

---

isolated vessel. At the same time 120 prisoners from the *Neptune* were transferred to
another hulk in Cape Town harbour.

[75] Hattersley, *The Convict Crisis*, pp. 45–46.

[76] Paul Pickering, 'Loyalty and Rebellion in Colonial Politics: The Campaign against
Convict Transportation in Australia', in Phillip Buckner and R. Douglas Francis
(eds.), *Rediscovering the British World* (Calgary: University of Calgary Press, 2005),
pp. 87–107.

[77] For the league practice of getting up religious demonstrations 'where they assembled the
scum of all creeds, and the sweepings of all sects', see John Almack, *Character Motives
and Proceedings of the Anti-Corn Law Leaguers* (London: John Ollivier, 1843), p. 60.

[78] *South African Commercial Advertiser*, 30 January 1850.

[79] *South African Commercial Advertiser*, 29 October 1849; founded by George Greig in
1824, the *South African Commercial Advertiser* survived the governor's efforts to close it
down in 1827, BPP 1826–1827 (470) XXI.775.

[80] Kristen McKenzie, '"Franklins of the Cape": The South "African Commercial
Advertiser" and the Creation of a Colonial Public Sphere, 1824–1854', *Kronos*, 25
(1998/99), 3.

[81] G. C. Moore Smith (ed.), *The Autobiography of Lieutenant-General Sir Harry Smith*
(London: Murray, 1903), p. 612.

resigned their seats and, though they were replaced (some refused the offer), it was not so easy to breach the blockade of supplies from merchants and the edict from banks and insurance offices that they would conduct no business with anyone who opted out of the anti-convict pledge.[82] The bitterness of the dispute was extended, and to some extent was coordinated by means of, churches, chapels, missions and the Jewish synagogue. The *South Australian Register* reported that an elder of the Dutch Reformed Church was compelled to resign when all his fellow elders refused to worship with him:[83] '[A]ll look upon the conduct of these men as highly sinful ... There is not any one of the various religious denominations in South Africa which would not regard it in the same light.'[84] Smith advised Earl Grey that the resistance to the disembarkation of the *Neptune* was much stronger than he had anticipated, that it included objections from 'every religious persuasion', including the Anglican bishop of Cape Town and leaders of the Dutch Reformed Church, and advised a strategic retreat.[85] After consulting the Prime Minister, Grey agreed to do so.

Churches led the way in formulating petitions to Governor Smith against the arrival of convicts, as they had done against the introduction of juvenile offenders from Parkhurst in 1842.[86] Of the fifty-five petitions Smith submitted with his despatches of 24 May and 14 June 1849, thirty-eight or about 70 per cent were prepared by clergy and adherents of Cape Colony's many churches, including the Anglican bishop of Cape Town and clergy, the Roman Catholic bishop and clergy of the Western Provinces, along with clergy and people of the Baptist, Congregational, Dutch Reformed, Episcopal, Lutheran, Moravian, Presbyterian, Wesleyan and Native Independent Congregations of the London Missionary Society. Many refer to the injury likely to be caused to missionary work on the frontier by the arrival of British criminals. A group of thirteen ministers objected that convicts would constitute a 'direct and palpable aggression on the moral condition, low as it is of the numerous South African tribes'.[87] Representatives of the Dutch Reformed Church, the largest in the city, pleaded for the introduction

[82] George McCall Theal, *History of South Africa since September 1795*, 5 vols. (London: Swan Sonnenschein, 1908), vol. 3, p. 75.

[83] *South Australian Register*, 10 January 1850, p. 4.   [84] Ibid.

[85] Smith to Earl Grey, 24 May 1849, *Reception of Convicts at Cape of Good Hope*, BPP 1850 (1138) XXXVIII.223, p. 4.

[86] George Hough, Senior Colonial Chaplain, and A. Faure, V. D. M., Senior Minister of the Dutch Reformed Church and eighteen others, 'Petition from the Religious Ministers at the Cape', 14 November 1842, BPP (217) 1849 XLIII.1, p. 15.

[87] 'Memorial of ... Ministers of the Gospel Resident in Cape Town and Its Vicinity', 16 April 1849, *Reception of Convicts at Cape of Good Hope*, p. 12.

of 'the moral and religious emigrant' to enhance the character of the races of the colony, 'many of whom are yet in heathen darkness'.[88] For the London Missionary Society (LMS), the Rev. John Philip (1775–1851) and the Rev. Joseph Freeman deplored the damage caused by the arrival of convicts to 'progress from heathenism to Christianity, and from barbarism or savage life to civilization'.[89] Through the LMS, Philip sought to advance missionary projects such as limiting white settlement in Xhosa territory, opposing the pass system designed to enhance control of the Khoisan workforce by white masters, and advocate on behalf of Xhosa chiefs.[90] For their part, the Native Independent Congregation (LMS) wished to avoid the arrival of savage whites including those they labelled 'political offenders, Irish traitors, and traversers'.[91] At Colesberg, the Dutch Reformed, Anglican and Congregational churches combined to protest 'political convicts from the mother-countries', likely to degrade the reputation of the colony.[92] Signing on behalf of his clergy, even the Irish Dominican, Raymond Griffith (1798–1862), Roman Catholic Vicar Apostolic of the Cape of Good Hope, Western District, protested, albeit rather less forcefully, on the grounds that 'evil is not to be done that even good may come from it'.[93] Further anti-convict petitions were submitted to Governor Smith by the elders and deacons of the Dutch Reformed Church at Pietermaritzburg, Natal on 18 August 1849, and the presbytery of Albany on 30 November 1849.[94] Seven missionaries of the Moravian Missionary Institution of Genadendal, declared that the arrival of convicts would ruin 'the fruits of so many years' missionary labour'.[95] This was supported by 472 mission residents of Genadendal, who objected to the influx of criminals, 'scattering the seeds of infamy throughout a colony unprotected by rural police'.[96]

A sophisticated response to the convict crisis was provided by the South African Auxiliary of the British and Foreign Bible Society (BFBS)

---

[88] 'Memorial of the Consistory of the Dutch Reformed Church of the City of Cape Town', 17 April 1849, Ibid.
[89] 'Memorial of the Rev. John Philip, D.D. and the Rev. Jos. C. Freeman, London Missionary Society', 20 April 1849, Ibid., p. 14.
[90] Andrew C. Ross, *John Philip (1775–1851): Missions, Race and Politics in South Africa* (Aberdeen: Aberdeen University Press, 1986).
[91] 'Memorial of the Ministers, Elders, and Deacons of the Native Independent Congregations, connected with the London Missionary Society, at Kat River', 25 April 1849, *Reception of Convicts at Cape of Good Hope*, p. 16.
[92] 'Memorial of the ... Ministers ... of Colesberg', 27 April 1849, Ibid., p. 19.
[93] 'Memorial of the Roman Catholic Bishop and Clergy of the Western Provinces of the Colony', 28 May 1849, Ibid., 27.
[94] For both petitions see Ibid., pp. 93, 135.
[95] H. G. Smith to Earl Grey, 5 January 1849, encl. 1 and 2, Ibid., p. 32.   [96] Ibid., p. 33.

in a pamphlet printed in Cape Town following a special meeting on 20 July 1849.[97] Auxiliaries of the non-denominational society had been formed in Cape Town, Graham's Town and Salem where their work included providing Bibles and written materials for Protestant missions and settlers along the frontier.[98] Mission propaganda represented this activity as critical to advance a moral occupation in partnership with converts such as 'The Christian Hottentot' who exclaimed: 'We are tame men now ... I thank God, in the name of every Hottentot ... that I have seen the face of Englishmen.'[99] All this was put at risk by the arrival of dissolute whites. Choosing to ornament their title page, not with an extract from scripture but a quotation from Archbishop Whately's 'Remarks on Transportation', the Society appealed to 'fellow-subjects in other British settlements' to support their rejection of the white plague and all its moral pollution.[100]

Rather late in the day, Anglican clergy chose to intervene in the convict crisis with the intention of calming the more turbulent elements. The leading newspaper in the Eastern Cape was the *Grahamstown Journal*, which provided loyal support to Governor Smith against radicals, such as John Philip of the LMS, who had the backing of the *South African Commercial Advertiser*, edited by Philip's son-in-law, John Fairbairn. The rebuff to Governor Smith by the Anti-Convict Association was seen as discourteous, and a more respectful address was presented to him by a group of 114 moderate protestors including leading clergy. Signatories included the Rev. William Long, colonial chaplain and minister for Graaff-Reinet; the Rev. Charles Orpen (1791–1856), physician, humanitarian and Anglican minister for Colesburg;[101] the Rev. Edmund Payne, Anglican minister for Somerset East; John Edwards (1804–1887), the first Wesleyan minister appointed to Port Elizabeth; and other respectable colonists. They attested that they disapproved of attempts to supply food and the necessities of life to the 'poor unfortunate Convicts now on board the ship Neptune', but would not accept convicts as settlers: 'We need a population of superior men, surrounded and intermingled as we

[97] British and Foreign Bible Society, *An Earnest and Respectful Appeal to the British and Foreign Bible Society by Its South African Auxiliary on Behalf of the Injured Colony of the Cape of Good Hope (with Reference to Convict Transportation)* (Cape Town: Saul Solomon, 1849). I thank Chris Holdridge for providing me with a copy.

[98] George Browne, *The History of the British and Foreign Bible Society from Its Institution in 1804 to the Close of Its Jubilee in 1854*, 2 vols. (London: British and Foreign Bible Society, 1859), vol. II, p. 248.

[99] Ibid., vol. II, p. 246.   [100] *An Earnest and Respectful Appeal*, p. 24.

[101] Emma L. Le Fanu, *Life of the Reverend Charles Edward Herbert Orpen ... for Some Years Chaplain to the First Church of the Established Religion of England and Ireland in Colesberg, South Africa* (Dublin: Charles Westerton, 1860).

are with barbarous tribes and nations, and we wish to encourage, by all means in our power, free Emigration from the mother country.'[102] This 'population of superior men' was, presumably, men like themselves, religiously observant free emigrants, not Irish or Catholic if possible and loyal subjects of the Crown. Loyalty was in short supply in the Cape, as Archdeacon N. J. Merriman (1809–1882), later Anglican bishop of Grahamstown, observed when reflecting on the feeling among the people on the Queen's birthday at the height of the anti-convict crisis.[103]

The voices of the colonists were amplified in the British Parliament by supporters who included Charles Bowyer Adderley (1814–1905), a long-time opponent of transportation and advocate for free emigration.[104] Adderley took up the cause of the Cape in Parliament, in gratitude for which he would later be honoured with a handsome library chair. He was also nominated as a representative for the Colony of Victoria as an advocate for the Australasian Anti-Transportation League. As part of a concerted propaganda campaign, the Cape anti-convict movement has been defined by its unity, patriotism and loyalism, reflected in the title of the pioneering study by Alan Hattersley, as well as the gestures of solidarity across class and creed and liberal historiography of the move-ment. Yes, as Holdridge argues, claims to loyalism and unity effaced other forms of dissent outside the carefully curated activities of the Anti-Convict Association.[105] In 1908, with the pains of the South African War still raw, the former missionary and historiographer George McCall Theal looked back at the anti-convict protest as a precious moment of colonial solidarity when, having abandoned slave labour, the colony chose poverty rather than advancing economically on the backs of con-vict labour. Theal praised the 'intelligent patriotism' of the people and admired the 'great advance in liberal ideas' excited by the convict debate.[106] But the solidarity of petition and popular meetings papered over deep divides in the settler community between British and Dutch, Calvinist and Evangelical Protestant, high and low church Anglicans, European and native African Methodists, not to mention the complex dynamics of a mixed population of settlers, former slaves and indigenous

---

[102] *Grahamstown Journal*, 2 March 1850.

[103] Nathaniel James Merriman, H. M. Matthew and Douglas Harold Varley (eds.), *The Cape Journals of Archdeacon N. J. Merriman, 1848–1855* (Cape Town: Van Riebeeck Society, 1957), p. 50.

[104] Adderley, *A Century of Experiments on Secondary Punishment*; Charles Bowyer Adderley, *A Tract on Tickets of Leave* (London: Parker, 1857); Charles Bowyer Adderley, *Transportation Not Necessary* (London: LSE Library, 1850).

[105] Holdridge, 'Putting the Global Back'.

[106] Theal, *History of South Africa*, vol. 3, p. 69.

Khoikhoi. The latter occupied a space somewhere outside the unified 'people in South Africa' that the colonists claimed to have created in the course of anti-convict agitation.[107] In the Cape, Bishop Gray may well have been glad of the distraction of the convict protest since his own clergy were divided between an older generation of chaplains and missionaries, including Evangelicals who resented the arrival of a bishop and his party of high church clergy. While supporting the anti-convict cause, none of Gray's party signed the anti-transportation petition to the governor.[108]

The protest was successful, and by 21 February 1850 the decision to make the Cape a penal colony was revoked and the *Neptune* ordered to proceed to Van Diemen's Land. On the evening of her departure, 'general illuminations' were displayed in Cape Town with the churches central to celebrations as they were central to the success of the campaign. In the absence of colonial assemblies, it was the churches which made a political mobilization possible and effective. Friday, 8 March was set aside for 'a day of general devotion to return thanks to Almighty God for relieving the Colony from a convict settlement'.[109] The Anti-Convict Association also wound up its secular affairs. Reported in the Hobart press, this can have done little to endear the colonists of Van Diemen's Land to their status as the empire's only remaining penal settlement. As Mitchel astutely pointed out, the Australian colonists were also armed against the arrival of more convicts. Besides the *Neptune*, stranded at the Cape, two or three transports, including one holding his fellow conspirators, John Martin and Kevin O'Doherty, were on their way to Van Diemen's Land, 'for on Britain's convict-ships the sun never sets'.[110]

News of the resistance by the Cape to the convict arrivals was transmitted by way of the stately exchange of shipping between southern ports, carrying reports of the convict crisis in the London papers as well as those from the Cape. The London *Daily News* expressed the views of many: 'Of all the heartless freaks of the colonial office' stated one article, reprinted in Launceston, 'this is probably the worst'.[111] Without a legislative assembly to represent popular opinion, colonists were not in any position to reject the convicts, though they could and did make their

[107] The phrase 'people in South Africa' comes from the *Cape Town Mail*, 26 January 1850, p. 2; Holdridge, 'Putting the Global Back', 152.

[108] James Alexander, *Sketches of English Church History in South Africa* (Cape Town: Juta, 1887), p. 99.

[109] *The Irish Exile and Freedom's Advocate* (Hobart) 6 April 1850, p. 4.

[110] *The Colonist*, 6 May 1852, p. 4.   [111] *Launceston Examiner*, 6 April 1850, p. 6.

objections known.[112] The *Neptune* arrived in the port of Hobart on 5 April 1850 to renewed protests and petitions, with the now familiar arguments: 'Religion, humanity, patriotism, all unite', said the *Argus*, in resisting the dumping of convicts in Van Diemen's Land.[113]

John McEncroe

In New South Wales, the most radical opponent of transportation, reflecting his experience living in the United States, was the Catholic chaplain, John McEncroe. While openly referring to his oath of loyalty to the sovereign, taken as a graduate of Maynooth, McEncroe's speeches became more political as the anti-transportation campaign gathered steam. Protesting the arrival of the *Neptune*, he accused Earl Grey of colluding 'with the squatters of the north and the officials of the south with a view to forcing convicts upon Australia'.[114] He relished his role as 'one of the oldest members of the League, and one of the first combatants in the anti-transportation struggle'.[115] In these meetings he did not allude to religious or moral arguments against transportation, but simply lent the authority of the cloth to the proceedings, as did other clergy.

McEncroe was persuasive because he had so much direct experience of the convict system. Having founded the *Freeman's Journal* in Sydney in 1850, McEncroe thereby created a vehicle through which to address the Irish Catholic audience more directly.[116] The *Journal* gave expansive coverage of the great public meeting, said to have assembled more than 6,000 people in Barrack Square on 26 September 1850, at which McEncroe made one of his most significant speeches. He reminded the people that he had volunteered to go to Norfolk Island and saw himself as 'the prisoners' friend', but that he opposed the penal system as 'the degradation and curse of this noble land'.[117] He further raised the spectre of slavery with a snatch of verse from the Irish poet Thomas Moore (1779–1852), with a small change to the final line:

---

[112] The House of Assembly was established in 1856 when Tasmania became a self-governing colony. The six-member Van Diemen's Land Legislative Council, which was advisory only, was created in 1825.

[113] *The Argus*, 10 February 1851, p. 4.

[114] *Sydney Morning Herald*, 1 July 1852, p. 1; *Maitland Mercury*, 6 August 1851, p. 3, where McEncroe attended a meeting protesting against Earl Grey's plan; or *The Argus* (Melbourne), 17 April 1852, p. 4, where he endorsed the consensus.

[115] *Sydney Morning Herald*, 1 July 1852, p. 1.

[116] The title is adapted from the *Freeman's Journal* (founded 1763), the major nationalist newspaper in Ireland.

[117] *Freeman's Journal*, 26 September 1850, p. 1.

> I would rather homeless roam,
> Where freedom and my God may lead
> Than be the sleekest slave at home
> That crouches to this convict creed.[118]

Before allowing the *Nelson* to land, he urged his fellow colonists to follow the example of the American colonists and claim their freedom. On this occasion, the Rev. Dunmore Lang did not try to surpass McEncroe's heady rhetoric but moved a resolution to congratulate the colonists of the Cape of Good Hope on their successful resistance to the convict menace.

Among the early anti-transportationists, the two ecclesiastics, McEncroe and Lang, were the most radical advocates for a more independent Australia flowing from the repudiation of the convict legacy.[119] In this they were capturing the popular mood reflected in colonial memoirs of the 1840s, such as that of 'emigrant mechanic' Alexander Harris (1805–1874), son of a Nonconformist minister. Harris opposed the execution of the men found guilty of the 1838 Myall Creek massacre, which he regarded as pandering to British humanitarians who lacked knowledge of frontier conditions.[120] Yet he opposed both flogging and the 'horrid iniquities of the ultra penal settlements', where men were herded together or sent to the wilderness 'whither the sound of holy counsel and spiritual caution never reached'.[121] He supported efforts to appeal to the innate moral code and sense of fairness of working men, sending religious advisers who would uplift the convicts and constrain the worst impulses of the masters.[122] In New South Wales, the anti-transportationists included many free emigrants like Harris who felt caught between the interests of large capital in the colony and distant imperial policymakers and do-gooders in London.[123]

Turning the focus back to Van Diemen's Land, the colonists now feared a permanent stain on their characters because of the association with convict labour, and without the expectation of responsible

---

[118] *Freeman's Journal*, 26 September 1850, p. 3, citing 'The Fire-Worshippers', Thomas Moore, *The Poetical Works of Thomas Moore* (London: Simpkin, 1867), p. 89. The original has 'crouches to the conqueror's creed!'

[119] Though, according to Birchley, Lang went much further than McEncroe on this issue; Birchley, *John McEncroe*, p. 97.

[120] Alexander Harris, *Settlers and Convicts; or, Recollections of Sixteen Years' Labour in the Australian Backwoods by an Emigrant Mechanic* (London: C. Cox, 1847), p. 398. John Metcalfe, 'Harris, Alexander (1805–1874)', ADB. Harris signed a petition for the reprieve of the convict stockmen found guilty of the massacre.

[121] Ibid., 415.   [122] Ibid., 416.

[123] Alan Lester, 'British Settler Discourse and the Circuits of Empire', *History Workshop Journal*, 54.1 (2002), 24–48.

government opening up to settlers elsewhere in the empire.[124] With the end of transportation to New South Wales, and the practical refusal of other colonies to accept them in the wake of the voyage of the *Neptune*, Van Diemen's Land became, for a while, the only colony – other than the island hulks of Bermuda and Gibraltar – receiving convicts.

The *Neptune* arrived in Van Diemen's Land in April 1850 and in August the Launceston Anti-Transportation Association held its first meeting. On 25 October another was held in the Cornwall Assembly Rooms, where, as the *Cylopedia of Tasmania* put it, 'nearly all the clergy of the different denominations and leading citizens expressed their views'.[125] Following the first meeting in Launceston, the Rev. John West approached colleagues in Hobart with a plan to create a cross-colonial 'Anti-Transportation League'.[126] Over the course of the year, this initial call for solidarity was extended to New South Wales, South Australia, Victoria and New Zealand, who all set up Anti-Transportation Associations and agreed to support Van Diemen's Land's struggle to abandon its status as a penal colony.[127] With trans-Tasman support from New Zealand, the movement declared itself the Australasian Anti-Transportation League, with its own executive, annual conference, pageantry, propaganda and priestly supporters, as well as a delegation in London. Both Molesworth and Robert Lowe (now back in London) agreed to support the anti-transportation cause, as indeed they had been doing since Molesworth's time in Newgate.

John West

The intellectual and spiritual head of the Australasian League was John West, soon to become historian of the movement.[128] He provided the Australasian League with its motto: 'the Australias are one', designed the banner of the Australasian League, sewn in silk by women of Launceston in 1851, which was widely copied in bunting and banners across the continent. The flag of the Australasian League, also used by colonial branches, depicted the Southern Cross on a British blue ensign; if there was any doubt of the Christian significance of this, it should be dispelled by the Van Diemen's Land Anti-Transportation League pledge, the letterhead of which included both the Southern Cross flag and the motto

[124] Ibid., 24–48.
[125] Anonymous, *Cyclopedia of Tasmania: An Historical and Commercial Review* (Hobart: Maitland and Krone, 1900), p. 15.
[126] West, *History of Tasmania*, vol. I, p. 296.   [127] Ibid., p. 345.
[128] Ratcliffe, *The Usefulness of John West*, pp. 409–424.

of the Christian Emperor Constantine: '*In hoc signo vinces*' (by this sign you will conquer).[129]

West had a rapid rise to public prominence. He had arrived in Hobart in 1838 with his wife and young family to take up an appointment as itinerating missionary for the Congregationalist Colonial Missionary Society. By 1839, divesting himself of his obligations to the Society,[130] he had moved to Launceston where he founded his own Independent Chapel in St John's Square. An entrepreneur and social and literary activist in the Dissenting tradition, West was soon as active as a journalist as he was as a minister, helping to establish the *Examiner* in 1842, which became a vehicle for the anti-transportation movement as did West's *History of Tasmania* (1852). In 1854, he was invited by his fellow Congregationalist John Fairfax (1804–1877) to take an editorial role in the *Sydney Morning Herald*, which he was establishing as the city's major metropolitan daily newspaper.

To what extent did West's Dissenting faith impinge on his commitment to the anti-transportation movement? Certainly, Dissenters had been central to other liberal and humanitarian causes, notably anti-slavery which Congregationalists (usually called Independents in the United States) supported.[131] However, it would be a mistake to make too many connections between the two traditions and Paul Pickering is surely right to draw attention instead to the parallels with the strategies of the Anti-Corn Law League.[132] The cause of anti-transportation was essentially a loyalist and political movement, which made considerable use of religious language and imagery to enhance the prestige and respectability of the cause. On the other hand, it would be just as reasonable to suggest that the Anti-Corn Law League drew its methods

129 'Australasian League Letters, with printed letter-head', 17 July 1851; 'Van Diemen's Anti-Transportation League pledge', SLNSW MS Aa 25/3; Constantine's vision of a cross of light above the sun prompted him to make Christianity the religion of the empire following the Battle of Milvian Bridge in 312.

130 For John West's case, 'Minutes of Colonial Missionary Society', 13 January 1840, pp. 188–195, London School of Oriental and African Studies Library, Colonial Missionary Society Records.

131 John R. McKivigan, *The War against Proslavery Religion* (Ithaca, NY: Cornell University Press, 1984), pp. 26, 48–49. Before the 1830s, Congregationalists supported amelioration rather than abolition. In the northern United States, the sects who made the earliest commitment to anti-slavery were the Quakers, Freewill Baptists and some independent Presbyterians.

132 Paul Pickering, '"And Your Petitioners & C": Chartist Petitioning in Popular Politics 1838–48', *English Historical Review*, 118.466 (2001); Paul Pickering, 'A Wider Field in a New Country: Chartism in Colonial Australia', in Marion Sawer (ed.), *Elections Full, Free and Fair* (Sydney: Federation Press, 2001), pp. 28–44; Pickering, 'Loyalty and Rebellion in Colonial Politics', pp. 87–107.

and practice, including the mass meetings (often held out of doors), the petitions, conferences and delegations, from the practice of the many, small and large Dissenting communities who gathered around the anti-Corn Law cause or, later, the Chartist petitions. Religious activism and political activism were common expressions of the communitarian working classes, and the anti-transportation movement needs to be included as one of a range of movements that galvanized the poor and emigrating masses in the popular politics of the 1840s and 1850s.

West's own account of the history of the Anti-Transportation League from 1847 to 1852, printed while the outcome of the struggle was still unresolved, formed the final sections of the first volume of his *History of Tasmania*.[133] West eloquently satirized the vacillation of the government as 'upstart theory and fitful experiment without end', cataloguing the sorry progression from the condemnation of private assignment by Molesworth in 1838, through Lord Russell's supposed stopping of transportation in 1840, Captain Maconochie's mark system in 1841 and Lord Stanley's probation scheme in 1842 and finally Mr Gladstone's North Australian colony in 1845.[134] Earl Grey's revolutions were the most confusing of all, having announced total abolition in 1847 followed by declaring that all would be sent to Van Diemen's Land in 1848. Against this, West provided a rhetoric of gentlemanly, Christian solidarity, strong on family values and the future of the youth of the colony.

In fact, the cause was not so unanimous as West would have us believe and both sides used the language of religion to promote their cause.[135] There was significant resistance to the anti-transportation juggernaut, much of it principled and based on the economic loss to the colony as well as belief in the reformative powers of transportation, with clergy, at least initially, to be found on both sides of the debate. There were also different layers of dissent, with religious, regional and political interests framing their opposition in terms of distinctive local issues and concerns.[136] In 1851, when Molesworth commissioned a return listing every memorial on convict discipline and transportation up to that date,[137] a majority (six out of eleven) in New South Wales favoured the arrival of Exiles, including employers and magistrates from Moreton Bay, Darling Downs and Wide Bay; in Van Diemen's Land a minority (two out of eight) petitioned for the continuation of private assignment, but six were

---

[133] West, *History of Tasmania*, vol. I, pp. 265–316.   [134] Ibid., p. 286.
[135] Shaw, *Convicts and the Colonies*, 346.
[136] For Protestant and Catholic positions, see Michael Roe, *Quest for Authority in Eastern Australia, 1835–1851* (Melbourne: Melbourne University Press, 1965), pp. 110–111.
[137] *Memorials or Representation on Convict Discipline*, BPP 1851 (262) XLV.471.

against including two vehement petitions from Anglican clergy led by Marriott, and Dissenting clergy, including John West, which specifically condemned the probation system for encouraging unnatural crime; in South Australia, New Zealand, Cape of Good Hope and Mauritius, they were all against, including a strong petition by the Evangelical Alliance in Wellington, New Zealand. The exception was Western Australia, where seven out of eight meetings of colonists, landowners and stockholders were enthusiastic about the arrival of convicts.

Not all meetings of the League were models of united equanimity; many disagreed that the moral argument was entirely on the side of the anti-transportationists. On the part of the many former convicts and their families, there was particular distaste for the anti-transportationists' exaggerated claims of the vice of convicts and the moral damage they were said to have inflicted on the purity of the free community.[138] In Port Phillip, where the need for labour remained high, landowners supported the exiles. At an anti-transportation meeting held in the district in March 1847, the pastoralist Edward Curr (1820–1889),[139] an English-born Catholic educated at Stonyhurst who had a deep interest in Aboriginal language and culture, protested to the clergy present for their unthinking support of the anti-transportation cause.[140] Curr's humanitarian bona fides are not beyond question even though James Stephen had initially provided him with a warm introduction to Colonel Arthur when Curr arrived in Van Diemen's Land as director of the Van Diemen's Land Company.[141] They soon quarrelled over issues which included the Company's harsh treatment of convicts and violent reprisals against Aborigines.[142] Curr's interests aligned with labour-hungry pastoralists and he had been one of the first to welcome Earl Grey's exiles to Port Phillip. He reminded the Port Philip meeting of the exiles' good qualities and criticized the clergy for lacking the Christian spirit of forgiveness. To the interjection of 'No political parsons', he said he was surprised to see clergy convening the meeting since he had total faith in the reformative potential of convicts who had benefitted from the scheme: '[H]e presumed the Reverend gentleman to whom he had referred had read in the

[138] Mclaughin, 'Against the League', 76–104.
[139] Harley W. Forster, 'Curr, Edward Micklethwaite (1820–1889)', ADB; Edward M. Curr, *The Australian Race*, 4 vols. (Melbourne: John Ferres, 1886).
[140] *Port Phillip Patriot and Morning Advertiser*, 2 March 1847, p. 2.
[141] James Stephen to Arthur, 16 September 1825, SLNSW Arthur Papers A2164: 541, 'He is a Roman Catholic; & for that reason (hearty protestant tho' I am) he has a large share of my sympathy. If is depended on me, there would be no civil distinctions between Christians.'
[142] Geoff Lennox, 'Van Diemen's Land Company', *The Companion to Tasmanian History* (Hobart: Centre for Tasmanian Historical Studies, 2006), n.p.

bible that the sins of the fathers were visited upon the children, and had forgotten that the Redeemer came not to call the just, but sinners to repentance.'[143]

Following the Molesworth SC, there had been widespread affront taken at the slights it projected on the moral standing of the colonists, the claims of sexual depravity on behalf of the convicts and callous mastery by the free settlers. In New South Wales, there was hostility to all those who testified to the Molesworth Committee, including the Catholic Vicar General, Dr Ullathorne, as discussed in Chapter 6.[144] In 1839, Launceston clergy and laity published 'An Answer to the Calumnies of the English Press being the Testimony of the Lieutenant Governor and of the Resident Ministers of the Various Communions of Van Diemen's Land upon the Moral and Religious Character of the Free Population of the Colony'.[145] There were subscription lists drawn up of those who supported the pro-transportation cause, including a number of respectable clergy. In Northern Van Diemen's Land, the Baptist government catechist, Henry Dowling and the Rev. J. Simpson, a Wesleyan preacher, spoke in defence of the 'moral and religious condition of the inhabitants' in a public meeting held in Launceston in April 1839.[146] Five months later, the names of both appear in the list of those who signed the Pro-Transportation Petition.[147] The Rev. S. Martin was one of those who signed a petition imploring the Queen to continue transportation and, variously, defending the prospect for reformation of convicts under the assignment system, and the reasonableness of the rate of flogging.[148] Besides defending their self-respect, the pro-transportation lobby in Van Diemen's Land had been set up to try and restore the practice of private assignment. It had quickly become apparent that there was no government support for this and by the time the *Neptune* arrived there were few calling for the continuance of transportation under any conditions.

The anti-transportation campaign had, then, from the beginning the strong character of a moral crusade, taken against the perceived economic self-interest of the island colony. The 'Song for the Australasian League', written to celebrate the signing of the anti-transportation covenant in July 1851, has this rejection of pecuniary motives front and centre:

---

[143] *Port Phillip Patriot and Morning Advertiser*, 2 March 1847, p. 2.
[144] 'That Roman Catholic Meeting: Dr Ullathorne before the Transportation Committee', *The Australian*, 15 January 1839, p. 2.
[145] Anonymous, *Answer to Calumnies*.
[146] *Launceston Advertiser*, 4 April 1839; Ratcliffe, *Usefulness of John West*, p. 312.
[147] *Launceston Advertiser*, 25 September 1839; Ratcliffe, *Usefulness of John West*, p. 488.
[148] *Launceston Advertiser*, 4 April 1839; and, on the rate of flogging, 18 April 1839.

Ours is no mercenary aim,
And nought shall save from scorn and shame
The man who yields this land to be
The home of crime or slavery.[149]

West would later suggest that there had been no opposition to the abandonment of convictism: 'The parents – the women of Van Diemen's Land – the clergy, singly – all sects together and in their separate churches, kept up by petitions a constant fire.'[150] This reflects the wording of the petition of April 1850, written in response to the arrival of the *Neptune* which West included as an appendix to his history; the plea came from 'the parents of 20,000 children', the clergy and the magistrates; that is, those charged with the education, guardianship and moral guidance of the colony.[151] West continued to show a genius for articulating a form of words which steered the movement towards the high moral ground, securing consensus and collaboration and avoiding potentially damaging divisions.

West circumvented the reality of division in the movement by emphasizing unity above all else – and to a large extent the strategy was politically astute and effective. The Congregationalists had pioneered non-sectarian Christian activism in the missionary movement and the consensus that united Exeter Hall at home was galvanized to ensure a solid coalition against the London advocates of continued transportation. As in Cape Colony, both Anglican and Catholic bishops of Van Diemen's Land opposed transportation, primarily on humanitarian grounds; the one remaining voice of opposition was Bishop Broughton in New South Wales, who had earlier defended Lt Governor Arthur's penal system against Archbishop Whately. Finally, even Broughton changed his mind providing a letter which was included in an appendix to the instructions to the London delegation of the Australasian League.[152] Broughton was never a very effective speaker and was always too conscious of his own rights and dignity to earn much popularity.[153] His letter to the League probably managed to annoy almost everyone by first explaining why he had refused to allow the League to use an Anglican schoolroom to hold their meeting, before drawing up the shreds of his

---

[149] 'A Song for the Australasian League, July 1851', John West Newspaper Cuttings, SLNSW 365/W.
[150] West, *History of Tasmania*, vol. 1, p. 292.   [151] Ibid.
[152] Australasian League Executive Board, Letter of Instructions to the London Delegates of the Several Colonies of Australia (Sydney: Daniel, 1851), appendix.
[153] For example, when demanding precedence over other Catholic bishops and archbishops: Bishop Broughton to Sir Charles Fitzroy, 22 May 1850, *Letter from Bishop of Sydney in Relation to Rank*, BPP 1851 (105) XXXV.65.

former episcopal authority, 'having once held the spiritual charge over all the Colonies to which your League extends'. However, he did offer them support:

[I] am fully persuaded that transportation, carried on, as it must now be, in the face of so strenuous and general an opposition, must defeat its own object, which is to represent the growth of crime ... It cannot be supported if England cause herself to be regarded as the author of a continual wrong.[154]

This was a grudging admission that Broughton found the abandonment of transportation to be inevitable, not because it was the right policy but simply because it was the view of nearly everyone else. The letter appeared in the colonial press, but the *Argus* provided the editorial rider: 'We are no admirers of political parsons, but the transportation question is a social one, and not a political.'[155] It was the end of an era in many ways. The following year Broughton sailed for England and never returned. He died on 20 February 1853 in the home of Lady Gipps, widow of his old schoolfriend, the former governor of New South Wales, and was buried in Canterbury Cathedral.[156]

No Political Parsons

The cry 'no political parsons' was raised at different points in the anti-transportation campaign, generally to explain why there should be an exception to the general rule that excluded clergy from the podium. At a meeting to form the Anti-Transportation League, held in Launceston in 1847, it was alleged that 'political parsons had done much injury to the colony (applause)', and again in Launceston, when arguing against the plan to move convicts from New South Wales to Van Diemen's Land, a speaker noted, he 'had no love of political parsons'.[157] As in Britain and Ireland, clergy who engaged in political questions were subject to reproach, particularly from Whigs and Radicals. When four Van Diemen's Land clergy offered an address to Governor Arthur on the occasion of his retirement, the *Cornwall Chronicle* objected, 'We hate political parsons – they are the curse of a community.'[158] Against the Rev. Dunmore Lang, the former convict surgeon Thomas Parmeter declared: 'No political parson, can search the Hearts, or reform the

[154] Australasian League Executive Board, *Instructions to the London Delegates*, appendix.
[155] *The Argus* (Melbourne), 12 May 1851, p. 2.
[156] K. J. Cable, 'Broughton, William Grant (1788–1853)', *ADB*.
[157] *Launceston Examiner*, 30 October 1847, p. 3; *Cornwall Chronicle* (Launceston), 3 February 1849, p. 345; *The Argus*, 12 May 1851, p. 2.
[158] *Cornwall Chronicle* (Launceston), 22 July 1826, p. 2.

manners of his Congregation.'[159] And when Bishop Broughton intervened in the education debate, he was called 'A political parson of the most dangerous description' and 'the worst of all political priests'.[160] So what was it that made this campaign different, and why did clergy feel free to participate?

Once the movement was underway, there was a concerted push to create petitions that would resonate with those in government. As Lt Governor of the colony with the most significant penal population, Denison in Van Diemen's Land bore the brunt of the defence of Earl Grey's transportation dreams. His considered view, expressed in a confidential dispatch of 2 May 1850, was that both the evils allegedly caused by transportation and also the benefits to be created by its abolition were greatly exaggerated. Resignedly, he forwarded a petition on 18 December 1850 from the bishop and clergy of the Church of England, who might in other times have been numbered among the defenders of government policy.[161] By the standards of the secular anti-transportation petitions this was a modest affair, with just thirty-seven signatures, but these included the bishop, archdeacons and clergymen of the 'United Church of England and Ireland in Tasmania'. This may have been a particular trial to Denison because his wife was friendly with both Bishop Nixon and Archdeacon Marriott; their children played together and when Marriott married, Denison's wife regaled the family with the details.[162]

Referring to themselves as 'ministers of peace', the clerical petition invoked the 'appalling evils resulting from transportation', regretted plans to make Van Diemen's Land a 'permanent penal colony' and condemned the continued arrival of convicts on the grounds that this would perpetuate divisions in society, 'seriously impeding the efforts of your Majesty's petitioners to promote the extension and continuance of Christian peace and love, according to their appointed duty'.[163] These views were in accord with Marriott's printed letter addressed to Lt Governor Denison in 1847, arguing that exclusive penal colonies were morally unjustifiable.[164] His objections were both to a penal colony 'left to grow into a colony of emancipists alone', and a free colony 'made to

---

[159] Thomas Parmeter, M. D.'Lines to a clergyman', *Sydney Gazette* (27 October 1835), p. 4.

[160] Defending him against these slurs, *The Tasmanian* (Hobart), 2 September 1836, p. 5.

[161] Denison to Earl Grey, 18 December 1850, encl. 33, BPP 1851 (1361 & 1418) XLV.1, 265, pp. 113–114.

[162] William Denison, *Varieties of Vice-Regal Life*, 2 vols. (London: Longmans, 1870), vol. I, p. 93.

[163] 'Petition of the United Church of England and Ireland in Tasmania', BPP 1851 (1361 & 1418) XLV.1, 265, p. 14.

[164] Marriott, *Penal Colony*.

bear the burthen of the crimes of its Father-land'.[165] Denison's response
to the latter is not recorded, but his official correspondence suggests
he found the resistance of the established clergy to the policy of
the government to be as welcome as that of the members of his own
Legislative Council. In Launceston, a clerical gathering was led by the
Anglican bishop of Melbourne, Charles Perry (1807–1891), encouraging
anti-transportation petitions on the grounds that as long as Tasmania
remained a convict settlement, 'Victoria must suffer all the evils of
convictism, without any of the advantages supposed to flow from that
system.'[166] This was a notable concord between rival church parties in
the Australian colonies since Marriott and Nixon were both high churchmen and Perry an Evangelical who differed from Nixon on almost all
points. Yet here they were united in opposition to the convict menace.

It was the duty of the governors to support the home government and
not attach themselves to one side or other of a colonial dispute. Mostly
they succeeded, though FitzRoy in New South Wales became very close
to the anti-transportation lobby and Denison seems to have relished his
minority role as supporter of transportation, on both economic and
moral grounds. In forwarding the petition signed by 144 employers of
labour, Denison stated that he fully concurred with its overall argument
that transportation was necessary for the economic health of the colony
and rejecting arguments that this impinged on its moral standing.[167] In
July 1851, Denison summarized the overall position that, firstly 'a large
numerical proportion' of the employers of labour opposed transportation, giving his view that they included many who had an 'erroneous and
exaggerated idea' of the alleged moral effects on the community and
others who believed it had not been a significant economic benefit either.
He agreed that the labouring classes opposed transportation, as did the
'professional men', who included the clergy, the merchants and the
landowners. Those who supported transportation were a minority who
believed – rightly, in Denison's opinion – that the loss of transportation
would lead to a drastic rise in wages and the consequent economic ruin
of the colony.[168]

The petitions from across Van Diemen's Land tended to be more or
less respectful in tone, stressing their loyalty and frequently referring to
religion and the rights supposedly ignored by the government. '[T]he
disregard of the moral, religious, and social welfare of this colony,
evinced by you in continuing to inundate it with the crime of the British

---

[165] Ibid., 5.   [166] *Launceston Examiner*, 22 February 1853, p. 5.
[167] Denison to Grey, 27 March 1851, BPP 1852 (1517) XLVI.183, p. 1.
[168] Denison to Grey, 14 July 1851, Ibid., p. 5.

Empire has spread alarm and indignation throughout the Australian colonies', wrote eight petitioners from Van Diemen's Land on 29 May 1851.[169] To Denison's annoyance, they also regularly accused him of underestimating their importance and failing to signal the numerical strength of the opposition to transportation. Denison would continue to denigrate the credentials and standing of the anti-transportation movement, including the formation of the Australasian League in 1851, warning the government about attempts to exaggerate its importance: 'Here, however, very little regard is paid to it'.[170] He was similarly dismissive of the protests against the arrival of two convict ships, *Lady Kennaway* and the *Blackfriars*, noting that the convicts from the *Cornwall* were so eagerly sought after 'as to make a solemn protest of this kind rather farcical'.[171] But Denison was losing ground and, despite the strong demand for labour, quiet protests from branches of the Australasian League continued with each new arrival.[172]

As the delegate for Van Diemen's Land to the Australasian League and the only cleric, John West was able to generate respectable support for the anti-transportation movement and sympathy for clergy who chose to participate. At the Melbourne launch of the Australasian League in 1851, one participant affirmed the role played by clergy in the anti-slavery movement, and called on 'members of that profession in Australia' to enter 'heart and soul' into the anti-transportation cause.[173] Many proceeded to do so. In South Australia, founded as a free colony, the meeting to establish a branch of the League attracted all the leading clergy and included two delegates from the Australasian Conference, including West, who addressed the meeting. Reflecting the inclusive policy pursued by churches in the Cape, all five motions were either moved or seconded by the clergy representing all the leading

---

[169] Thomas D. Chapman, Memorial to Earl Grey, 29 May 1851, Ibid., p. 8. When Tasmania was plunged into economic depression, Denison sounded rather pleased to be able to report to his mother that his 'poor old colony' it was mired in bankruptcies and disaster. 'My poor old colony, Van Diemen's Land, is in a very miserable condition. I kept warning the people of what would be the result of the cessation of transportation and the blow has now come upon them.' Denison to Mrs Denison, 5 February 1857, Denison, *Varieties*, vol. 2, p. 379.

[170] Denison to Earl Grey, 14 July 1851, BPP 1852 (1517) XLVI.183, p. 5; Denison to Earl Grey, 14 June 1851, '[A]ll the reports of the progress of the Australian League against transportation are gross exaggerations.' Ibid., vol. I, p. 159.

[171] Denison to Earl Grey, 15 July 1851, BPP 1852 (1517) XLVI.183, p 7.

[172] Denison received written protests following the arrival of the *Cornwall*, the *Aurora*, the *Blenheim* and the *Rodney*, all of which arrived in November and December 1851. Ibid., pp. 7, 64, 67, 71.

[173] Australasian League, *The Inauguration of the Australasian League: Held at the Queen's Theatre, Melbourne, on February 1st, 1851* (Melbourne: Samuel Goode, 1851), p. 27.

denominations. The Anglican bishop of Adelaide moved 'That the cessation of transportation to the Australian Colonies is essential to their honour, happiness, and prosperity'; the Rev. Mr Stow followed, with support from the Rev. Mr Symons, 'That this meeting rejoices in the union of Victoria, Van Diemen's Land and New South Wales, in on great confederation, to secure by moral means the deliverance of these fair regions from the curse of convictism'. Others were proposed by the Rev. Daniel James Draper (1810–1866), Wesleyan Methodist minister of Pirie Street Church, seconded by Father George Backhaus (1811–1882), minister to Adelaide's German Catholic community and the Rev. John Gardner (1809–1899) of the Free Presbyterian Church.[174] This privileging of clerical voices can hardly be accidental and was calculated to demonstrate West's most powerful weapon – that the 'Australias' were united in their opposition, that the campaign to defeat transportation was a moral and ethical one which garnered support across the denominational spectrum and that it was the first step in greater unity across the colonies. Other clergy took the lead in motions recorded in support of the anti-transportation cause. At Port Macquarie in northern New South Wales, founded as a penal settlement in the 1820s, the Rev. William McKee expressed the alarm of his fellow colonists at suggestions that the northern districts might be separated into a district 'forming a place for British criminals'. He objected to any place which would, in the words of the motion, 'disgrace us in the eyes of our fellow colonists' and 'infallibly bring guilt and ruin upon ourselves and the colony generally'.[175]

The most sophisticated and extensive response made by the Anti-Transportation Association was prepared by Charles Cowper, chairman of the Committee of the New South Wales Association for Preventing the Revival of Transportation to These Colonies. This included the 'federal petition' from all the Australian colonies as well as New Zealand directed against the continuance of transportation to Van Diemen's Land. Cowper noted that this petition had gathered 10,200 signatures in the version forwarded by Cowper to Governor FitzRoy, though he noted that another 10,000 had signed in South Australia alone. Besides the petition itself, he included the proceedings of the Conference of the Australasian League, held from late April to 3 May 1851. Along with a set of guiding principles and regulations, this conference generated the lengthy 'Letter of Instructions', issued by the executive of the Australasian League to

[174] Young to Grey, 8 September 1851, encl.: 'Anti-Transportation Meeting (Adelaide)', 1 September 1851, BPP 1852 (1517) XLVI.183, p. 250
[175] Fitzroy to Grey, 20 March 1851, encl., 'Anti-Transportation Meeting at Port Macquarie', BPP 1852 (1517) XLVI.183, p. 84.

the London delegates heading to promote the cause at the fountainhead of imperial power.

Cowper was a pastoralist and politician who became aligned with the liberal faction opposing transportation on the New South Wales Legislative Council. As the son of the colonial chaplain, he was closely associated with the interests of the Church of England.[176] The New South Wales movement was pragmatic, informed and liberal – but, like the Van Diemen's Land movement, it made strategic use of religious language to add moral weight to its testimonials. The fullest and most eloquent expression of the principles of the Australasian League were incorporated into the 'Letter of Instructions to the London delegates', drawn up following the Sydney Conference of the League, held in April and May 1851. The details of this were said to have been finalized by John West, and indeed it bears the mark of his easy, moralizing style.[177] The 'Instructions' stressed that all religious authorities deplored the presence of crime and criminals in their midst and supported the cause:

The people of Great Britain need not be told that Ministers of every religious persuasion, and parents of every rank, feel that no earthly consideration can, or ought to, reconcile them, to expose their families, or their flocks, to the contagion of crime.[178]

The London delegates were instructed to 'tell them that we love our native country, and rejoice in her share of her heritage of glory, that we offer our filial duty and manly affiance, but, that we offer them on this condition, that we, and our children, and their country, shall be free'.[179] Part of the impassioned speech made by Sir Richard Broun on behalf of the starving Irish and Scots seeking to emigrate to North America was quoted, in which Broun wrote: 'England has no right to cast out amongst other nations, or upon naked shores, either her poverty or her crime. This is not the way in which a great and wealthy People, a MOTHER OF NATIONS, ought to colonise.'[180] The letter concludes by calling for a 'great moral victory' as well as closer union and the overcoming of the

[176] John M. Ward notes that he was known as the 'Member for the Church of England' because of his support for church schools; John M. Ward, 'Cowper, Sir Charles (1807–1875)', *ADB*.

[177] *The Courier* (Hobart), 21 May 1851, p. 2. 'It is understood that the Rev. John West remains to perfect certain details and settle certain addresses and letters of instruction to the London Board of the League'.

[178] Australasian League Executive Board, *Instructions to the London Delegates*, p. 2.

[179] Ibid., p. 6.

[180] Sir Richard Broun, 'The Baronetage of Scotland and Ireland (7 November 1844)', *Simmonds's Colonial Magazine*, 4 (1844): 1–12.

burdens 'imposed by a despotic Minister'.[181] The direct, if still respectful, rebuff to Earl Grey suggests the limits of colonial patience had been reached. The antis may well have thought that their protest, so carefully scripted and buoyed by arguments from every quarter, was irrefutable and that transportation must now fall.

Alas, it was not enough. While Cowper, West and the other leaders of the League were convinced that they had assembled an unassailable case, the Colonial Office continued to support Lt Governor Denison, who never wavered in his support for transportation. As Denison made clear in his covering letters to Earl Grey, the anti-transportationists were vulnerable for their exaggeration of the statistics and the dubious use they made of the moral evidence. Other opponents remained quiet, but not George Hull (1787–1879), a large landowner who had also served as assistant commissary general in Van Diemen's Land, who penned a lengthy, outraged letter deploring the abuse of statistics by the members of the Australasian League, pointing out that 'I am the father, Sir, of nine sons and four daughters, with ten grandchildren, who all have reason to be proud of this land of their birth.'[182] His letter included testimonials for the hard work, integrity and decency of the former convict tenants on his property, the fabrication of statistics by the League, naming the bishop of Adelaide and the Rev. John West as prime offenders. At the same time, he pointed to the donations to Bible societies in Van Diemen's Land, the safety of its roads and the success of its convict residents: 'It cannot be known in England that it is almost [a] universal practice of this "immoral" community to place the Bible or some other book of devotion on the table as a part of the breakfast equipage; or to assemble the family, servants and all, then, or immediately afterwards, when the master, mistress, or some one of the family reads and prays.'[183] The image of the whole of free and convict Van Diemen's Land spending their meal times in prayer is as much of a fantasy as the hell-hole image evoked by the Anti-Transportation League, but both parties used religion to define the moral boundaries of their respective visions.

Earl Grey remained impervious to both prayers and petitions and continued to seek alternative destinations for the convicts he claimed to have reformed. Against the evidence, he maintained that transportation was a boon to both the colonies and to the convicts themselves, reflected in his policies which required the convicts to repay a portion of their

---

[181] Australasian League Executive Board, *Instructions to the London Delegates*, p. 6.
[182] Denison to Grey, 11 October 1851, encl., George Hull to Denison, 4 October 1851, BPP 1852 (1517) XLVI.183, p. 59.
[183] Ibid., p. 63.

ticket of leave, insisting that colonies which may have considered accepting convict labour had to pay for it, and quibbling over paying any additional costs for policing and judicial establishments in the penal colonies.[184] He believed that the best mode of penal discipline began with separate confinement and religious instruction at home, followed by penal labour and transportation to the colonies. He defended this belief in a retirement project of many hundreds of pages which provided his account of his policy and why he was right and the anti-transportation movement was wrong.[185]

In line with other political campaigns, the resolution came not with a triumph of one side or another but with regime change. The collapse of Lord John Russell's Liberal government saw Grey's departure as secretary of state for war and the colonies, an office he had held from July 1846 to 21 February 1852. His successors were much less averse to acknowledging the role played by the colonial opposition to transportation in bringing about an end to the system. An Order in Council revoking the status of Van Diemen's Land as a penal colony was passed on 29 December 1853, to universal rejoicing in the 'Empire's gaol'. In the House of Lords, Grey attempted to condemn the measure, but was outvoted.[186] As to the moral and religious argument, much of which had focussed on the reformation of convicts, the outcome of this remained uncertain.

Conclusion

Despite tacit and overt hostility to 'political parsons', the clergy were active participants in the anti-transportation movement and they can be found, on both sides of the argument, in all colonies threatened by Earl Grey's decision to open up the empire to receiving British convicts. Clergy participated in three major ways, all of them effective in lending dignity to the proceedings: convening and chairing meetings, signing petitions and writing, on behalf of their flocks, to government and ecclesiastical officialdom. The particular strategies taken by different clergy tended to reflect the theological and ecclesiological traditions of their respective churches. The anti-transportation campaign began in Van Diemen's Land, which was most affected by the attempt to renew the transportation of convicts and which was the largest and most important of the empire's penal colonies. There it was led by the Rev. John West,

---

[184] Shaw, *Convicts and the Colonies*, p. 347.
[185] Grey, *The Colonial Policy of Lord John Russell*.
[186] Shaw, *Convicts and the Colonies*, p. 351. For colonial celebrations, see Holdridge, 'Pageantry'.

who infused the movement with its non-denominational, liberal and moral character. Although they made up the smallest of the Protestant sects in the colonies, it was not surprising to find Congregationalists in pole position, as they had been on other imperial campaigns, from anti-slavery to broader political movements to widen the franchise, liberalize the press and remove religious impediments to participation in civil affairs. West also led the campaign to unite the separate colonies in a movement to protect their common interests.

In the Cape Colony and in New Zealand, clergy who participated in petition making were anxious to point to the implications for the missionary movement of the arrival of those they perceived as degraded whites, who would fail to set an appropriate Christian standard of behaviour for emerging tribes. In Van Diemen's Land, clerical petitions were more likely to raise moral issues, such as the opposition to the perceived association between the probation gang system and unnatural crime. The most significant clerical activity was that in the Cape Colony, where the churches acted to coordinate petition writing, acting as representatives for the whole community and its moral stance against the arrival of convicts, including juveniles from Parkhurst and the Irish Exiles from Bermuda who precipitated the convict crisis of 1849.

The Anglican clergy, who included an important group of newly consecrated bishops to the colonies of New South Wales, Van Diemen's Land and the Cape Colony, lent prestige and social standing to the movement Initially, the only bishop to remain attached to the pro-transportation cause was the Anglican bishop of Sydney, Richard Grant Broughton. When the anti-transportationists finally persuaded him to add a letter of support to the great federal petition, sent to London in 1851, it was reasonable to think that all sectors had been conquered. In Van Diemen's Land, Bishop Nixon and Archdeacon Marriott secured a united front for the Anglican clergy, all the more surprising because of the divisions raging between high and low churchman in this most fractious of Australian colonial seas. They were soon joined by the Evangelical Anglican bishop of Melbourne, Charles Perry, securing a united episcopal front and a resounding rupture between the formerly established church and the colonial government.

Among the Catholic clergy, the most radical voice was provided by Archdeacon McEncroe, whose American experience had inclined him towards democracy and whose pastoral duties within the convict system, including the vicissitudes of Norfolk Island, had convinced him that there was no justification for maintaining a system so demoralizing, inconsistent and inhumane. He was the successor to earlier Catholic clergy, including Archdeacon Ullathorne and Bishop Willson, who had provided effective witness to humanitarian abuses within the convict system. Catholics had their own counter-narrative to the vice and immorality of convictism, one which celebrated their survival despite the neglect and abuse of the British authorities. They were to embrace the opportunities for federalism and religious autonomy in the rising colonies. Collectively, the clergy were most significant at this stage of the anti-transportation movement as symbols of their wider communities. It was John West's genius to recognize this and to have the focus and energy to maintain a coalition of the willing to end the transport of convicts to the eastern colonies of Australia. Recognizing their central role, the churches participated joyfully in the celebrations for the ending of transportation to Van Diemen's Land and New South Wales, as they had done when the *Neptune* was seen off at the Cape. Nevertheless, convict transportation was not yet at an end as the focus of the campaign – and the convicts – turned to the hulks.

10 'Floating Hells': Bermuda, Gibraltar and the Hulks, 1850–1875

> Bermuda is the solitary exception, under the British Crown, where these dens of infamy and pollution are permitted to exist ... [In America] I found no such thing as a hulk existing and the surprise of all the prison officers in the United States was great, that in an English colony, at the present day, such hells of abomination could be tolerated longer.[1]
>
> (Rev. J. M. Guilding, 1860)

> It is hardly possible to conceive a state of things more abominable than that which commonly occurs on board transport ships bearing convicts to Bermuda, Gibraltar, or Western Australia. These ships are in truth floating hells.[2]
>
> (Thomas Beard, 1861)

This chapter considers religious aspects of the campaign to end transportation and the use of hulks in the convict establishments of Bermuda and Gibraltar. In Bermuda, this campaign was stimulated by the public denunciation by the Rev. John Melville Guilding (1830–1898), government chaplain from 1856 to 1865. As successive governors sought to modernize the system, anti-transportationists represented convict labour in the immoral and unhygienic confines of the hulks as a blight on the reputation of the empire. A series of religious issues troubled the secular management of convict labour in Bermuda. There were humanitarian and security anxieties over the arrival of significant numbers of Irish convicts, including political prisoners as well as pauper victims of the Irish Famine, the majority of whom were Roman Catholics. There was sectarian wrangling about who had religious oversight over convicts and colonists in Bermuda and the extent to which convicts were entitled to priests and ministers of their own persuasion. Finally, the clash between secular and religious management of convict labour came to a head in the dispute between Guilding and the superintendent of convict labour over access to schooling and reformation of the convict labour force.

---

[1] *Spectator*, 2 June 1860, p. 521.
[2] 'A Dialogue Concerning Convicts', 158–159, commissioned and edited by Dickens from his friend, Thomas Beard.

Combined with the liability of the hulks to periodic outbreaks of epidemic disease, these religious entanglements hastened the decision to transfer all convicts to shore-based accommodation and break up the hulks in all locations at home and abroad. The hulks therefore formed the last bastion of resistance in the long campaign to end the transportation of British and Irish convicts in the empire.

Bermuda, 1824–1865

Between 1824 and 1865, about 9,000 convicts were transported to Bermuda from Britain and Ireland. Although it was one of the smallest of the overseas repositories for Britain's convict population (only Gibraltar was smaller) it was the most lethal. The warm conditions, confined space and poor hygiene below decks ensured there was a high death rate from epidemic disease. Relative to other British penal colonies there have been few accounts of the Bermuda convicts, though Clare Anderson is currently adding to our knowledge of this intriguing site.[3] While Clara Hallett has written the only monograph-length study, and Bermuda has been scrutinized as part of the system of prison hulks in the United Kingdom and British colonies.[4] Vic Gatrell regarded Bermuda as 'the British hulk establishment's most notorious outpost', and Alyson Brown has discussed its role in the removal of those involved in the Chatham Prison riots of January 1861.[5] Despite this formidable reputation, the Bermuda hulks had their religious side. An important addition to knowledge about convict life and labour in Bermuda comes from the excavations conducted by Chris Addams and Mike Davis in 1982, with permission from the Bermuda government, in the area where the *Dromedary* hulk was once anchored. Using an unconventional suction dredge, marine archaeologists recovered thousands of items which reflect the material culture of the convict world above.[6] One striking finding from

---

[3] Clare Anderson, 'The Convict Hulks of Bermuda', Carceral Archipelago staffblogs.le.ac.uk/carchipelago/2014/06/26/the-convict-hulks-of-bermuda/ (Accessed 5 April 2018).

[4] C. F. E. Hollis Hallett, *Forty Years of Convict Labour* (Bermuda: Juniperhill, 1999; Chris Addams and Michael Davis, *Convict Establishment, Bermuda* (Bermuda: Dromedary Foundation Publications, 1998); Wilfrid Oldham and W. Hugh Oldham, *Britain's Convicts to the Colonies* (Sydney: Library of Australian History, 1990); Edward Cecil Harris, *Bermuda Forts 1612–1957* (Bermuda: Bermuda Maritime Museum Press, 2001); Shaw, *Convicts and the Colonies*, pp. 332–333.

[5] Gatrell, *Hanging Tree*, p. 493; Alyson Brown, 'A "Receptacle of Our Worst Convicts": Bermuda, the Chatham Prison Riots and the Transportation of Violence', *Journal of Caribbean History*, 37.2 (2003), 233–255.

[6] Addams and Davis, *Convict Establishment, Bermuda*. Over 500 artefacts from the Dromedary excavation were provided for the Convict Hulks exhibition, Hyde Park

the Dromedary excavation was the number of religious objects identified, including carved tokens in the form of bibles and crucifixes, which may have been used for gambling or as part of an internal currency for the exchange of valuables such as alcohol, tobacco or food. Religion was part of the emotional landscape of these working communities. A careful religious census of the Bermuda prisoners conducted on 1 August 1858 shows that 64.3 per cent professed themselves Church of England, 26.2 per cent Roman Catholic and 4.1 per cent Presbyterian, including four members of the Free Church of Scotland (who had initiated the count) and two Jews (see Table 10.1).[7] Jewish observances mattered in Bermuda, and in 1859, M. Marks petitioned the governor to send Passover biscuits to his son, the convict John Marks.[8] Among the 1,252 prisoners, most claimed a specific sect or denomination suggesting the resilience of religious markers of identity even for those at the margins of Victorian society.

Gibraltar, 1842–1875

Gibraltar, like Bermuda, came to receive convict labour rather by default when alternatives – slaves in one case, and native Spanish labourers in the other – were deemed politically inadvisable. In the wake of the American War of Independence Gibraltar was considered as one of many options for an alternative site for the transportation of British convicts. It was considered again in 1831 after the disastrous fallout from the overloading of convicts in Van Diemen's Land under the probation system. The first use of convict labour at Gibraltar occurred in 1842 when 200 convicts were despatched to build a breakwater and fortifications including the Line Wall and the New Mole.[9] Convicts remained in use until 1875 after which they were withdrawn, largely on economic grounds, because it was calculated that Spanish day labourers were more efficient than convict labour. Stephen Constantine notes that the local administration had very

---

Barracks Museum, Sydney, 4 August 2007–26 July 2009, sydneylivingmuseums.com.au/stories/convict-hulks (Accessed 8 April 2015).

[7] By 1860, the number of Roman Catholics had fallen to 194 out of 1,009 prisoners (19 per cent); Murray to Newcastle, 24 January 1861, encl. comptroller's report, BPP 1861 (2785) XL.425, p. 13.

[8] M. Marks on behalf of his son John Marks, 'Letters Relating to the Convict Department in Bermuda, 1859', TNA CO 37/169 1959.

[9] George Hills, *Rock of Contention: A History of Gibraltar* (London: Robert Hale, 1974), p. 381.

Table 10.1 *Religious denominations of the Bermuda convicts, 11 August 1858*

Prisons	Church of England	Church of Rome	Church of Scotland	Free Church of Scotland	Methodists	Baptists	Presbyterians	Relief Church	Independents	Dissenters	Jews	Heathens	H[indu?] Religion	Bible Christians	Total
Boaz Island	349	84	9	1	4	3	5	1	1	4	2	1	13	0	477
Medway	365	207	14	3	10	4	13	0	0	6	0	0	8	1	631
Tenedos	92	37	6	0	3	1	1	0	0	1	0	0	3	0	144
Total	806	328	29	4	17	8	19	1	1	11	2	1	24	1	1,252
%	64.3	26.2	2.3	0.32	1.36	0.64	1.52	0.08	0.08	0.88	0.16	0.08	1.92	0.08	100

Source: 'Minute by Mr Elliot', 5 October 1858, TNA CO 37/166: 96v.

little say over the deployment of convicts and this ensured they were less controversial than they proved at other sites, including Bermuda.[10]

Convicts came to Gibraltar from all over the empire to work on the fortifications, eventually obtaining over 700,000 tons of stone for the New Mole alone.[11] The first transport arrived in October 1842 and thereafter numbers rose to about 1,000. Convicts were initially housed in hulks but were then provided with shore-based accommodation. There were perennial debates about the relative economy of the Gibraltar convict establishment and its benefit to the navy. As in Bermuda, there were disputes between the military and civilian authorities about the quality of the labour performed by convicts and their control.[12] In 1852, a confidential Colonial Office breakdown of the cost of accommodating prisoners at home or abroad demonstrated the thriftiness of both Bermuda and Gibraltar, with the latter costing £14.40 per prisoner per year and the former £21.90. This was good value, even when the £6,000 it cost to transport prisoners to Bermuda and Gibraltar was taken into consideration, and less than the cost per prisoner in remote Van Diemen's Land (£21.60) and Western Australia (£57.73) with their expensive infrastructure for probation, religious instruction and transportation (see Table 10.2). Cheapest of all would be to keep them in Irish prisons (£11.30 per prisoner), but – unsurprisingly – no one suggested this.

In Gibraltar, the navy approved of convicts as a solution to their labour needs and preferred them to Spanish workers. Civilians, less concerned with issues of military security, preferred the cheaper and more accessible free labour from the unlimited reserves of the Spanish mainland.[13] Convicts were still being promoted as a solution in the 1870s, though by 1863 the number actually employed was averaging 862 annually at a cost of £25,082. In justifying the expense, Harry Blair, the comptroller of convicts, took pains to emphasize the good behaviour of the men, the low rates of recidivism of those returned to England and their exemplary economy when compared with Spanish day labourers.[14] The chaplain's report was prepared by the elderly Canon Robert Alder (1796–1873), a former Methodist missionary who had converted to Anglicanism late in

---

[10] Stephen Contantine, *Community and Identity: The Making of Modern Gibraltar since 1704* (Manchester: Manchester University Press, 2009).
[11] Darren Fa and Clive Finlayson, *The Fortifications of Gibraltar 1068–1945* (Oxford: Osprey, 2006), p. 40.
[12] McConville, English Prison Administration, p. 203.   [13] Ibid.
[14] Harry Blair, 'Report of the Comptroller Gibraltar Prison', 1 January 1864, BPP 1864 (3305), p. 18: 'I am yet able to prove that the cost of 276 prisoners is far below that of 211 civilians.'

Table 10.2 *Abstract of 1852 vote for prisons and transportation in Great Britain and Ireland and the colonies*

	Annual £	Annual £ per prisoner
General superintendence at home	16,200	
Prisons in Great Britain for 7,824 convicts	220,900	28.2
Prisons in Ireland for 4,796 convicts	54,300	11.3
Total for 12,620 prisoners in prisons in the United Kingdom	**291,400**	23.1
Prison at Bermuda for 1,750 convicts	38,400	21.9
Prison at Gibraltar for 900 convicts	13,000	14.4
Prisons at Van Diemen's Land for 5,000 convicts in detention	108,000	21.6
	86,600	57.7
Prisons in Western Australia for 1,500 convicts	7,600	
New South Wales, superintendence of ticket-of-leave men		
Total for 9,150 prisoners in detention in the colonies	**253,600**	27.7
Removal of prisoners within the realm	12,400	
Transport of prisoners to Bermuda and Gibraltar	6,000	
Transportation to Australia	95,000	
Total for removal and transportation	**113,400**	
Recapitulation		
Prisons in the United Kingdom 16,200 prisoners	291,400	17.9
Prisons in the colonies 9,150 prisoners	253,600	22.7
Removal and transportation	113,400	
Total	658,400	

Source: T. Frederick Elliot, 'Transportation, November 1852', Table No. 5, p. 35, TNA Confidential Print CO 885/2/15.

life after service in Canada.[15] Alder provided a lengthy account for Governor Sir William Codrington. Despite having charge of 910 prisoners supported by two schoolmasters, Alder had no complaints:

I am well satisfied, that not only has much evil and mischief been prevented, but that some of these fallen ones have been raised up, that the weak in purpose and effort in regard to well-doing have been strengthened and that a measure of general religious and educational improvement has taken place.[16]

Although Alder does not mention them, the convict establishment supported a Roman Catholic clergyman (£100), and a Presbyterian minister

[15] G. S. French, 'Alder, Robert', *DCB*.
[16] 'Chaplain's Report, Gibraltar Prison', 11 January 1864, BPP 1864 (3305) XL.475, p. 36.

Table 10.3 *Gibraltar prison: religion of the prisoners, 1863*

Religion of the prisoners	
	Number
Protestants	617
Presbyterians	61
Roman Catholics	225
Jews	3
Mahometan	1
Total	907

Source: *Annual Report of the Convict Establishment at Gibraltar for 1863*,
BPP 1864 (3305) XL.475, p. 23.

(£50), in addition to the Protestant chaplain (£300), scripture reader
(£150) and two schoolmasters (£276), for a total cost of £876, which
was generous by comparison with both Tasmania and Western Australia
(see Table 10.2). The Catholic chaplain was certainly necessary, since
225 of the 907 prisoners confined there in 1863 were Catholic, including
Irish soldiers convicted for offences against military discipline (see
Table 10.3).

As part of the hulk system, convicts sent to Bermuda or Gibraltar were
not, technically, seen as having undergone transportation. In the legal
imaginary the watery zone of the hulks moored in ports and harbours
around the British Isles had simply been extended across the Atlantic. In
an interview to the Select Committee on Transportation (1856), Horatio
Waddington, under secretary at the Home Office, stated that prisoners
sent to Bermuda and Gibraltar 'may be considered as in this country'
under the same conditions as prisoners at Portland and Dartmoor.[17]
This meant that both Bermuda and Gibraltar were less vulnerable to
settler-led protests about their presence than other British overseas possessions. T. Frederick Elliot, assistant under secretary for the colonies,
assured the same SC that efforts had been made to improve discipline at
both Bermuda and Gibraltar, and integrate them to 'improved' prison
establishments at home.[18] Questions nevertheless continued to be raised
in Parliament about the reformatory character of hulks in Bermuda and
Gibraltar, by now regarded as an essential component of penal discipline.[19] Religious provision to Gibraltar was substantially less than to the

---

[17] 'Testimony of H. Waddington', 17 April 1856, *SC on Transportation* (First Report), BPP
   1856 (244) XVII.1, p. 5.
[18] 'Testimony of T. F. Elliott', 21 April 1856, Ibid., BPP 1856 (244) XVII.1, p. 34.
[19] Hansard, HL Deb, vol. 222, col. 21, April 1856.

reformatory regimes of Van Diemen's Land and Western Australia.[20] The Gibraltar convict station was finally closed on 15 May 1875 at which stage there were only 127 employed, all of whom were repatriated to England.

The use of hulks to accommodate British prisoners dates from the eighteenth century and was always intended to be temporary.[21] Half a century later, in 1842, five hulks moored at Woolwich, Chatham, Devonport and Portsmouth were still being used to house 70 per cent of home-based prisoners in England, a figure which only began to decline with the opening of the new penitentiaries at Parkhurst and Pentonville.[22] Hulks were retained for both financial and strategic purposes, especially for their role in providing labour for admiralty or ordinance work. They were also used for special groups of prisoners, including women (the *Anson* hulk on the Derwent River in Hobart)[23] and juveniles (the *Bellerophon* at Sheerness and the *Euryalus* at Chatham). Others were used to hold prisoners awaiting transportation, stores, schoolrooms and hospital ships in sites such as Bermuda (from 1799), Malta (1800), Nova Scotia (1813), Barbados (1814), Ireland (1817), Van Diemen's Land (1824), New South Wales (1825), Gibraltar (1842) and Victoria (1852).[24] This had benefits for the government in that dangerous prisoners could be removed overseas and additional capacity could be created at short notice and removed again when no longer needed. The prison hulks were for a long time in the hands of a single overseer, Duncan Campbell (1726–1803). There were perennial problems of escape and breaches of discipline as well as outbreaks of disease which released more souls than either pardons or escapes.[25] From 1814 the hulks were made into a government-run operation under John Henry Capper, a Home Office clerk, who was appointed 'Superintendent of ships and vessels employed for the confinement of offenders under sentence of transportation' or just 'Superintendent of Convicts', later assisted by his nephew. Under

---

[20] See Table 11.1 at the end of Chapter 11.

[21] For the history of the hulk system, see William Branch Johnson, *The English Prison Hulks* revised edn (Chichester: Phillimore, 1970).

[22] McConville, *English Prison Administration*, p. 198. especially Table 7.1.

[23] The Dunkirk at Portsmouth, which served as a women's hulk from 1784 to 1791, was the only other hulk used to house women. Other prison ships and hulks were used as prison hospitals, or to house supplies such as coal, or to cope with emergencies, such as when the *Neptune* was stranded in Cape Town Harbour. 'Convict Hulks', Digital Panopticon, www.digitalpanopticon.org/Convict_Hulks (Accessed 12 August 2018); Johnson, *The English Prison Hulks*, p. 29.

[24] List of sites and dates from the 2007 'Convict Hulks' exhibition, Hyde Park Barracks, Sydney, sydneylivingmuseums.com.au/stories/convict-hulks (Accessed 8 April 2015).

[25] Oldham and Oldham, *Britain's Convicts to the Colonies*, p. 40.

Capper's control, prisoners on board the hulks were supposedly subject to the same regime of classification and moral management as that for prisoners on shore. In reality, although Capper was not immune to convict protests, conditions were grim, classification impossible and punishments brutal.[26]

Religion and the Hulks

Despite the conditions, the hulks were not free from moral and religious surveillance which increased in the last decades of the transportation era. While Capper was directed to ensure that the hulks were run as economically as possible, a visiting chaplain played a key role in providing recommendations, based on their conduct, for transportation to Bermuda or elsewhere in the convict system.[27] This was particularly pertinent in the case of juveniles. In addition to advocacy from Bristol philanthropist Mary Carpenter (1787–1873), demanding separate reformatories for young offenders,[28] there was a long tradition of regarding ships and the sea as an ideal way to accommodate recalcitrant youth.[29] This is one explanation for the deployment of HMS *Euryalus*, a prison hulk moored at Chatham, which was used for young offenders from 1825 to 1843. Under Earl Grey's scheme of assisted emigration, juvenile offenders were transported to Western Australia or Van Diemen's Land once they reached the age of fifteen; after 1838, the Parkhurst Act established a separate prison for young offenders and they were no longer transported but sent to the state-run Parkhurst penitentiary (though they could be transported or sent to an adult prison such as Millbank if they reoffended or were regarded as 'incorrigible'). H. J. Dawes, who was chaplain to the juveniles on the *Euryalus*, reported 'progressive improvement in their department' and less tyrannizing by boys over each, which he hoped might be attributable to effective religious instruction. At Woolwich, the Rev. T. Price reported that the prisoners on board the *Justitia* had been quiet and orderly, which he attributed in part to the effectiveness of his preaching which he sustained

---

[26] For convict protests from the hulks, 'Criminal Petitions for Mercy 1819–1839', TNA HO 17; Briony Paxman, '"A Floating Hell": Life on Early 19th Century Hulks', *Records and Research* (2018; Kew: National Archives, 2018). http://blog.nationalarchives.gov.uk/blog/ (Accessed 26 January 1918).

[27] For two recommendation lists prepared by Henry John Capper and David Jones chaplain for convicts on board the *Discovery* at Deptford, TNA, HO 17/73/191.

[28] Mary Carpenter, *Reformatory Schools for the Children of the Perishing and Dangerous Classes* (London: Gilpin, 1851).

[29] Phil Carradice, *Nautical Training Ships* (Stroud: Amberley, 2009).

both in chapel and before they made their departure to New South Wales: '[M]any have been deeply affected under the preaching of the Word, and I trust brought truly to see "the error of their way."'[30] While convicts performed useful labour, public scandal dogged the hulks at home and in the colonies. Ultimately it would prove impossible to integrate the Bermuda convicts into the new system of penitentiaries and reformatory labour which came to the fore following the end of convict transportation to eastern Australia.

The creation of paid, professional chaplains attached to all the various prisons within the British penal system led to increasingly problematic relations between the secular and spiritual officers of penal establishments. Under both private and Home Office administration, chaplains had a vested interest in emphasizing the good effects of the innovations they supplied. They commented on access to religious instruction and schooling, attendance and good behaviour (usually compulsory) at divine service, and other indicators of moral improvement, including a reduction in swearing, trade in alcohol and tobacco with outsiders and other forbidden practices. Henry Wynter stated with confidence that he was addressing the root cause of crime by his pastoral ministry in the *Fortitude* hulk: 'I trust that the idle habits and religious ignorance to which the dishonest practice of the Convicts may to a great extent be traced, are in a considerable measure removed by their detention at this hulk.'[31] At Portsea, William Tate reported that the convicts demonstrated 'the greatest decency of demeanour and apparent attention' at divine service, contrition and true penitence for their former behaviour and that the sick prisoners in hospital were not only thankful for the attention they received but 'disposed to listen to his instructions and exhortations'.[32] Reports of this kind, universally extolling convict behaviour, suggest that chaplains lacked both candour and independence, opening them up to ridicule by more sceptical critics such as the writer and social commentator Charles Dickens.

Capper ran the hulks profitably, and presented the chaplains' reports as evidence of the moral improvement of the convicts in his charge. A relentless drive for economy, unimpeded by effective review, was a major factor in the lamentable conditions revealed by a parliamentary inquiry in 1847.[33] Although limited to the hulks at Woolwich, the inquiry

[30]   T. Price to Capper, 5 July 1835, *Reports Relating to Convict Establishments*, BPP 1836 (51) XLI.1, p. 3.
[31]   Henry Wynter to Capper, 6 July 1835, Ibid., p. 2.
[32]   William Tate to Capper, 9 January 1836, Ibid. p. 6.
[33]   *Inquiry into the Hulks at Woolwich*, BPP (831) XVIII.1.

led to the resignation of Capper and his nephew, with superintendence of the hulks transferred to Herbert Voules, another Home Office clerk, later inspector of prisons for the northern district. Voules and Joshua Jebb were soon reporting that conditions on the hulks were irredeemable and that they must close.[34] In this resolve they were greatly aided by the chaplains, newly invigorated as guardians of convict moral and physical welfare.

Throughout the 1830s, while the Bermuda hulks remained in Capper's charge, the chaplains' reports were brief, token and complaisant. This reflects the view of the Colonial Office that regarded the system as predominately one of labour management. The hulks were therefore the last places where the reformatory gales that had blown through the old gaols and penal colonies were allowed to flow. Several factors changed the assumption that the hulks were beyond reform: firstly, in Bermuda, the recurrence of epidemics of such severity that the government felt bound to act. Secondly, the challenge to the viability of the service created by the Irish Famine and the transportation of paupers, rather than able-bodied labourers which compromised the unspoken policy of 'labour and economy first'. And thirdly, the arrival of some distinguished administrators and chaplains, determined to either drive through change or abolish the hulks altogether. It was a new instalment in the anti-transportation battle.

The complicity of the chaplains working under Capper on the hulks is evident from their reports, from 1830 (when there was no chaplain's report) until 1846. From 1843, there were Anglican convict chaplains at two stations and, from 1848, a Catholic chaplain, all paid for out of imperial funds.[35] The reports were mostly written by the Rev. Robert Mantach (1795–1853), a career prison officer with a large family, who was also the longest serving gaol chaplain in the service by the time of his retirement, shortly before his death in 1853. Mantach had a bleak view of convict human nature that rendered him suspicious of attempts to reform the men and seemingly impervious to the violence and disease that were their perennial companions in the Bermuda hulks. In 1830 and 1831 there were violent clashes among the prisoners, including a number of assaults on officers as well as an outbreak of dysentery which led to the

---

[34] McConville, *English Prison Administration*, p. 393.
[35] *Return of Grants, Endowments, and Appropriations for Religious Instruction or Education for Bermuda, 1843–52*, BPP 1852–1852 (937) LXV.127, p. 129; Protestant chaplains received £320 in 1843 rising to £400 in 1852; the Catholic chaplain received £100 in 1848, rising to £200 in 1849.

deaths of twenty-six men.[36] On 1 July 1830, the Bermuda chaplain Robert Whitehead approved the return of 'a number of abandoned and atrocious characters', measures to suppress the sale of spirits, and the cheerful progress of the school, evening prayers and divine service.[37] Ignoring the violence, Mantach's report simply looked to the positive, extolling the prisoners, 'old and young' who spent their Sunday afternoon, 'some with their Alphabet or Spelling Book in their hands, and not a few with the Bible or New Testament'.[38]

The chaplains were initially always members of the Church of England reinforced with occasional visits from distant bishops. Despite its location in the North Atlantic the bishop with responsibility for Bermuda from 1825 to 1839 was based in Nova Scotia, over 1,300 kilometres away. In 1835, John Inglis (1777–1850), third bishop of Nova Scotia,[39] visited Bermuda and offered to preach a sermon in each of the hulks. Four years later, in July 1839, the Rev. William Tate, chaplain to the Portsmouth dockyard, reported: 'The general attention of these misguided men at Divine Service is most decent and commendable; and their usual appearance, both on board and when out of work, is that of an orderly body of men.'[40] In 1839, the Anglican diocese was divided when Aubrey George Spencer was made bishop of Newfoundland and Bermuda. With rising expectations of religious emancipation, Catholic and Dissenting clergy also made their appearance. The first Catholic chaplain's report from Bermuda was made by the Rev. J. G. Murray, who had been in the post for just nine months but reported, in a single sentence: 'every detail connected with this Establishment has been conducted in a manner characterized by the utmost quiet, regularity, and contentment'.[41] From Ireland Island, Bermuda, the veteran Anglican chaplain Robert Mantach remained positive, delighted to have received supplies of books that enabled him to distribute the scriptures to the prisoners.[42]

The following year, Capper followed Lord Russell's instruction to restrict the numbers transported to New South Wales and Van Diemen's

---

[36] John Henry Capper, 'Report', 24 July 1830, *Reports Relating to Convict Establishments*, BPP 1830–1831 (162) XVII.439, p. 1.
[37] 'Report of Robert Whitehead', 1 July 1830, Ibid., pp. 10–11.
[38] 'Report of Robert Mantach', 30 June 1830, Ibid., p. 11.
[39] John Inglis's vast diocese included Nova Scotia, New Brunswick, South Walesick, Prince Edward Island, Newfoundland and Bermuda; Judith Fingard, 'Inglis, John', *DCB*.
[40] 'Report of William Tate', 5 July 1839, *Reports Relating to Convict Establishments*, BPP 1840 (125) XXXVIII.543, p. 2.
[41] 'Report of J. G. Murray', 29 July 1839, Ibid.
[42] 'Report of R. Mantach', 1 July 1839, Ibid., p. 3.

Land and provide convicts with work in the hulks either at home or in Bermuda. This was challenging, not least because those kept behind were often too ill and infirm to be put to hard labour. The public works at Bermuda were, in Capper's opinion, sufficient to require the labour of 1,000 prisoners for at least another five years but problems included the constant threat of disease and the risk of breaches in regulation 'arising chiefly from their obtaining spirits clandestinely from the free black population on shore'.[43] Capper's report for 1840 included the usual bland and acquiescent reports from chaplains. In fairness to them, from 1840 to 1842 the stipend received by the chaplain to the Bermuda hulks was a modest £40, too little to do more than provide a part-time attendance at services and not enough to support a family.[44] The same returns show that the salary of the chaplain to the naval dockyard was £400 and the bishop of Newfoundland and archdeacon of Bermuda received £400.[45]

The pattern of reporting and assurances, once established, remained set for some time. Capper continued to focus on running the hulks economically. The chaplains formed an integral part of hulk management because, together with the surgeons, they acted as internal auditors for the health, safety and physical, social and spiritual wellbeing of the prisoners. In Australia, a return on the provision of religious services in 1840 indicates progress had been made to provide support for convicts with chaplains and schoolteachers and facilities for religious services, schools and visitation.[46] In Bermuda, Robert Mantach pleaded for religious books for private reading, since 'much time that is otherwise misspent would be employed in reading were there a sufficient number of useful books to supply each ship with a small library'.[47] On 1 July 1845, Mantach assured the superintendent of convicts that other than some excitement connected with restrictions on the use of tobacco, 'quietness and obedience have pervaded the establishment'.[48] From Gibraltar, the chaplain to the forces, J. Buchanan, was singing from the same hymn sheet: 'I am happy to say that the Prisoners ... are going on satisfactorily', while asking for a 'lending library of good books'.[49] Little disturbed the positive tenor of

---

[43] Ibid., p. 5.
[44] 'Chaplain to the Convict Hulks Bermuda, 1840–41', *Return ... for Religious Instruction or Education in Colonies, 1840–42*, BPP 1845 (356) XXXV.171, p. 29.
[45] Ibid.
[46] *Correspondence on Advancement of Religion in Australia*, BPP 1840 (243) XXXIII.239.
[47] 'Report of R. Mantach', 1 July 1840, BPP 1841 (100) XVIII.629, p. 9.
[48] 'Report of R. Mantach', 1 January 1845, BPP 1846 (326) XXXIV.491, p. 5.
[49] 'Report of J. Buchanan', 6 July 1845, Ibid., p. 2.

Mantach's reports, though in 1846 he reported on 'much embarrassment' following the escape of some convicts.[50]

The winds of change were blowing through the convict system. By the Act for Abolishing the Office of Superintendent of Convicts Under Sentence of Transportation [1846] the management of convicts overseas was passed from the superintendent of convicts to 'such Person or Persons as shall be for that Purpose appointed', which for the time being meant the surveyor general of prisons, Joshua Jebb.[51] The concentration of so much power in Jebb's hands at home attracted some criticism, which was partly vented in public through the press. Overseas, including Bermuda and Gibraltar, responsibility for the hulks was put in the hands of the colonial governors. The incoming governor of Bermuda immediately seized his opportunity. In 1849, Capper's uncritical reports on the hulks were replaced by Jebb's rigorous and damning analyses of abuses by officers and the deficiencies of the prisoners, 'the refuse of all the convicts confined in the Government prisons'.[52] Jebb firmly recommended that all the hulks should be closed, that they were impossible to secure and provide appropriate separation for the men and they did not even have the advantage of cost effectiveness. They were expensive to outfit and even more expensive to maintain.[53] As with the earlier stages of the anti-transportation movement, despite Jebb's injunction, it would be some time before this happened and first there were attempts to 'reform' the system along the lines of shore-based 'separate' prisons at home.

Elliot and the Irish Prisoners

On 1 January 1847, Sir Charles Elliot (1801–1875) wrote to Earl Grey to report that he had arrived at Government House in Bermuda.[54] Governor Elliot, who had just completed a term as administrator of Hong Kong, was something of a catch for Bermuda, an able administrator who threw himself with characteristic energy into his new role. The *Bermuda Royal Gazette* published his speech on the Opening of Parliament, an institution which dated from 1620 following the tempestuous founding

---

[50] 'Report of R. Mantach', 1 January 1846, Ibid., p. 3.
[51] Eric Stockdale, 'The Rise of Joshua Jebb, 1837–1850', *British Journal of Criminology*, 16, no. 2 (1976): 164–170; Jebb's ascendancy was facilitated by the tragic deaths of both William Crawford and Whitworth Russell in 1847, the latter while visiting Pentonville, the former by his own hand while visiting Millbank Penitentiary.
[52] *Manager of Convict Hulk Establishment Report, 1849*, BPP 1850 (1178) XXIX.13, p. 2.
[53] Ibid., p. 4.   [54] Elliot to Grey, 1 January 1847, TNA CO 37/116.

of the colony by Sir George Somers (1554–1610).[55] Elliot planned to be an enlightened ruler, alive to the prospects for trade and the advantages of the warm climate for growing crops in advance of those available in Britain. The richness of the crops in Bermuda were also contrasted with the terrible news of those Elliot called 'our fellow subjects in parts of the United Kingdom'. The president of the council, Thomas Butterfield, voted to give £500 for the relief of victims of the famine in Ireland and Scotland, a gesture which was warmly received.[56] In practical terms, Elliott was responsive to the demands of the Colonial Office to employ convicts. In 1846, an additional three hundred prisoners were deployed by the admiralty on the naval dockyards and, under Elliot, the convict establishment grew in size and elaboration. At Earl Grey's request, he agreed to double the magnitude of the convict establishment, assuring him 'there was work for two thousand men for twelve years'.[57]

Elliott was also asked to consider the implementation of Captain Maconochie's mark system. Of the governors consulted about implementing Maconochie's scheme in some form as part of the management of their convict establishments, Elliot was one of the most enthusiastic.[58] In a dispatch of February 1847 he outlined the means by which he hoped to implement the mark protocol in the Bermuda hulks.[59] Elliot also wanted to improve the educational standard of the people, forwarding Mantach's list of the books in the libraries of the hulks and seeking to improve it.[60] This was a belated response to a vigorous request from Edward Feild (1801–1876), the bishop of Newfoundland, during his visitation to Bermuda in April 1845, who had asked Governor Reid for facilities to allow the convict chaplain to assist with the education of the black population as well as the construction of a residence on Ireland Island and a new chapel.[61] Besides delivering a charge to the clergy, Feild had preached in each of the convict hulks and tried to assert exclusive privileges for the Church of England over the convict establishment, warning Reid about the dangers of 'latitudinarian principles', which presumably applied to other Protestants, as well as the 'Romish Bishop' in Nova Scotia, who was

---

[55] 'Opening of the Colonial Parliament', *Royal Gazette* Extra, TNA CO 37/111: 388.
[56] Elliot to Grey, 28 April 1847, TNA CO 37/ 116: 394–399.
[57] Shaw, *Convicts and the Colonies*, p. 333.
[58] For the consultation with Governor Elliot on the mark system, see Denis to Benjamin Hawes, 7 February 1828, TNA CO 37/122, p. 26; 'Captain Maconochie's Mark System', TNA CO 37/126: 32–43.
[59] Elliot to Grey, February 1847, TNA CO 37/116: 178–85v.
[60] Robert Mantach, 'Abstract of Books in the Library for the Use of the Guards and Convicts at Bermuda, 31 October 1846', TNA CO 37/144.
[61] Feild to Reid, 4 April 1845, TNA CO 37/111/14: 124.

extending his authority to Bermuda.[62] Feild later attempted to refuse use of the Garrison Grave Yard at St George and the grave yard at Ireland Island by ministers other than the Church of England. Lord Grey, having given permission by despatch to the relevant authorities, advised that it was 'out of his power' to make an alteration.[63]

Recognizing the reality of the need for toleration, Elliot wanted to promote convict schools with as much non-sectarian thoroughness as he could and asked for books of instruction from the British and Foreign School Society. He proposed that there should be a Board of Visitors and initially suggested that it consist of the Anglican bishop or his deputy, the senior minister of the Roman Catholic Church and the Church of Scotland or any other persuasions. On reflection, he decided against this, noting: 'Visitors should not do more upon religious subjects than to ascertain that the prisoners had the consolation and advice of the Ministers of the persuasion to which they belonged.'[64] In one year, therefore, Elliot had launched a trial of Maconochie's mark system, provided for a more diverse religious ministry and more effective schooling for the convicts. What could go wrong?

Irish prisoners arrived in Bermuda in significant numbers from the late 1840s, many of them paupers who had committed minor property offences.[65] In June 1848, Governor Elliot expressed his unhappiness at their physical condition:

It will be remarked with anxiety, on examining the list of 704 prisoners, sent from Ireland, in the *Medway* and *Bangalore*, that many of them were convicted of stealing food, and agrarian offences; the first, no doubt, chiefly attributed to the dreadful calamity which befell the poorer classes of people during the last two years, and the last in a high degree to the inflammatory practices of others, in the time of desperate need.[66]

Elliot saw the presence of these men as a humanitarian problem for which he hoped to find an honourable solution. The Irish also aroused security concerns; a number were likely to be sympathetic to violent political causes, in close proximity to the politicized Irish in the nearby United States. Elliot immediately tried to remove all the juveniles, describing them as 'friendless men in humble stations of life' who might

---

[62] Feild to Reid, 4 April 1845, attaching: 'The Bishop's Patent, Charge Delivered to the Clergy of Bermuda by Edward Feild Bishop of Newfoundland at His First Visitation on the Feast of St Matthias, 1845', TNA CO 37/111/14: 146.
[63] Grey to Elliot, 14 January 1851, TNA CO 37/133/37: 320–321.
[64] Elliot to Grey, 1 March 1847, TNA CO 37/ 116: 204–205.
[65] Elliot to Grey, 22 June 1848; 3 July 1848; 1 November 1848; 8 February 1849, BPP 1849 (217) XLIII.1, pp. 49–52
[66] Elliot to Grey, 22 June 1848, BPP 1849 (217) XLIII.1, p. 49.

be sent to Australia on ticket-of-leave. Elliot stressed the youth of the Irish prisoners and harsh sentences for crimes of need: 'it will shock H. M. Government to learn that twelve of them are under sixteen years of age, and that one thirteen-year-old has been sentenced to 15 years' transportation for sheep stealing'.[67]

Irish prisoners were also problematic because of anxieties about their religion and the perceived risk (from the Protestant point of view) of proselytization by the Catholic priests permitted to minister to prisoners on the hulks. Elliot was concerned when a prisoner wished to convert to Roman Catholicism, ruling that a private ceremony was acceptable but not a public baptism in the Roman Catholic church. Prisoners were to be provided with the 'utmost practical liberty of conscience', but this should not upset the peace of the prison.[68] In 1851, Elliott ruled against the legitimacy of a marriage ceremony performed by the Catholic chaplain, the Rev. Thomas Lyons (d.1853),[69] who had issued bans of marriage on board the *Medway* between the colonists James Dunbar Bell, a Roman Catholic, and Eleanor June Roberts, a Wesleyan Methodist.[70] Lyons was interviewed by Governor Elliot who dismissed him, despite his otherwise excellent conduct, because of what he saw as a serious impropriety. Grey intervened to ensure that Lyons was able to resume his mission which was a triumph for common sense. Clearly uncomfortable dealing with Irish Catholic priests in a penal context, Elliot complained to Earl Grey in 1851 that since 1848 there had been four Roman Catholic priests chosen at the convenience of the Roman Catholic bishop of Halifax. He asked Grey to approach 'some moderate and liberal minded Roman Catholic laymen of influence in England' in order to secure a 'temperate and judicious Roman Catholic Minister of English birth' for service in Bermuda.[71] Meanwhile the hulks continued to float in a liminal state as far as religious establishment was concerned.

The reputation of the Bermuda hulks as a 'floating hell' does not reflect reality in a number of ways, including the physical treatment of the men engaged, for forty years, to work on the Bermuda docks.[72] A summary of the numbers and causes of death among convicts was

---

[67] Elliot to Grey, 3 July 1848, BPP 1849 (217) XLIII.1, p. 49.

[68] Gov. Charles Elliot to Earl Grey, 11 January 1849, TNA CO 37/126: 51–53.

[69] Lyons died of yellow fever on 13 November 1853, contracted while ministering to convicts on the prison hulks, and was buried in the Saint John the Evangelist churchyard.

[70] Elliot to Earl Grey, 6 December 1850, TNA CO 37/133: 283.

[71] Elliot to Grey, 8 March. 1851, TNA CO 37/135: 152

[72] Hallett, *Forty Years of Convict Labour*, pp. 53–54.

compiled by the medical superintendent, Dr Charles Edwards, at the time of the convict establishment's closure in 1863.[73] Mortality varied from as low as two out of 299 prisoners (0.6 per cent) in 1824, to as high as sixty-seven out of 1,941 (3.5 per cent) in 1848. Yellow fever caused spikes of mortality of 10.1 per cent (1843), 15.6 per cent (1853) and 3.0 per cent (1856), which was much higher than rates for British prisons but lower than those recorded for the people in the town who had no access to medical and hospital treatment. Another bad year for the convict death toll was in 1848, when over 700 prisoners were transported for 'crimes' which were the result of famine conditions in Ireland. Many of these men were so ill on arrival that they died in considerable numbers; few were fit to work. In some distress, Governor Elliot provided the medical report: of 704 prisoners who had arrived on the *Medway* and the *Bangalore*, forty-four had died.[74] Elliot was pleased that many recovered their health in Bermuda after a stay in its newly built convict hospital. It was from this group that Elliot chose 250 Irish prisoners to be sent direct to other colonies on tickets-of-leave.[75]

As with other prisons, visitors provided an independent assessment of the Bermuda hulks. In 1859, Anthony Trollope recorded his view of convict conditions, stressing the high quality of the rations which compared favourably with those in the military and navy: 'he has a glass of grog, exactly the same amount that a sailor has; and he has an allowance of tobacco money, with permission to smoke at midday and evening'.[76] Discipline on the Bermuda hulks was tightly regulated but of no greater severity than that meted out to the enlisted men of the navy and army who also worked in the Bermuda forts.[77] There was considerably more freedom and independence possible to men who quartered in the hulks, despite all its attendant discomforts, than in the more regulated conditions of the new penitentiaries being constructed by Captain Jebb, where they were perpetually under the eye of the chaplain and the prison governor. Backhouse and Walker reported that men transported to Van Diemen's Land from Bermuda indicated that they preferred the Bermuda hulks where they had fresh rations three times a week, a generous allowance of rum, a shilling a week reserved for them and a return to

[73] Dr Charles Edwards, 'General Abstract' CO 37/ 186:170–180, cited by Ibid., 53.
[74] Elliot to Grey, 2 November 1848, TNA CO 37/123: 116.
[75] Elliot to Grey, 22 June 1848; 3 July 1848; 1 November 1848; 6 February 1848, BPP 1849 (217) XLIII.1, pp. 49–51.
[76] Anthony Trollope, *The West Indies and the Spanish Main* 4th edn (London: Chapman & Hall, 1859), pp. 350, 355, 361, 362.
[77] Harris, *Bermuda Forts*, pp. 27–36.

England at the end of their sentences.[78] Prisoner rights were supported by Governor Elliot who, from 1847, ordered that no prisoner could be flogged without personal authorization from him. Under his direction, 'special punishment' had to be medically supervised and had to be discontinued if it was thought the prisoner could not endure it. The same restrictions applied to solitary confinement. The regime was still harsh: Elliott ordered forty men to be flogged in the eighteen months from 1 December 1847, when his order came into effect, to 30 June 1849.[79]

The conditions in the Bermuda hulks for convicts were subject to inquiries by the House of Commons Select Committee on Transportation in 1838. In his testimony, Colonel W. B. Tylden seems to have been rather mystified by questions about the incidence of unnatural crime. In answer to the question, 'Was it supposed at all that unnatural crime existed in the hulks?', he replied: 'No, it was not; I never heard an instance of it. I may add that from their being constantly at work, it gave the men habits of industry.'[80] In 1847, the running cost of the Bermuda establishment was £31,353 per annum. While provisions for 100 officers, 1,700 healthy and 100 sick convicts made up about half this amount, £706 was set aside for religious instruction, a modest increase since the days of Mantach.[81] From 1852, prisoners were slowly transferred from the hulks to onshore accommodation where better conditions for classification, religious instruction and hygiene might be anticipated.

Despite the construction of the new shore-based facility, about a third of the Bermuda prisoners continued to be accommodated in hulks, where they were exposed to both the ravages of yellow fever and to sexual predation in the unregulated sleeping accommodation below decks. The hulks were therefore anathema to prison reformers who had been advocating classification, supervision and regulation of prisoners since the days of John Howard. These ongoing health and moral issues raised in government inquiries about Bermuda provide the context for the dispute between the convict superintendent, Captain William Montagu Isaacson George Pasco (1806?–1872/73), and the convict chaplain, the Rev. John Melville Guilding (1830–1898).

---

[78] Backhouse and Walker, 'Report on Macquarie Harbour', *Molesworth SC on Transportation*, BPP 1837 (518) XIX.1, appendix, p. 8.
[79] Harris, *Bermuda Forts*, p. 29.
[80] 'Testimony of W. B. Tylden', 15 March 1838, *Molesworth SC on Transportation* BPP 1837–1838 (669) XXII.1, p. 87.
[81] 'Cost of the Bermuda Establishment', 1847, TNA CO 37/126:76.

Rev. John Melville Guilding

Guilding came to Bermuda in 1856 and served until 1863 as the govern-ment chaplain with responsibility for the convicts. He represented the new breed of religious prison officer, keen to see the old corruption exchanged for the finely graded moral progress of the separate system. His posting was a kind of homecoming to the British West Indies since he had been born into a clerical dynasty in Saint Vincent, where both his father and grandfather had been ministers. His father, the Rev. Lans-down Guilding (1797–1831), was a gifted artist and naturalist who read papers to the Linnean Society and corresponded with Charles Darwin. Guilding was a modern man in other ways, having graduated as a theological associate from the new King's College, London, in 1851.[82] Ordained in 1853, he served as assistant curate in Crayke, Yorkshire, then All Souls, Langham Place, London (then, as now, an important seat of Evangelical Anglicanism in London), before heading to Bermuda.

Guilding was not the first chaplain of the convict establishment, but he was the one who did most to lead reform. As resident chaplain, he lived on shore on Boaz Island and visited the two large hulks where about 1,400 prisoners were housed as well as those in hospital. Unlike those of his predecessor, Guilding's reports are full and detailed and continue until the closure of the convict establishment in 1863.[83] The reports reflect a high view of his spiritual and pastoral responsibility for the prisoners and make clever political use of public opinion to advance penal reform. From 1858, Guilding was required to maintain a character book for all the prisoners and other duties along the lines of those required of religious instructors in the Van Diemen's Land probation system. He wrote to Governor Freeman Murray, outlining the scale of his duties and requesting the services of an assistant chaplain.[84] Guild-ing's request was refused, however he did acquire a scripture reader to assist in visiting schools and providing religious education for the prisoners.

After four years attempting to bring change, Guilding's 1860 report struck a new note in which he bewailed the government's failure to transfer prisoners out of the hulks and to house them in a shore prison,

---

[82] The AKC was the original three-year programme of King's College, London, founded in 1829 as an Anglican response to the founding of the secular London University (now University College London) in 1826.

[83] Guilding, 'Chaplain's Reports', TNA CO 37/160 (1857), 165 (1858), 169 (1859), 174 (1860), 178 (1861), 182 (1862), 186 (1863). Reports were printed with *Annual Reports on Convict Establishments of Bermuda and Gibraltar.*

[84] J. M. Guilding to Freeman Murray, 3 November 1858, TNA CO 37/166: 276–278.

'according to the practice of the best model prisons in England'.[85] He declared the hulks of Bermuda to be the scandal of the empire, comparing 'these hells of abomination', with the model prisons of Auburn and Philadelphia in the United States, which he had recently visited while on holiday. Guilding stated that prisoners could not be reformed in such an environment, that the stifling heat made them unfit for occupation and drove the men to acts of desperation such as the prison riot on 1 June, during which one prisoner was slain and twenty-four were wounded. *The Spectator*, which picked up Guilding's report from the colonial Blue Books, used it to denounce the hulks, detailing all the most lurid episodes in the history of transportation. Nothing was omitted: the pestilential convict voyages, the mutinies on Norfolk Island, the outrage of Judge Burton about how convictism 'took out the heart of a man and gave him the heart of a beast', or the cannibalism of Alexander Pearce.[86] Good questions were asked about why, following the 1848 bill which was intended to do away with them and the construction of the shore prison on Boaz Island, convicts were still housed in the hulks: 'It almost seems as if the horrors, revealed twenty-two years before Sir William Molesworth's committee, are coming into life again.'[87]

On his return from leave, Governor Freeman Murray made a prompt response to Guilding's claims, which he confessed to read, 'with some astonishment'.[88] He called Guilding 'a young man of very good ability and great zeal', but said that his account of convict life between decks bore little connection to reality and suggested that he had been 'enormously imposed upon' by some of the prisoners.[89] In July 1860, he reported that he had personally made a number of surprise visits to the hulks, purposely selecting hot nights for the purpose, and reviewing every convict; all was perfectly tranquil and the attending officers diligent.[90] Guilding did not back down and his 1861 report included thinly veiled accusations against the quality of the prison officers, calling for 'a superior class of men', to take on these roles: 'without such men chaplains may preach and schoolmasters instruct in vain'.[91]

---

[85] Guilding, 'Chaplain's Report', TNA CO 37/160/ 174 (1860).
[86] Anonymous, 'Convict Establishments in 1860', *Spectator*, 33.2 June (1860), 521–522.
[87] Ibid., 522.
[88] Murray to Newcastle, 23 March 1860, *Convict Establishment at Bermuda*, BPP 1860 (2700) XLV.269, p. 5.
[89] Ibid.
[90] Murray to Newcastle, 11 July 1860, *Annual Reports on Bermuda and Gibraltar, 1860*, BPP 1861 (2785) XL.425, pp. 3–4.
[91] Guilding to Murray, 'Fifth Chaplain's Report for 1860', 10 January 1861, Ibid., p. 18.

There the matter may have lain to rest had not the conservative politician Henry Herbert (1831–1890), 4th Earl of Carnarvon, regarded Guilding's report as an opportunity to discomfit the government for its mismanagement of the convict question. Carnarvon was just beginning his interest in penal reform, which would lead in due course to more rigorous sentencing and the implementation of penal servitude at home in place of transportation.[92] In the House of Lords, Carnarvon referred to Guilding's report on the hulks where 'there is no safety for life, no supervision over the bad, no protection to the good', unnatural crime was rife and violence below decks at a level which could not be controlled by the few guards.[93] In parliament, Carnarvon tried again in April 1861 asking the Secretary of State for the Colonies: '[w]hether any Measures had been taken to investigate the Truth of the Charges made by the chaplain of the Bermuda hulks'.[94] The last nails were at last being driven into the coffin of transportation.

Although reproved by the governor for his indiscretion, Guilding continued to press reforms, promoting schools for the prisoners, as was the norm elsewhere. In February 1858, the governor provided a commentary on a fierce battle that had been waged between Guilding and the deputy superintendent of convicts, Captain Pasco, over this seemingly inconsequential issue.[95] There were questions of status involved here. Pasco was a naval officer with a distinguished service career, son of Rear-Admiral John Pasco.[96] By the time he took up his post as deputy superintendent of convicts at Bermuda, he had served in the British Navy with distinction for over thirty years and had his own views on the hierarchy of command and the proper place of the convict chaplain within that hierarchy. In the controversy over the Bermuda schools, General Freeman Murray (1803–1885), who served as governor from 1854 to 1859, made clear that he supported the chaplain. The governor hoped he could make Pasco acknowledge the importance of prison schools. Unfortunately, the effect of trying to force Pasco to give way on this matter, led to an all-out war, in the course of which Elliot felt obliged to suspend him.

---

[92] Harling, 'The Trouble with Convicts', 80–110.

[93] Hansard, HL Deb vol. 160, col. 181–182, 26 July 1860.

[94] Hansard, HL Deb, 23 April 1861; See also Lord Naas, again referring to Guilding's report, Hansard, HC Deb, vol. 158, col. 1611–1614, 22 May 1860.

[95] Freeman Murray to under secretary of state, 27 February 1858, TNA CO 37/165: 124–125.

[96] Richard O'Byrne, *A Naval Biographical Dictionary* (London: John Murray, 1849), p. 870.

In miniature, the conflict between the chaplain and the deputy superintendent of convicts, reflects the deeper divide between military administrators, who regarded convicts as a labour force, and penal reformers,
who believed that punishment should include both punitive and reformative elements. Pasco, not unreasonably, pointed out that the level of
educational provision (once in twelve days) was so modest that it served
little purpose. He frankly believed it should make way for the primary
object of the convict establishment, which was to serve the public works
of the naval dockyard:[97] '[I]t appears to me that the moral culture of the
men at School . . . and the successful progress of the works are incompatible, and that one must . . . yield to the other.'[98] For this report, Pasco was
roundly condemned by Thomas Elliot (1808–1880), the assistant under
secretary for the colonies (succeeding James Stephen who retired in
1847).[99] Guilding was also vindicated by the governor, who noted that
the time spent by the prisoners in school was used partly for instruction
and 'partly to [let] them write their letters and attend to other personal
matters for which there is no opportunity on their days of labor (sic)'.[100]
There was no problem in Pasco expressing his opinion that it was more
important that the men should work than be 'improved', but his
thwarting of the chaplain, even when reproved by the governor, as well
as attempting to humiliate the schoolmasters (for example, by requiring
them to mess with the wardens), was, Elliot suggested, 'unworthy'.[101] To
the Colonial Office, Guilding stated that he embraced the opportunity to
classify, reform and convert the prisoners: 'It is sufficient, if I can shew
your Excellency that no means have been left untried by me for the moral
improvement and instruction of the Prisoners.'[102]

Despite the constant interruptions, Guilding reported satisfactory progress in the three schools on Bear Island, *Medway* and *Tonedos* hulks,
where good numbers were making 'superior progress' (see Table 10.4).

He attributed the high proportion of non-readers on the *Tonedos* to the
fact that half were Irish Roman Catholics, 'who are commonly inferior in
education to the English Prisoner'.[103] Figures on attendance at school,
use of the prison library and the number of letters written by prisoners
continued to improve, as indicated in subsequent reports from the convict schoolmaster.[104] In 1860, the number of volumes in the library

[97] 'Pasco Report', NA CO 37/165: 132.   [98] 'Pasco Report', NA CO 37/165: 133.
[99] Elliot, 'Memorandum on Annual Report of Bermuda Convict Establishment for 1857',
     TNA CO 37/165: 188–192.
[100] Ibid.   [101] Ibid.
[102] Rev. J. M. Guilding, Chaplain's Report, 10 January 1858, TNA CO 37/165: 138.
[103] Rev. J. M. Guilding, Chaplain's Report, 10 January 1858, TNA CO 37/165: 150.
[104] 'Schoolmaster's Return', 31 December 1860, BPP 1861 (2785) XL.425, p. 22.

Table 10.4 *School report, Bermuda convict establishment, 1858*

School	No. [of prisoners] on books	Can't read	Can't write	Neither read nor write	Superior progress
Boaz Island	192	9	7	5	24
Medway	671	19	19	19	163
Tonedos	159	18	20	18	6

Source: Chaplain's Report for 1858, TNA CO 37/165:150.

reached 1,377 of which almost 600 had been added in the previous year; the prisoners had written 1,732 letters and received 1,710 in return.[105] Under challenging conditions, Guilding was lifting expectations of prisoner welfare, using the benchmark of the 'Portland Rules', devised for the H. M. Prison Portland which housed the convict labour force assembled to construct the breakwaters and other defences of Portland Harbour prior to transportation. At Portland, prisoners were allowed half a day in school per week in addition to evening classes and there were two schoolmasters for seventy men, compared with four for the 1,000 in Bermuda. Guilding complained of the challenges he when the Portland Rules were ignored: 'I despair of ever doing anything for the moral benefit of the Prisoners, while they are systematically disregarded in all their Reformatory Principles and Regulations.'[106] But the end was near. Despite receiving prisoners sentenced for participation in the 1861 riots in Chatham Convict Prison, Bermuda had worn out its usefulness.[107] Having the appetite neither for further scandal nor for the expense of upgrading the facilities for effective surveillance and instruction, it made better sense to remove the prisoners and recall the officers, including the chaplain and schoolmasters.

Conclusion

The hulks constituted the longest-running element of the British convict service. They provide a link between the earlier era of Atlantic transportation and the later one, which included Bermuda, Gibraltar and the network of floating prisons in Great Britain and Ireland. As in Van Diemen's Land under the probation system, the arrival of salaried,

[105] Ibid.
[106] Rev. J. M. Guilding, Chaplain's Report, 10 January 1858, TNA CO 37/165:138.
[107] Brown, 'A "Receptacle of Our Worst Convicts"', 233–255.

professional chaplains was one factor accelerating first reform, and then abolition of the hulks. Joshua Jebb's implacable hostility to the hulks was also important in breaking down the view, common to the military and naval managers appointed to manage the convict establishment, that labour extraction was more important than reform.

It would be wrong to conclude that the utilitarians were ultimately successful in the transformation of prison education reflected in this case study of the prison schools of Bermuda. The changes were more in line with the recommendations of the Evangelical utilitarians and were not secular. If anything, the role of the chaplains (Protestant and Roman Catholic) was enhanced by the creation of the penitentiary system and their appointment to prisons designed by Jebb and his followers. The rise of professional prison officers, including governors, warders, schoolmasters and probation officers, meant that the privileged role of the chaplain and educator, in the manner enjoyed by the Rev. J. M. Guilding was changing. The post-transportation penitentiaries, such as the grim outposts in places like Dartmoor, put a renewed emphasis on harsh conditions, including penal labour, and much less on religion and education as part of the 'moral machinery' which Guilding had hoped to entrench in Bermuda for the prisoners under his care. In the wake of the 1859 prison riot, there was increasing distaste for maintaining the convict hulks, despite the attraction they continued to have for naval administrators. Convict transportation to Bermuda ended in 1861 with the last convict removed to Western Australia – the very last port of call for convicts and the site of discussion in the following chapter.

11 'Reformatory Colony': Western Australia, 1850–1868

> If any plan can, humanly speaking, carry out the merciful object in view – Reformation not Punishment – it is this – & it deserves the support of every humane, patriotic Xtian man.[1]
>
> (Rev. John Wollaston, 6 April 1851)

> [A]s English prisons, when ruled in conformity with benevolent and Christian principles, may become reformatories, so may a colony, ruled in the same way, become a reformatory also.[2]
>
> (Bishop Matthew Hale, 1857)

Other than Gibraltar, Western Australia was the last location which received convicts direct from Britain – none came from Irish ports – anywhere in the empire. As convict transportation ended elsewhere, Western Australia became a node for the transfer of prisoners, including those who came from Bermuda in 1862.[3] It was distinctive in other ways as well and was affected by the decisive shift in government policy away from reformative and towards punitive systems of penal policy. Nevertheless, religion and reformatory methods were strongly invoked in the initial stages of the transport of convicts to Western Australia. This chapter will examine the attempt to create what Bishop Matthew Blagdon Hale (1811–1895) called a 'reformatory colony' rather than a 'penal settlement', where convicts might be governed by the benevolent and Christian principles that he believed was a realizable ideal in British prisons.[4] It will assess the views of clergy and religious instructors drawn in to work with prisoners and how they slowly became disenchanted with

---

[1] Wollaston, 6 April 1851, Wollaston Journals, iii, 219, Rev. John Ramsden Wollaston, 'Diaries', 3 vols., CUL RCMS 288 [Hereafter 'Wollaston Journals']. For archival records relating to Western Australia in this chapter, I am indebted to Rowan Strong.

[2] Mathew B. Hale, *The Transportation Question, or Why Western Australia Should Be Made a Reformatory Colony, Instead of a Penal Settlement* (Cambridge: Macmillan, 1857), p. 12.

[3] McConville, *English Prison Administration*, p. 395. Only prisoners sentenced to transportation were transferred from Bermuda to Western Australia. Those sentenced to penal servitude were returned to Britain. Convicts transported to Van Diemen's Land remained there.

[4] Hale, *The Transportation Question*, p. 12.

convictism. This disillusionment was a factor in ensuring clergy supported moves to end the practice of transportation to even this distant outpost of empire.

Convicts to Western Australia

To judge by the overheated invective directed against the convict menace in the course of the anti-transportation campaign, there was no appetite for the return of convicts anywhere in the empire. A confidential Colonial Office memo dated 10 January 1857 declared: 'There does not exist on the globe any formed society of large extent which is willing to relieve Great Britain of her criminals.'[5] Of five less settled options, only one was considered acceptable, namely Swan River, established in 1829 and renamed Western Australia in 1832, one of the few places to have remained positive about receiving convicts in any form.[6] Initially the commissioners of Pentonville thought it too small and isolated to be a good destination for their reformed men.[7] Nevertheless, it was better than nothing and Western Australia was made a colony for the receipt of convicts by order-in-council on 1 May 1849. Even before this, boys from Parkhurst had been shipped there as 'apprentices' to a generally positive reception.[8]

Prisoners sent to Western Australia formed a distinct cohort, rather different from those sent to the penal colonies of the east of the continent.[9] They were all male and mostly at the end of their terms, having served part of their sentence in Great Britain. The Pentonville graduates came with their own guard of Chelsea pensioners, who were looking for a place to retire, and a board of visiting magistrates to hear grievances. The convicts were also paid for their labour. There were positive reports, including from visiting clergy, about the quality and reformed character of the convicts who arrived in the first years. Regrettably, there was a subsequent turn to more punitive conditions which disgraced the idealism of the Western Australian experiment, much of it under Governor John Stephen Hampton (1810–1869), a former surgeon superintendent

---

[5] W. F. E. (Walter Elliot), 'Question of the Places in the British Dominions Available for the Reception of Convicts', TNA Confidential Print, Miscellaneous No. XXXVI: 2.

[6] Ibid. The other options were the Falkland Islands (too unproductive), the Hudson's Bay Territory, Vancouver Island and Albert River at the bottom of the Gulf of Carpentaria.

[7] Shaw, *Convicts and the Colonies*, p. 353.

[8] For the 1,500 Parkhurst apprentices sent to Western Australia from 1842 to 1849, A. W. Gill, *Forced Labour for the West: Parkhurst Convicts 'Apprenticed' in Western Australia 1842–1851* 2nd edn (Maylands: Blatellae Books, 1997). 'Apprentices' were also sent to New Zealand.

[9] Shaw, *Convicts and the Colonies*, pp. 353–358. Gillian O'Mara, *Convict Records of Western Australia* (Northbridge: Friends of Battye Library, 1990); J. S. Battye, *Western Australia* (Oxford: Clarendon Press, 1924).

and comptroller general of convicts in Van Diemen's Land, who reintro-
duced the dark cells, flogging and punitive chain gangs.[10] Hampton's
term as governor covered the last years of transportation to Western
Australia, from 1862 to 1868, but the return to harsh physical punishments is a reminder of the vulnerability of convicts within even exemplary penal arrangements. Nevertheless, the project was deemed a
success: financially, administratively and even morally. Between 1850
and 1868, 37 convict ships carrying 9,636 convicts, together with their
guards, disembarked in Western Australia.[11] Many free settlers came as
well and, in no small degree, it was the convicts who helped the struggling colony to turn around its economic fortunes.

The Western Australian convicts have had relatively few historians
other than those attracted to a few set pieces, such as the brutality
(possibly exaggerated) under Governor Hampton,[12] or the spectacular
escape on 17–19 April 1876 of six Irish political prisoners transported on
the *Hougoumont*, the last convict transport to arrive in Australia.[13] What
research there has been is tied up in edited collections, unpublished
theses and some archaeology.[14] However Western Australia is significant
for its effective implementation of probation and the ticket-of-leave
system in the period when, according to Seán McConville, reformative
methods in penal policy in Britain 'underwent an almost total eclipse'.[15]

---

[10] Shaw, *Convicts and the Colonies*, p. 356. For the Howard League's intervention on behalf
of convicts alleging 'cruel and illegal punishments' under Hampton, see BPP 1867–1868
(482) XLVIII.429. For Hampton on Norfolk Island, see Chapter 7.

[11] Bateson, *Convict Ships*, p. 396.

[12] William Edgar notes a number of revisionist assessments of Hampton's reputation.
William J. Edgar, 'The Convict Era in Western Australia: Its Economic, Social and
Political Consequences', (Murdoch University, 2014), p. 15.

[13] Ciarán Fee, 'Robert Cranston and the Catalpa Escape', *The Bell (Journal of Stewartstown
and District Local History Society)*, 10 (2006), 3–18; Keith Amos, *The Fenians in Australia,
1865–1880* (Sydney: University of New South Wales Press, 1988); Geoffrey Bolton,
'The Fenians Are Coming, the Fenians Are Coming', in Robert Reece (ed.), *The Irish in
Western Australia* (Nedlands: University of Western Australia Press, 1981), pp. 284–303.

[14] Alexandra Hasluck, *Unwilling Emigrants: A Study of the Convict Period in Western Australia*
(Melbourne: Melbourne University Press, 1959); Charles Thomas Stannage (ed.),
Convictism in Western Australia (Nedlands: University of Western Australia, 1981);
Jacqui Sheriff and Anne Brake (eds.), *Building a Colony: The Convict Legacy*
(Nedlands: University of Western Australia Press, 2006). For the theses, see Cherry
Gertzel, 'The Convict System in Western Australia, 1850–1870', (BA Honors thesis,
University of Western Australia, 1949); William J. Edgar, 'The Convict Era in Western
Australia: Its Economic, Social and Political Consequences', (PhD thesis, Murdoch
University, 2014); For the archaeology, Martin Gibbs, 'The Archaeology of the
Convict System in Western Australia', *Australasian Historical Archaeology*, 19 (2001),
60–72; Sean Winter, *Transforming the Colony: the Archaeology of Convictism in Western
Australia* (Newcastle-upon-Tyne: Cambridge Scholars, 2017).

[15] McConville, *English Prison Administration*, p. 347.

Although Joshua Jebb asserted that both reform and punishment were compatible objectives in a well-designed prison system, politicians in Britain pandered to the public demand that criminals be made to suffer and that pain, not scripture, was necessary to deter criminals. As discussed in Chapter 10 Lord Carnarvon had led the attack on the Bermuda hulks which ended transportation to those islands. By 1862, when Carnarvan chaired the SC to inquire into local prisons, even penal servitude was held to be insufficiently punitive and witnesses openly queried whether prison could or should even attempt to reform as well as punish.[16] In the new prisons, religious instruction and secular education were reduced to what McConville calls a 'decorative role'.[17] Edmund Frederick Du Cane (1830–1903) served as visiting magistrate at convict stations in Western Australia before returning to Britain to administer the new system of penal servitude; in 1869 he became director of convict prisons with additional responsibility for colonial convict prisons. Du Cane scarcely bothered to disguise his contempt for the religious element in prison management, noting in his chapter on penal servitude: 'the exertions of the ministers of religion bear perhaps as much fruit as in the world outside'.[18] In this hostile environment, Western Australia has particular interest as the last major attempt to implement reform as a primary object of transportation, and to do so with the usual implements of hard work tempered by chaplains, religious instructors, schoolteachers, books, bibles and prison visiting.

Reformation Not Punishment

The Anglican hierarchy was initially cautious when they heard the news that convicts might be sent to Western Australia. A petition to the governor for increased state support for Anglican religious services in the Swan River Colony in 1841 had been rebuffed by a counter petition declaring 'compulsory measures are contrary to the spirit of Christianity'.[19] After the debacle of the probation system in Van Diemen's Land, they were aware that to be successful there would need to be sufficient chaplains and trained schoolmasters if the prisons were to be places of reform. From Adelaide, Bishop Augustus Short (1802–1883) wrote to the SPG secretary, Ernest Hawkins (1802–1868), praying that if Swan

---

[16] Ibid., 347, 444.   [17] Ibid., 408.
[18] Edmund F. Du Cane, *The Punishment and Prevention of Crime* (London: Macmillan, 1885), p. 160; McConville, *English Prison Administration*, p. 409.
[19] *Report of the Statistics of Western Australia in 1840* (Perth: F. Lochee, 1841), appendix, p. ii.

River was to be 'inundated with Convicts like Van Diemen's Land', then at least the SPG needed to attempt to 'secure proper religious instruction and superintendence'.[20] This was wise since Western Australia was seriously depressed, free emigration was at a standstill and the few clergy already in the colony were stretched to breaking point catering to colonists and the missions to the Aborigines.

As a window into the conditions in Swan River, the journal of the Anglican colonial chaplain, Archdeacon John Ramsden Wollaston (1791–1856), is an important source, revealing as it does the transition from an impoverished free settlement to one underpinned, and ultimately flourishing, on the strength of convict labour for public works.[21] On 6 April 1851, Wollaston made his first visit to the newly settled penal settlement at Fremantle 'with strong prejudices against the convict establishment', but was tremendously impressed both by the devotion of the men and the reformatory ideals they embodied.[22] Exulting that such a system had never before been tried in the colonies (indicating he knew very little about earlier experiments, such as those of Maconochie on Norfolk Island or even Lord Stanley's probation system), he was moved by the devotion and demeanour of the ten convicts who attended the communion service at Fremantle Church celebrated by the chaplain, the Rev. Matthew Fletcher: 'If any plan can, humanly speaking, carry out the merciful object in view – Reformation not Punishment – it is this – & it deserves the support of every humane, patriotic Xtian man.'[23] Wollaston admired everything: the cleanliness and 'reasonable comfort', the 'excellent library' under the chaplain's charge which was well used, even the grim punishment cell in which he was shut up momentarily but which, he was assured, was 'hardly used', with punishment in chains only meted out to the refractory. He was impressed by the barracks being constructed entirely by prison labour on the hill above Fremantle which was designed to hold 500 men.[24] Not only, he felt assured, would the system 'be the means, under God, of reclaiming many a sinner from the

---

[20] Short to E. Hawkins, Adelaide 23 April 1850, Wollaston Journals, iii, 178.

[21] Rowan Strong, 'The Reverend John Wollaston and Colonial Christianity in Western Australia, 1840–1863', *Journal of Religious History*, 25.3 (2001), 261–285.

[22] Wollaston Journals, 6 April 1851, iii, 219.

[23] Ibid. Fletcher travelled out with *Scindian*, the first convict transport, which arrived in Western Australia on 1 June 1850.

[24] For a detailed description of the Fremantle site drawn from the Blue Books, see Anonymous, 'The New Convict Establishment in Western Australia', in William Chambers (ed.), *Chambers's Edinburgh Journal* (18; Edinburgh: Chambers, 1852), 106–108.

Error of his ways', it was modern and progressive: 'It is the Pentonville plan carried out *here*'.[25]

Pentonville was also interested in Western Australia, which was now the only site for transportation for British prisoners in the empire. The Rev. Joseph Kingsmill, the distinguished prison chaplain at Pentonville, wrote a series of 'chapters on Australia', one of his many writings intended to provide training and encouragement for prison officers and to support reformatory penal systems.[26] His 'advice to prisoners sentenced to transportation' fully captured the optimistic spirit of this last age of transportation, one where the convicts went hopefully to new lives. At the request of Governor Charles Fitzgerald (1791–1887), Kingsmill provided a list of books thought suitable for the Fremantle establishment, though it is not certain how many of those made their way to Western Australia to augment the excellent library Wollaston admired on his visit.[27] Even if some were diverted, the convicts would have had a library unmatched by any other prison outside Pentonville itself. Besides works of religious devotion and emulation, there were biographies, books of natural history, astronomy, geography, music, machinery and travel. Convicts could read about shipwrecks and enjoy an extensive collection of travel writing, voyaging in their imaginations from Africa to Asia to the Arctic and beyond, as well as Kingsmill's own *Chapters on Convicts*. By 1854, when Kingsmill produced a third edition of *Chapters on Prisons*, he was already contemplating the end of the reformative experiment in Western Australia which, given the numbers, had only ever been a partial solution.[28] It was nevertheless a world away from the shoddy hand-me-downs and dreary religious propaganda of other penal stations: it took years to assemble a decent library for Bermuda (Chapter 10).[29]

Yet a few months later, Wollaston's journal records his unhappiness that the influx of strangers into Fremantle had made it increasingly licentious, not a suitable place for the Aboriginal school he had

---

[25] Wollaston Journals, 6 April 1851, iii, 219.
[26] Kingsmill wrote extensively on prison and was one of the most celebrated of the prison chaplains of the era. In addition to *Chapters on Australia* he published *Advice to Prisoners* (1849); *Chapters on Prisons and Prisoners* 2nd edn (1852); *The Officer* 3rd edn (1853); *On the Present Aspect of Serious Crime* (1856); *The Sabbath: Thoughts for Thinking Men of the Industrial Classes on the Sabbath Question* (1856); *The Prisoner's Manual of Prayer* (1860); *The First Steps to Ruin, as Collected from Statements Made by Convicts Respecting the Causes of Their Crimes* (1857).
[27] Pakington to Fitzgerald, 14 August 1851, SROWA 41/1178/22: 23–24.
[28] Joseph Kingsmill, *Chapters on Prisons and Prisoners* 3rd edn (London, 1854), p. 204.
[29] In contrast, there was an excellent library at Port Arthur, though developed largely after the ending of convict transportation; Keith Adkins, 'Books, Libraries and Reading in Colonial Tasmania', *Papers and Proceedings (Tasmanian Historical Research Association)*, 53.3 (2006), 158–169.

sponsored. For this he did not blame the convicts, convinced that the penal establishment was perfectly designed for their reformation, but rather the arrival of mechanics from other colonies.[30] The Colonial Office was inclined to agree and, anxious to avoid the outbreak of scandal and claims of demoralization, they were for once open to the need to provide additional clergy, to both bond and free, at the delicate stage when convicts were being introduced into the colony.[31] Stipends were supplied for three Anglican chaplains, in addition to that already provided for Wollaston, with the Catholics receiving, belatedly, rather less.

The issue of salaries to be paid to religious officers at convict establishments continued to rankle and mirrored sectarian rivalries over access to resources, though not so rancorous as the disputes in Van Diemen's Land. In the United Kingdom, Parliament balked at payments to Protestant chaplains in Irish prisons, where the overwhelming majority of prisoners were Catholic. In Western Australia, Governor FitzGerald objected to giving a salary of £200 to the Catholic chaplain appointed to the convict establishment at Fremantle on the grounds that this was disproportionate given the Church of England chaplain received £250 a year to serve a higher number of prisoners.[32] By 1863, salaries and allowances for religious instruction at the Fremantle Convict Establishment, Perth Prison and outstations would reach over £2,000 for Protestant and £637 for Catholic clergy, and £1,300 for thirteen Protestant chaplains attached to convict outstations, the successors to the probation stations of Van Diemen's Land, where many lessons had been learned (see Table 11.1). Further government funding was provided for the construction of extensions to existing churches on the basis that they were being attended by ticket-of-leave men.[33] The finest church was that for the Fremantle prison, constructed on the model of Pentonville by convict labour. Bishop Short, who visited Fremantle on 20 June 1852, expressed his pleasure in a letter to the SPG secretary at the participation of the 300 prisoners: 'It is an affecting sight, so many fellow men under sentence for crime! And when the psalmody burst forth from a trained body of them, the effect to me was quite overpowering; to hear the sounds of praise issuing from lips trained perhaps to blasphemy, and poured forth I would fain hope, from hearts hardened to ignorance and sin.'[34] The Reverend James Brown served as chaplain of the Fremantle

[30] Wollaston to Hawkins, 21 June 1851, Wollaston Journals, iii, 249.
[31] H. Merivale to Sir C. E. Trevelyan, 4 August 1851, SROWA 41.1178/22: 93–95.
[32] Fitzgerald to Earl Grey, 7 January 1852, SROWA 41.1178/22: 133.
[33] Newcastle to Governor Fitzgerald, 26 January 1853, SROWA 41/1178/27: 11–12.
[34] Bishop Short to Hawkins, 6 August 1852, Wollaston Journals, iii, 271–272, 273, 274.

Table 11.1 *Salaries and allowances for religious instruction to convicts in Gibraltar, Tasmania and Western Australia, 1863–1864*

		£	£
Gibraltar			
	Salary for one chaplain	300	
	Salary for one scripture reader	150	
	Salaries for two schoolmasters	276	
	Allowance to Roman Catholic clergyman	100	
	Allowance to Presbyterian minister	50	
	Total Gibraltar		876
Tasmania			
	Salary for one Protestant chaplain	325	
	Allowance to chaplain, Female Factory	30	
	Allowance to chaplain, Hobart Town	40	
	Salary for one schoolmaster	100	
	Salary for one clerk of church	9	
	Forge for chaplain's horse	39 10s	
	Total Church of England	543 10 s	
	Salary for one Roman Catholic chaplain	275	
	Allowance to Roman Catholic chaplain, Female Factory	30	
	Allowance to Roman Catholic chaplain, Hobart Town	39 10s	
	Forage for chaplain's horse		
	Total Church of Rome	384 10s	
	Total Tasmania		928
Western Australia			
	Salary for one Protestant chaplain, Convict Establishment	400	
	Salary for one Protestant chaplain, Perth Prison	240	
	Salaries for thirteen Protestant chaplains outstations, at £100 each	1300	
	Allowance to religious instructor to road parties	150	
	Total Church of England	2,090	
	Salary for one Roman Catholic chaplain, Convict Establishment	200	
	Salary for one Roman Catholic chaplain, Champion Bay	50	
	Visiting chaplains, depots and road parties	387	
	Total Church of Rome	637	
	Total Western Australia		2,727
	Grand total		4,581

Source: Salaries and Allowances or Religious Instruction to Convicts, 1863–64, BPP 1863–1864 (285) XXXVII.523.

convict establishment from 1853 to 1855 and his diary and biennial reports show that he took his duties seriously and was committed to the moral reformation of the prisoners. He also secured an organ for the prison chapel.[35]

The colony already had a Catholic bishop, the erratic John Brady whom we have already encountered in Chapter 6 in relation to Norfolk Island. After refusing the latter posting and serving in New South Wales, Polding recommended Brady as vicar general of Western Australia where he arrived in 1843, the year after the colony had begun to receive its first consignment of juvenile prisoners. Demonstrating the extent to which the penal colonies could provide a forum for the mad, incompetent, improvident and morally compromised, Brady claimed in Rome that Western Australia held two million Aborigines ripe for conversion and eight thousand Europeans, half of them Catholic – all nonsense. The ensuing disaster was too much, even for Bishop Polding (who had saved Brady from Norfolk Island) and Brady was formally dismissed in 1852.[36] Fremantle's prison chapel served the Anglican establishment; it was not until 1861 that a Catholic chapel was opened in the Northern Association ward of the prison.

With the Catholics descending into ecclesiastical civil war, the field was open to the majority Anglicans at the time that transportation of convicts to Western Australia began in 1850. At first this meant the tiny number of colonial chaplains, the Rev. John Burdett Wittenoom (1788–1855) and the Rev. John Wollaston. As the colony's prospects improved following the influx of labour, it received that mark of establishment esteem, an Anglican bishop. With funding from the Colonial Bishoprics Fund, Matthew Hale was consecrated bishop of Perth at Lambeth Palace Chapel on 25 July 1857. No stranger to colonial service, Hale had served on the committee of the SPG recommending clergy for the Van Diemen's Land probation system and at one stage sought a post as missionary to the West Indies. In 1850, Hale fulfilled his ambition of a missionary posting when he accompanied Bishop Short to Adelaide where he founded the Poonindie Natives' Training Institution, one of the most successful and innovative of all colonial attempts to missionize the Aborigines.[37] Hale's diary, which proceeds in fits and starts (it has no

[35] Alex Grose, 'Pious Labours: Reformation and Reverend Brown's Chaplaincy', *Fremantle Studies*, 8 (2014), 62–77.

[36] Kathleen O'Donoghue, 'Brady, John (1800–1871)', ADB; Christopher Dowd, *Rome in Australia: The Papacy and Conflict in the Australian Catholic Missions, 1834–1884*, 2 vols. (Leiden: Brill, 2008), vol. I, pp. 125–161.

[37] Mathew B. Hale, *The Aborigines of Australia* (London: Society for Promoting Christian Knowledge, 1889).

entries for the sad years following 1845 when his beloved wife, Sophia Clode, died) is an important source for the history of Anglicans in South Australia.[38] A worthy protégé of Short's, Hale was an active, thinking Christian pastor with a love of technology (he studied mathematics at Cambridge), including the new photography which he deployed on recording the Aboriginal members of the Poonindie community.[39] When he began diarizing again it was to record the excitement of new projects: the Aboriginal mission, the convict establishment in his new diocese, or the thrill of acquiring a new lithographic printing press, which worked beautifully to print circulars for parishioners.[40]

With his readiness for new things, Hale was initially both hopeful and positive about the convict experiment in Western Australia. On the voyage to Australia he wrote a treatise arguing for the benefits of 'reformist transportation' compared with the punitive practices of the past.[41] The title stated the thesis he wished to argue: 'Why Western Australia Should Be Made a Reformatory Colony, Instead of a Penal Settlement'. Why indeed? Penal settlements evoked the old chest of horrors, the chain gangs and flogging, the sexual abuse and demoralization of settler and servant. In Van Diemen's Land, Archdeacon Marriot had eloquently argued that there could be no theological justification for the creation of penal colonies, that they were 'incompatible with God's kingdom'.[42] Hale began by apologizing for addressing the question of transportation at all, accepting that it was the duty of a clergyman to focus his attention on spiritual matters. But with the old catcalls of 'no political parson' no doubt ringing in his ears, he proceeded regardless, noting that the outcry against transportation had been so prolonged and hostile that it was a wonder that the practice had been continued in any form.[43] His basic argument was that the new, reformatory system had now replaced the hulks and chain gangs of New South Wales and Van Diemen's Land, on which a universal condemnation had been pronounced.[44] Under the system in operation in Western Australia, reformed men were released into the community, to be assimilated as citizens and effective employees. He provided a surprisingly modern interpretation of the problems with the 'assimilation' theory of penal transportation, including a perceived rise in crime attributed to the former convicts. What was lacking, according to Hale, were sufficient religious ministers and resources to

---

[38] Hale Diary, Hale Papers, 1835–1891, University of Bristol Archives (UOBA) DM130/Box 1 [Hereafter 'Hale Diary'].
[39] Jane Lydon and Sari Braithwaite, 'Photographing "the Nucleus of the Native Church" at Poonindie Mission, South Australia', *Photography and Culture*, 8.1 (2015), 37–57.
[40] Hale Diary, 29 August 1860.   [41] Hale, *The Transportation Question*.
[42] Marriott, *Penal Colony*.   [43] Hale, *The Transportation Question*, p. 3.   [44] Ibid., 2.

complete the reformation of prisoners following their release. Isolated and with easy access to drink, the men committed breaches of their ticket-of-leave conditions and were trapped in a cycle of reoffending. He asked for a 'supply of devoted men' to come to the colony and support the work.[45] With sufficient ministers, he was full of hope for a new form of penal colony: '[A]s English prisons, when ruled in conformity with benevolent and Christian principles, may become reformatories, so may a colony, ruled in the same way, become a reformatory also.'[46]

Hale pleaded for high levels of religious intervention both in prison and once men were released to work in the community. This required government support for the payment of salaries to clergy and school-teachers, as well as the construction of churches and chapels. The challenge was that the view of some parliamentarians, stridently backed by figures such as Charles Dickens and advocates for harsher sentencing, was that chaplains were ineffective as evaluators of the potential of prisoners to reoffend. In the 1856 SC on Transportation, several witnesses were quizzed in relation to the capacity of the chaplain to perceive when prisoners were deceiving them. There was a particular concern about boys leaving Parkhurst and arriving in British colonies. Although the chaplain attempted to follow up on the boys, he could provide them neither with jobs or a new way of life, particularly in the absence of a home, or intact family, to receive them.[47] Captain Irwine S. Whitty, former governor of Parkhurst Prison, testified about the system for discharging young men. Asked 'How far, in your experience, is the judgement of the chaplain in these matters to be attended to?', he replied strongly in the affirmative. When asked 'You must be aware that there is a very strong feeling in the public which is encouraged by works of fiction and other causes, that a certain amount of hypocrisy and judicious temperance of conduct in a prison may enable a criminal to gain, not only the favour of the authorities, but a remission of sentence?' To this he responded that the chaplains and governors observed the men's conduct and knew them as well as was possible.[48]

In their defence, prison chaplains were far from the naïve dupes that some members of the Select Committee appear to have assumed. The Rev. Joseph Kidd Walpole (1806–1862), chaplain of the *Stirling Castle*, the invalid hulk at Gosport, was one of those interviewed in 1856. Walpole had served as a missionary with the SPG in Madras before heading to New South Wales where, from 1845 to 1848, he was chaplain of the penal establishment and Benevolent Asylum in Sydney.

---

[45] Ibid., 74.   [46] Ibid., 12.
[47] *SC on Transportation, First Report* BPP 1856 (244) XVII.1, pp. 58–59.   [48] Ibid., p. 86.

He returned to England in 1848 and acted as chaplain to the hulks as well as serving ten months at Dartmoor. Walpole was therefore a highly experienced, career prison chaplain. He believed that transportation should be resumed, though he realized this was unlikely. 'I think that there, as everywhere, there ought to be proper spiritual superintendence provided with convicts sent out; because, if they do badly and run wild, they would do so in those countries from other causes.'[49] Walpole spoke warmly of the capacity and influence of the chaplains in the penal colonies:

I knew many families in New South Wales who were the children of convicts, who had fallen under the influence of the chaplains who were sent out there first. There was a band of very good men indeed, laborious devoted men, and they rendered most essential service to those first convicts who went out; and there were families in various parts of the country who were settled in agricultural farms, and very well conducted and well brought up; and I have heard many of them ascribe the origin of their welldoing to the care they experienced from those first convict chaplains. There were Dr Cowper, Mr Cartwright, Mr Hassell, Mr Vincent, and several others; so that I think always where prisoners are sent to these new and wild countries, there ought, among other things, to be an organization for spiritually superintending them, and benefitting them in that way.[50]

Men such as Walpole were given the responsibility of trying to follow up on prisoners leaving prison. They received little credit for this. Sir C. Cresswell was typical in complaining of the lightness of sentencing and the gullibility of the chaplain: 'A man goes into gaol, and, by playing the hypocrite for twelve months, succeeds in getting the good opinion of the chaplain and the gaoler, and has a fair prospect of a ticket-of-leave, which relieves him from any further suffering under the sentence.'[51] Chaplains were often the most important source of information for the subsequent behaviour of men after they left prison, but the amount of information they could obtain was limited. The reality was that claimed rates of recidivism in colonial penal establishments in Australia, which could be as low as 10 per cent, were a fraction of those facing the managers of modern prison populations in the UK.[52]

---

[49] 'Evidence of J. K. Walpole', 12 June 1856, Ibid., p. 70.
[50] 'Evidence of J. K. Walpole', 12 June 1856, Ibid.
[51] 'Evidence of Sir C. Cresswell', 16 June 1856. Ibid., p. 102.
[52] In the UK, from October 2016 to December 2016, short-sentenced prisoners had a re-offending rate of 64.5 per cent within a year: *Proven Reoffending Statistics Quarterly Bulletin*, 25 October 2018. For historical data, 'Recidivism', Digital Panopticon, www.digitalpanopticon.org/Recidivism (accessed 3 December 2018).

While clergy at home remained positive about the need for chaplains in prison and for clergy to follow up as ex-convicts moved into the community, experience dulled the appetite for this in Western Australia. In 1853, Wollaston confided to his journal that 'respectable people of the Upper Class are moving away – where they can – who once thought to make this colony the permanent residence of their children. They now dread the prospect of leaving them in a penal colony'.[53] Chaplains nevertheless continued to do their duty, ministering in remote and challenging locations as new probation stations and itinerating missions were opened up. Among those who corresponded with the SPG, the Rev. George Pownall (later the first dean of Perth) advised that he conducted an evening 'recreation' for the ticket-of-leave men as an alternative to the pub. This involved a formula of tea, coffee, newspapers, chess and dominoes, but the men themselves had put together a music class, which was self-supporting.[54] The Rev. Henry Thornhill reported on a Bible class attended by ten young men, three of them on ticket of leave.[55] The Rev. James Stuart Price at Pinjarrah was active catechizing in people's homes, reporting that there were about 200 ticket-of-leave men employed as servants, some of whom attended the services he provided at Pinjarrah, Serpentine and Mandurrah.[56] All reflected on the challenges of a bush ministry complicated by the presence of recently released prisoners or those working for the government on public works, often in remote locations.

In time, even brave Bishop Hale lost heart. In September 1860, he tore himself away from the pleasures of his lithographic printing press to travel to Fremantle from Perth.[57] He preached in the Church of St John the Evangelist in the morning from the first lesson: 'Spread it before the Lord' (Isaiah 37: 14). Sadly, it might have been: 'the day of small things' (Zechariah 4:10). There were only fifteen communicants and his only comment was: 'Singing very bad'. In the prison chapel, where Bishop Short had been so impressed by the singing, Hale was disappointed that only 393 prisoners attended the evening service. While Bishop Hale struggled to put the best face on the continued practice of convict transportation to Western Australia, forces were gathering to end this final vestige of the system.

---

[53] Wollaston Journal, 16 May 1853, iii, 348.
[54] Rev. George Pownall to Bullock, 8 June 1858, BodL USPG/ E/5.
[55] Rev. Henry Thornhill to E. Hawkins, 12 Jun 1860, BodL USPG/ D/30c: 393–395,
[56] Rev. James Stuart Price, 31 December 1862, BodL USPG/ E/12.
[57] Hale Diary, 2 September 1860.

Northern Australia continued to have theoretical attractions for arm-chair penal colonists, such as the Rev. George Sculthorpe Morris (1812–1889), who had served as a convict chaplain at Oatlands in Van Diemen's Land.[58] After his return to England he wrote pamphlets supporting the continuance of transportation, but solely to new colonies.[59] In his *Thoughts on Transportation* (1853), Morris argued that transportation could not continue to settled colonies when it was not thought fit to release prisoners 'among ourselves'.[60] Instead, he thought they should be deployed to open up territory in northern Australia from prisons established on offshore islands. In a Christian gloss, he suggested that the men might intermarry with the Malays, Christian instruction would be provided for all, and the offspring of these mixed marriages would be brought up in the Christian faith. On the key question of reformation, he argued in a subsequent letter to Earl Grey 'that convicts have turned out worse than emigrants' in all penal settlements.[61] As evidence for this, he cited the account of Mrs Meredith's *Home in Tasmania* (1852), who complained that prisoner women were of far lower grade than the men and not to be trusted as servants. (While she does make this point, Meredith devotes much more space to extolling the virtue and reliability of convict servants generally and the complete safety of her 'home in Tasmania'.)[62] In Western Australia, Morris made selective use of criminal statistics to suggest that the rate of reoffending had increased since the arrival of convicts. Reviewing both works, the *Argus* agreed with Morris on the danger of convicts but opposed the suggestion that new penal colonies be created, whether on offshore islands in the Cape of Carpentaria or elsewhere.[63]

In Westminster, Charles Adderley, member of the London delegation of the Anti-Transportation League, called for the final eradication of transportation in all its forms.[64] His 1857 tract on tickets of leave (i.e., Earl Grey's exile system) included a bravura condemnation of all the ways that transportation, including its latest supposedly reformative iteration in Western Australia, had failed, and a pocket history of

---

[58] *Cable Index.*
[59] G. S. Morris, *Transportation* (London: W. H. Dalton, 1856); Reviewed The Argus (Melbourne) 30 May 1857, p. 4.
[60] G. S. Morris, *Convicts and Colonies* (London: Hope, 1853), p. 5.
[61] Morris, *Transportation*, p. 8.
[62] Mrs Charles Meredith, *My Home in Tasmania* (London: John Murray, 1852), pp. 45–48 (on convict virtue); p. 153 (on low grade of prisoner women servants).
[63] *The Argus* (Melbourne), 30 May 1857, p. 4.
[64] In the context of the *Neptune* crisis Charles Adderley had written Adderley, *Transportation*.

transportation from the time of colonial America onwards. It is a long quotation, but it does cover a long history:[65]

> They ask us to forget all the variations through which the system has been forced to pass – the early American struggles – the loudly-condemned assignments – the phase of 'three stages' – that of 'five stages' – the decomposition of the whole theory in the rottenness of Norfolk Island – the rebellion of the Cape – the demoralization of Van Diemen's Land – the late remonstrance from Western Australia – the news of today from Cayenne – the witness of the French experience, given by their highest law officer M. Bérenger. They say, Burn all the Blue-books, and reports of Select Committees, and the pamphlets of Molesworth and Whately, and take the wishes of Lord Grey against his own great experience. We must suppose all the Ministers who have conducted every stage of the experiment to have been mere fools and blunderers, and all the world to have forgotten them – colonies which have now obtained free constitutions to be willing to submit to what they resented when subject to despotic control – the globe, peopled as it now is, to be freer for the purpose that when it was comparatively empty – distance to have the same terrors in these days of steam and electricity as when Robinson Crusoe was a hero of romance – and the notion of gold being discoverable everywhere, to have a homoeopathic influence on the thirst for gold, curative instead of stimulative. We must conceive the judges to be the best counsellors against the change of a system which they have been accustomed to administer; and forget that, as a class, they have historically opposed all such changes, from Romilly's downwards. When we have consented to all this demand, we may set up transportation again, and trust to our advisers that 'it is the only rational thing to do'.[66]

What worked best, Adderley concluded, were establishments at home: cheaper, more effective and independent of the entanglements that were poisoning the path to self-government of the settler colonies and the false claims and falser hopes of reformation of penal reformers.

Wollaston had enthused that the Fremantle Establishment was an opportunity to 'build Pentonville in the colonies'. The design of the building allowed for expansion with the classification of prisoners and access to services being paramount. The major prison complex included the grand Protestant (Anglican) chapel discussed earlier.[67] The Protestant chaplain's house was located next to the warden's house beside the main prison entrance.[68] A Catholic chapel was installed some time later and a house provided, not so close to the entrance, for the Catholic

---

[65] Adderley, *Tickets of Leave*.   [66] Ibid., 8.
[67] 'Plan of the Convict Grant, Fremantle 1857–58'; 'Convict Establishment, Fremantle, Western Australia: Elevant Plan and Section of Chapel'; 'Cottage Barracks for Pensioner's Guard', TNA MPG 1/722.
[68] 'Convict Establishment, Fremantle, W. Australia. Plan of Entrance Buildings', TNA MPG 1/722.

chaplain. The cottage barracks for the pensioner's guard to the convict establishment were handsomely designed and sited slightly further away from the main prison. With some care, the convict depot was integrated into the original plan of the town of Fremantle with King's Square, which included Saint John's Church of England (1843), and Queen's Square to the north.[69] The primacy given to religion and rehabilitation is reflected not just in the architecture but also in the high status, salary and accommodation of the religious officers. In short, the system put in place in Western Australia was one of the most reformative ever attempted in the empire. On the whole it was successful in its aim of supporting the growth of the colony and reforming the prisoners who laboured towards this end.

Nevertheless, as Wollaston also realized, the convicts were far from the reformed characters they had been promised. The convicts sent to Western Australia were mostly serious offenders who had earned their right to transportation by good behaviour in prison. Unlike the earliest days of the convict system in eastern Australia, only felons were transported, and this meant men whose offences ranged from lesser degrees of murder through to arson, grand theft, major sexual offences and crimes involving violence. The breakdown of the prison population has been analyzed by Tom Stannage and Sandra Taylor who conclude that the Western Australian convicts were more likely to be Scottish or English rather than Irish, Protestant (53 per cent) rather than Catholic (19 per cent), urban rather than rural in origin, as well as being better educated and more likely to be married than convicts sent to the east.[70] They were also more likely to have committed crimes with violence and to be serving longer sentences. Over half were sentenced to more than seven years.[71] Ongoing research by Barry Godfrey and Lucy Williams suggests that about 80 per cent of the last convicts to arrive in Western Australia went on to reoffend. They suggest that rather than celebrating the rehabilitation of the few, it would be better to regard transportation as allowing

---

[69] 'Plan of the Town of Fremantle, Western Australia to Accompany Topographical Return to 30 June 1851 [showing the Convict Depot]', TNA MPG 1/722. The original town plan was devised by John Septimus Roe in 1833; St John's Church was built at the request of colonists before the arrival of the convicts.

[70] Sandra Taylor, 'Who Were the Convicts? A Statistical Analysis of the Convicts Arriving in Western Australia, 1850/51, 1861/62 and 1866/68', in Charles Thomas Stannage (ed.), *Convictism in Western Australia* (Nedlands: University of Western Australia, 1981), pp. 19–45.

[71] For statistics, see Tom Stannage, 'Interpreting Convicts in Western Australia', Unpublished Lecture (1978), 'Convict Profile', Fremantle Prison, www.fremantleprison.com.au/History/ (Accessed 22 August 2018).

sufficient reform for society to progress, while ensuring a lifetime of social deficit for those transported.[72]

While initially hopeful of turning around the lives of those transported, the arrival of large numbers of convicts in Western Australia led to a rise in the rate of low-level crime, especially vagrancy and drunkenness, as well as attracting disruptive elements from other colonies.[73] The aspirational character of the Western Australian convict project is stressed by Michal Bosworth in her study of convict Fremantle.[74] From 1850 to 1887, it was acknowledged that a trip to Western Australia was a reward for good behaviour for those subjected to long prison terms in Britain. Hence the paradox that the WA prisoners were both more skilled and better behaved – less Irish and less Catholic – than other convicts, despite having been convicted for more serious crimes than those in the east.[75] Fremantle would never earn the dire reputation that tarnished earlier penal colonies in New South Wales, Van Diemen's Land and Norfolk Island.

The tide of convictism would seem to have inexorably gone out, with even its strongest supporters, such as Colonel Denison departing to new responsibilities or, like Bishop Broughton, coming around to the opposing side. At the same time, there was growing enthusiasm for increasing severity for home-based punishments led by the hawkish Earl Carnarvon.[76] The construction of increasing numbers of penitentiaries to the design of Joshua Jebb meant that the absolute need to transport convicted prisoners was declining as accommodation could now be provided for them at home, without the expense of transporting and maintaining convict establishments abroad. But there was to be one last shake of the transportation tree in the wake of the London garroting panic of 1856.[77]

---

[72] Barry Godfrey and Lucy Williams, 'The Story of Australia's Last Convicts', *The Conversation*, January 8, 2018.

[73] Barry Godfrey and David J. Cox, '"The Last Fleet": Crime, Reformation, and Punishment in Western Australia after 1868', *The Australian and New Zealand Journal of Criminology*, 41.2 (2008), 236–258; revising Braithwaite, 'Crime in a Convict Republic', *Modern Law Review*, 64.1 (2001), 11–50.

[74] Michal Bosworth, *Convict Fremantle: A Place of Promise and Punishment* (Crawley: University of Western Australia Press, 2004).

[75] R. and G. O'Mara Erickson, 'Convicts in Western Australia, 1850–1887', *Dictionary of Western Australians, Vol. IX* (Crawley: University of Western Australia Press, 1994).

[76] Séan McConville, *English Local Prisons 1860–1900: Next Only to Death* (London: Routledge, 1994), pp. 52–53.

[77] Jennifer Davies, 'The London Garotting Panic of 1862: A Moral Panic and the Creation of a Criminal Class in Mid- Victorian England', in V. A. C. Gatrell, B. Lenman and G. Parker (eds.), *Crime and the Law: A Social History of Crime in Western Europe since 1500* (London: Europa, 1980), pp. 190–213.

Anti-Transportation and the Garrotting Panic

Back in London, the fear of untamed criminal types wandering at large and terrorizing the metropolis was sparked by an attack on a Member of Parliament, Hugh Pilkington, as he walked home on 17 July 1862. The ensuing media panic, accompanied by the view that there had been unsatisfactory arrangements for supervision of convicts following discharge, put transportation back on the agenda. Sir George Grey (1799–1882) was charged with a Royal Commission seeking possible sites for ensuring criminals were once again sent to the penal colonies rather than having them stay at home.[78] The result was legislation requiring criminals to report to police and provide certificates of good behaviour, which might come from an employer or clergyman. But the colonies resolved to block any move to revive transportation, including Grey's recommendation that, with some exceptions, all convicts sentenced to penal servitude should be sent to Western Australia.[79]

The journalist Howard Willoughby (1839–1908) was one of the first to write against any moves to resume transportation, despite its effectiveness in reforming prisoners and its generally benign character. In a tract that was originally published in the Melbourne *Argus*, Willoughby argued that despite its 'many excellent points' which had none of the faults of the old assignment system, or the brutality of Norfolk Island, transportation in Western Australia was neither penal nor reformatory:

It will scarcely be denied, that for the moral reformation of the convict it is necessary that he should be preserved from constant contamination, and that religious influences should be brought to bear upon him. Now, in West Australia, a man is herded with twenty or thirty criminals, all of whom may be worse than himself. He is obliged to consort with them at meals, at work and at night. As to religious instruction, the men, after they leave Fremantle Gaol, receive none; for they march to church, when they are near one, and the Sabbath reading of prayers by the warders when they are not, are but mockeries.[80]

On the question of the reformatory character of the system, where evidence suggested that most convicts did not reoffend, Willoughby thought the colony had simply been lucky. In a protracted discussion, he showed that the financial cost to both Britain and the colony far outweighed the benefits of abolishing transportation altogether. This

---

[78] *RC into Acts relating to Transportation and Penal Servitude* (Grey Committee), BPP 1863 (3190) XXI.1.
[79] Ibid., p. 35.
[80] Howard Willoughby, *Transportation: The British Convict in Western Australia: A Visit to the Swan River Settlements* (London: Harrison 1865), p. 36.

calculation was echoed by the figures compiled by Elliot at the Colonial Office in 1852 (see Table 10.2). Because Western Australia had a small population which could not support the men as they finished their sentences, most departed for the eastern states and did not help to consolidate Western Australia. Willoughby went on to denounce the system: 'The free colonies have spurned transportation as an accursed thing, those who have had the longest trial of it have cast it off with execration. Is another land to be exposed now to a repetition of the scenes which these would so gladly forget?'[81]

The threat of a renewal of transportation was enough to spark a new round of meetings and petitions. These were feeble in comparison with the outrage and thousands of signatures attached to the 'federal petition' of the Australasian League in 1851, but just as firm in their resolve. It is interesting to compare the claims made in the sequence of petitions against transportation in 1849, in response to Lord Grey's request to the colonies seeking those willing to accept convicts, with those received in 1863 and 1864. As before, the governors despatched the petitions to London with the distinction that few bothered to express their personal opposition to the anti-transportation movement. In 1856 Denison was appointed governor of New South Wales and governor general of all five Australian colonies, a title he retained until his posting to Madras in 1862. His passing removed the last governor who supported transportation against the majority views of the colonists and their elected representative institutions. The latter were responsible for anti-transportation petitions from New South Wales, Victoria, South Australia, Tasmania and Queensland, as well as the first Australian Intercolonial Conference, held in Melbourne in June 1863.[82] All opposed the renewal of transportation, with Queensland writing specifically to scotch the suggestion from Judge John Byles (1801–1884), in a charge to the grand jury at the winter assize in Maidstone reported in the *Times*,[83] that 'Queensland was desirous to receive transported convicts.'[84] Byles's motives were humane as he was seeking an alternative to the intolerable conditions in county jails and the extreme difficulty ex-prisoners faced trying to secure employment.[85]

---

[81] Ibid., 64.
[82] *Memorials in Favour of or against Transportation to Australia*, BPP 1863 (505) XXXVIII.805.
[83] *Times*, 2 December 1862.
[84] The motion against transportation made by the Intercolonial Conference was reported in *The Star* (Ballarat), 6 June 1863, p. 3.
[85] Carolyn A. Conley, *The Unwritten Law* (Oxford: Oxford University Press, 1991), p. 143.

The second round of petitions arrived in 1864 and 1865.[86] In Victoria Governor C. H. Darling (1809–1870), a career military officer with early experience in New South Wales when he served his uncle, Governor Sir Ralph Darling (1772–1858) as personal secretary, gave his support to those opposing any continuance of transportation. F. K. Crowley condemns the younger Darling for failing to act with appropriate detachment, as would be expected of a governor, and thus justifiably being recalled.[87] Yet, his identification with the rising liberal democracy was not unreasonable and he is likely to have had a much better sense of the public mood, and especially the need to push back against the lobbying from the wealthy elite. Darling forwarded three petitions from Victoria, the first was from a public meeting held at Rushworth, claiming that continued transportation to Western Australia would affect all the Australian colonies 'socially, politically, and morally' since 'from past experience' expirees and ticket-of-leave holders would find their way to Victoria. The home government 'are virtually forcing upon us, for their own protections, a class of criminals with whom they, with all the experience of modern civilization, are powerless to contend against'.[88] The second petition came from the mayor and councillors of Heathcote, who objected to the 'inundation' of the colony with the worst class of criminals attracted to the discoveries on the gold fields. The third was a set of resolutions from the Legislative Council (upper house) and Assembly (lower house) in Victoria, claiming that the arrival of convicts threatened to break apart the empire, 'so long as any convicts are transported from Great Britain to the shores of Australia, the feelings of attachment of the people of Victoria to the Crown will be mingled with deep scenes of unmerited wrong'.[89] From South Australia Governor Dominick Daly (1798–1868) also sent three petitions, which made pointed reference to the very different standing of the colonists whose objections were forwarded from the parliaments of New South Wales, Victoria, South Australia and Tasmania, as well as from the delegates of the intercolonial conference.[90] There appears to have been just one, rather bleating appeal from Western Australian colonists to retain transportation. By 1865 the

---

[86] *Petitions against Continuance of Transportation*, BPP 1864 (3357) XLI.69; *Correspondence Relating to Discontinuance of Transportation*, BPP 1865 (3424) XXXVII.911; *Letters from Gentlemen Connected with the Colony of Western Australia*, BPP 1865 (247).

[87] F. K. Crowley, 'Darling, Sir Charles Henry (1809–1870)', ADB.

[88] 'Petition against Transportation, Rushworth Victoria', [1863] BPP 1864 (3357) XLI.69, p. 3.

[89] 'Petition against Convict Transportation to Western Australia, Victorian Legislative Council and Assembly', BPP 1864 (3357) XLI.69, p. 5.

[90] Mayor of Adelaide, 'Petition against Convict Transportation to Western Australia', BPP 1864 (3357) XLI.69, p. 6.

signatories were concerned mostly with the vain attempt to secure compensation for the supposed loss of their convict labour supply.[91] Without attempting extravagant expressions of loyalty, the colonists were no longer willing to accept policies that led to benefits for those at 'home' and not themselves. In contrast to the petitions forwarded with despatches in the 1850s, neither religious or moral arguments feature, and the clergy are conspicuous by their absence from those chairing meetings and formulating motions.

As the petitions began arriving in the Colonial Office, resolute opposition to transportation was also forthcoming from experts at home. Since Bentham and Whately, no political economist had thought transportation was an effective or economical punishment. Sir Robert Richard Torrens (1814–1884) was a significant figure in the colonial settlement of South Australia.[92] When he read a paper before the British Association for the Advancement of Science in Newcastle on 29 August 1863, he had retired to England after serving as the first premier of South Australia, where his main reform was the creation of the system of land title that bears his name. Speaking of the garrotting panic, Torrens asserted that the fear of criminals at loose in Britain was not a sufficient reason to continue the practice of transportation anywhere in Australia, including Western Australia. His paper consists of a thorough rebuttal of three grounds which were usually advanced in support of transportation: as a deterrent, as a reformatory influence and as a means of founding colonies. In relation to the first, he argued that there was no evidence that punishment in any form inflicted in the penal colonies had any affect on the crime rate in Britain: 'From the year 1788 to 1852 every conceivable form of penal discipline was tried in New South Wales, Tasmania and Norfolk Island – the Road Gang System, the Solitary System, the Separate System, the probation system, the Maconochie or Mark System, – and the result of this sixty-four years' experimentising proved an entire failure.'[93] Also a failure, were all the various attempts to make transportation reformatory, largely because the major influence on the convicts who ended up in Western Australia was neither the penitentiary nor the religious instructor but the other convicts.

[91] *Letters from Gentlemen Connected with the Colony of Western Australia*; the signatories were: Ross D. Mangles, Henry A. Sanford, Wm Felgate, Sir James Stirling, Thomas Carter, John T. Smith, Wm Burges, Robt. M. Habgood, Alexander Andrews, Charles Gosnell, Henry Rt. Grellet.

[92] Douglas J. Whalan, 'Torrens, Sir Robert Richard (1814–1884)', *ADB*.

[93] Robert Torrens, *Transportation Considered as a Punishment and as a Mode of Founding Colonies* (London: William Ridgway, 1863), p. 7.

The End of Transportation

And so, at last, transportation did end. Although the last convicts were transported to Western Australia in 1867, those that were serving out their sentences and, in some cases, those who reoffended, continued to be a charge on the British Government. As we saw in Chapter 10, the convict establishment at Bermuda was closed in 1863 and at Gibraltar in 1875. Convicts from Bermuda and Gibraltar who had completed their sentences were brought back to England upon discharge, but those who were transported to Australia served out their sentences and mostly settled there.[94] Even as late as 1895, the British Government continued to pay for the surviving transported convicts, notably invalids, lunatics and paupers. As transportation ended, there no longer needed to be separate home and overseas administrations, and the chaplains and religious instructors who had served the older convict establishments with a duty to reform convicts were discharged.[95]

Another casualty of the end of transportation were the cellular chapels, schools and barracks required by the separate system. Many experienced and humane prison officers were, as we have seen, disturbed by the mental impact of the enforced isolation this inflicted on vulnerable people. More importantly, it proved impossible to prevent all communication between prisoners without savage reprisals (which were a feature of Auburn Prison in New York where the silent system originated). In his testimony to the 1863 SC on Prison Discipline, John Perry (1802–1870), the inspector of prisons for the southern district, provided a detailed commentary on prison schools, noting that in large prisons 'there is almost always a schoolmaster' and in the smallest the chaplain 'does the duty'. While chapels were often subdivided (and, in Perry's opinion, very ineffectively so), it was less common for school-rooms, though often chapels were used for school. It was also his opinion that partitions in chapels were of little use in preventing communication, since the prisoner regularly bypassed all impediments placed in their way. In addition, the prisonrs 'were apt to go to sleep during the service from the closeness of the confinement in which they were; and they had great facilities for doing so, by sinking down upon their seats, so that they could not be seen by the chaplain'.[96] One of the places where cellular schoolrooms were implemented, as well as cellular chapel, was at Parkhurst Prison on the Isle of Wight, which was changed into a convict prison for boys awaiting

---

[94] 'Evidence of William James Forsythe', *Prisons Committee: Minutes of Evidence* (London: HMSO, 1895), p. 461.
[95] Ibid.   [96] *HL SC on Gaols and Prison Discipline*, BPP 1863 (499) IX.1, p. 136.

transportation to Australia by the Parkhurst Act of 1835.[97] There is something cheering about this subversion of the cellular penitentiary by prisoners – a bright spot in a dreary episode in the role of the church in enforcing the will of the state at home and abroad. In the event, Perry was one of the few individuals who confronted Lord Carnarvon and attempts to drive the prison system in a more punitive direction. Against Carnarvon, Perry continued to press his view that 'moral reformation' should be the primary object of imprisonment and that mere punishment was 'morally prejudicial' and that instruments designed to deliver punishment and no other benefit, such as the crank and treadwheel, should be abolished.[98] The convict depots constructed in Western Australia reflect the decline of the reputation of the separate system, and there were no attempts to install the stifling and ineffective partitioned sleeping stalls that blighted the Van Diemen's Land probation stations.[99]

Although Sir George Grey's committee had recommended the revival of transportation on a large scale, the colonists were totally opposed to this and eventually even Carnarvon accepted that it was not viable under these conditions. Paradoxically, one reason for the abandonment of transportation was that it was deemed insufficiently punitive to satisfy politicians and the voting public. The claimed horrors of transportation, while real enough for those who endured them, were largely a projection of the different campaigns aimed either at continuing transportation by assuring the public it was sufficiently punitive, or alternately, ending it, for its alleged humanitarian and moral abuses. The one determined effort to make transportation truly reformative and a mirror, in the colonies, to the penitentiaries at home was the probation system. Probation was sound enough in principle, indeed so sound that it remains the basis for many modern penal systems which succeeded it. While theoretically committed to schooling and religious instruction for prisoners, legislators were unwilling to support probation in the light of rising costs and its perceived moral failings. In 1852, in a lengthy memorandum summarizing the history of transportation, Thomas Frederick Elliot (1808–1880), who had succeeded James Stephen as assistant under secretary for colonies in 1847, strongly hinted that there was very little additional cost involved in providing accommodation for all prisoners in Britain and Ireland and abandoning transportation, which now cost substantially

---

[97] For an image of the probationary ward with its cellular school, see *Illustrated London News*, 13 March 1846.

[98] McConville, *English Local Prisons*, p. 105.

[99] Martin Gibbs, 'Landscapes of Redemption: Tracing the Path of a Convict Miner in Western Australia', *International Journal of Historical Archaeology*, 14.4 (2010), 599.

more per prisoner to sustain than to keep the same prisoners in Great Britain. Indeed, it cost very much less to keep them in Irish prisons (see Table 10.2).[100]

Abandoning transportation meant a resolute end to reformative experiments designed to assure colonists that prisoners could be made into better people, less likely to reoffend by sending them to the other side of the world. Demonstrating more effectively than anything else the essentially political character of British penal policy, Carnarvon's knee-jerk reaction to the garrotting panic was to sponsor the passage of the draconian Security from Violence Bill (1863), which allowed the infliction of 150 lashes in instalments of fifty – something long outlawed in the penal colonies. Those under sixteen would receive seventy-five strokes, inflicted in three lots of twenty-five.[101] For critics, it seemed like a return to the severity that had been overthrown by the dismantling of the Bloody Code a century earlier.[102] The passion and religious commitment of reformers such as Matthew Davenport Hill and Alexander Maconochie, and the consistent reports of chaplains and schoolteachers were ignored. The British opted instead for an increasingly severe system of penal servitude: hard fare, hard work and isolation. While transportation continued for non-Europeans in the British Empire, for British and Irish prisoners the empire of hell was no more.

---

[100] Elliot, 'Transportation', TNA CO 885/2/15: 33. Elliot's figures show that it cost almost twice as much to support convicts in Western Australia than in England and almost three times as much to support the prisoners in Van Diemen's Land under the probation system.

[101] McConville, *English Local Prisons*, p. 61. McConville points out that Carnarvon passed this law without, in all probability, even witnessing a flogging.

[102] For resistance to the bill, see Ibid., 64. For a less sanguine view, see Davies, *The London Garotting Panic of 1862.*

12 Conclusion
'This Great Scheme of Human Redemption'

> It must also be remembered, that the flourishing communities now spreading over Australia, and which promise, at no distant date, to become a great nation, are in fact the creation of the system of transportation.[1]
>
> (Earl Grey, 1850)

> It remains for those who have this important question before them to determine whether this great scheme of human redemption is not better imitated and aided by continuing that system rather than by compulsory labour under confinement.[2]
>
> (Lucas Horrox, 1861)

This book has addressed a long-standing lacuna in the history of the British penal empire, namely the impact of religion and religious affiliation on the campaign to reform and then to end the transportation of convicts from Britain and Ireland. It has brought together arguments and methodology from the new imperial religious history to address old debates about the social and political development of convict transportation. By attending to religious arguments that were raised in favour and against transportation, it has highlighted some of the convict system's lesser known but most significant features. For more than eighty years, punishment was never the exclusive object of penal discipline. It was always moderated by the functional demands of deploying convict labour and, increasingly as the century progressed, the rhetoric – and sometimes the reality – of social and religious reform. This is unexpected since, at the time when the first consignments of convicts were sent on their southern journeys, Britain was barely emerging from the 'age of Draco' in penal discipline. Transportation has traditionally been regarded as a vestige of the old regime, with an atavistic commitment to retribution, terror and pain, rather than reform, in punishment. By focussing on religious arguments from all points of the denominational compass and including anti-transportation campaigns waged across the settler empire,

---

[1] Henry George Grey, *Speeches ... On ... a Bill for the Better Government of Convict Prisons* (London: George Woodfall, 1850), p. 46.
[2] Gibbs, 'Landscapes of Redemption', 186.

306

this study has pushed back against the formidable stereotype, outlined in Chapter 1, of transportation as an 'empire of hell'.

This is not to question the very real suffering and degradation of the 185,000 British and Irish convicts transported to penal establishments between 1788 and 1875 or their impact on indigenous people and the colonial landscape. The work of convict historians continues to disclose how convicts supplied the imperial demand for labour to secure and extend the frontier of Britain's remote settler colonies and naval bases. As humanitarian opponents of transportation stressed, convicts contributed to the destruction of indigenous society in penal colonies, even though they did not choose to initiate these fatal contacts. Saxe Bannister (1790–1877), the former attorney general of New South Wales, denounced convict colonization as a system of extermination of the original inhabitants and demoralization of nearby regions: 'from island to island outwards, our runaway conicts and unchecked sailors are still covering the whole ocean with our worst vices'.[3] The agency and identity of convicts is reflected not just in the impressive infrastructure they created, largely for the benefit of settler colonists who came in their wake, but also in the way they represented their servitude, through memoirs, newspapers, letters and literature, some of it facilitated by the teaching and preaching of clergy and religious instructors. From the 1830s, the contested ideal of reformative transportation was mediated through chaplains, religious instructors, scripture teachers and committed laypeople at the highest levels of government at home and in the colonies. As discussed in Chapter 2, the convict colonies were conceived in the age of atonement, when a dark vision of human nature dominated British cultural politics. This book suggests that religious interventions and collusions in convict transportation were integral to the age of reform and not an aberration from it.

This concluding chapter will look briefly at the changing fashions in the historical assessment of transportation, as well as contemporary efforts to judge the success of some of its most controversial features, particularly the attempt to reform as well as punish convicts. It will address three questions: firstly, was transportation reformative? Secondly, how have academic and nationalist interpretations of the convict past impacted on religious elements of the transportation debate? And thirdly, what is the continuing legacy of convictism and religious attempts to reform convicts? Even when all parties came together, as they did to crush the continuance of transportation in the eastern

---

[3] S. Bannister, *On Abolishing Transportation* (London: Wilson, 1837), p. 42.

colonies of Australia, the lure or prospect of reform continued to attract supporters for transportation.

Reformative Transportation

For religious authorities, reform lay at the heart of the debate about convict transportation. Whether or not transportation really did lead to reform is something of a non-question, since so much depended on the point of view of the interrogator but few issues were so hotly contested throughout the transportation era. For its most outspoken critics, such as Molesworth, Whately or Adderley, there were no advantages to transportation that outweighed the innate corruption of the system of assigned labour. Colonial authorities such as the Arthur, Denison and the Rev. J. D. Lang, argued that transportation frequently did lead to individual reform, if by this is meant avoidance by convicts of serious crime after their release. Some historians agree – but argue that reform had its limits.[4] While there were many individual success stories, for other convicts transportation was followed by a life of low-level nuisance crime, especially drunkenness and vagrancy.[5] This suggests that neither the worst fears of the colonists regarding convict depravity nor the loftiest expectations of government ministers of convict reform were realistic. Importantly, it is only in recent times and following the availability of 'big data' that criminologists have been able to make an accurate assessment of long-term rates of recidivism. Contemporaries, by contrast, had no real way of knowing for sure and shameless manipulation of the statistics to support a particular point of view, such as Judge Burton's charge to the jury in 1835, was characteristic of anti-transportation polemic.

Reformative or not, transportation to Australia appears to have led to enhanced social outcomes for convicts and their children when compared with long-term incarceration in home-based penitentiaries under conditions of penal servitude in Britain and Ireland. Convict agency rather than victimhood is stressed by most academic historians, with the notable exception of Robert Hughes, who have published in recent decades.[6] Successful rehabilitation was an exceptional feature of

---

[4] Godfrey and Cox, 'The Last Fleet', 236–258; Braithwaite, 'Crime in a Convict Republic', 11–50. For an adventurous attempt to trace convict after lives, see Frost and Maxwell-Stewart, *Chain Letters*.
[5] Godfrey and Cox, 'The Last Fleet', 253.
[6] The original research was led by J. B. Hirst, *Convict Society and Its Enemies* (Sydney: Allen & Unwin, 1983); Harling, 'The Trouble with Convicts', Footnote 7.

transportation to Australia, and was not matched elsewhere, for example in the case of French convicts, many of them recidivists, transported to French Guyana and New Caledonia.[7] Earl Grey reflected this view when he responded in the House of Lords to news of the very large petitions which had been assembled by the Australasian League: 'He was firmly persuaded that the system now in operation was that which led to the least evils, because they knew that in the Colonies the great majority of those who were sent out as convicts, though they might not be improved in heart, were, at all events, improved in conduct.'[8] Grey's views echo those of the doyen of the history of convict transportation, A. G. L. Shaw, who agreed that overall the system was not only effective in reducing recidivism but also considerably less punitive in its effect than the system of penal servitude which replaced it.[9] Christian penal reformers looked to achieve something more than the 'least of all evils'; they wanted a penal system whose implicit and explicit values aligned with doctrinal norms, including the internal, spiritual reformation of the criminal.

Transportation ended not because it failed to reform criminals but because it was opposed by all colonies where the British government attempted to send them. Shipowners who brought former convicts from Bermuda to American ports were fined and required to return them to Bermuda; the Australian colonists rejected their convicts, largely on social grounds. This was despite well-authenticated reports; for example, by the journalist Howard Willoughby (1839–1908) in relation to Western Australia, that the convicts were rarely violent, were highly motivated not to reoffend and appeared to enjoy rather than lament their final period of labour in the healthy climate of Western Australia.[10] Similarly, in Bermuda, although the rate of disease and the sub-tropical climate meant that it was always a hardship station, the conditions were comparable with those of other sites of forced labour on the hulks and dockyards. It also failed because the religious arguments used to defend its claims to reform as well as punish criminals, were no longer supported by leading clerics in the colonies or at home.

---

[7] For the transportation of the 'living plague' of repeat offenders, see Stephen A. Toth, *Beyond Papillon: The French Overseas Penal Colonies, 1854–1952* (Lincoln: University of Nebraska Press, 2006), p. 35 For failed penitential experiments, including transportation, Anderson (ed.), *A Global History of Convicts*, p. 344.

[8] Hansard, HL Deb, vol, 116., col. 740–769, 9 May 1851. Lord Grey's remarks are at the end of the debate at col. 769.

[9] Shaw, *Convicts and the Colonies*, p. 359.

[10] Willoughby, *Transportation*; Suzanne G. Mellor, 'Willoughby, Howard (1839–1908)', ADB.

Debating Transportation

Since the abolition of convict transportation from Britain and Ireland, debate has continued about its morality, effectiveness and legacy.[11] Despite the rancour with which it was eliminated from the settler colonies, aspects of the system were widely admired and discussed at International Prison Congresses,[12] while both France and Germany implemented schemes which borrowed elements from the British experience, including its use of religious instruction and education to reform convicts.[13] Escaped French convicts from New Caledonia were soon proving a nuisance to the former penal colonies of Australia and elsewhere in the Pacific.[14]

Over fifty years ago, Michael Roe argued that anti-transportation, together with politics, land policy and education, was a key field over which religious and political interests fought for authority in eastern Australia prior to 1851.[15] He called the resulting consensus 'moral enlightenment', ignoring the racial and gendered assumptions which underlay British settler discourse.[16] There needed to be new tools for this debate, some of which have been developed in the course of this study. When Kathleen Wilson proposed a new imperial history of Britain and its empire, she cautioned that it was 'very much a work in progress', but showcased studies of cultural categories such as gender, class, race and how they advanced mainstream imperial histories with their focus on military and political matters.[17] Imperial religious history is also a work in progress as historians continue to be fascinated by missionaries, humanitarianism and trusteeship, but have been slow to press their claims into other fields of the imperial past. Yet, in a significant review essay, Tony Ballantyne suggested that a growing body of research was transforming the understanding of Christianity in the imperial project: 'It is increasingly clear that religion stood at the heart of imperial culture and acted as

[11] Roberts, 'Beyond the Stain', 205–279.
[12] Briony Neilson, 'The Paradox of Penal Colonization: Debates on Convict Transportation at the International Prison Congresses 1872–1895', *French History and Civilization: Papers from the George Rudé Seminar*, 6 (2015), 198–211.
[13] Fitizpatrick, 'New South Wales in Africa?', 59–72.
[14] Russell Brennan and Jonathan Richards, "The Scum of French Criminals and Convicts": Australia and New Caledonia Escapees', *History Compass*, 12.7 (2014), 559–566; Alexis Bergantz, '"The Scum of France': Australian Anxieties towards French Convicts in the Nineteenth Century', *Australian Historical Studies* 49.2 (2018), 150–166.
[15] Roe, *Quest for Authority*, pp. 193, 205–206.
[16] For a different perspective, allying colonial anti-transportation with anti-humanitarian loyalist networks, see Lester, 'British Settler Discourse', 28.
[17] Kathleen Wilson, *A New Imperial History* (Cambridge: Cambridge University Press, 2004), p. 26.

a central feature of the contested terrains of colonial cultures, from Punjab to Polynesia.'[18] Like claims for convict reform, the 'moral enlightenment' achieved by the cessation of convict transportation was heavily constrained, particularly its impact on indigenous people.

Initially, as discussed in Chapter 2, it was the Evangelicals who framed the discussion about the standing of transportation. From the eighteenth century, Christian and secular utilitarians were opposed to transportation and favoured the enlightened solution of the penitentiary, but construction was inhibited by cost as much as the usefulness of convict labour to settler colonialism. Evangelicals within the established church then moved to support the next best solution, which was to seek to create penal colonies which would entrench Evangelical values in the empire. In New South Wales, they were highly successful in this endeavour with every colonial chaplain being endorsed by the Evangelical party and many of their societies and principles being advanced by their leading representative, the Rev. Samuel Marsden. Even the parliamentary attacks of William Wilberforce were moderated by the belief that the system would receive the condemnation it deserved at the hands of Commissioner Bigge. In fact this did not happen. Bigge was ordered to make transportation an 'object of real Terror',[19] not to abolish it; his religious reforms all concerned the settler community, not those who came in chains. The most important Evangelical attempt to make transportation the equal to the reformative machine that was the penitentiary was that of Colonel Arthur in Van Diemen's Land. Chapter 4 showed how Arthur's effective and authoritarian rule was underpinned by his Evangelical faith. Accused of creating 'hell on earth', he was supported to the last by his Evangelical friends. When the first great debate about convict transportation was launched by Archbishop Whately, it was Arthur, in collaboration with Bishop Broughton, who provided an effective justification for the continuance of the system he had created – not 'hell on earth' so much as a penal purgatory.

After the Evangelicals, it was the Quakers who provided the most thorough investigation of the practice of transportation in the penal colonies. James Backhouse and George Washington Walker visited every convict site across New South Wales, Van Diemen's Land and Norfolk Island over the course of their extended visitation to Australia. Their work was supported financially and morally by the London meeting and they were tasked with supporting Elizabeth Fry's investigation of the

---

[18] Tony Ballantyne, 'Religion, Difference, and the Limits of British Imperial History', *Victorian Studies*, 47.3 (2005), 451.
[19] Bathurst to Bigge, 6 January 1819, *Instructions to Bigge*, p. 4.

conditions of convict women. In the great fight against slavery, the Quakers in both America and Britain had been the staunchest supporters of abolition, dominating the river of anti-slavery that was Thomas Clarkson's map of the movement. Not so with convict transportation. After the most minute examination, Backhouse and Walker continued to recommend reformative interventions that left the practice of transportation essentially untouched. Indeed, they were staunch supporters of the reforms created by Colonel Arthur, including his plans to confine all prisoners within the natural penitentiary of Tasman's peninsula.

The first salvo in the campaign to abolish transportation was fired by Archbishop Whately who explained to Earl Grey that the transportation question was not 'purely political', but was 'closely connected with morality', to the extent that it justified an archbishop taking an interest in it.[20] From this point it can be argued, with Whately, that the campaign to end convict transportation became a religious as much as a political issue. Chapter 6 examined the very different intellectual and theological roots of Whately's thoughts on penal reform, how they had their origins in the Christian utilitarianism of predecessors such as Paley and Chalmers. The real significance of Whately is that he was influential with the rising Whigs who would soon triumph in the polls, bringing in an age of unprecedented political, legal and social reform. Whately objected to transportation because he believed it was ineffective in reducing crime and impeded effective remedies for social maladies, including education for the poor and free emigration. Whately's influence was wielded out of all proportion to the time he devoted to this subject because it was magnified by the Molesworth SC on Transportation. Whately provided radical Whigs, who were hostile to convict transportation and keen to promote free emigration and systematic (rather than convict) colonization, with archiepiscopal authority. Attacked by Colonel Arthur and Bishop Broughton, who opposed his Liberal Anglican churchmanship as much as his utilitarian arguments, Whately retaliated with an effective pamphlet campaign that captured the mood of policymakers which was swinging against claims for both the utility and morality of transportation.

The major vehicle for the attack on the reputation of the settler colonists and employers of convicts was the Molesworth SC on Transportation. Debate about the morality of transportation was spiced with sexual panic and sectarianism, as Protestants and Catholics provided different accounts of the 'horrors of transportation', separately

---

[20] Whately, *Secondary Punishments*, p. 2.

supporting the bombastic claims of the Molesworth Committee. Chapter 7 reflected on the bitter exchange between Judge Burton, for the Protestant establishment, and Father Ullathorne, for post-emancipation Catholics. Burton saw convict society in New South Wales as the problem, in which convicts, emancipists and settlers alike were racing towards crime. Like metropolitan humanitarians, Burton considered convicts to be the deplorable source of violence against Aborigines, such as those engaged in wholesale slaughter in the Myall Creek massacre of 1838. While Burton demanded more Anglican religious instructors to remedy the problem, Ullathorne was more successful in securing Catholic chaplains. In this he had the support of the Liberal regime in the colony of New South Wales as much as the government in Westminster. The 'horrors of transportation' were ameliorated by the liberal balm of equitable distribution of government funding to the major denominations and dismantling the vestiges of church establishment in New South Wales and Van Diemen's Land.

The Molesworth SC recommended the abolition of private assignment and suspending transportation of convicts to New South Wales. But Molesworth's barbs had no impact on Arthur, who progressed to ever higher colonial duties and unimpeached Evangelical reputation. Attempts to create liberal reforms of transportation continued, of which the most exciting was the experiment conducted by Captain Maconochie on Norfolk Island. Chapter 8 considered the religious roots of Maconochie's system, its borrowings from Richard Whately (and Wiliam Paley) and school reformers, who suggested the moral regime of labour-based (rather than time-based) sentencing, and the use of disciplinary regimes based on a symbolic economy. If Whately was a Liberal Anglican, then Maconochie can be viewed as a Liberal Presbyterian, whose system was supported by those who admired his tolerance, positivity and belief in the reforming power of labour. While Maconochie's regime was relatively short-lived, the most significant investment in religiously-based reform was the probation system, considered in Chapter 9. The many flaws in the implementation of that scheme meant that it was denounced within and without the penal colonies by clergy and lay colonists alike. The ripple-on effect of the failure of probation was significant, bringing to an end the religious consensus that had supported transportation within the established church. With rising hysteria about unnatural crime, the sacking of the Lt Governor of Van Diemen's Land and the outraged refusal of its Anglican bishop to accept the credentials of convict religious instructors, the system was doomed.

The campaign to end convict transportation was a late arrival in the hitherto genteel pamphlet exchanges on the merits of transportation.

The anti-convict campaign sparked by attempts to revive convict transportation to New South Wales and extend it to other colonies, including
the Cape Colony, was discussed in Chapter 10. Church and missionary
leaders argued that corrupt whites would damage missionary goals
already complicated by ongoing frontier warfare in the Cape and unregulated emigration in the Pacific. Clergy participated actively in this campaign and the Rev. John West was the acknowledged moral leader of the
movement. Religious leaders supported West's Australasian League
because they were persuaded that penal colonies were incompatible with
God's plan, as argued by Archdeacon Marriott in Van Diemen's Land.
But they also chose pragmatically to ally themselves with the rising
democratic elements in the colonies, who were dominated by recent,
free emigrants and who opposed the interest of the large-scale employers
of labour. The central role played by the churches was recognized in the
'Jubilee' marking the cessation of transportation to Van Diemen's Land
in 1853, during which public thanksgiving services were held in Hobart
at St David's Anglican Cathedral, Chalmer's Free Church, the Independent Chapel, Baptist Chapel and St George's Anglican Church.[21] In
Launceston, St John's Square with its churches was the centre of celebrations, including religious services, a memorial arch, cake for the
children, a loyal procession, the lighting of bonfires, tar barrels and
rockets, and dinner for about 100 native-born colonists.[22]

Two further religious campaigns were involved in the ending of transportation on the hulks and the penal establishments of Bermuda, Gibraltar and Western Australia. In Bermuda, Governor Elliott was active in
attempts to reform the convicts, including by implementing Captain
Maconochie's mark system. But the Rev. J. M. Guilding provided support for those who opposed the continuation of the hulks and convict
transportation in any form, raising the spectre of the moral failure of both
Norfolk Island and the probation system. Western Australia is the last
and best case for the implementation of reformative transportation, and it
initially had the support of Bishop Matthew Hale. In its initial phase, this
scheme was indeed reformative and provided opportunities for those
who had shown a willingness to comply with prison discipline in Britain.
The last days of transportation in Western Australia saw a return to the
abuses of earlier stages of transportation, but, of all the many attempts to
reform criminals through transportation, it was one of the most successful. That this story is not better known is largely because of the legacy of

---

[21] *Colonial Times*, 11 August 1853, p. 2; Argus 14 June 1853, p. 6;
[22] *Examiner* (Launceston), 10 August 1903, p. 7.

the 'horrors of transportation' and its implied rebuke to the standing of the colonists, free and unfree.

Legacies of Transportation

Australia was born in the cradle of convict transportation and, like the conflicted relationship of the United States and the West Indies to slavery, this has had a profound impact on national history-writing. American historians writing in the wake of the Civil War imagined themselves as the heirs to two revolutions: the first American Revolution (1775–1783) overthrew the British tyrant and created a single nation from the separate colonies. The second was the American Civil War (1861–1865) which facilitated the advance of bourgeois democracy and its partnership with capitalism by ridding the Republic of encumbrances to a free market in labour and goods such as slavery and tribalism. There was no slavery in Australia, but to some degree convictism was its economic equivalent, albeit on a significantly smaller scale. Anti-transportation was a revolution, supported by all creeds and classes, but like all revolutions it did come at a cost. Among the consequences of the abolition of convict transportation was the economic decline of Van Diemen's Land, much as Denison observed and indeed predicted.[23] There was no compensation to convict masters, though an ineffective attempt to mount one was made by a group of employers in Western Australia.[24] The most important consequence was the emotional one of 'shame' at Botany Bay or the 'stain' of convictism,[25] which continues to shape the historiography of the anti-transportation movement. As David Roberts has shown, initial assessments were uniformly laudatory.[26] The swing to nationalism in the 1970s sparked changes in perspective, with Babette Smith continuing the nationalist tradition of compensatory acclamation for the convict achievement and condemnation of convict administrators, clergy and abolitionists.[27]

The anti-transportation movement may have been a victim of its own success. Rhetorical tropes used to bring down transportation – the

[23] Denison to Mrs Denison, 5 February 1857, Denison, *Varieties*, vol. 2, p. 379; Henry Reynolds, '"That Hated Stain": The Aftermath of Transportation in Tasmania', *Historical Studies*, 14:53 (1969), 19–31.
[24] *Western Australia. Copy of Any Letters from Gentlemen Connected with the Colony of Western Australia to the Secretary of State for the Colonies*, BPP 1865 (247).
[25] Hirst, *Convict Society*, pp. 189–217
[26] David Roberts 'Beyond the Stain: Rethinking the Nature and Impact of the Anti-Transportation Movement', *Journal of Australian Colonial History*, 14 (2012), 205–279.
[27] Smith, Babette, *Australia's Birthstain: The Startling Legacy of the Convict Era* (Sydney: Allen & Unwin, 2008).

demoralisation of convict society, the horrors of transportation and unnatural crime – proved difficult to sheath once their purpose had been met. The word 'convictism', to mean a system of forced labour parallel to that of slavery, first appeared in the 1830s in the writing of the former New South Wales magistrate, and Tory polemicist, James Mudie's *Felonry of New South Wales* (1837).[28] Mudie aimed to attack Governor Richard Bourke and fellow colonial liberals such as Roger Therry, decrying humane interventions on behalf of convicts and former convicts as 'convictism' and 'emancipistism'.[29] The term was quickly picked up by the quarterlies to denigrate convict colonisation and promote 'moral' colonisation by free settlers to New Zealand and South Australia, described as 'entirely free of convicts and convictism'.[30] By the time Mrs Meredith published an account of her life as a minister's wife in Tasmania in 1853, a reviewer in the *Westminster Review* thought mainly of her dismal role as the manager of 'her slaves', the convicts: 'it would have been the gem of Australasia, but for the presence of Convictism'.[31] Without multiplying the examples, the social taint of 'convictism' was an early consequence of the anti-transportation campaign and it related less to the perceived dangers of convicts than to the corruption of all levels of polite society who had made use of their labour. Free colonists were keen to avoid the suggestion that, like the West Indian planters in relation to slavery, they were motivated financially to support the system. On the contrary, they argued, the convict system was an expensive imposition on both the colony and the Crown without delivering any economic benefits to them.

Examining the anti-humanitarian campaigns waged in the 1840s and 1850s by settlers in the Cape Colony, New South Wales and New Zealand, Alan Lester has argued that transportation was taken up by humanitarians at home, who were persuaded by the arguments of Richard Whately and others that private assignment was tantamount to slavery.[32] The SC on Aborigines in British Settlements (1836) took aim at the moral standing of settler colonists, the masters of convict 'slaves', in much the same way as the anti-slavery campaign had targeted slave owners, representing them as a stain on the character of the British nation. Kirsten McKenzie points out that transportation was originally abolished against the wishes of employers in New South Wales, outraged

---

[28] Mudie, *Felonry of New South Wales*, p. 93.   [29] Ibid.
[30] Thomas Horton James, *Six Months in South Australia with Some Account of Port Philip and Portland* (London: Cross, 1838), p. 39; *Dublin Review* 6 (1838), p. 462.
[31] *The Westminster Review*, 59 (1853), 602, reviewing Meredith, *My Home in Tasmania*.
[32] Lester, 'British Settler Discourse', 45, Footnote 9.

Legacies of Transportation 317

by the accusations of the Molesworth SC.[33] It was the shame created by the evidence, much of it highly coloured, that associated them with the moral depravity of slave ownership and prison discipline, which turned the tide in the convict transportation debate. Whereas most clergy and respectable colonists supported the transportation system in the form created by Sir George Arthur in Van Diemen's Land, they perceived the rising tide of humanitarian criticism as an attack on themselves. Against Lester, Reid suggests that settler discourse was rather different in Van Diemen's Land.[34] Colonial abolitionists were not moved by a narrowly defensive view of Britishness, so much as 'undoubted compassion for, and humanitarian sympathy with, the plight of the suffering convict', coupled with an assertive view of male political rights.[35] These views were underpinned and validated by religious arguments across the denominational spectrum, to the extent that the rise and fall of convict transportation cannot be understood without the religious context provided by the preceding chapters.

Postscript: 'This Great Scheme of Human Redemption'

This study began with John Mitchel's diabolical evocation of his own experience of penal transportation in the British empire. Yet – as both Mitchel himself and the convict Martin Cash were able to demonstrate – there were occasional opportunities for escape.[36] Particularly interesting reflections on the convict experience in Western Australia have been uncovered by archaeologist Martin Gibbs and a team of students.[37] Gibbs studied the landscapes associated with a gentleman convict, Joseph Lucas Horrocks (1805–1866), transported to the Colony of Western Australia in 1852, granted a ticket of leave in 1853 and a conditional pardon in 1856.[38] Having been emancipated, Horrocks's skills as mining engineer were deployed by the convict department to build what Gibbs calls an 'ideal industrial community' at the Gwalla Estate near Northampton in the colony's mid west. Investigating the Lynton Convict Hiring Depot, 500 kilometres north of Perth, which operated from 1852 until being abandoned in 1856, Gibbs reports that there was a village for the pensioner guards including a commissariat

---

[33] McKenzie, *Scandal in the Colonies*, pp. 149–151.
[34] Reid, *Gender, Crime and Empire*, pp. 245–246.   [35] Ibid., 246.
[36] Famous for escaping twice from Port Arthur, Cash's life was romanticized by James Lester Burke (ed.), *The Adventures of Martin Cash* (Hobart Town: "Mercury" Steam Press Office, 1870).
[37] Gibbs, 'Landscapes of Redemption'.
[38] Wendy Birman, 'Horrocks, Joseph Lucas (?–1865)', *ADB*.

store, lockup, and hospital as well as prisoner barracks with cookhouse, blacksmith's forge, well and closets. Gibbs notes that the functionality of this site, which lacked a chapel and was integrated into the free settlement, contrasts with convict sites in eastern Australia studied by James Kerr.[39] A similar open, functional character can be observed from plans for the convict depot at Toodyay, which operated between 1850 and 1875.[40]

In the east, a series of government inquiries and moral panic about unnatural crime led to insistence on a high degree of formal separation and classification at all probation stations. Typically, there were individual cells, guards, a chapel and boundaries; most were established as far away from free settlements as possible. A very different landscape was presented in the series of mining sites associated with Horrocks. He was forty-nine, married and a respectable Manchester merchant when he was convicted of forging and uttering two bills of exchange and transported for fourteen years, arriving in Fremantle in January 1852. Horrocks seems to have been a man of considerable entrepreneurial gifts and Methodist leanings. In 1863, at his Gwalla mining settlement, Horrocks built a non-denominational church with separate pulpits for Anglicans and Nonconformists and open to all.[41] A text inscribed on a cement tablet – prominently displayed – made its purpose very plain: 'My house shall be called a house of Prayer for All People' (Isaiah 56:7).[42] Horrocks himself acted as minister until his death and was buried in the cemetery adjacent when he died at the age of fifty-five, six years after being transported to the colony. Churches have been identified at other mining sites associated with Horrox, anticipating the ongoing influence of Methodism in Western Australian mining communities.[43] A remarkable letter from Horrocks to the Colonial Secretary dated

---

[39] James Semple Kerr, *Design for Convicts* (Sydney: Library of Australian History, 1984).

[40] 'Plan of Convict Grant Toodyay', TNA MPG 1/722; Sean Winter, 'A Preliminary Report on Archaeological Investigations at Two Western Australian Regional Convict Depots', *Australian Archaeology*, 73.1 (2011): 65–68.

[41] 'Church and Cemetery, Gwalla', 1 July 2017, Heritage Council Western Australia, inherit.stateheritage.wa.gov.au (Accessed 1 September 2018).

[42] Isaiah 56:7 (KJV): 'Even them will I bring to my holy mountain and make them joyful in my house of prayer: their burnt offerings and their sacrifices shall be accepted upon mine altar; for mine house shall be called a house of prayer for all people.' For the origins of the Gwalla Church (modern Northampton, WA), J. M. Drew, 'Early Northampton: An Undenominational Church', *Journal and Proceedings of the Western Australian Historical Society*, 2, no. 9 (1932): 30–36. Drew does not mention that Horrocks was a convict.

[43] Gibbs, 'Landscapes of Redemption', 602. Gibbs is referring to Wanerenooka mine, established in 1855. See also Raelene Frances, 'Christianity on the Coalfields: A Case Study of Collie in the Great Depression', in Tonkin, John (ed.), *Religion and Society in Western Australia, Studies in Western Australian History*, 9 (1987), 115–124.

17 October 1860, speaks in favour of continued transportation to Western Australia.[44] Against the claims of colonists in the east, Horrocks argued for the 'incalculable benefit' of transportation for both colony and mother country. Far from an 'empire of hell', he called transportation 'a great scheme of human redemption', preferable in every way to the forced labour and confinement in Britain and Ireland which replaced it.[45]

[44] J. L. Horrocks to Colonial Secretary, 17 October 1862, Colonial Secretary's Office, vol. 494, pp. 183–196; Gibbs, 'Landscapes of Redemption', 186.
[45] Cited by Ibid.

Bibliography

A Archives

Australia

National Library of Australia, Canberra
Diary of John Ward, convict, 1841–1844, MS 3275
Tasmanian Archives and Heritage Office (TAHO), Hobart
Backhouse and Walker, 'Report on Tasman's Peninsula', November 1834, CSO1 807–17244.
Durham Correspondence Misc. 62/1/A 1087/1 128
Ferguson, Chaplain's Cottage, Norfolk Island, PWD266/1/1912
Lingard, Protestant Clergyman's Quarters, Norfolk Island, PWD266/1/1913
Lingard, Plans for Divine Service, Norfolk Island, PWD266/1/1914
State Library of New South Wales (SLNSW), Sydney
Arthur Papers, Vol. 4, 1821–1855, A2164
Australasian Anti-Transportation League, Letters January–July 1851, Aa 25
Backhouse, James, Papers, 1834–1842, Ab 124
Backhouse and Walker, 'Reports', B706-7
Bourke Papers, Miscellaneous 1831–1834, MLMSS 404–411.
Cook, Thomas, 'An Exile's Lamentations', A1711
Knopwood, Robert, 'Prayers for Convicts Condemned to Death', 1822, DLMS 51
Lang, John Dunmore, Letters received, 1825–1893, MLMS 3016
Marsden Papers, A1992, A1998
MacNamara, Francis, 'A Convict's Tour to Hell', C967
Naylor, Rev. T. B., Papers, 1829–1849, DLMS 134, DLMSQ 363.
Norfolk Island Convict Papers, c. 1842–1867, MLMSS 102, Q168
Pearce, Alexander, 'Narrative of the Escape of Eight Convicts from Macquarie Harbour in September 1822', 1824, DLMS 3
Rogers, Thomas and W. Foster Rogers, 'Man's Inhumanity', c.1912–1914, C214
Rogers, Thomas, Letterbook, 1844–1847, A323
Sharpe, Rev. Thomas, Papers; Journal on Norfolk Island, 1837–1840, B217, B218
West, Rev. John, Newspaper cuttings relating to anti-transportation, 1850–1851, 365/W.

Ireland

National Library of Ireland, Dublin
Convict Register, 1849, MS 3,016
Catholic Clergymen on Convict Ships, 1848–1852, Mayo Papers, MS 11,823
Letter from Elizabeth Fry to John Henry Cropper, 16 September 1835, MS 24,961

United Kingdom

University of Bristol Library, Bristol
Hale, Mathew Blagden, Diary, DM130/1–20
University Library, Cambridge
Backhouse and Walker, Reports, RCMS 2738/3/1–2
Wollaston, Rev. John Ramsden, Diaries, 1841–1856 (Typescript), RCMS 288
School of Oriental and African Studies Library, London
Colonial Missionary Society, Board Minutes, 1836–1839
Colonial Missionary Society, Home Correspondence, Box 1
Library of the Religious Society of Friends, London
Backhouse, James, 'Letters', 1831–1856, MS Vol. 375, 39
Epistles from the Yearly Meeting of Friends
Meetings of Ministers and Elders, 1802–1839
Meeting for Sufferings, 1823–31
The National Archives (UK), London

Admiralty
ADM 101   Surgeons' Journals

Colonial Office
CO 37/116–35   Despatches from Charles Elliot, Bermuda
CO 37/165–66   Despatches from Freeman Murray, Bermuda
CO 37/173   Letters Relating to the Convict Department in
                  Bermuda
CO 201/280   Offices: AA Company, Church Missionary Society,
                  Rev. Mr Ullathorne
CO 201/29   Offices: Rev. J. D. Lang, Scotch Church
CO 201/291   Offices: Australian Agricultural Company, S. P. G.
CO 201/7   Norfolk Island
CO 201/127   Appendix to Commissioner Bigge's Report 1822:
                  Ecclesiastical Establishments, Schools &
                  Charitable Societies
CO 325/28   Governor George Arthur: Memoranda on New South
                  Wales and Tasmania Clergy, 1826–30.
CO 885/2/9   Rev. T. B. Beagly Naylor to Lord Stanley,
                  Confidential Print

CO 885/2/12   T. W. C. Murdoch, 'Transportation', Confidential Print

Home Office
HO 17/30–40   Criminal Petitions, Series I
HO 45/335   Convict Discipline
HO 45/1792   Convicts to New Zealand

Privy Council
PC 1/67–   Unbound Papers: In-letters relating to Convicts and
                   Prisons

Bodleian Library, Oxford
United Society for the Propagation of the Gospel (USPG) Archive
Oriel College Library, Oxford
Richard Whately, Letters and Other Papers, Vol. 4, 1837–1852

B British Parliamentary Papers and Official Publications

Annual Reports

1816–47	Reports of J. H. Capper
1817–43	Report of the Committee of the General Penitentiary at Millbank
1843–50	Reports from the Commissioners of Pentonville Prison
1858–64	Annual Reports on Convict Establishments at Bermuda and Gibraltar
1865–69	Annual Reports on Convict Establishments at Western Australia and Tasmania
1863–68	Annual Report of Convict Establishment at Gibraltar
1869–81	Directors of Convict Prisons: Reports on ... Gibraltar, Western Australia and Tasmania

Select Committees and Royal Commissions

1810–11	*SC on Penitentiary Houses, First Report (Holford Committee)*, BPP 1810–1811 (199, 207) III.567, 691
1812	*SC on Transportation*, BPP 1812 (341) II.573
1819	*SC on Millbank Penitentiary*, BPP 1819 (80) XVII.333
1819	*SC on Gaols and Other Places of Confinement*, BPP 1819 (579) VII.1
1822	*Commissioner Bigge on the State of the Colony of NSW*, BPP 1822 (448) **XX**.539
1823	*Instructions to Bigge*, BPP 1823 (532) XIV.633
1823	*Commissioner Bigge on Judicial Establishments of NSW and VDL*, BPP 1823 (330 X.515
1823	*Commissioner Bigge on Agriculture and Trade [and Ecclesiastical Establishments]*, BPP 1823 (136) X.607

(cont.)

1826–27	*SC on Criminal Commitments and Convictions,* BPP 1826–1827 (534) VI.5
1828	*Report by Macquarie to Bathurst,* BPP 1828 (477) XXI.538
1831	*SC on Secondary Punishments (Evidence),* BPP 1831 (276) VII.519
1831–32	*SC on Secondary Punishments (Report),* BPP 1831–1832 (547) VII.559
1834	*W. Crawford on Penitentiaries in USA,* BPP 1834 (593) XLVI.349
1835	*SC HL on Gaols and Houses of Correction,* BPP 1835 (438) XI.1 (First Report)
1836	*SC Aborigines in British Settlements,* BPP 1836 (538) VII.1
1837	*SC on Aborigines in British Settlements (Aborigines Report),* BPP 1837 (425) VII.1
1837	*Molesworth SC on Transportation (Minutes),* BPP 1837 (518) XIX.1
1837–38	*Molesworth SC on Transportation (Report),* BPP 1837–1838 (669) XXII.1
1843	*Letter on Convict Discipline, by Sir J. Graham, to Committee of Visitors of Parkhurst Prison,* BPP 1843 (171) XLII.447
1847	*Inquiry into the Hulks at Woolwich,* BPP (831) XVIII.1
1847	*HL SC on Execution of the Criminal Laws (Juvenile Offenders and Transportation) First Report (447) Second Report,* BPP 1847 (447 & 534) VII.1,637
1850	*Select Committee on Prison Discipline,* BPP 1850 (632), XLVII.1
1850	*Colonel Jebb on Prisons,* BPP 1850 (1176) XXIX.151
1851	*Colonel Jebb on Convict Prisons,* BPP 1851 (1409 & 1419) XXVIII.1, 213
1854	*RC into Birmingham Borough Prison,* BPP 1854 (1809) XXXI.1
1856	*SC on Transportation, First Report (244), Second Report (296), Third Report (355), Evidence (404),* BPP 1856 (244) XVII.1; BPP 1856 (296) XVII.189; BPP 1856 (355) XVII.397,492; BPP 1856 (404) XVII.561
1861	*SC on Transportation,* BPP 1861 (286) XIII.505
1863	*RC on Penal Servitude (Grey Committee),* BPP 1863 (3190) XX.1, 283
1863	*HL SC on Gaols and Prison Discipline,* BPP 1863 (499) IX.1

Returns and Estimates

1830	*Return of Expense of Convicts in Hulks in England and Bermuda, 1820–1829,* BPP 1830 (600) XXIII.17
1831–32	*Return of the Salary Paid to the Chaplain of Every Prison in England and Wales,* BPP 1831–1832 (622) XXXIII.533
1835	*Gaol Chaplains: Return of Salaries Paid to Chaplains in Gaols, Hours of Attendance, Emoluments from Other Sources,* BPP 1835 (200) XLV.187
1845	*Return of Colonial Bishops and Archdeacons; and of Grants, Endowments and Appropriation for Religious Instruction or Education in Colonies, 1840–1842 (Religious Instruction in Colonies),* BPP 1845 (356) XXXV.171
1852–53	*Return of Numbers of Prisoners of each Religious Denomination in Prisons in England, Scotland and Ireland (Religion in Prison, 1852–1853),* BPP 1852–1853 (908 908–I) LXXXI.317, 333
1852–53	*Return of Grants, Endowments, and Appropriations for Religious Instruction or Education for Bermuda, 1843–52,* BPP 1852–1852 (937) LXV.127
1863–64	*Salaries and Allowances for Religious Instruction to Convicts in Convict Establishments in Colonies, for 1863–1864,* BPP 1863–1864 (285) XXXVII.523

Correspondence and Governor's Despatches

Aborigines

1831   *Correspondence Concerning Military Operations against Aboriginal inhabitants of Van Diemen's Land*, BPP 1831 (259)

1839   *Despatches Relative to the Massacre of Aborigines in 1838*, BPP 1838 (526) XXXIV.391

Bermuda, Gibraltar and the Cape Colony

1849   *Return of Correspondence with Governors of Cape of Good Hope Respecting Transportation of Convicts*, BPP 1849 (217) XLIII.1

1850   *Despatches Relative to Reception of Convicts at Cape of Good Hope*, BPP 1850 (1138) XXXVIII.223

1850   *Despatches Relative to Convict Discipline and Employment of Colonial Convicts in Formation and Improvement of Roads at Cape of Good Hope*, BPP 1850 (104) XXXVIII.387

1860   *Papers Relative to the Convict Establishment at Bermuda*, BPP 1860 (581) XLV.269

1860   *Papers Relating to Convict Establishment at Bermuda*, BPP 1860 (2700) XLV.269

Van Diemen's Land, Maconochie and Eardley Wilmot

1834   *Correspondence on Secondary Punishment (Australia) (Backhouse on Macquarie Harbour)*, BPP 1834 (82) XLVII.121

1837–38   *Report on State of Prison Discipline in Van Diemen's Land (Maconochie's Report)*, BPP 1837–1838 (121) XL.237

1837–38   *Convict Discipline in Van Diemen's Land (Franklin's Despatch)*, BPP 1837–1838 (309) XLII.15

1843   *Correspondence between Secretary of State and Governor of Van Diemen's Land on Convict Discipline*, BPP 1843 (158) XLII.353, 451

1845   *Correspondence between Secretary of State and Governor of Van Diemen's Land on Convict Discipline (Forster's Regulations)*, BPP 1845 (659) XXXVII.329

1846   *Correspondence between Secretary of State and Colony of Van Diemen's Land on Convict Discipline and Relief*, BPP 1846 (36) XXIX.291

1846   *Correspondence between Secretary of State for Colonies and Lieutenant Governor of Van Diemen's Land, on Convict Discipline (Eardley Wilmot, Gladstone; Major Childs; Pentonville Prisoners in VDL, Report of Dr Hampton)*, BPP 1846 (402) XXIX.363

1846   *Convict System (Norfolk Island). (Gipps on Maconochie on Norfolk Island)*, BPP 1846, House of Lords (40 and 94) VII.425, 599.

1847   *Correspondence on Convict Discipline and Transportation (Rev. Beagly Naylor on Norfolk Island) (785); Eardley Wilson to Gladstone on Probation (785); Fitzroy to Gladstone on Renewal of Transportation (800); Eardley Wilmot to Gladstone (811)), BPP 1847 (785) XLVIII.93; BPP 1847 (800 and 811) XLVIII.297, 313*

(*cont.*)

1847–48	*Convict Discipline and Transportation (Grey to Fitzroy, Break up of Norfolk Island; LaTrobe's Report)*, BPP 1847–1848 (941) LII.7
1847	*Correspondence between Secretary of State and Sir E. Wilmot, Relative to Recall of Latter from Government of Van Diemen's Land*, BPP 1847 (262 and 400) XXXVIII.513

Convict Discipline, Secondary Punishments and Transportation, New South Wales, Norfolk Island, Western Australia

1834	*Secondary Punishments (Australia). Further Correspondence (Magistrates on flogging)*, BPP 1834 (614) X.297
1839	*Transportation and the Assignment of Convicts (Gipps on Molesworth SC)*, BPP 1839 (76), XXXIV.551
1849	*Correspondence on Convict Discipline and Transportation (FitzRoy on Break Up Convict Establishments in NSW)*, BPP 1850 (1022 and 1121) XLIII.63
1849	*Letter from E. S. Hall, August 1849, on Transportation and Convict Discipline*, BPP 1850 (40) XLV.397
1850	*Correspondence on Convict Discipline and Transportation (Exiles; Hashemy; Renewal of Transportation; Maori Petition)*, BPP 1850 (1153, 1285) XLV.11, 155
1851	*Correspondence on Convict Discipline and Transportation (Anglican Petition)*, BPP 1851 (1361 and 1418) XLV.1, 265
1852	*Correspondence on Convict Discipline and Transportation. (Denison; Protests on Convict Ships)*, BPP 1852 (1517) XLVI.183
1857	*Correspondence on Convict Discipline and Transportation in Australian Colonies (Western Australia; Despatches from Governor Kennedy; Tasmania Reduction of Salaries; Expense of Maintaining British Convicts)*, BPP 1857 (2197) XIV.543
1865	*Western Australia. Letters from Gentlemen Connected with the Colony of Western Australia to the Secretary of State for the Colonies*, BPP 1865 (247) XXXVII.367
1867–68	*Letter from Howard Association Forwarding Memorial from Convicts at Fremantle, Western Australia Alleging Infliction of Cruel and Illegal Punishments by Governor*, BPP 1867–1868 (482) XLVIII.429

Memorial and Petitions for and against Transportation

1847	*Memorials on Transportation*, BPP 1847 (169 692 741) XXXIX.281, 453, 539
1851	*Petitions on Convict Discipline and Transportation Presented to HM from Australia or Van Diemen's Land since 1838*, BPP 1851 (130, 262 and 280) XLV.437, 471, 527
1863	*Memorials in Favour of or against Transportation to Australia; Resolution Adopted by Conference of Delegates from NSW, Victoria, South Australia and Tasmania at Melbourne*, BPP 1863 (505) XXXVIII.805
1864	*Despatches from Governors of Australian Colonies, with Petitions against Continuance of Transportation*, BPP 1864 (3357) XLI.69
1865	*Correspondence with Governments of Australian Colonies Relating to Discontinuance of Transportation*, BPP 1865 (3424) XXXVII.911

Religion

1837	*Religious Instruction, Australia. Despatches to Australian Colonies, since 1 April 1835, relating to Enlargement of Means of Religious Instruction and Public Worship*, BPP 1837 (112) XLIII.21
1837–38	Correspondence on Religion in Australia, BPP 1837–1838 (75) XL.115
1840	Correspondence on Advancement of Religion in Australia, BPP 1840 (243) XXXIII.239
1850	Correspondence and Papers Relating to Cases in Which Bishops in Australian Colonies Attempted to Exercise Ecclesiastical Jurisdiction Over Clergy, BPP 1850 (175)
1851	Letter from Bishop of Sydney to Governor General of Australian Colonies, in Relation to Rank and Precedence of Bishops Appointed by Pope within H. M. Australian Dominions, BPP 1851 (105) XXXV.65

C Newspapers and Magazines

Magazines: *Dublin Review, Edinburgh Magazine, Fraser's Magazine, London Review, Quarterly Review, Quarterly Theological Review, Westminster Review.*
United Kingdom: *Leeds Times, London Times, Liverpool Mercury, Manchester Guardian, Spectator, The Atlas*
New South Wales: *Australian, Colonist, Sydney Gazette, Sydney Herald* (*Sydney Morning Herald* after 1842), *Sydney Monitor*
Port Philip: *Port Philip Gazette*
Van Diemen's Land: *Colonial Times, Cornwall Chronicle, Hobart Town Advertiser, Hobart Town Courier, Launceston Advertiser, Tasmanian, True Colonist*
The Cape Colony: *Cape Town Mail; South African Commercial Examiner*

D Published Primary Sources

Adderley, Charles Bowyer, *Transportation Not Necessary* (London: LSE Library, 1850).
A Tract on Tickets of Leave (London: Parker, 1857).
A Century of Experiments on Secondary Punishment (London: Parker, 1863).
Alumnus, 'Catholic Church Norfolk Island', *Australasian Chronicle* (12 August 1841), 2.
Anley, Charlotte, *The Prisoners of Australia: A Narrative* (London: Hatchard, 1841).
Anonymous, A member of the Whip Club (ed.), *Lexicon Balatronicum: A Dictionary of Buckish Slang, University Wit and Pickpocket Eloquence Compiled Originally by Captain Grose* (London: Chappel, 1811).
'Secondary Punishments', *Law Magazine*, 7 (1832), 1–43.
An Answer to the Calumnies of the English Press: Being the Testimony of the Lieutenant-Governor, and of the Various Communions of Van Diemen's Land, upon the Moral and Religious Character of the Free Population of That Colony (Launceston: Dowling, 1839).

Benevolence in Punishment, or Transportation Made Reformatory (London: Seeley, 1845).

'The New Convict Establishment in Western Australia', in William Chambers (ed.), *Chambers's Edinburgh Journal* (Edinburgh: Chambers, 1852), vol. 18, pp. 106–108.

Epistles from the Yearly Meeting of Friends, Held in London to the Quarterly and Monthly Meetings in Great Britain, Ireland and Elsewhere, from 1681 to 1857, 2 vols. (London, 1858).

'Convict Establishments in 1860', *The Spectator*, 33 (1860), 521–522.

Cyclopedia of Tasmania: An Historical and Commercial Review (Hobart: Maitland, 1900).

Arthur, George, *Defence of Transportation, in Reply to the Remarks of the Archbishop of Dublin in His Second Letter to Earl Grey* (London: Cowie, 1835).

Arthur, George, and William Grant Broughton, *Observations Upon Secondary Punishments ... to Which Is Added a Letter upon the Same Subject by the Archdeacon of New South Wales* (Hobart Town: Ross, 1833).

Atkins, Thomas, *Reminiscences of Twelve Years' Residence in Tasmania and New South Wales* (Malvern: Advertiser Office, 1869).

Australasian League Executive Board, *Letter of Instructions to the London Delegates of the Several Colonies of Australia* (Sydney: Daniel, 1851).

Australasian League, *The Inauguration of the Australasian League: Held at the Queen's Theatre, Melbourne, on February 1st, 1851* (Melbourne: Goode, 1851).

Backhouse, James, *Extracts from the Letters of James Backhouse, 10 Parts* (London: Harvey, 1837–1841).

A Narrative of a Visit to the Australian Colonies (London: Hamilton, 1843).

A Narrative of a Visit to the Mauritius and South Africa (London: Hamilton, 1844).

Backhouse, Sarah, and James Backhouse, *Memoir of James Backhouse, by His Sister* (York: Sessions, 1870).

Beard, Thomas, and Charles Dickens, Charles, 'A Dialogue Concerning Convicts', *All the Year Round*, 5 (1861), 156–159.

de Beaumont, Gustave, and Alexis de Tocqueville, *On the Penitentiary System in the United States and Its Application in France*, trans. Francis Lieber (Philadelphia: Carey, 1833).

Système Pénitentiaire Aux États-Unis Et De Son Application En France Suivi D'un Appendice Sur Les Colonies Pénales 3rd edn (Paris: Gosselin, 1845).

Beccaria, Cesar Bonesana, *An Essay on Crimes and Punishments ... with a Commentary by Mons. de Voltaire*, trans. Edward D. Ingraham (London: Almon, 1767).

Bell, Andrew, *An Abridged Edition of the Work of the Rev. Andrew Bell* (Edinburgh: Oliver & Boyd, 1833).

Benbow, William, *The Crimes of the Clergy, or the Pillars of Priest-Craft Shaken* (London: Benbow, 1823).

Benson, George, *The Horrors of Transportation Contained in the Life & Sufferings of George Benson* (Bristol: Author, 1843).

Bentham, Jeremy, *Panopticon versus New South Wales: Or, the Panopticon Penitentiary System, and the Penal Colonization System, Compared* (London: Baldwin, 1812).

Bentham, Jeremy, *Writings on Australia, V. Third Letter to Lord Pelham*, ed. T. Causer and P. Schofield, pre-publication version (London: The Bentham Project, 2018).

British and Foreign Bible Society, *An Earnest and Respectful Appeal to the British and Foreign Bible Society by Its South African Auxiliary on Behalf of the Injured Colony of the Cape of Good Hope (with Reference to Convict Transportation)* (Cape Town: Solomon, 1849).

British Ladies' Society for Promoting the Reformation of Female Prisoners, *A Concise View of the Origin and Progress of the British Ladies Society for Promoting the Reformation of Female Prisoners* (London: The Society, 1840).

Broughton, W. G., *A Charge Delivered to the Clergy of Van Diemen's Land at the Primary Visitation Holden in the Church of St David in Hobart Town on Thursday the 15th of April 1830* (Hobart: Ross, 1830).

Browne, George, *The History of the British and Foreign Bible Society from Its Institution in 1804 to the Close of Its Jubilee in 1854*, 2 vols. (London: British and Foreign Bible Society, 1859).

Browne, Rev. W. H., *Jail Manual, or, a Selection of Prayers for the Use of Persons Confined in Jails or Penitentiaries or under Sentence of Hard Labour* (Launceston: Dowling, 1834).

Browning, Colin Arrott, *The Convict Ship* (London: Smith, Elder, 1844).

The Convict Ship and England's Exiles: In Two Parts 3rd edn (London: Hamilton, Adams, 1848).

Broxup, John, *Life of John Broxup Late Convict at Van Diemen's Land* (Leeds: J. Cook, 1850).

Burke, James Lester (ed.), *The Adventures of Martin Cash* (Hobart Town: 'Mercury' Steam Press Office, 1870).

Burton, William Westbrooke, *The State of Religion and Education in New South Wales* (London: Cross, 1840).

Buxton, Charles (ed.), *Memoirs of Sir Thomas Fowell Buxton* (London: Murray, 1848).

Buxton, Thomas Fowell, *An Inquiry, Whether Crime and Misery Are Produced or Prevented, by Our Present System of Prison Discipline* 5th edn (Edinburgh: Constable, 1818).

Callow, Edward, *Five Years' Penal Servitude: By One Who Has Endured It* (London: R. Bentley & Son, 1877).

Carpenter, Mary, *Reformatory Schools for the Children of the Perishing and Dangerous Classes, and for Juvenile Offenders* (London: Gilpin, 1851).

Our Convicts, 2 vols. (London: Longman, 1864).

Carvosso, Benjamin, 'Methodism in Van Diemen's Land', *Wesleyan Methodist Magazine*, 49 (1831), 243–251.

Chalmers, Thomas, *On Political Economy in Connection with the Moral State and Moral Prospects of Society* 2nd edn (Glasgow: Collins, 1832).

Chaplain, Rev. W. C. of the New Bayley Prison Manchester, *The Prisoner's Select Manual of Devout Exercises: Including Forms of Visitation and Select Psalms* (Manchester: Swindells, 1791).

Clark, Robert Lindsey (ed.), *Travels of Robert and Sarah Lindsey*. (London: Harris, 1886).

Clarke, Marcus Andrew Hislop, *For the Term of His Natural Life* (London: Bentley, 1874).

Clarkson, Thomas, *The History of the Rise, Progress and Accomplishment of the Abolition of the African Slave-Trade by the British Parliament*, 2 vols. (London: Longman, 1808).

Clay, John, *Twenty-Five Sermons Preached to the Inmates of a Gaol* (London: Rivington, 1827).

Clay, W. L., *Our Convict Systems* (London: Macmillan, 1862).

Clay, Walter Lowe, *The Prison Chaplain: A Memoir of the Rev. John Clay ... Late Chaplain of the Preston Gaol, with Selections from His Reports and Correspondence, and a Sketch of Prison Discipline in England* (Cambridge: Macmillan, 1861).

Colonial Committee of Correspondence, *Report of the Statistics of Western Australia in 1840* (Perth: Lochee, 1841).

Conybeare, W. J., 'Church Parties, Past and Present', *Edinburgh Review*, 98 (1855), 273–342.

'Church Parties, Ed. Arthur Burns', in Stephen Taylor (ed.), *From Cranmer to Davidson: A Church of England Miscellany* (Woodbridge: Boydell, 1999), pp. 213–386.

Cook, Thomas, *The Exile's Lamentations* (North Sydney: Library of Australian History, 1978).

Cowper, William Macquarie, *The Autobiography and Reminiscences of William Macquarie Cowper, Dean of Sydney* (Sydney: Angus & Robertson, 1902).

Cunningham, Peter Miller, *Two Years in New South Wales: Comprising Sketches of the Actual State of Society in That Colony*, 2 vols. (London: Henry Colburn, 1827).

Curr, Edward M., *The Australian Race: Its Origin, Languages, Customs, Place of Landing in Australia, and the Routes by which It Spread Itself over that Continent*, 4 vols. (Melbourne: Ferres, 1886).

Davenport-Hill, Rosamond, and Florence Davenport Hill, *A Memoir of Matthew Davenport Hill, the Recorder of Birmingham* (London: Macmillan, 1878).

Denison, William, *Varieties of Vice-Regal Life*, 2 vols. (London: Longmans, 1870).

Du Cane, Edmund F., *The Punishment and Prevention of Crime* (London: Macmillan, 1885).

Easy, Henry, *Horrors of Transportation: Or the Danger of Keeping Bad Company, or Being Careless in the Choice of Companions* (Bristol: Wright, 1847).

Ferguson, Adam, *Principles of Moral and Political Science*, 2 vols. (Edinburgh: Strachan, 1792).

An Essay on the History of Civil Society 8th edn (Philadelphia: Finsley, 1819).

Fitchett, William Henry, *The New World of the South*, 2 vols. (London: Smith, Elder, 1913.

Fitzpatrick, William John, *Memoirs of Richard Whately, Archbishop of Dublin: With a Glance at His Contemporaries & Times*, 2 vols. (London: Bentley, 1864).

Forster, Thomas Hay, *Account of a Voyage in a Convict Ship with Notes of the First Itinerating Missionary in Tasmania* (London: SPCK, 1850).

Fox, Lady Mary, and Richard Whately (eds.), *Account of an Expedition to the Interior of New Holland* (London: Bentley, 1837).

Frost, John, *The Horrors of Convict Life, Two Lectures, 31 August 1856* (London: Holyoake, 1856).

Fry, Elizabeth Gurney, *Observations on the Visiting, Superintendence and Government of Female Prisoners* (London: Arch, 1827).

'Elizabeth Fry and Convict Ships [Letter from Elizabeth Fry to James Backhouse, 23 June 1832]', *The Journal of the Friends Historical Society*, 25 (1928), 22–24.

Fulton, Henry, *A Letter to the Rev. W. B. Ullathorne in Answer to a Few Words to the Rev. Henry Fulton* (Sydney: Stephens & Stokes, 1833).

Gibson, Chris B., *Irish Convict Reform: The Intermediate Prisons, a Mistake* (Dublin: McGlashan & Gill, 1863).

Glancey, Michael F. (ed.), *Characteristics from the Writings of Archbishop Ullathorne* (London: Burns & Oates, 1889).

Gouger, Robert (ed.), *A Letter from Sydney, the Principal Town of Australasia [by Edward Gibbon Wakefield]* (London: Cross, 1829).

Grey, Henry George [Earl Grey], 'Secondary Punishments – Transportation', *Edinburgh Review*, 58 (1834), 336–362.

Speeches . . . On the Second and Third Readings of a Bill for the Better Government of Convict Prisons (London: Woodfall, 1850).

The Colonial Policy of Lord John Russell's Administration 2 vols. 2nd edn (London: Bentley, 1853).

Griffiths, Arthur, *Memorials of Millbank and Chapters in Prison History* (London: Chapman & Hall, 1884).

Gurney, Joseph John, *Notes on a Visit Made to Some of the Prisons in Scotland and the North of England in Company with Elizabeth Fry* (London: n.p., 1819).

Hale, Mathew B., *The Transportation Question, or Why Western Australia Should Be Made a Reformatory Colony, Instead of a Penal Settlement* (Cambridge: Macmillan, 1857).

The Aborigines of Australia: Being an Account of the Institution for Their Education at Poonindie, South Australia (London: Society for Promoting Christian Knowledge, 1889).

Harris, Alexander, *Settlers and Convicts* (London: Cox, 1847).

Harris, Edward Cecil, *Bermuda Forts 1612–1957* (Bermuda: Bermuda Maritime Museum Press, 2001).

Hodges, John George, *Report of the Trial of John Mitchel for Felony* (Dublin: Thom, 1848)

Holford, George, *Thoughts on the Criminal Prisons of This Country* (London: Rivingtons, 1821).

The Convict's Complaint in 1815, and the Thanks of the Convict in 1825 (London: Rivingtons, 1825).

Howard, John, *The State of the Prisons in England and Wales, with Preliminary Observations, and an Account of Some Foreign Prisons* (Warrington: William Eyres, 1777).

An Account of the Principal Lazarettos in Europe (Warrington: William Eyres, 1789).

Howitt, William, *Colonization and Christianity: A Popular History of the Treatment of the Natives by the Europeans in All Their Colonies* (London: Longman, 1838).

Land, Labour, and Gold, 2 vols. 2nd edn (London: Longman, 1858).

Humanitas, *Secondary Punishments Discussed . . . By and Emigrant of 1821* (London: Cochrane, 1835).

Innes, Frederick Maitland, 'The Convict System of Van Diemen's Land', *Monthly Chronicle*, 5:27 (1840), 431–449.

Secondary Punishments. The Merits of a Home and of a Colonial Process, of a Social and of a Separate System, or Convict Management Discussed (London: John Ollivier, 1841).

Ison, John L., *Appeal to the Secretary of State Relative to the Dismissal of the Rev. John L. Ison, from His Chaplaincy at Norfolk Island* (Oatlands: Private, 1850).

James, John Angell, *The Anxious Inquirer after Salvation: Directed and Encouraged* (Companions for a Quiet Hour; London: Religious Tract Society, 1835).

James, Thomas Horton, *Six Months in South Australia with Some Account of Port Philip and Portland* (London: Cross, 1838).

Johnson, Richard, *An Address to the Inhabitants of the Colonies Established in New South Wales and Norfolk Island* (London: The Author, 1792).

Kelsh, Thomas, *'Personal Recollections' of the Right Reverend Robert William Willson, D. D. (First Bishop of Hobart Town)* (Hobart: Davies, 1882).

King, Charles Adolphus, *A Warning Voice from a Penitent Convict* (London: Birt's Wholesale Song & Book Warehouse, 1840).

Kingsmill, Joseph, *Chapters on Prisons and Prisoners* 2nd edn (London: Longman, 1852).

Knopwood, Robert, *The Diary of the Reverend Robert Knopwood, 1803–1838*, edited by Mary Nicholls (Hobart: Tasmanian Historical Research Association, 1977).

Lancaster, Joseph, *The British System of Education* (London: Longman, 1810).

Lang, John Dunmore, *Transportation and Colonization* (London: Valpy, 1837).

Brief Sketch of My Parliamentary Life and Times (Sydney: Sherriff, 1870).

Laurie, P., *Prison Discipline and Secondary Punishments* (London: Whittaker, 1837).

Le Fanu, Emma L., *Life of the Reverend Charles Edward Herbert Orpen* (Dublin: Westerton, 1860).

Loveless, James, et al., *A Narrative of the Sufferings of J. Loveless, J. Brine, and T. & J. Standfield, Four of the Dorchester Labourers: Displaying the Horrors of Transportation*(London: n.p., 1838).

Macarthur, James, *New South-Wales, Its Present State and Future Prospects* (London: n.p., 1837).

Macaulay, Thomas Babington (1849), *The History of England from the Accession of James II*, vol. 1 (London: Longman).

Maconochie, Alexander, *Considerations on the Propriety of Establishing a Colony in One of the Sandwich Islands* (London: Richardson, 1816).

A Summary View of the Statistics and Existing Commerce of the Principal Shores of the Pacific Ocean (London: Richardson, 1818).

Australiana. Thoughts on Convict Management (London: Parker, 1839).

Supplement to Thoughts on Convict Management (Hobart Town: MacDougall, 1839).

'Criminal Statistics and Movement of the Bond Population of Norfolk Island, to December, 1843', *Journal of the Statistical Society*, 8:1 (1845), 1–49.

The Mark System of Prison Discipline (London: W. H. Compton, 1847).

Norfolk Island (London: Hatchard, 1847).

Comparison between Mr Bentham's Views on Punishment and Those Advocated in Connexion with the Mark System (Marylebone: Compton, 1847).

Norfolk Island (London: John Ollivier, 1848)

On Colonel Arthur's General Character and Government [1837–1838] (Adelaide: Sullivan's Cover, 1989).

Maginn, William, 'Archbishop Whately's Secondary Punishments Dissected', *Fraser's Magazine*, 6 (1832), 566–575.

Marriott, Fitzherbert Adams, *Is a Penal Colony Reconcileable with God's Constitution of Human Society and the Laws of Christ's Kingdom?* (Hobart Town: s. n., 1847).

Marsden, Samuel, *The Letters and Journals of Samuel Marsden, 1765–1838*, edited by J. R. Elder (Dunedin: Otago University Council, 1932).

Maurice, Frederick Denison, *Social Morality* 2nd edn (London: Macmillan, 1872).

Mayhew, Henry, and John Binny, *The Criminal Prisons of London and Scenes of Prison Life* (New York: Kelley, 1862).

Measor, C. P., *The Convict Service* (London: Hardwicke, 1861).

Melville, Henry Saxelby, *The History of the Island of Van Diemen's Land, 1824–1835* (London: Smith & Elder, 1835).

The Present State of Australia ... With Practical Hints on Emigration, Prison Discipline and Suggestions for Obviating the Difficulties Attending the Transportation of Convicts (London: Willis, 1851).

Meredith, Mrs Charles, *My Home in Tasmania* (London: John Murray, 1852).

Miller, Linus W., *Notes of an Exile to Van Dieman's Land* (Fredonia, NY: McKinstry, 1846).

Mitchel, John, *Jail Journal, Or Five Years in British Prisons* (New York: The "Citizen", 1854).

The Last Conquest of Ireland (Perhaps) (Glasgow: Cameron & Ferguson, 1876).

Molesworth, William, *Report from the Select Committee of the House of Commons on Transportation: Together with a Letter from the Archbishop of Dublin on the Same Subject* (London: Hooper, 1838).

Moore, Thomas, *The Poetical Works of Thomas Moore* (London: Simpkin, 1867).

Morris, G. S., *Convicts and Colonies: Thoughts on Transportation & Colonization, with References to the Islands and Mainland of Northern Australia* (London: Hope, 1853).

Transportation, Considered from Home and Colonial Points of View (London: Dalton, 1856).

Mudie, James, *The Felonry of New South Wales: Being a Faithful Picture of the Real Romance of Life in Botany Bay* (London: Whaley, 1837).

Nicholls, Mary (ed.), *Traveller under Concern: The Quaker Journals of Frederick Mackie on His Tour of the Australasian Colonies, 1852–1855* (Hobart: University of Tasmania, 1973).

New Zealand Association, *The British Colonization of New Zealand* (London: Parker, 1837)

Nihill, Daniel, *Prison Discipline in Its Relation to Society and Individuals: As Deterring from Crime, and as Conducive to Personal Reformation* (London: Hatchard, 1839).

Nixon, Norah (ed.), *The Pioneer Bishop in Van Diemen's Land, 1843–1863: Letters and Memories of Francis Russell Nixon* (Hobart: s.n., 1853).

Page, Thomas, *The Horrors of Transportation: Containing the Life, and Sufferings of Thomas Page* ([London]: n.p., 1846).

Paley, William, *The Principles of Moral and Political Philosophy* (London: Faulder, 1785).

Paley, William, and Richard Whately, *A View of the Evidences of Christianity: In Three Parts* (London: Parker, 1859).

Parry, Edward, *Memoirs of Rear-Admiral Sir W. Edward Parry, Kt* 3rd edn (London: Longman, 1857).

Platt, Joseph, *The Horrors of Transportation as Related by Joseph Platt* (Birmingham: Pratt, 1850).

Pratt, Josiah, and John Henry Pratt, *Memoir of the Rev. Josiah Pratt* (London: Seeleys, 1849).

Prison Discipline Society, *Fourth Report* (London: Bensley, 1822).

Eighth Report (London: Bensley, 1832).

Ritchie, Daniel (ed.), *The Voice of Our Exiles, or, Stray Leaves from a Convict Ship* (Edinburgh: John Menzies, 1854).

Rogers, Thomas, *Review of Dr. Hampton's First Report on Norfolk Island* (Hobart: Henry Dowling, 1849).

Correspondence Relating to the Dismissal of the Rev. T. Rogers from His Chaplaincy at Norfolk Island (Launceston: Dowling, 1849).

Ross, William, *The Fell Tyrant, or, the Suffering Convict R_S* (London: Ward, 1836).

Russell, John Russell Earl, *Essays on the Rise and Progress of the Christian Religion in the West of Europe* new edn (London: Longmans, Green, 1873).

Simeon, Charles, *A Collection of Psalms and Hymns from Various Authors, Chiefly Designed for the Use of Public Worship* (Cambridge: Page, 1835).

Memoirs of the Life of the Rev. Charles Simeon, edited by William Carus (London: Hatchard, 1847).

Society for Diffusing Information on the Subject of Capital Punishment and Prison discipline, *The Origin and Object of the Society for the Diffusion of Knowledge Upon the Punishment of Death* (London: McCreery, 1812).

An Account of the Maison de Force at Ghent from the Philanthropist, May 1817 (London: Taylor, 1817).

Stanley, Arthur Penrhyn (ed.), *The Life and Correspondence of Thomas Arnold* 6th edn (London: Fellowes, 1846).

Stephen, James, 'The Clapham Sect', *Edinburgh Review*, 80:161 (1844), 204–307.

Strickland, E., *The Australian Pastor: A Record of the Remarkable Changes in Mind and Outward State of Henry Elliott* (London: Wertheim, 1862).

Therry, Roger, and an unpaid magistrate, *Observations on the "Hole and Corner Petition" in a Letter to the Right Honorable Edward G. Stanley* (Sydney: n.p., 1834).

Timpson, Thomas, *Memoirs of Mrs. Elizabeth Fry* (London: Aylott, 1847).

Torrens, Robert, *Transportation Considered as a Punishment and as a Mode of Founding Colonies* (London: Ridgway, 1863)

Trollope, Anthony, *The West Indies and the Spanish Main* 4th edn (London: Chapma, 1859).

Ullathorne, W., *On the Management of Criminals: A Paper Read before the Accademica of the Catholic Religion* (London: Richardson, 1866).

Ullathorne, William Bernard, *The Catholic Mission in Australasia* (Liverpool: Rockliff, 1837).

The Horrors of Transportation Briefly Unfolded (Dublin: Coyne, 1838).

A Reply to Judge Burton, of the Supreme Court of New South Wales, on 'The State of Religion' in the Colony (Sydney: Duncan, 1840).

On the Management of Criminals (London: Richardson, 1866).

The Autobiography of Archbishop Ullathorne: With Selections from His Letters, 2 vols. (London: Burns & Oates, 1891–1892).

From Cabin-Boy to Archbishop: The Autobiography of Archbishop Ullathorne (London: Burns & Oates, 1941).

Wakefield, Edward Gibbon, *Facts Relating to the Punishment of Death in the Metropolis* (London: Ridgway, 1831)

Wesley, Charles, *Hymns and Sacred Poems* 2nd edn (Bristol: Farley, 1743).

Wesley, John, *The Works of the Rev. John Wesley*, vol. 1, 4th edn (London: Mason, 1837).

West, John, *The History of Tasmania*, 2 vols. (Launceston: Dowling, 1852).

Whately, E. Jane, *Life and Correspondence of Richard Whately, D. D. Late Archbishop of Dublin*, 2 vols. (London: Longmans, 1866).

Whately, Richard, 'Transportation', *London Review*, 1:1 (1829), 112–139.

Thoughts on Secondary Punishments in a Letter to Earl Grey ... To Which Are Appended, Two Articles on Transportation to New South Wales, and on Secondary Punishments; and Some Observations on Colonization (London: Fellowes, 1832).

Remarks on Transportation and on a Recent Defence of the System in a Second Letter to Earl Grey (London: Fellowes, 1834).

Substance of a Speech on Transportation Delivered in the House of Lords on the 19th of May, 1840 (London: Fellowes, 1840).

Miscellaneous Lectures and Reviews (London: Parker, 1861).

Wheeler, Daniel, and Daniel Wheeler the Younger, *A Memoir of Daniel Wheeler, with an Account of His Gospel Labours in the Islands of the Pacific* (Philadelphia: Association of Friends for the Diffusion of Religious and Useful Knowledge, 1859).

Wilberforce, William, *An Appeal to the Religion, Justice, and Humanity of the Inhabitants of the British Empire in Behalf of the Negro Slaves in the West Indies* (London: Hatchard, 1823).

Wilkes, G. A., and A. G. Mitchell (eds.), *Experiences of a Convict Transported for Twenty-One Years by J. A. Mortlock* (Sydney: Sydney University Press, 1965).

Willoughby, Howard, *Transportation: The British Convict in Western Australia: A Visit to the Swan River Settlements* (London: Harrison, 1865)

Wilton, C., and N., Pleydell, *Twelve Plain Discourses Addressed to the Prisoners of the Crown in the Colony of New South Wales* (Sydney: Stephens, 1834).

Yonge, Duke, *A Manual of Instruction and Devotion, for the Use of Prisoners* 4th edn (London: Society for Promoting Christian Knowledge, 1827).

E Published Secondary Sources

Adamson, Christopher, 'Evangelical Quakerism and the Early American Penitentiary Revisited: The Contributions of Thomas Eddy, Roberts Vaux, John Griscom, Stephen Grellet, Elisha Bates, and Isaac Hopper', *Quaker History*, 90:2 (2001), 35–58.

Addams, Chris, and Michael Davis, *Convict Establishment, Bermuda* (Bermuda: Dromedary Foundation Publications, 1998).

Adkins, Keith, 'Books, Libraries and Reading in Colonial Tasmania', *Papers and Proceedings (Tasmanian Historical Research Association)*, 53:3 (2006), 158–169.

Adkins, Keith, 'Convict Probation Station Libraries in Colonial Tasmania', *Script and Print* 34.2 (2010), 87–92.

Akenson, Donald H., *A Protestant in Purgatory: Richard Whately, Archbishop of Dublin* (Hamden, CT: Archon, 1981).

Discovering the End of Time: Irish Evangelicals in the Age of Daniel O'Connell (Montreal: McGIll-Queens University Press, 2016).

Alexander, Alison, *Tasmania's Convicts: How Felons Built a Free Society* (Sydney: Allen & Unwin, 2010).

Allars, Kenneth G., 'William Westbrooke Burton', *Journal of the Royal Australian Historical Society*, 37:5 (1951), 257–294.

Allen, Matthew, 'The Myth of the Flogging Parson: Samuel Marsden and Severity of Punishment in the Age of Reform', *Australian Historical Studies*, 48:4 (2017), 486–501.

Amos, Keith, *The Fenians in Australia, 1865–1880* (Sydney: University of New South Wales Press, 1988).

Anderson, Atholl, and Peter White, 'Prehistoric Settlement on Norfolk Island and Its Oceanic Context', *Records of the Australian Museum, Supplement,* 27 (2001), 135–141.

Anderson, Clare, 'Transnational Histories of Penal Transportation: Punishment, Labour and Governance in the British Imperial World, 1788–1939', *Australian Historical Studies*, 47:3 (2016), 381–397.

(ed.), *A Global History of Convicts and Penal Colonies* (London: Bloomsbury, 2018).

Anderson, Joseph Jocelyn, *Recollections of a Peninsular Veteran* (London: E. Arnold, 1913).

Andersson, Stefan, 'Religion in the Russell Family', *Russell: The Journal of Bertrand Russell Studies*, 13:2 (1993), 113–224.

Atkins, Gareth, 'Anglican Evangelicalism', in Jeremy Gregory, *The Oxford History of Anglicanism, Vol. 2* (Oxford: Oxford University Press, 2017), pp. 452–473.

Atkinson, Alan, *The Europeans in Australia: A History, Vol. 2, Democracy* 2nd edn (Sydney: University of New South Wales Press, 2016).

Badcock, Sarah, and Judith Pallot, 'Russia and the Soviet Union from the Nineteenth to the Twenty-First Century', in Clare Anderson (ed.), *A Global History of Convicts and Penal Colonies* (Cambridge: Cambridge University Press, 2018), pp. 271–306.

Bailey, Brian J., *Hellholes: An Account of History's Most Notorious Prisons* (London: Orion, 1995).

Ballantyne, Tony, 'Religion, Difference, and the Limits of British Imperial History', *Victorian Studies*, 47:3 (2005), 427–455.

Entanglements of Empire: Missionaries, Māori, and the Question of the Body (Durham, NC: Duke University Press, 2014).

Barnett, Michael N., *Empire of Humanity: A History of Humanitarianism* (Ithaca, NY: Cornell University Press, 2010).

Barr, Colin, and Rose Luminiello, '"The Leader of the Virgin Choirs of Erin": St Brigid's Missionary College, 1883–1914', in Timothy McMahon, Michael DeNie and Paul Townsend (eds.), *Ireland in an Imperial World* (Houndmills London: Palgrave Macmillan, 2017), pp. 155–178.

Barrett, John, *That Better Country: The Religious Aspect of Life in Eastern Australia 1835–1850* (Melbourne: Melbourne University Press, 1966).

Barry, J. V., 'Pioneers in Criminology XII – Alexander Maconochie (1787–1860)', *Journal of Criminal Law and Criminology*, 47:2 (1956), 145–161.

Alexander Maconochie of Norfolk Island: A Study of a Pioneer in Penal Reform (Melbourne: Oxford University Press, 1958).

Bateson, Charles, *The Convict Ships, 1787–1868* 2nd edn (Glasgow: Brown, Son & Ferguson, 1969).

Battye, J. S., *Western Australia: A History from Its Discovery to the Inauguration of the Commonwealth* (Oxford: Clarendon Press, 1924).

Beale, Paul (ed.), *Eric Partridge. Slang and Unconventional English* 8th edn (London: Routledge, 1984).

Bebbington, David W., *Evangelicalism in Modern Britain: A History from the 1730s to the 1980s* (London: Unwin Hyman, 1989).

Benton, Lauren A., and Lisa Ford, *Rage for Order: The British Empire and the Origins of International Law, 1800–1850* (Cambridge, MA: Harvard University Press, 2016).

Bergantz, Alexis, '"The Scum of France": Australian Anxieties towards French Convicts in the Nineteenth Century', *Australian Historical Studies* 49.2 (2018), 150–166.

Bethell, Ben, 'An Exception Too Far: "Gentleman" Convicts and the 1878–9 Penal Servitude Acts Commission', *Prison Service Journal*, 232:39 (2017), 40–45.

Biagini, Eugenio F., *Liberty, Retrenchment and Reform: Popular Liberalism in the Age of Gladstone, 1860–1880* (Cambridge: Cambridge University Press, 1992).

Birchley, Delia, *John McEncroe: Colonial Democrat* (Melbourne: Collins Dove, 1986).

Blackton, C. S., 'New Zealand and the Australian Anti-Transportation Movement', *Historical Studies: Australia and New Zealand*, 1 (1940), 116–122.

Blackton, Charles Stuart, 'The Australasian League 1851–1854', *Pacific Historical Review*, 8:4 (1939), 385–400.

Blain, Michael, Leonie Cable and K. J. Cable (eds.), *Cable Clerical Index* (Project Canterbury, c. 2011, http:/anglicanhistory.org).

Blakely, Curt R., *Prisons, Penology and Penal Reform: An Introduction to Institutional Specialization* (New York: Peter Lang, 2007).

Bolton, Geoffrey, 'The Fenians Are Coming, the Fenians Are Coming', in Robert Reece (ed.), *The Irish in Western Australia* (Nedlands: University of Western Australia Press, 1981), 284–303.

Bonk, Andrew, 'Losing Faith in the Civilizing Mission: The Premature Decline of Humanitarian Liberalism at the Cape, 1840–60', in M. Daunton and R. Halpern (eds.), *Empire and Others* (London: UCL Press, 1999), pp. 364–383.

Bosworth, Michal, *Convict Fremantle: A Place of Promise and Punishment* (Crawley: University of Western Australia Press, 2004).

Bourdieu, Pierre, 'The Forms of Capital', in J. G. Richardson (ed.), *Handbook for Theory and Research for the Sociology of Education* (Westport, CT: Greenwood, 1985), pp. 241–258.

Boyce, James, *Van Diemen's Land* (Melbourne: Black Inc, 2008).

Bradley, Ian, *The Call to Seriousness: The Evangelical Impact on the Victorians* (London: Jonathan Cape, 1976).

Braithwaite, John, 'Crime in a Convict Republic', *Modern Law Review*, 64:1 (2001), 11–50.

Brand, Ian, *Penal Peninsula: Port Arthur and Its Outstations, 1827–1898* (West Moonah: Jason Publications, 1978).

Macquarie Harbour Penal Settlements 1822–1833 and 1846–1847 (West Moonah: Jason Publications, 1984).

The Convict Probation System: Van Diemen's Land 1839–1854, edited by M. N. Sprod (Hobart: Blubber Head Press, 1990).

Port Arthur 1830–1877 (Launceston: Regal, 1996)

Brennan, Russell, and Jonathan Richards, '"The Scum of French Criminals and Convicts": Australia and New Caledonia Escapees', *History Compass*, 12:7 (2014), 559–566.

Brent, Richard (1987), *Liberal Anglican Politics: Whiggery, Religion and Reform, 1830–1841* (Oxford: Clarendon, 1987).

Brown, Alyson, '"A "Receptacle of Our Worst Convicts": Bermuda, the Chatham Prison Riots and the Transportation of Violence', *Journal of Caribbean History*, 37:2 (2003), 233–255.

'Challenging Discipline and Control: A Comparative Analysis of Prison Riots at Chatham (1861) and Dartmoor (1932)', in Helen Johnston (ed.), *Punishment and Control in Historical Perspective* (Houndmills: Palgrave Macmillan, 2008).

Brown, Christopher Leslie, *Moral Capital: Foundations of British Abolitionism* (Chapel Hill: University of North Carolina Press, 2006).

Brown, Ford K., *Fathers of the Victorians* (Cambridge: Cambridge University Press, 1961).

Brownrigg, Jeff, 'The Legend of Frank the Poet: Convict Heritage Recovered or Created?', *Journal of Australian Colonial History*, 18 (2016), 1–22.

Burns, Arthur, 'The Authority of the Church', in Peter Mandler (ed.), *Liberty and Authority in Victorian Britain* (Oxford: Oxford University Press, 2006), pp. 179–200.

Burroughs, Peter, 'Lord Howick and Colonial Church Establishment', *Journal of Ecclesiastical History*, 25:4 (1974), 381–405.

Butler, Cuthbert, *The Life and Times of Bishop Ullathorne, 1806–1889* (London: Burns, Oates, and Washbourne, 1926).

Byrnes, Dan, '"Emptying the Hulks": Duncan Campbell and the First Three Fleets to Australia', *Push from the Bush*, 24 (1987), 2–23.

Carey, Hilary M., 'Subordination, Invisibility and Chosen Work: Missionary Nuns and Australian Aborigines, c.1900–1949', *Australian Feminist Studies*, 13:28 (1998), 251–267.

God's Empire: Religion and Colonialism in the British World, c.1801–1908 (Cambridge: Cambridge University Press, 2011).

'Clerics and the Beginning of the Anti-Transportation Debate', *Journal of Australian Colonial History*, 14 (2012), 241–249.

'"Reforming the Guilty": Legacies of Sectarianism and the Politics of the Convict Past in Australia', in Timothy Stanley (ed.), Religion after Secularization in Australia (Houndmills: Palgrave Macmillan, 2015), pp. 33–48.

Carradice, Phil, *Nautical Training Ships: An Illustrated History* (Stroud: Amberley, 2009).

Chalmers, Thomas, *On Political Economy in Connection with the Moral State and Moral Prospects of Society* 2nd edn (Glasgow: Collins, 1832).

Champ, Judith F., *William Bernard Ullathorne: A Different Kind of Monk* (Leominster: Gracewing, 2006).

Christopher, Emma, '"The Slave Trade Is Merciful Compared to [This]": Slave Traders, Convict Transportation and the Abolitionists', in Emma Christopher, Cassandra Pybus and Marcus Rediker (eds.), *Many Middle Passages. Forced Migration and the Making of the Modern World* (Berkeley: University of California Press, 2007), pp. 109–128.

Claeys, Gregory, *Imperial Sceptics: British Critics of Empire 1850–1920* (Cambridge: Cambridge University Press, 2010).

Clark, Anna, *The Struggle for the Breeches: Gender and the Making of the British Working Class* (London: Rivers Oram Press, 1995).

Clark, C. M. H., *A History of Australia II. New South Wales and Van Diemen's Land, 1822–1838* (Melbourne: Melbourne University Press, 1968).

Clark, J. C. D., *English Society, 1660–1832: Religion, Ideology and Politics during the Ancien Régime* 2nd edn (Cambridge: Cambridge University Press, 2000).

'Church, Parties and Politics', in Jeremy Gregory (ed.), *The Oxford History of Anglicansim, Volume II: Establishment and Empire, 1662–1829* (Oxford: Oxford University Press, 2017), pp. 289–313.

Clay, John, *Maconochie's Experiment* (London: John Murray, 2001).

Clout, Hugh, 'Alexander Maconochie: Britain's First Professor of Geography', *Bloomsbury Project* (University College London, ucl.ac.uk/bloomsbury-project, 2009)

Clune, Frank, *The Norfolk Island Story* (Sydney: Angus and Robertson, 1967).

Coffey, John, *Exodus and Liberation: Deliverance Politics from John Calvin to Martin Luther King Jr* (Oxford: Oxford University Press, 2013).

Collingwood, P. J., 'Prison Visitation in the Methodist Revival', *London Quarterly & Holborn Review*, 180 (1955), 285–292.

Collini, Stefan, *Public Moralists: Political Thought and Intellectual Life in Britain 1850–1930* (Oxford: Clarendon, 1991).

Colwell, James, *The Illustrated History of Methodism: Australia, 1812–55. New South Wales and Polynesia, 1856–1902* (Sydney: W. Brooks, 1904).

Conley, Carolyn A., *The Unwritten Law: Criminal Justice in Victorian Kent* (Oxford: Oxford University Press, 1991).

Conlon, Anne, '"Mine Is a Sad yet True Story": Convict Narratives 1818–1850', *Royal Australian Historical Society Journal*, 55 (1969), 43–82.

Contantine, Stephen, *Community and Identity: The Making of Modern Gibraltar since 1704* (Manchester: Manchester University Press, 2009).

Cruickshank, Joanna, '"Appear as Crucified for Me": Sight, Suffering, and Spiritual Transformation in the Hymns of Charles Wesley', *Journal of Religious History*, 30:3 (2006), 311–330.

Cullen, J. H., 'Bishop Willson', *Australasian Catholic Record*, 29:1–3 (1952), 20–27, 117–124, 205–214.

'Bishop Willson and Norfolk Island', *Tasmanian Historical Research Association Papers and Proceedings*, 1:2 (1952), 4–10.

Cullen, John, 'Norfolk Island: Its Catholic Story', *Advocate (Melbourne)*, 13 September 1928, p. 9.

Currie, Robert, Alan D. Gilbert, and Lee Horsley, *Churches and Churchgoers: Patterns of Church Growth in the British Isles since 1700* (Oxford: Clarendon Press, 1977).

Daly, R. A., 'Archdeacon McEncroe on Norfolk Island, 1838–42', *Australasian Catholic Record*, 36:4 (1959), 285–305.

Dandelion, Pink, *An Introduction to Quakerism* (Cambridge: Cambridge University Press, 2007).

The Quakers: A Very Short Introduction (Oxford: Oxford University Press, 2008).

Davies, Jennifer, 'The London Garotting Panic of 1862: A Moral Panic and the Creation of a Criminal Class in Mid-Victorian England', in V. A. C. Gatrell, B. Lenman and G. Parker (eds.), *Crime and the Law: A Social History of Crime in Western Europe since 1500* (London: Europa, 1980), pp. 190–213,

De Beaumont, Gustave, and Alexis de Tocqueville, *Système Pénitentaire Aux États-Unis Et De Son Application En France Suivi D'un Appendice Sur Les Colonies Pénales* (Paris: Gosselin, 1833).

On the Penitentiary System in the United States and Its Application in France, trans. Francis Lieber (Philadelphia: Carey, 1833).

Devereaux, Simon, 'The Making of the Penitentiary Act, 1775–1779', *The Historical Journal*, 42:2 (1999), 404–433.

De Vito, Christian G., and Alex Lichtenstein, 'Writing a Global History of Convict Labour', *International Review of Social History*, 58:2 (2013), 285–325.

(eds.), *Global Convict Labour* (Leiden: Brill, 2015).

Dow, S., A., and A. Hutton, 'Thomas Chalmers and the Economics and Religion Debate', in D. Hum (ed.), *Faith, Reason and Economics: Essays in Honour of Anthony Waterman* (Winnipeg: St John's College Press, 2003), pp. 47–58.

Dowd, Christopher, *Rome in Australia: The Papacy and Conflict in the Australian Catholic Missions, 1834–1884*, 2 vols. (Leiden: Brill, 2008).

Draper, Tony, 'An Introduction to Jeremy Bentham's Theory of Punishment', *Journal of Bentham Studies*, 5:1 (2002), 1–17.

Drenth, Annemieke van, and Francisca de Haan, *The Rise of Caring Power: Elizabeth Fry and Josephine Butler in Britain and the Netherlands* (Amsterdam: Amsterdam University Press, 1999).

Edmonds, Penelope, 'Travelling "under Concern": Quakers James Backhouse and George Washington Walker Tour the Antipodean Colonies, 1832–41', *Journal of Imperial and Commonwealth History*, 40:5 (2012), 769–788.

Elbourne, Elizabeth, 'The Foundation of the Church Missionary Society: The Anglican Missionary Impulse', in John Walsh, Colin Haydon and Stephen Taylor (eds.), *The Church of England c.1689–c.1833: From Toleration to Tractarianism* (Cambridge: Cambridge University Press, 1993), pp. 247–264.

'Early Khoisan Uses of Mission Christianity', in Henry Bredekamp and Robert Ross (eds.), *Missions and Christianity in South African History* (Johannesburg: Witwatersrand University Press, 1993), pp. 65–96.

Blood Ground: Colonialism, Missions and the Contest for Christianity in the Cape Colony and Britain, 1799–1853 (Montreal: McGill-Queen's University Press, 2002).

Elbourne, Elizabeth, and Robert Ross, 'Combating Spiritual and Social Bondage: Early Missions in the Cape Colony', in Richard Elphick and Rodney Davenport (eds.), *Christianity in South Africa* (Cape Town: Maskew Miller Longman, 1997), pp. 31–50.

Emsley, Clive, *Crime and Society in England, 1750–1900* 5th edn (Harlow: Longman, 2018).

Evans, E. J., 'Some Reasons for the Growth of English Rural Anti-Clericalism c.1750–c.1830', *Past & Present*, 66:101 (1975), 84–109.

Evans, R., '"Creating an Object of Real Terror": The Tabling of the First Bigge Report', in Martin Crotty and David A. Roberts (eds.), *Turning Points in Australian History* (Sydney: University of New South Wales Press, 2009), pp. 48–61.

Fa, Darren, and Clive Finlayson, *The Fortifications of Gibraltar 1068–1945* (Oxford: Osprey, 2006).

Fee, Ciarán, 'Robert Cranston and the Catalpa Escape', *The Bell (Journal of Stewartstown and District Local History Society)*, 10 (2006), 3–18.

Fitzpatrick, K., 'Mr Gladstone and the Governor: The Recall of Sir John Eardley Wilmot from Van Diemen's Land', *Historical Studies*, 1:1 (1940), 31–45.

Fitzpatrick, Matthew, 'New South Wales in Africa? The Convict Colonialism Debate in Imperial Germany', *Itinerario*, 37:1 (2013), 59–72.

Fletcher, Brian H., 'Australia's Convict Origins', *History Today*, 42:10 (1992), 39–43.

   'Christianity and Free Society in New South Wales 1788–1840', *Journal of the Royal Australian Historical Society*, 86:2 (2000), 93–113.

Fludernik, Monica, '"Stone Walls Do (Not) a Prison Make": Rhetorical Strategies and Sentimentalism in the Representation of the Victorian Prison Experience', in Jason W. Haslam and Julia M. Wright (eds.), *Captivating Subjects: Writing Confinement, Citizenship, and Nationhood in the Nineteenth Century* (Toronto: University of Toronto Press, 2005), pp. 144–174.

Follett, Richard R., *Evangelicalism, Penal Theory, and the Politics of Criminal Law Reform in England, 1808–30* (New York: St. Martin's Press, 2000).

Ford, Lisa, and David A. Roberts, 'New South Wales Penal Settlements and the Transformation of Secondary Punishment in the Nineteenth-Century British Empire', *Journal of Colonialism and Colonial History*, 15:3 (2014).

   'Legal Change, Convict Activism and the Reform of Penal Relocation in Colonial New South Wales: The Port Macquarie Penal Settlement, 1822–26', *Australian Historical Studies*, 46:2 (2015), 174–190.

Forsythe, Bill, 'The Aims and Methods of the Separate System', *Social Policy and Administration*, 14:3 (1980), 249–256.

   'Foucault's Carceral and Ignatieff's Pentonville – English Prisons and the Revisionist Analysis of Control and Penality', *Policing and Society*, 1:2 (1990), 141–158.

Forsyth, W. D., *Governor Arthur's Convict System: Van Diemen's Land 1824–36: A Study in Colonization* 2nd edn (Sydney: Sydney University Press, 1970).

Foucault, Michel, *Discipline and Punish: The Birth of the Prison*, trans. Alan Sheridan (London: Allen Lane, 1977).

Frances, Raelene, 'Christianity on the Coalfields: A Case Study of Collie in the Great Depression', [Paper in: John Tonkin (ed.). Religion and Society in Western Australia], *Studies in Western Australian History*, 9 (1987), 115–124.

Fry, Elizabeth, 'Elizabeth Fry and Convict Ships [Letter from Elizabeth Fry to James Backhouse, 23 June 1832]', *The Journal of the Friends Historical Society*, 25 (1928), 22–24.

Gascoigne, John, *The Enlightenment and the Origins of European Australia* (Cambridge: Cambridge University Press, 2002).

Gatrell, V. A. C., *The Hanging Tree. Execution and the English People, 1770–1868* (Oxford: Oxford University Press, 1996).

Gibbs, Martin, 'The Archaeology of the Convict System in Western Australia', *Australasian Historical Archaeology*, 19 (2001), 60–72.

'Landscapes of Redemption: Tracing the Path of a Convict Miner in Western Australia', *International Journal of Historical Archaeology*, 14:4 (2010), 593–613.

Gibson, Mary, 'Gender and Convict Labour: The Italian Case in Global Context', in Christian Giuseppe de Vito and Alex Lichtenstein (eds.), *Global Convict Labour* (Leiden: Brill, 2015), pp. 317–319.

Gibson, Mary, and Ilaria Poerio, 'Modern Europe, 1750–1950', in Clare Anderson (ed.), *A Global History of Convicts and Penal Colonies* (Cambridge: Cambridge University Press, 2018), pp. 337–370.

Gilchrist, Catie, 'Space, Sexuality and Convict Resistance in Van Diemen's Land: The Limits of Repression?', *Eras Journal*, 6 (2004), n.p.

Gill, A. W., *Forced Labour for the West: Parkhurst Convicts 'Apprenticed' in Western Australia 1842–1851* 2nd edn (Maylands: Blatellae Books, 1997).

Giustino, David de, 'Finding an Archbishop: The Whigs and Richard Whately in 1831', *Church History*, 64:2 (1995), 218–236.

Gladwin, Michael, 'Flogging Parsons? Australian Anglican Clergymen, the Magistracy, and Convicts, 1788–1850', *Journal of Religious History*, 36:3 (2012), 386–403.

Anglican Clergy in Australia, 1788–1850: Building a British World (Woodbridge: Boydell and Brewer, 2015).

Glancey, Michael F. (ed.), *Characteristics from the Writings of Archbishop Ullathorne* (London: Burns & Oates, 1889).

Glucklich, Ariel, *Sacred Pain: Hurting the Body for the Sake of the Soul* (Oxford: Oxford University Press, 2001)

Godfrey, Barry, and David J. Cox, '"The Last Fleet": Crime, Reformation, and Punishment in Western Australia after 1868', *The Australian and New Zealand Journal of Criminology*, 41:2 (2008), 236–258.

Godfrey, Barry, and Lucy Williams, 'The Story of Australia's Last Convicts', *The Conversation* (January 8, 2018), theconversation.com/the-story-of-australias-last-convicts-89723.

Graber, Jennifer, *The Furnace of Affliction: Prisons & Religion in Antebellum America* (Chapel Hill: University of North Carolina Press, 2011).

Grocott, Allan M., *Convicts, Clergymen and Churches: Attitudes of Convicts and Ex-Convicts towards the Churches and Clergy in New South Wales from 1788–1851* (Sydney: Sydney University Press, 1980).

Habermas, Jürgen, *The Structural Transformation of the Public Sphere: An Inquiry into a Category of Bourgeois Society*, trans. Thomas Burger (Cambridge: Polity, 1989).

Hall, Catherine, *Macaulay and Son: Architects of Imperial Britain* (New Haven, CT: Yale University Press, 2012).

Hallett, C. F. E. Hollis, *Forty Years of Convict Labour* (Bermuda: Juniperhill, 1999).

Hamm, Thomas D., *The Transformation of American Quakerism: Orthodox Friends, 1800–1907* Bloomington: Indiana University Press, 1988).

Hardwick, Joe, *An Anglican British World: The Church of England and the Settler Empire, c. 1790–1860* (Manchester: Manchester University Press, 2014).

Harling, Philip, 'The Trouble with Convicts: From Transportation to Penal Servitude, 1840–67', *Journal of British Studies*, 53:1 (2014), 80–110.

Harrington, Jack, 'Edward Gibbon Wakefield, the Liberal Political Subject and the Settler State', *Journal of Political Ideologies*, 20:3 (2015), 333–351

Harris, Edward Cecil, *Bermuda Forts 1612–1957* (Bermuda: Bermuda Maritime Museum Press, 2001).

Haslam, Jason W. and Wright, Julia M., *Captivating Subjects: Writing Confinement, Citizenship, and Nationhood in the Nineteenth Century* (Toronto: University of Toronto Press, 2005).

Hasluck, Alexandra, *Unwilling Emigrants: A Study of the Convict Period in Western Australia* (Melbourne: Melbourne University Press, 1959).

Hattersley, Alan F., *The Convict Crisis and the Growth of Unity: Resistance to Transportation in South Africa and Australia 1848–1853* (Pietermaritzburg: University of Natal Press, 1965).

Hazzard, Margaret, *Punishment Short of Death: A History of the Penal Settlement at Norfolk Island* (Melbourne: Hyland House, 1984).

Henriques, U. R. Q., 'The Rise and Decline of the Separate System of Prison Discipline', *Past & Present*, 54 (1972), 61–93.

Hills, George, *Rock of Contention: A History of Gibraltar* (London: Robert Hale, 1974).

Hilton, Boyd, *The Age of Atonement: The Influence of Evangelicalism on Social and Economic Thought 1785–1865* (Oxford: Clarendon, 1988).

'Whiggery, Religion and Social Reform: The Case of Lord Morpeth', *The Historical Journal*, 37:4 (1994), 829–859.

A Mad, Bad, and Dangerous People?: England, 1783–1846 (Oxford: Clarendon Press, 2006).

Hirst, John, 'The Australian Experience: The Convict Colony', in Norval Morris and David J. Rothman (eds.), *The Oxford History of the Prison: The Practice of Punishment in Western Society* (Oxford: Oxford University Press, 1995), pp. 235–265.

'Anti-Transportation', in Graeme Davison, John Hirst and Stuart Macintyre (eds.), *The Oxford Companion to Australian History* (Oxford: Oxford University Press, 2001).

Hoare, Merval, 'A Religious Presence', in Raymond Nobbs (ed.), *Norfolk Island and Its Second Settlement, 1825–1855* (Sydney: Library of Australian History, 1991), pp. 138–157.

Norfolk Island: A Revised and Enlarged History 1774–1998 (Rockhampton: Central Queensland University Press, 1999).

Holdridge, Chris, 'Putting the Global Back into the Colonial Politics of Anti-transportation', *Journal of Australian Colonial History*, 14 (2012), 272–279.

'The Pageantry of the Anti-Convict Cause: Colonial Loyalism and Settler Celebrations in Van Diemen's Land and the Cape Colony', *History Australia*, 12:1 (2015), 141–164.

Hole, Robert, *Pulpits, Politics and Public Order in England, 1760–1832* (Cambridge: Cambridge University Press, 1989).

Horton, David M., *Pioneers in Penology: The Reformers, the Institutions, and the Societies, 1557–1900*, 2 vols. (Lampeter: Edwin Mellen Press, 2006).

Howse, Ernest Marshall, *Saints in Politics: The 'Clapham Sect' and the Growth of Freedom* (London: Allen and Unwin, 1971).

Hughes, Robert, *The Fatal Shore: A History of the Transportation of Convicts to Australia, 1787–1868* (New York: Knopf), 1986.

Huon, Dan, 'By Moral Means Only: The Origins of the Launceston Anti-Transportation Leagues, 1847–1849', *Papers and Proceedings: Tasmanian Historical Research Association*, 44:2 (1997), 92–119.

Ignatieff, Michael, *A Just Measure of Pain: The Penitentiary in the Industrial Revolution, 1750–1850* (London: Macmillan, 1978).

Ingram, J. K., *A History of Political Economy*, (First pub. 1888) (Cambridge: Cambridge University Press, 2013).

Innes, Joanna, 'Politics and Morals: The Reformation of Manners Movement in Later Eighteenth-Century England', in Eckhart Hellmuth (ed.), *The Transformation of Political Culture* (Oxford: Oxford University Press, 1990), pp. 57–118.

Isba, Anne, *The Excellent Mrs. Fry: Unlikely Heroine* (London: Continuum, 2010).

Isichei, Elizabeth, *Victorian Quakers* (Oxford: Oxford University Press, 1970).

Jackman, Greg, 'From Stain to Saint: Ancestry, Archaeology, and Agendas in Tasmania's Convict Heritage – a View from Port Arthur', *Historical Archaeology*, 43:3 (2009), 101–112.

Johnson, William Branch, *The English Prison Hulks* revised edn (Chichester: Phillimore, 1970).

Jones, Tod E., *The Broad Church: A Biography of a Movement* (New York: Lexington, 2003).

Jones, Tudor (ed.), *Protestant Nonconformist Texts, Vol. 1: 1550–1700* (Aldershot: Ashgate, 2006).

Kamerling, Henry, *Capital and Convict: Race, Region and Punishment in Post-Civil War America* (Charlottesville: University of Virginia Press, 2017).

Karskens, Grace, *The Rocks: Life in Early Sydney* (Carlton: Melbourne University Press, 1997).

Kent, John, *Elizabeth Fry* (London: B. T. Batsford, 1962).

Kerr, James Semple, *Design for Convicts: An Account of Design for Convict Establishments in the Australian Colonies during the Transportation Era* (Sydney: Library of Australian History, 1984).

Kersher, Bruce, 'Perish or Prosper: The Law and Convict Transportation in the British Empire, 1700–1850', *Law and History Review*, 21:3 (2003), 527–584.

Kiernan, Thomas Joseph, *Transportation from Ireland to Sydney: 1791–1816* (Canberra: The Author, 1954).

Kinealy, Christine, *A Death-Dealing Famine: The Great Hunger in Ireland* (London: Pluto Press, 1997).

Koditschek, Theodore, *Liberalism, Imperialism and the Historical Imagination: Nineteenth-Century Visions of a Greater Britain* (Cambridge: Cambridge University Press, 2011).

Kriegel, A. D., 'A Convergence of Ethics: Saints and Whigs in British Antislavery', *Journal of British Studies*, 26:4 (1987), 423–450.

Lancaster, Joseph, *The British System of Education: Being a Complete Epitome of the Improvements and Inventions Practised at the Royal Free Schools, Borough-Road, Southwark* (London: Longman, 1810).

Lang, John Dunmore, *Transportation and Colonization; or, the Causes of the Comparative Failure of the Transportation System in the Australian Colonies* (London: Valpy, 1837).

Brief Sketch of My Parliamentary Life and Times: From 1st August 1843 Till the Late Dissolution of Parliament (Sydney: Sherriff, 1870).

Larsen, Timothy, 'Defining and Locating Evangelicalism', in Timothy Larsen and Daniel Treier (eds.), *The Cambridge Companion to Evangelical Theology* (Cambridge: Cambridge University Press, 2007), pp. 1–14.

A People of One Book: The Bible and the Victorians (Oxford: Oxford University Press, 2011).

Larsen, Timothy, and Michael Ledger-Lomas(eds.), *The Oxford History of Protestant Dissenting Traditions, Vol. III the Nineteenth Century* (Oxford: Oxford University Press, 2017).

Laslett, Peter, *The World We Have Lost* (London: Methuen, 1965).

Lennox, G. R., 'A Private and Confidential Despatch of Eardley-Wilmot', *Tasmanian Historical Research Association Papers and Proceedings*, 29 (1982), 80–92.

Lester, Alan, 'Colonial Settlers and the Metropole: Racial Discourse in the Early 19th-Century Cape Colony, Australia and New Zealand', *Landscape Research*, 27 (2002), 39–49.

'British Settler Discourse and the Circuits of Empire', *History Workshop Journal*, 54:1 (2002), 24–48.

Lester, Alan, and Fae Dussart, 'The Genesis of Humanitarian Governance: George Arthur and the Transition from Amelioration to Protection', in Alan Lester and Fae Dussart (eds.), *Colonization and the Origins of Humanitarian Governance: Protecting Aborigines across the Nineteenth-Century British Empire* (Cambridge: Cambridge University Press, 2014), pp. 37–76.

Levy, Michael C. Ivan, *Governor George Arthur: A Colonial Benevolent Despot* (Melbourne: Georgian House, 1953).

Lydon, Jane, 'Anti-Slavery in Australia: Picturing the 1838 Myall Creek Massacre', *History Compass* (15 May 2017) doi.org/10.1111/hic3.12330.

Lydon, Jane, and Sari Braithwaite, 'Photographing "the Nucleus of the Native Church" at Poonindie Mission, South Australia', *Photography and Culture*, 8:1 (2015), 37–57.

Mack, Phyllis, *Visionary Women. Ecstatic Prophecy in Seventeenth-Century England* (Berkeley: University of California Press, 1989).

MacRaild, Donald, 'Transnationalizing "Anti-Popery": Militant Protestant Preachers in the Nineteenth-Century Anglo-World', *Journal of Religious History*, 39 (2015): 224–243.

Maddox, Alan, 'On the Machinery of Moral Improvement: Music and Prison Reform in the Penal Colony of Norfolk Island', *Musicology Australia*, 34:2 (2012), 185–205.

Maxwell-Stewart, Hamish, 'The Search for the Convict Voice', *Tasmanian Historical Studies*, 6:1 (2001), 75–89.

'Convicts', *The Companion to Tasmanian History* (Hobart: Centre for Tasmanian Studies, 2006).

'"Like Poor Galley Slaves": Slavery and Convict Transportation', in Maria Suzette and Fernandes Dias (eds.), *Legacies of Slavery: Comparative Perspectives* (Newcastle upon Tyne: Cambridge Scholars, 2007), pp. 48–61.

Closing Hell's Gates: The Death of a Convict Station (Sydney: Allen & Unwin, 2008).

'Convict Transportation from Britain and Ireland 1615–1870', *History Compass*, 8:11 (2010), 1221–1242.

'The Rise and Fall of Penal Transportation', in Paul Knepper and Anja Johansen (eds.), *The Oxford Handbook of the History of Crime and Criminal Justice* (Oxford: Oxford University Press, 2016), pp. 655–671.

'Transportation from Britain and Ireland, 1615–1875', in Clare Anderson (ed.), *A Global History of Convicts and Penal Colonies* (London: Bloomsbury, 2018), pp. 183–210.

'"And all my great hardships endured"?: Irish Convicts in Van Diemen's Land, in Nial Whelehan (ed.), *Transnational Perspectives in Modern Irish History* (London: Routledge, 2015), pp. 69–87.

Maxwell-Stewart, Hamish, and Ian Duffield, 'Skin Deep Devotion: Religious Tattoos and Convict Transportation to Australia', in Jane Caplan (ed.), *Written on the Body: The Tattoo in European and American History* (London: Reaktion, 2000), pp. 118–135.

McConville, Seán, *A History of English Prison Administration, vol. I 1750–1877* (London: Routledge & Kegan Paul, 1981).

Irish Political Prisoners, 1848–1922: Theatres of War (London: Routledge, 2003).

McConville, Séan, *English Local Prisons 1860–1900: Next Only to Death* (London: Routledge, 1994).

McCoy, Ted, *Hard Time: Reforming the Penitentiary in Nineteenth-Century Canada* (Edmonton: Athabasca University Press, 2012).

McCulloch, S. C., 'Sir George Gipps and Captain Alexander Maconochie: The Attempted Penal Reforms at Norfolk Island, 1840–44', *Historical Studies Australia and New Zealand*, 7 (1957), 387–406.

McGowen, Randall, 'A Powerful Sympathy: Terror, the Prison, and Humanitarian Reform in Early Nineteenth-Century Britain', *Journal of British Studies*, 25 (1986), 312–334.

'"He Beareth Not the Sword in Vain": Religion and the Criminal Law in Eighteenth-Century England', *Eighteenth-Century Studies*, 21:2 (1987), 192–211.

'The Well-Ordered Prison: England, 1780–1985', in Norval Morris and David J. Rothman (eds.), *The Oxford History of the Prison: The Practice of Punishment in Western Society* (Oxford: Oxford University Press, 1995), pp. 71–99.

'The Problem of Punishment in Eighteenth-Century England', in Simon Devereaux and Paul Griffiths (eds.), *Penal Practice and Culture, 1500–1900: Punishing the English* (Houndmills: Palgrave Macmillan, 2004), pp. 210–231.

McGuire, James, *What Works: Reducing Reoffending: Guidelines from Research and Practice* (Chichester: Wiley, 1995).

McKenzie, Andrea, 'From True Confessions to True Reporting? The Decline and Fall of the Ordinary's Account', *The London Journal*, 30:1 (2005), 55–70.

McKenzie, Kirsten, '"Franklins of the Cape": The South "African Commercial Advertiser" and the Creation of a Colonial Public Sphere, 1824–1854', *Kronos*, 25 (1998/99), 88–102.

Scandal in the Colonies: Sydney and Cape Town, 1820–1850 (Carlton: Melbourne University Press, 2004).

McKerrow, Ray E., 'Archbishop Whately, Human Nature, and Christian Assistance', *Church History*, 50 (1981), 166–181.

McKivigan, John R., *The War against Proslavery Religion: Abolitionism and the Northern Churches, 1830–1865* (Ithaca, NY: Cornell University Press, 1984).

McLaughlin, Ann, 'Against the League: Fighting the "Hated Stain"', *Tasmanian Historical Studies*, 5:1 (1995), 76–104.

McLaughlin, Trevor, *Barefoot & Pregnant? Irish Famine Orphans in Australia* (Melbourne: Genealogical Society of Victoria, 2001).

Meredith, John, and Rex Whalan, *Frank the Poet* (Melbourne: Red Rooster, 1979).

Meyering, Isobelle Barrett, 'Abolitionism, Settler Violence and the Case against Flogging', *History Australia*, 7:1 (2010), 6.1–6.18.

Milton, John, *Paradise Lost*, edited by William Kerrigan, James Rumrich and Stephen M. Fallon (New York: Random House, 2011).

Moore, John, 'Alexander Maconochie's "Mark System"', *Prison Service Journal*, 198 (2011), 38–46.

Morris, Norval, *Maconochie's Gentlemen: The Story of Norfolk Island & the Roots of Modern Prison Reform*, vol. 1 (Oxford: Oxford University Press, 2002).

Morris, Norval and David J. Rothman, 'Perfecting the Prison', in Norval Morris and David J. Rothman (eds.), *The Oxford History of the Prison: The Practice of Punishment in Western Society* (Oxford: Oxford University Press, 1995).

Neal, D. J., *The Rule of Law in a Penal Colony: Law and Power in Early New South Wales* (Melbourne: Cambridge University Press, 1991).

Neilson, Briony, 'The Paradox of Penal Colonization: Debates on Convict Transportation at the International Prison Congresses, 1872–1895', *French History and Civilization: Papers from the George Rudé Seminar*, 6 (2015), 198–211.

Nicholas, Stephen (ed.), *Convict Workers: Reinterpreting Australia's Past* (Cambridge: Cambridge University Press, 1988).

Nicholls, Mary (ed.), *Traveller under Concern: The Quaker Journals of Frederick Mackie on His Tour of the Australasian Colonies, 1852–1855* (Hobart: University of Tasmania, 1973).

Nobbs, Raymond, *Norfolk Island and Its Second Settlement, 1825–1855* (Sydney: Library of Australian History, 1991).

Nunn, Cameron, 'Pure Minds, Pure Bodies, Pure Lips: Religious Ideology and the Juvenile Convict Institutions at Carter's Barracks and Point Puer', *Journal of Religious History* 40.2 (2016), 161–184.

O'Connor, Tamsin, 'A Zone of Silence: Queensland's Convicts and the Historiography of Moreton Bay', in Ian Duffield and James Bradley (eds.), *Representing Convicts: New Perspectives on Convict Forced Labour Migration* (London: Leicester University Press, 1997).

O'Donnell, Ruán, 'Hellship: Captain Richard Brooks and the Voyage of the Atlas', in Tadhg Foley and Fiona Bateman (eds.), *Irish-Australian Studies* (Sydney: Crossing Press, 2000), pp. 164–174.

O'Mara, Gillian, *Convict Records of Western Australia: A Research Guide* (Northbridge: Friends of Battye Library, 1990).

Oats, William Nicolle, *Backhouse and Walker: A Quaker View of the Australian Colonies 1832–1838* (Sandy Bay: Blubber Head Press, 1981).

A Question of Survival: Quakers in Australia in the Nineteenth Century (St Lucia: University of Queensland Press, 1985).

Oldham, Wilfrid, and W. Hugh Oldham, *Britain's Convicts to the Colonies* (Sydney: Library of Australian History, 1990).

Outhwaite, R. B., *The Rise and Fall of the English Ecclesiastical Courts, 1500–1860* (Cambridge: Cambridge University Press, 2006).

Page, Anthony, 'Rational Dissent, Enlightenment and Abolition of the British Slave Trade', *The Historical Journal*, 54:3 (2011), 741–772.

Paley, William, *The Principles of Moral and Political Philosophy* (London: Faulder, 1785).

Paley, William, and Richard Whately, *A View of the Evidences of Christianity: In Three Parts* (London: J. Parker, 1859).

Palmer, Beth, and Adelene Buckland, *A Return to the Common Reader: Print Culture and the Novel, 1850–1900* (Farnham: Ashgate, 2011).

Pascoe, C. F., *Two Hundred Years of the S. P. G.: An Historical Account of the Propagation of the Gospel in Foreign Parts, 1701–1900*, 2 vols. (London: SPG, 1901).

Paxman, Briony, '"A Floating Hell": Life on Early 19th-Century Hulks', *Records and Research* (Kew: National Archves, 2018).

Penn, Nigel, '"Close and Merciful Watchfulness": John Montagu's Convict System in the Mid-Nineteenth-Century Cape Colony', *Cultural and Social History*, 5:4 (2008), 465–480.

Peters, Edward, 'Prison before the Prison', in Norval Morris and David Rothman (eds.), *The Oxford History of the Prison* (New York: Oxford University Press, 1998), pp. 17–21.

Picker, Gregory, 'A State of Infancy: The Anti-Transportation Movement in New Zealand, 1848–1852', *New Zealand Journal of History*, 34:2 (2000), 226–240.

Pickering, Paul, 'A Wider Field in a New Country: Chartism in Colonial Australia', in Marion Sawer (ed.), *Elections Full, Free and Fair* (Sydney: Federation Press, 2001), pp. 28–44.

'"And Your Petitioners &c": Chartist Petitioning in Popular Politics 1838–48', *English Historical Review*, 118:466 (2001), 368–388.

'Loyalty and Rebellion in Colonial Politics: The Campaign against Convict Transportation in Australia', in Phillip Buckner and R. Douglas Francis (eds.), *Rediscovering the British World* (Calgary: University of Calgary Press, 2005), pp. 87–107.

Porter, Andrew, 'Trusteeship, Anti-Slavery, and Humanitarianism', in *The Oxford History of the British Empire, Vol. III: The Nineteenth Century* (Oxford: Oxford University Press, 1999), pp. 198–221.

'Evangelical Visions and Colonial Realities', *The Journal of Imperial and Colonial History*, 38:1 (2010), 145–155.

Radzinowicz, L., *A History of English Criminal Law and Its Administration from 1750*, 4 vols. (London: Stevens, 1948–1968).

Rashid, Salim, 'Richard Whately and Christian Political Economy at Oxford and Dublin', *Journal of the History of Ideas*, 38:1 (1977), 147–155.

'Richard Whately and the Struggle for Rational Christianity in the Mid-Nineteenth Century', *Historical Magazine of the Protestant Episcopal Church*, 47 (1978), 293–311.

Ratcliffe, Patricia Fitzgerald, *The Usefulness of John West: Dissent and Difference in the Australian Colonies* (Launceston: Albernian, 2003).

Reece, Bob, *Exiles from Erin: Convict Lives in Ireland and Australia* (Basingstoke: Macmillan, 1991).

Irish Convict Lives (Sydney: Crossing Press, 1993).

The Origins of Irish Convict Transportation to New South Wales (Houndmills: Palgrave, 2001).

Reid, Kirsty, *Gender, Crime and Empire: Convicts, Settlers and the State in Early Colonial Australia* (Manchester: Manchester University Press, 2007).

'The Horrors of Convict Life: British Radical Visions of the Australian Penal Colonies', *Cultural & Social History*, 5:4 (2008), 481–495.

Reilly, Ciarán, 'An Inhospitable Welcome? Emigration to the Cape of Good Hope During the Great Irish Famine', *Breac: A Digital Journal of Irish Studies*, (2018), breac.nd.edu/articles/.

Reynolds, Henry, 'That Hated Stain': The Aftermath of Transportation in Tasmania, *Historical Studies*, 14:53 (1969), 19–33.

Fate of a Free People (Ringwood; Harmondsworth: Penguin 1995).

Richmond, Barbara, 'John West and the Anti-Transportation Movement', *Papers and Proceedings (Tasmanian Historical Research Association)*, 2 (1951–1952).

Ridden, Jennifer, 'The Forgotten History of the Protestant Crusade: Religious Liberalism in Ireland', *Journal of Religious History*, 31:1 (2007), 78–102.

Ritchie, John, 'Towards Ending an Unclean Thing: The Molesworth Committee and the Abolition of Transportation to New South Wales 1837–40', *Australian Historical Studies*, 17 (1976), 144–164.

Ritchie, John, and John Thomas Bigge, *The Evidence to the Bigge Reports: New South Wales under Governor Macquarie*, 2 vols. (Melbourne: Heinemann, 1971).

Roberts, David A., 'A "City on a Hill": Religion and Buildings on the Frontier Mission at Wellngton Valley, New South Wales', *Australian Religion Studies Review*, 23:1 (2010), 91–114.

'Beyond the Stain: Rethinking the Nature and Impact of the Anti-Transportation Movement', *Journal of Australian Colonial History*, 14 (2012), 205–279.

'Remembering "Australia's Glorious League": The Historiography of Anti-Transportation', *Journal of Australian Colonial History*, 14 (2012), 205–215.

'The "Illegal Sentences Which Magistrates Were Daily Passing": The Backstory to Governor Richard Bourke's 1832 Punishment and Summary Jurisdiction Act in Convict New South Wales', *The Journal of Legal History*, 38:3 (2017), 231–253.

Roberts, Stephen H., *The Squatting Age in Australia, 1835–1847* (Melbourne: Melbourne University Press, 1964).

Rodgers, Nini, *Ireland, Slavery and Anti-Slavery: 1612–1865* (Houndmills: Palgrave Macmillan, 2007).

Roe, Michael, *Quest for Authority in Eastern Australia, 1835–1851* (Melbourne: Melbourne University Press, 1965).

Romilly, Samuel, *Observations on the Criminal Law of England as It Relates to Capital Punishments* (London: Cadell & Davies, 1810).

Rose, June, *Elizabeth Fry* (London: Macmillan, 1980).

Ross, Andrew C., *John Philip (1775–1851): Missions, Race and Politics in South Africa* (Aberdeen: Aberdeen University Press, 1986).

Ross, Robert, *The Borders of Race in Colonial South Africa* (Cambridge: Cambridge University Press, 2014).

Ryan, Lyndall, *Tasmanian Aborigines: A History since 1803* (Crows Nest: Allen & Unwin, 2012).

Sarat, Austin, *Pain, Death, and the Law* (Ann Arbor: University of Michigan Press, 2001).

Scotnicki, Andrew, *Criminal Justice and the Catholic Church* (Plymouth: Sheed & Ward, 2008).

Scott, Ernest, 'The Resistance to Convict Transportation in Victoria, 1844–53', *Victorian Historical Magazine*, 1 (1911), 101–142.

Seay, Scott D., *Hanging between Heaven and Earth: Capital Crime, Execution Preaching, and Theology in Early New England* (DeKalb: Northern Illinois University Press, 2009).

Sellin, Thorsten, 'Paley on the Time Sentence', *Journal of Criminal Law and Criminology*, 22:2 (1931), 264–266.

Shaw, A. G. L., 'Sir John Eardley-Wilmot and the Probation System in Tasmania', *Papers and Proceedings (Tasmanian Historical Research Association)*, 11:1 (1963), 5–19.

Convicts and the Colonies: A Study of Penal Transportation from Great Britain and Ireland to Australia and Other Parts of the British Empire (London: Faber, 1966).

Sir George Arthur, 1784–1854 (Melbourne: Melbourne University Press, 1980).

Sheriff, Jacqui, and Anne Brake (eds.), *Building a Colony: The Convict Legacy* (Nedlands: University of Western Australia Press, 2006).

Skotnicki, Andrew, 'God's Prisoners: Penal Confinement and the Creation of Purgatory', *Modern Theology*, 22 (2006), 85–110.

Slee, June, and John Ward, *Crime, Punishment and Redemption: A Convict's Story* (Canberra: National Library of Australia, 2014).

Smith, Babette, *Australia's Birthstain: The Startling Legacy of the Convict Era* (Sydney: Allen & Unwin, 2008).

Smith, G. C. Moore (ed.), *The Autobiography of Lieutenant-General Sir Harry Smith* (London: Murray, 1903).

Snell, K. D. M., and Paul S. Ell, *Rival Jerusalems: The Geography of Victorian Religion* (Cambridge: Cambridge University Press, 2004).

Stannage, Charles Thomas (ed.), *Convictism in Western Australia* (Nedlands: University of Western Australia, 1981).

Stoneman, David, 'Richard Bourke: For the Honour of God and the Good of Man', *Journal of Religious History*, 38:3 (2013), 341–355.

Stott, Anne, *Wilberforce: Family and Friends* (Oxford: Oxford University Press, 2013).

Strachey, Giles Lytton, *Eminent Victorians* (London: Chatto & Windus, 1918).

Strange, Carolyn, 'The Undercurrents of Penal Culture: Punishment of the Body in Mid-Twentieth Century Canada', *Law and History Review*, 19:2 (2001), 343–385.

Strong, Rowan, 'The Reverend John Wollaston and Colonial Christianity in Western Australia, 1840–1863', *Journal of Religious History*, 25:3 (2001), 261–285.

Anglicanism and the British Empire, c.1700–1850 (Oxford University Press, 2007).

Victorian Christianity and Emigrant Voyages to British Colonies c.1840–c.1914 (Oxford: Oxford University Press, 2017).

Summers, Anne, *Female Lives, Moral States: Women, Religion and Public Life in Britain, 1800–1930* (Newbury: Threshold, 2000).

Taylor, Sandra, 'Who Were the Convicts? A Statistical Analysis of the Convicts Arriving in Western Australia, 1850/51, 1861/62 and 1866/68', in Charles Thomas Stannage (ed.), *Convictism in Western Australia* (Nedlands: University of Western Australia, 1981), pp. 19–45.

Temple, Philip, *A Sort of Conscience: The Wakefields* (Auckland: Auckland University Press, 2002).

Theal, George McCall, *History of South Africa since September 1795*, vol. 3 (London: Swan Sonnenschein, 1908).

Thompson, John, *Probation in Paradise. The Story of Convict Probationers in Tasman's and Forestier's Peninsulas, Van Diemen's Land, 1841–1857* (Hobart: Artemis, 2007).

Throness, Laurie, *A Protestant Purgatory: Theological Origins of the Penitentiary Act, 1779* (Aldershot: Ashgate, 2008).

Tolen, Rachel J., 'Colonizing and Transforming the Criminal Tribesman – the Salvation Army in British India', *American Ethnologist*, 18:1 (1991), 106–125.

Tomlinson, Heather M., 'Penal Servitude 1846–1865: A System in Evolution', in Victor Bailey (ed.), *Policing and Punishment in Nineteenth-Century Britain* (London: Croom Helm, 1981), pp. 126–149.

Toth, Stephen A., *Beyond Papillon: The French Overseas Penal Colonies, 1854–1952* (Lincoln: University of Nebraska Press, 2006).

Townsend, Norma, 'The Molesworth Enquiry: Does the Report Fit the Evidence?', *Journal of Australian Studies*, 1:1 (1977), 33–51.

Tucker, H. W., *The Spiritual Expansion of the Empire* 4th edn (London: SPG, 1900).

Tuckwell, W., *Pre-Tractarian Oxford: A Reminiscence of the Oriel 'Noetics'* (London: Smith, Elder & Co., 1909).

Tuffin, R., et al., 'Landscapes of Production and Punishment: Convict Labour in the Australian Context', *Journal of Social Archaeology*, 1:18 (2018), 50–76.

van der Veer, Peter, *Imperial Encounters: Religion and Modernity in India and Britain* (Princeton, NJ: Princeton University Press, 2001).

Vaughan, Géraldine, '"Britishers and Protestants": Protestantism and Imperial British Identities in Britain, Canada and Australia from the 1880s to the 1920s', *Studies in Church History*, 54 (2018): 359–373.

Virgin, Peter, *The Church in an Age of Negligence: Ecclesiastical Structure and Problems of Church Reform 1700–1840* (Cambridge: James Clarke, 1989).

Waldersee, James, *Catholic Society in New South Wales, 1788–1860* (Sydney: Sydney University Press, 1974).